MASTERS
of the
TALMUD

ALSO BY ALFRED J. KOLATCH

Best Baby Names for Jewish Children
A Child's First Book of Jewish Holidays
Classic Bible Stories for Jewish Children
The Complete Dictionary of English and Hebrew First Names
The Concise Family Seder
El Libro Judio del Por Que
The Family Seder
How to Live a Jewish Life
Great Jewish Quotations
The Jewish Book of Why
The Jewish Child's First Book of Why
The Jewish Heritage Quiz Book
The Jewish Mourner's Book of Why
The Jonathan David Dictionary of First Names
Let's Celebrate Our Jewish Holidays!
The New Name Dictionary
Our Religion: The Torah
The Second Jewish Book of Why
These Are the Names
This Is the Torah
Today's Best Baby Names
What Jews Say About God

MASTERS

of the

TALMUD

Their Lives and Views

Alfred J. Kolatch

JONATHAN DAVID PUBLISHERS, INC.
Middle Village, New York 11379

Jonathan David Publishers, Inc.
68-22 Eliot Avenue
Middle Village, New York 11379

www.jdbooks.com

2 4 6 8 9 10 7 5 3 1

Library of Congress Cataloging-in-Publication Data

Kolatch, Alfred J.
    Masters of the Talmud: their lives and views / Alfred J. Kolatch
      p. cm.
    ISBN 0-8246-0434-2
    1. Talmud—Biography—Dictionaries. 2. Tannaim—Biography—
Dictionaries. 3. Amoraim—Biography—Dictionaries. I. Title.

BM501.15 .K55 2003
296.1'2'00922—dc21
[B]   00-065761

Book design and composition by John Reinhardt Book Design

Printed in the United States of America

In Appreciation

Thanks are due many colleagues who have been available for consultation during the three years that this work has been in preparation. I am particularly grateful to Rabbi Emanuel S. Goldsmith, Rabbi Ben Zion Bergman, and my brother, Rabbi Arthur J. Kolatch, for sharing so generously of their knowledge and insight.

My gratitude also goes to Dr. Yehiel Kaplan, an ordained rabbi and specialist in Jewish law, for taking time from his busy schedule as a member of the Faculty of Law at the University of Haifa to prepare the Preface to this volume.

It would not have been possible to complete a work of this scope without the assistance of a superb editor. I extend my thanks to Judy Sandman for tirelessly checking and rechecking the manuscript for accuracy and consistency. Her commitment to the project has been greatly appreciated. I am also indebted to Diana Drew for carefully proofreading the manuscript and for making some very astute observations.

My thanks also go to John Reinhardt for his tasteful book design and to Mike Stromberg for his elegant jacket design.

To Marvin Sekler, Barbara Burke, Rachel Taller, and the entire staff of Jonathan David Publishers, I offer my sincere appreciation for their help in seeing this project through to fruition.

As always, my thanks to Thelma, Jonathan, and David for their contribution beyond measure.

Contents

~

Foreword

Books of historical data furnishing information on the tanna'im and amora'im—the scholars whose work is recorded in the Talmud—have been of great help to students throughout the ages. Brief documents of this nature have come down to us from the immediate post-Talmudic period—namely, the ge'onic period—up to the present time. Chronicles like *Seder Tanna'im ve-Amora'im* (anonymous authorship), and editions like Judah ben Kalonymos's *Yichusei Tanna'im ve-Amora'im* (recently published from a manuscript by the late Rabbi Judah Leib Maimon [1876–1962]), and more elaborate historical treatises on the Mishnah and Talmud (Frankel, Graetz, Weiss, Halevy, Yavetz, Bacher, Heiman, and others) are well known. A volume such as this is a welcome addition and, because of its popular approach and style, will be cherished by laypersons as well as scholars.

David ben [Shelomoh ibn Avi] Zimra, a sixteenth-century scholar, in a book entitled *Me-Harerei Nemerim*, sets down a few guiding rules for the student of the Talmud and emphasizes how important it is to know whether the scholar mentioned in a Talmudic discussion is a tanna or an amora; and if an amora, whether he is from Babylonia or Palestine. It is also important to know the relationship between the discussants: who is the master, who is the disciple, and who is the colleague.

The word *tanna* has two meanings:

1. The historical, namely, those who lived in the tannaitic period, which ends with the death of the editor of the Mishnah (219 or 220 C.E.).

This Foreword first appeared in *Who's Who in the Talmud* (Jonathan David Publishers, Inc., 1964), on which the more extensive *Masters of the Talmud* is based.

2. The functional, namely, those who recited tannaitic literature orally in the amoraic academies.

When we read, for instance, that Rav is a tanna and can take
issue with another tanna whose opinion is stated in a Mishnah or
baraita, it is tanna in the historical sense that is being used. This
means that Rav, who despite the fact that he was a member of the
first generation of Babylonian amora'im, belongs to the category
of tanna'im, since he was a disciple, and ordained (though not
fully) by Rabbi Yehudah ha-Nasi (the editor of the Mishnah). Similarly, it is said of Rav's uncle and teacher, Chiyya, that he is a tanna
and can oppose another tanna.

But, when we read very frequently in the Talmud that a tanna
taught in the presence of an amora, the reference is to a tanna in
the functional sense. This can be easily understood in view of the
fact that even after the Mishnah was committed to writing (Maimonides's opinion), they continued to study it orally in the amoraic
academies.

When studying the Talmud, it is easy to distinguish between an
amora ordained in the Babylonian academies and an amora ordained in the academies in Palestine. The name of the former is
always preceded by the title "Rav," while the latter is preceded by
the title "Rabbi." For example: Rav Huna, Rav Yehudah [bar
Yechezkel], Rav Nachman [bar Ya'akov], and Rav Chisda are
Babylonian amora'im. Rabbi Yochanan [bar Nappacha], Rabbi
Shimon ben Lakish, and Rabbi Abbahu are amora'im of Palestine.

It is sometimes possible to differentiate between a statement
made by the same scholar when he was merely ordained in the
Babylonian academies and the statements he made after traveling
to Palestine and receiving an additional ordination there. Such an
amora was Ze'eira. However, confusion occurs in the texts due to
the fact that the title "Rabbi" is abbreviated to "R̃".

The teacher-disciple relationship can be deduced from the chain
of traditions of a Talmudic dictum. When we come across a statement made by one amora in the name of another, or still another,
it is quite obvious that the first person named was a disciple of the
previous person named. When an amora quotes one amora at one
time and another amora at other times, it is an indication that he

studied under both. For instance, Rav Yehudah [bar Yechezkel], the founder of the Pumbedita academy, was a student of Rav, the founder of the Sura academy, and later a student of Shemu'el. Thus, he refers to both, and very often states that he forgot from whom he received the tradition.

The traditions in the academies in Palestine were brought down to the Babylonian academies by traveling scholars who became known as *nachotei*. The chief of such scholars was Ulla. Other famous traveling scholars were Rabbah bar [bar] Chana and Dimi. These, and many others, transmitted the teachings of their masters in the academies of Palestine to the scholars in the Babylonian academies.

Family relationships cannot be inferred unless expressly stated. However, the custom of naming a son after an earlier ancestor sometimes helps to trace such relationships.

The identification of a tanna or an amora, and the distinction between those who bear identical names, is of prime importance in checking one statement against another in order to prove its accuracy or its true meaning. However, this task at times becomes very difficult because of the scarcity of information. It is often difficult to ascertain whether there was only one, or more than one, scholar with the same name. The Talmud itself, and sometimes the commentators on the Talmud, devote much effort to unraveling these riddles.

The casual reader as well as the serious student of the Talmud will find much in this volume that will help clarify some of the problems indicated above.

SAMUEL K. MIRSKY

Samuel K. Mirsky, former Professor of Rabbinics at New York's Yeshiva University, died in 1966. He was editor of *Talpiot*, a quarterly publication under the auspices of Yeshiva University devoted to Jewish scholarship.

*P*reface

~~

In *Masters of the Talmud*, Rabbi Alfred J. Kolatch delves into the background of many of the major scholars—the tanna'im and amora'im—who were active primarily during the first five centuries of the Common Era. His concise and pithy biographies provide insight into the personalities of Sages who made concrete contributions to the evolution and development of a literature of singular importance in the annals of Hebrew jurisprudence, namely, the Talmud. These biographical sketches provide the student with a deeper understanding of the wisdom of the masters whose views and opinions are expressed in it.

The Talmud is an important link in the chain of development of Jewish law, which began, according to Jewish tradition, with the Revelation of the Torah to Moses on Mount Sinai. According to Mishnah *Avot*, the heritage was transmitted from Moses to Joshua, from Joshua to the Elders, from the Elders to the Prophets, and from the Prophets to the members of the Keneset ha-Gedolah—the Great Assembly.

Following the period of the Keneset ha-Gedolah, whose members were sometimes known as the "Scribes" and among whom Ezra the Scribe was one of the giants, a legal institution identified as the Sanhedrin assumed the role of the supreme judicial and legislative body governing the Jewish people. At its head were the *nasi* and the *av beit din*—president and deputy, respectively. The legal activity during this period was dominated by the *zugot*, five "pairs" of outstanding scholars who developed and interpreted Jewish law.

Subsequent to the leadership of Hillel and Shammai, the last of the *zugot*, a group of teachers known as tanna'im dominated the Jewish scholarly scene. Foremost among these was Yehudah ha-Nasi—Judah the Prince—who assembled all the Torah interpretations and rulings of scholars of his time, and compiled them into the Mishnah. The result of his efforts became the basis of discussions and analyses by the next group of Jewish scholars, known as amora'im, who held that the principles laid down by the tanna'im were binding.

The Talmud—actually two Talmuds, the Palestinian edition and the Babylonian edition—emerged from the discussions and debates of the amora'im in the Jewish academies established in Palestine and Babylonia. Although the amora'im accepted and respected the teachings set forth by their predecessors, they took the liberty of discussing the principles set forth in the Mishnah as well as their application. Talmudic debate usually follows a question-answer, explication-elucidation structure.

The wealth of information in Rabbi Kolatch's book offers a wide-ranging acquaintance with the spiritual giants of the Jewish people during the Talmudic period. Such familiarity will heighten the sensitivity of contemporary readers. The prophet Isaiah brought to our attention the fruitful benefit every individual derives from understanding his or her own spiritual heritage, from a familiarity with the rich past, from the inspiration provided by the legal and philosophical teachings of ancient Rabbis and Sages, and from the wisdom of the pillars of the Jewish people: ". . . [Y]our eyes will watch your teachers. . . . your ears shall heed that which reaches them; for they will tell you the way you should follow . . ." (*Isaiah* 30:20–21).

Rabbi Kolatch's book permits the reader to hear voices from the distant past expressed through the Talmud. By linking themselves with the creators of the Talmud, one of the loftiest endeavors of the Jewish people, readers enlighten and enrich their own vista.

A variety of selections from the Talmud make a substantial contribution to Jewish philosophical thought, especially in the area of faith and belief. In addition to the wonderful stories, the many examples of exalted conduct, and the deep wisdom of Jewish scholars represented in *Masters of the Talmud* have profound meaning for the contemporary reader. Let me point out several.

Rabbi Eliezer said: "Let the dignity of your friend [and his passion for learning] be as important to you as your own" (Mishnah *Avot* 2:10). This sentiment is demonstrated in the Babylonian Talmud

(*Yoma* 35b), which recounts a story told about Hillel, whose passion for knowledge will inspire students of today:

> Hillel labored for a daily wage of one-quarter dinar. He gave half of this to the watchman at the academy where he studied and used the other half to support himself and his family. One day Hillel wasn't able to muster his quarter dinar, and the watchman refused him entrance. Hillel hoisted himself to the roof of the academy and put his ear to the skylight, so as to be able to hear the words of Torah being taught by his masters Shemayah and Avtalyon. It was the eve of the Sabbath, in the middle of winter, and snow was falling. Shemayah said to Avtalyon: "Every day this building is well lit, and today it is dark." When they looked up, they saw the outline of the man on the roof, quickly brought him down, washed and cleaned him, and placed him in front of the fire to warm up.

The numerous words of wisdom ascribed to Hillel in the Talmud are as applicable to readers today as to Hillel's own students. Hillel said, for example, "He who reviews his studies one hundred times is not to be compared to one who has done so one hundred and one times" (*Chagigah* 9b). In Mishnah *Avot* 1:12 Hillel advises, "Be a disciple of Aaron, love peace, pursue peace, love mankind, and bring them close to Torah observance." "Do not separate yourself from the community," he cautions in *Avot* 2:2. The Talmud also describes Hillel's charitable acts, his hospitality to strangers, and his faith in the Almighty. So admired was the humility of Hillel that it was said of him, "Never will there be a man as modest as Hillel" (*Shabbat* 30b).

Rabbi Akiva ben Yosef's dedication to his students was legendary. When one of them fell ill, Akiva went to visit him. Said Rabbi Akiva, "Not visiting the sick is akin to the spilling of blood" (*Nedarim* 40a). One can discern the degree of Rabbi Akiva's love for humanity from his famous aphorism (Palestinian Talmud, *Nedarim* 9:4): "Love your neighbor as yourself is one of the greatest teachings of the Torah." Evidence of his deep concern for the sanctity of all human life can be gleaned from his view expressed in *Makkot*

7a: "If I were a member of the Sanhedrin, never would I have executed even a single person."

Jewish sources state that Rabbi Akiva sacrificed his life in order to sanctify God's name. When the Romans prohibited the study of Torah, he publicly flouted their decree, and was arrested and sentenced to death. When the hour of execution approached, Akiva prepared to recite the *Shema*. As he began the prayer, the Romans started combing his flesh with an iron rake. When asked how he could endure such intense pain, he replied: "All my life I was troubled, not knowing how I would ever be able to fulfill the commandment 'And you shall love the Lord your God with all your heart and all your soul and all your might' [which is part of the *Shema; Deuteronomy* 6:4–9]. Now that moment has arrived!" As Rabbi Akiva reached the final word, *Echad* ("One"), of the first sentence of the *Shema,* in which God's unity is affirmed, the last breath of life left him.

Among the numerous other Talmudic masters whose words resonate through the centuries are Abbayei and Rava, two of the most outstanding amora'im. Various sayings are ascribed to Abbayei, including: "One should always strive to be on the best of terms with his fellow Jews, his relatives, and all mankind, even the heathen in the marketplace, so that he may be beloved above [in heaven] and below [on earth], and well-received by all his fellow creatures" (*Berakhot* 17a).

From the biblical commandment "Love thy neighbor as thyself" (*Leviticus* 19:18), Abbayei concluded that if someone studies Scripture and Mishnah, attends to the needs of the disciples of the wise, is honest in business, and speaks pleasantly to his fellowman, people will say of him, "Happy is the father who taught him Torah; happy is the teacher who taught him Torah; and woe unto the people who have not studied the Torah. [And, they add,] [t]his man who has studied the Torah, look how fine his conduct is, how righteous are his deeds" (*Yoma* 86a). Concerning such people, Abbayei quoted the prophet Isaiah as saying, "You are my servant, Israel, in which I glory" (*Isaiah* 49:3).

Rava was a spiritual leader in the Babylonian city of Machoza. He ordered the Jewish citizens of Machoza to respect their wives (*Bava Metzi'a* 59b) and also instructed them to live a life of humility and modesty. He buttressed his demands by quoting a description of the trek of the Israelites through the desert as described in the book of *Numbers* 21:19: "Now, from the wilderness to Mattanah ["gift" in Hebrew], and from Mattanah to Nachali'el ["inheritance"], and from Nachaliel to Bamot ["the heights"]." Thus, concluded Rava, "When one makes himself as the wilderness, which is open and free to all [and is prepared to teach the Torah freely to all], the Torah becomes his gift (*mattanah*). And once he possesses it as a gift, God gives it to him as an inheritance (*nachal'iel*). And when God gives it to him as an inheritance, he ascends to great heights (*bamot*). But if he exalts himself immodestly, the Holy One, Blessed be He, casts him down. As it is written [in *Numbers* 21:20], "and from Bamot ['the heights'] to the valley" (*Eruvin* 54a, *Nedarim* 55a).

These are but a few examples of the wisdom of the Sages whose thoughts are expressed in the pages of the Talmud and whose insights continue to guide us today. The importance of Rabbi Kolatch's volume is that it unlocks the doors of the Talmud by making the lives and thinking of the ancient Rabbis more understandable and better appreciated. It will appeal to those just beginning Talmudic studies, but also to the experienced student who is interested in the history of the Talmudic era and the arguments presented by the tanna'im and the amora'im, as they considered the true meaning and intent of the Torah's commandments.

I will conclude on a personal note. As I write this Preface, I feel a sense of closure. Rabbi Alfred Kolatch was a student of my grandfather, Rabbi Dr. Yechiel Kaplan, a learned, cultured man, gentle and sensitive, who throughout his life embodied the spirit of the Torah and the moral lessons of the Sages of the Talmud. He taught Talmud in the Teachers Institute of Yeshiva University and was the author of *The Redaction of the Babylonian Talmud*. I am thankful for the opportunity, through this Preface, to honor my dear grandfather, whom I never met, but whose special traits I have heard about from many.

YEHIEL KAPLAN

Yehiel Kaplan, an ordained rabbi and doctor of jurisprudence, is a member of the Faculty of Law at the University of Haifa, Israel, where he specializes in Jewish Law and Family Law.

The Origin and Development of the Talmud

∽

The Torah, which according to tradition was dictated by God to Moses on Mount Sinai, is considered the greatest literary treasure of the Jewish people. The Talmud, for the most part a commentary on the Torah, is a monumental achievement in its own right.

Over the centuries, noted scholars and academicians, Jewish as well as non-Jewish, have sung the praises of the Talmud. In 1891, in the Preface to the English translation of his eleven-volume *History of the Jews*, historian and Bible scholar Heinrich Graetz wrote:

> The Babylonian amora'im [Talmudic scholars] created the dialectic, close-reasoning Jewish spirit, which in the darkest days preserved the dispersed nation from stagnation and stupidity. It was the eternal spring which kept the mind ever bright and active.

On December 29, 1920, Romanian-born Bible scholar Shalom Spiegel, who taught in Palestine and later at New York's Jewish Theological Seminary of America, delivered a lecture at the University of Chicago in which he said:

> The devil, according to Shakespeare, quotes Scripture. But if he is really as clever as he is reputed to be, he ought to quote the Talmud, as there is hardly any view of life for and against which one could not quote the Talmud.

The religious, civil, and ethical laws found in the Torah—referred to in English as the Five Books of Moses, in Hebrew as the *Chumash*, and in Greek as the Pentateuch—were the subjects of study in the academies of Palestine and Babylonia, the birthplace of the Talmud. The word *talmud* means "study" or "learning."

21

The tanna'im and amora'im—the scholars whose work ultimately became recorded in the Talmud—devoted their lives to the study of Torah. They delved into its text, analyzing and interpreting every verse, every word, every letter, trying to extract their innermost meanings and develop a definitive guide for proper Jewish living. These scholars found significant moral lessons even in the narrative portions of the Torah, beginning with Creation and ending with the death of Moses. No subject was alien to them, no aspect of life too remote to be examined.

All of the discussions, debates, and analyses of the tanna'im and amora'im comprise the two huge compendiums known as the Babylonian Talmud and the Palestinian (or Jerusalem) Talmud.

Historical Background

According to Talmudic tractate *Avot* (1:1), sometimes referred to in Hebrew as *Pirkei Avot* (in English, *Ethics of the Fathers*), "Moses received the Torah on Mount Sinai and transmitted it to Joshua, who transmitted it to the Elders. The Elders transmitted it to the Prophets, and the Prophets to the Men of the Great Assembly." Thus, the Torah that was read and studied in later generations was believed to be one and the same as the original Torah of Moses.

This has been the traditional view despite the fact that the whereabouts of the Torah of Moses were unknown for many centuries. From the time of the Revelation at Sinai, dated around 1250 B.C.E., until the reign of King Josiah in the early part of the seventh century B.C.E.—a span of six hundred years—no mention is made of such a Torah scroll.

Not until *2 Kings* 22:8 do we hear of the existence of a Torah scroll. At this point, the High Priest Chilkiah tells the scribe Shafan that he has discovered a scroll of the Torah in the Temple. Shafan informs King Josiah of the discovery, and the ecstatic king then summons all the people to appear at the Temple in Jerusalem, whereupon he reads to them the entire text of the scroll that had been found in the Temple (*2 Kings* 23:1–2). Scholars believe that the scroll was the book of *Deuteronomy*.

The next reference made to a public reading from a Torah scroll is to one held some two hundred years later, when Ezra, in the middle of the fifth century B.C.E., reads the Torah to the masses (*Nehemiah* 8). It is questionable whether the Torah used by Ezra (Mishnah *Keilim* 15:6) was the actual Torah dictated by God to Moses. The Talmud refers to many copies of the Torah that apparently were in existence at that time. However, one particular scroll—the Torah from which the High Priest read to the public on Yom Kippur—was considered to be the authentic Moses scroll.

This Azarah Scroll (*Sefer ha-Azarah*), also known as the Ezra Scroll (*Sefer Ezra*), was the official Temple scroll. It was never removed from the Temple precincts and was considered to always be in a state of purity. It is the text of this Torah scroll that tradition says was handed down from Ezra the Scribe to future generations and that eventually became the master from which all scrolls and codices were copied. The master scroll, although referred to, apparently was never found, and thus the trueness of current texts to the Torah of Moses is taken by traditionalists as an act of faith.

Other Torah scrolls kept in the Temple at that time were probably used for study purposes. But these were not guarded as was the *Sefer ha-Azarah*. They were kept in the storage area of the Temple together with gifts of food known as heave offerings (*terumot*), which were brought for the Priests by pilgrims to Jerusalem.

Ezra and Nehemiah

In 587 B.C.E., King Nebuchadnezzar of Babylonia captured Jerusalem and destroyed the First Temple, which had been built by King Solomon some four hundred years earlier. Zedekiah, the last king of Judah, was exiled to Babylonia in chains, along with many thousands of his compatriots. Judea ceased to be an independent nation, although Jews continued to live there. Jewish learning, once centered in Palestine (*Eretz Yisrael*, the Land of Israel), now found a haven in Babylonia.

In 539 B.C.E., King Cyrus of Persia defeated the Babylonian army, and the Persians became the dominant power in the region. In 538 B.C.E., Cyrus issued an edict permitting the Jewish exiles in Babylonia to return to Palestine and, if they wished, to reestablish their Temple. In 516 B.C.E., Zerubbabel, governor of Judah, completed the task of rebuilding. The new structure, the Second Temple, would remain standing for almost six hundred years before being destroyed by the Romans in 70 C.E.

Fifty years after the Temple was rebuilt by Zerubbabel, two figures dominated Jewish life: Ezra and Nehemiah. Both had been members of the Jewish community in exile in Babylonia, and both returned to Palestine. When Nehemiah, who had been cupbearer to Persian king Artexerxes I, heard that "Jerusalem's wall was full of breaches and its gates had been destroyed by fire" (*Nehemiah* 1:3), he asked the king's permission to help his fellow Jews rebuild the city's fortifications. Permission was granted, and Nehemiah was appointed governor of Jerusalem.

Ezra the Scribe was responsible for the religious instruction of the Jewish community, establishing schools, instituting the public reading of the Torah, and inaugurating the Keneset ha-Gedolah. Six hundred years later, Shimon ben Lakish recalled: "In ancient times, when the Torah was forgotten by Israel, Ezra came up from Babylonia [to Palestine] and restored it [by teaching it to the masses]" (*Sukkah* 20a). Yosei ben Chalafta said that had Moses not been chosen to receive the Torah from God, Ezra would have been selected (*Sanhedrin* 21b).

Keneset ha-Gedolah

According to tradition, it was under Ezra's leadership that a distinguished group of 120 Sages, including the prophets Haggai, Zechariah, and Malachi, formed the Keneset ha-Gedolah, known in English as the "Great Assembly." According to the Talmud (*Yoma* 69b and *Berakhot* 33a), the members of this body were called "great" because "they restored the crown of [God's] glory to its rightful place"; they are credited with instituting the *Shemoneh Esrei* and other prayers and rituals, including the *Kiddush* and *Havdalah*. It was during the period of the Keneset ha-Gedolah that the biblical canon was finalized. The members of the Keneset ha-Gedolah were the first to systematically study the biblical text, interpret it, and expound upon it. They extracted legal and moral lessons from each sentence, each word, even each letter. And all of these studies became the basis of the Oral Law—the *Mishnah* and, later, the *Gemara*.

The Sanhedrin

Derived from the Greek meaning "court," the term *Sanhedrin* refers to the great judicial body that functioned in Palestine during the Second Temple period (c. 520 B.C.E. to 70 C.E.). Scholars do not agree as to precisely how and when the Sanhedrin came into being, but according to a statement in *Avot*, it may have been an outgrowth of the Keneset ha-Gedolah.

The Sanhedrin was composed of two courts that governed Jewish religious and civil life under Roman rule: the Sanhedrin Gedolah, known in English as the "Great Sanhedrin," and the Sanhedrin Ketannah, known as the "Minor Sanhedrin."

Every well-populated city of Palestine had its own Sanhedrin Ketannah, consisting of twenty-three scholars who met to decide cases. Each Sanhedrin Ketannah handled major and minor cases, even homicides. Those that they were unable to adjudicate were referred to the Sanhedrin Gedolah in Jerusalem. The Sanhedrin Gedolah consisted of seventy-one members who met in the Temple's Lishkat ha-Gazit, the "Chamber of Hewn Stones."

Yosei ben Chalafta enumerates the qualities a scholar was expected to possess before he could become a member of the Sanhedrin (Tosefta *Chagigah* 2:9): He had to be a wise and modest man of pleasing appearance, impeccable moral character, and have many years of life experience.

The Zugot

From about 200 B.C.E. to the destruction of the Second Temple in 70 C.E., five pairs (*zugot*) of scholars, spanning five generations, dominated the study of Torah. Identified in the first chapter of *Avot*, they were:

1. Yosei ben Yo'ezer and Yosei ben Yochanan
2. Yehoshu'a ben Perachyah and Nittai of Arbela
3. Yehudah ben Tabbai and Shimon ben Shetach
4. Shemayah and Avtalyon
5. Hillel and Shammai

The first-named scholar of each pair was the *nasi* ("president") of the Sanhedrin. The second-named scholar served as the *nasi's* deputy and was referred to in Hebrew as the *av beit din*—"father of the court." The *av beit din* presided over the court when it was in session.

Originally, members of the Sanhedrin were selected from the elite segment of Jewish society consisting of wealthy landowners and *Kohanim* ("Priests"), who controlled the Temple sacrificial system. The Priests grew rich from the offerings brought to the Temple by the Jewish public.

This group was the backbone of the Sadducean party, from whose midst members of the Sanhedrin were generally chosen, although some members of the opposing political party, the Pharisees, also occupied seats on the court.

Following the destruction of the Second Temple in 70 C.E., the Sanhedrin was relocated to Yavneh. It was later moved to Sepphoris, in northern Israel, which in the time of Yehudah ha-Nasi had become a prime center of Jewish learning. However, the Sanhedrin would never regain the power and prestige it had enjoyed in Jerusalem and would be completely abolished when the patriarchate was dissolved, around 425 C.E.

Sadducees, Pharisees, and Essenes

Three religious-political parties were active toward the end of the Second Temple period: the Sadducees, the Pharisees, and a minor sect known as the Essenes.

From the writings of Jewish soldier and historian Josephus Flavius (c. 38–100 C.E.), and from the Talmud itself, we learn about the early dominance of the Sadducean party. The Sadducees were known in Hebrew as the Tzedokim or Tzedukim ("Righteous Ones"). Modern scholars believe the name was derived from Zadok, who, in the first chapter of *1 Kings*, is identified as the Priest upon whom King David called to anoint his son Solomon to succeed him as king of Israel. The prophet Ezekiel, himself a member of the Priestly family, commented that only the descendants of Zadok were worthy of performing Priestly functions (*Ezekiel* 44:15–16), including offering sacrifices brought by the Jewish public. The Priests, who received a portion of many of the sacrifices (with the remainder going to the offerer), became very wealthy and aligned themselves with other aristocrats.

The Sadducees followed the Torah to the letter, believing only in the authority of the Written Law; they did not believe in the resurrection of the dead or the immortality of the soul.

The Pharisees, on the other hand, accepted the Oral Law. Known in Hebrew as Perushim ("Separatists"), the Pharisees strictly observed the laws of ritual purity and tithing, and "separated" themselves from those who were not particular about these ritual matters and from the Sadducees.

The tenor of Jewish life underwent a change during the leadership of Shimon ben Shetach, a member of the third of the *zugot*, when he ousted the Sadducean members of the Sanhedrin and replaced them with Pharisees. Shimon is credited with initiating the written marriage contract and instituting elementary education for the young.

Shemayah and Avtalyon, who followed Shimon ben Shetach and Yehudah ben Tabbai, were persons of modest means, said by some to be proselytes or the sons of proselytes.

A generation later, under the leadership of Hillel, also a Pharisee, an important regulation was instituted to ease the ability of the poor to obtain loans. Hillel and other Pharisees assured the often distressed masses that their reward for righteous living awaited them in the world to come.

The leaders of the Pharisees were forerunners of the tanna'im, whose teachings are recorded in the Mishnah.

In addition to the Sadducees and Pharisees, a third religious-political party, known as the Essenes, flourished in Second Temple times. While the Sadducees and Pharisees were significant in number and are mentioned frequently in Talmudic literature, the Essenes, known in Hebrew as Isiyyim ("Pietists"), are not. We know about them primarily from the writings of the first-century C.E. Philo and Josephus. It is believed that the Essenes lived in an isolated community in Qumran, near the caves in which the Dead Sea Scrolls, believed by scholars to have been part of the Essene library, were discovered. The Essenes were opposed to ownership of property and strictly observed the laws of ritual purity.

Life in Babylonia

In 597 B.C.E., Nebuchadnezzar captured Jerusalem and exiled the first Jews to Babylonia, of which he was king. The Babylonian exile culminated in the destruction of the First Temple in 586 B.C.E., after which even more Jews were taken in captivity to Babylonia. Nebuchadnezzer did, however, allow the Jewish exiles to join a self-governing community under the leadership of the exilarch, known in Aramaic as the *reish galuta* ("head of the exile").

The office of *reish galuta* was hereditary: the man chosen to lead the Jewish community was to be a descendant of the ancient ruling dynasty of Judea, the house of David. The first exilarch was King Jehoiachin of Judah. Even after the power of the Babylonians in the region waned—they were succeeded by the Persians, the Syrians, and the Romans—the *reish galuta* was responsible for governing the Jews of Babylonia and mediating between the Jewish community and the ruling power.

The Jewish population of Babylonia was engaged in a variety of activities, and it was permitted to go about its business without interference. Those who lived on farms raised crops and cattle, while those who resided in cities were artisans of various types.

The *reish galuta* instituted strict market controls and appointed a marketing commissioner who regulated the economic life of the Jewish community, which included the collection of taxes, a portion of which was sent to the ruling power's treasury. The second/third-century Babylonian scholar Rav was appointed to this highly coveted position.

The *reish galuta* was responsible for the administration of justice both in civil and criminal matters. He appointed Jewish judges and administered a Jewish police force and penal system. The judges whom the exilarch appointed enjoyed immunity: they could not be sued for errors in judgment (*Sanhedrin* 4b). Although the *reish galuta* was not always a scholar, he was regarded by the Jews of Babylonia with great respect. Learned members of the *reish galuta*'s family often were selected to serve as judges and given the honorable title "Rabbana," meaning "our master" (*Pesachim* 115b and *Chullin* 92a).

When an ordinary Jew was given an *aliyyah* in the synagogue, he would ascend the pulpit to pronounce the Torah blessings. It is said that when the *reish galuta* was given an *aliyyah*, the Torah was carried to him.

The *reish galuta* was held in high regard by the governing powers, and the investiture of a new *reish galuta* was marked with great pomp and ceremony: the monarch would "lay hands" on the new appointee while trumpets were sounded. On the Sabbath following the exilarch's investiture, a special service was held in his honor. The *Yekum Purkan*, two prayers recited on the Sabbath in Ashkenazic synagogues following the Torah reading—one on behalf of the teachers of Israel and Babylonia, the other on behalf of the congregation—refers to the well-being of the *reish galuta*.

The first *reish galuta* of note is Huna, a third-century Babylonian amora. Yehudah ha-Nasi said that were Huna to come to Palestine, he would be subservient to Huna because Huna was descended from the House of David (Palestinian Talmud, *Kilayim* 9:3). Fourteen other exilarchs would serve during the Talmudic period.

Academies of higher learning were founded in Babylonia, the most famous of which were located in the cities of Sura, Nehardea, and Pumbedita. Many of the discussions in which the scholars of these academies engaged and their incisive Torah studies are recorded in the pages of the Talmud.

The Mishnah and the Tanna'im

The Hebrew term *mishnah* is derived from the root *shanah*, meaning "repeat," which characterizes the way in which the tradition was handed down from *tanna* ("teacher") to student, generation after generation: orally.

By the second century, however, the *tanna'im* (plural) feared that the vast oral tradition would be lost if it were not committed to writing. The most authoritative collection of Oral Law—and there were many such collections—was compiled in the third century by the esteemed scholar Yehudah ha-Nasi (Judah the Prince), usually referred to simply as "Rabbi." The compilation of Rabbi constitutes the official, accepted Mishnah that appears in the tractates of the Talmud.

The Mishnah, which is made up of the various *mishnayyot* (singular, *mishnah*) contained within each tractate, is divided into six "orders"—*Zera'im, Mo'ed, Nashim, Nezikin, Kodashim,* and *Tohorot.* In Hebrew, the Mishnah is sometimes referred to as *Shishah Sidrei Mishnah* ("Six Orders of the Mishnah") or by its acronym, *Shas.* Later the acronym came to be applied to the Talmud as a whole, which includes the Mishnah and its commentary, the Gemara.

Scholars were puzzled about the arrangement of the *massekhtot* ("tractates") within each order. For example, the tractate dealing with divorce (*Gittin*) precedes the tractate dealing with marriage (*Kiddushin*). It is popularly explained that the tractates were generally, though not always, arranged in order of length. *Gittin,* which has ninety pages, comes before *Kiddushin,* which has only eighty-two.

Some scholars posit that the Mishnah found in the Palestinian Talmud reflects an earlier version of Yehudah ha-Nasi's work. Talmudic authority Louis Ginzberg (1873–1953) believed the opposite: namely, that the Babylonian Talmud reflects an earlier version of the Mishnah than that of the Palestinian Talmud.

The tannaitic period drew to an end after the death of Yehudah ha-Nasi, in the early third century. At the end of his introduction to *Zera'im,* Maimonides counts 128 tanna'im whose teachings are found in the Mishnah. Other scholars place the number at 150.

Among the most prominent tanna'im, all of whom were Palestinian, were the disciples of Hillel and Shammai, Yochanan ben Zakkai, Gamli'el I, Gamli'el II, Yishma'el ben Elisha, Akiva ben Yosef and his disciples, Meir, Shimon bar Yochai, and, of course, Yehudah ha-Nasi.

The Tosefta

While Yehudah ha-Nasi completed the monumental task of compiling and editing the Mishnah, his brilliant disciples continued pursuing their studies, engaging in debate, and offering innovative interpretations of the Torah and Jewish tradition. Among the most outstanding of these scholars was Chiyya.

The teachings of these and other younger tanna'im were called *baraitot,* an Aramaic term meaning "external [to the Mishnah]."

ששה
סדרי משנה

ע ם
פירושי הראשונים
והאחרונים

הוצאת "אל המקורות" בע"מ
שנת התשי"ז
עיה"ק ירושלם תובב"א

The title page from an edition of the Mishnah published in Jerusalem in the Hebrew calendar year 5717 (1957). The large bold type reads *Shishah Sidrei Mishnah* ("Six Orders of the Mishnah"). The words beneath it indicate that the volume contains the interpretations of the *rishonim*, commentators who were active between the seventh and eleventh centuries, as well as those of the *acharonim*, who succeeded them.

31

The *baraitot* were gathered into a second collection of Oral Law called the *Tosefta*, which means "addition."

Although four times the length of the Mishnah, the Tosefta is arranged similarly. It is divided into the same six orders, with each order divided into the same *massekhtot*. These tractates are further divided into chapters and the chapters into individual laws.

The Amora'im

Once the Mishnah had been edited by Yehudah ha-Nasi, it soon became firmly established and itself the subject of intense scrutiny. The scholars who engaged in this formal study of the Mishnah were referred to as *amora'im*, meaning "speakers" or "interpreters."

Originally, an *amora* (singular) would stand alongside a tanna and explain in simpler terms the lesson being expounded by the tanna. Lessons often were presented in Hebrew, and the amora would translate the tanna's lecture into the vernacular Aramaic, which by the Second Temple period was the vernacular of both Palestinian and Babylonian Jews.

Gemara

In actuality, the amora'im did more than just translate the teachings of the tanna'im. They also commented and expanded upon the Mishnaic teachings, relating them directly to Jewish life and practice. Since the particulars of Torah commandments were not always spelled out in the Torah or Mishnah, the amora'im felt free to offer guidelines to be followed by all Jews. They offered instruction by way of two pedagogic methods: *halakhic* (legal) and *aggadic* (exegetical) interpretation.

The body of work in which the teachings of the amora'im, both halakhic and aggadic, are gathered is the Gemara, an Aramaic term meaning "learning." In the folios of the Talmud, an individual *gemara* commentary usually appears after each individual *mishnah* is presented. Note that the term Gemara is also sometimes used popularly as a synonym for the entire Talmud.

Halakhah, which derives from the Hebrew root meaning "to go," is the general, all-inclusive term for Jewish law—rituals, prayers,

The shaded area in this reproduction from the tractate *Bava Metzi'a* (115a) in the Babylonian edition of the Talmud shows a brief *mishnah* followed by a brief *gemara*. The commentary of Rashi appears in smaller type in the column at top right. The commentary in the left and bottom margins is known as *tosafot*, meaning "additions."

33

holiday observances, and so on. *Aggadah* (or *haggadah*, as the Babylonian scholars said) comprises such diverse subjects as hygiene, food, astrology, astronomy, folklore, even demonology. Included as well are legends and tales relating to the Messiah, the afterlife, man's relationship to God, and man's place in the universe.

In one of his essays on the Talmud, Emanuel Deutsch, the nineteenth-century German-Jewish orientalist, described *halakhah* as "emanating from the brain, *aggadah* from the heart. One is pure prose, the other poetry."

The Development of Halakhah

From the fifth century B.C.E. through the sixth century C.E., Jewish scholars studied, debated, and issued rulings that amplified the Torah text. Their overriding purpose was to ensure that the Jewish people remained loyal to the Covenant between God and Abraham by observing all the commandments (*mitzvot*) of the Torah. To the Rabbis of the Talmud this meant that a system of law had to be established, one that would train the Jewish people to serve God and their fellowmen as He had intended and protect them from alien influences.

The system used by Rabbis to uncover the underlying meanings of the Torah text is known as *hermeneutics*, from the Greek word meaning "to interpret." While the Sages insisted that the literal meaning of the text must be accepted as true and inviolable, they also validated allegorical and exegetical interpretations.

Though the rules are far older than Hillel, according to tradition it was Hillel who first articulated seven hermeneutical principles that could be used to explain biblical text. Yishma'el ben Elisha, who died a martyr's death during the Roman persecutions of 135 C.E., expanded on Hillel's rules and established thirteen principles for interpreting texts. Still later, Eli'ezer ben Yosei ha-Gelili expanded upon these thirteen principles and formulated thirty-two exegetical rules.

The thirteen hermeneutical principles of Yishma'el ben Elisha are included in the morning prayer service. Of the thirteen, the two that are the most commonly applied by students of the Bible are *kal va-chomer* and *gezeirah shavah*.

Using *kal va-chomer* (*a fortiori*, "for a stronger reason"), an inference deduced from a minor case is applied to a major case. The Tosefta (*Pesachim* 9:2) offers the following example: since silence is a good course for wise people to follow, how much more should this apply to ignorant people. Another example: if eating is prohibited on Tishah b'Av, which is not a holiday of biblical origin, how much more so is eating forbidden on Yom Kippur, whose observance is biblically mandated.

Gezeirah shavah means "comparison of texts." When the same phrase or word appears in two biblical passages, the lesson drawn in the first case applies in the second. For example, in *Kiddushin* 2a the Rabbis conclude that the "taking of a bride [in marriage]" becomes official with the transfer of money from the bridegroom to the bride (later, the giving of a ring by the groom to the bride). The Rabbis reached this conclusion by drawing an analogy between *Genesis* 23:13, in which Abraham, who wishes to acquire the cave of Machpelah from Ephron the Hittite as a burial plot for his wife Sarah, says, "I will give you money for the field; take [*kach*] it from me . . . ," and *Deuteronomy* 22:13, which says, "If a man takes [*yikach*] a wife . . ." Just as property is acquired through the payment of money, so is a wife.

Another important hermeneutical principle, offered in *Pesachim* 6b by Menashya bar Tachlifa in the name of Rav, states, *Ein mukdam u-me'uchar ba-Torah*, "There is no earlier or later in the Torah." In other words, the text of the Pentateuch is not presented in precise chronological order. For instance, *Numbers* 1:1 says that God spoke to Moses "on the first day of the *second* month in the second year following the Exodus from Egypt . . . ," while eight chapters later, in *Numbers* 9:1, it says that God spoke to Moses "in the *first* month of the second year following the Exodus . . ."

Using these principles and others, the tanna'im and amora'im examined the text of the Torah with microscopic precision to extract from it guidelines for Jewish daily living. In *Sanhedrin* 32b, for example, the Babylonian scholar Ashi ponders the verse, "Justice, justice shalt thou pursue . . ." (*Deuteronomy* 16:20). Puzzled by the repetition of the word *justice*, Ashi concludes that the first reference is to a just decision based on strict law and the second to justice arrived at through compromise. The Gemara supports this view by quoting Shimon ben Gamli'el II, who said, "The force of arbitration [hence, compromise] is greater than that of a legal ruling [by a judge] (*Sanhedrin* 5b)." In this manner, the amora'im encouraged the peaceful resolution of conflicts before an arbitrator rather than litigation before a court of law.

In the area of pure ritual, the amora'im also analyzed the Torah text and sought to explain some of their unusual findings. Thus, the amoraic disciples of the tanna Yishma'el ben Elisha (*Chullin* 115b) concluded that the biblical verse, "Thou shalt not boil a kid in its mother's milk," is repeated three times in the Torah (*Exodus* 23:19 and 34:26; *Deuteronomy* 14:21) in order to make three different points:

1. It is forbidden to eat meat and dairy foods together.
2. It is forbidden to derive any benefit from foods so prepared, meaning that one may not sell them or give them away as gifts.
3. It is forbidden to use the same pot to cook meat products and dairy products.

The masters of the Talmud believed that the Torah was an instrument to aid Jews in living full, productive lives, and they were not averse to expressing strong beliefs on issues of wide social interest. They demonstrated their concern for the poor and those in dire straits by enacting laws that were an expansion of Torah legislation.

Hillel, renowned for his compassion, was early to recognize the dangerous consequences that could result were certain laws to be carried out precisely as stipulated in the Torah; for example, the laws concerning *shemittah*—the sabbatical year—which falls every seventh year. *Deuteronomy* 15:2 states that in the seventh year all debts are cancelled. This law was especially difficult on the poor, who were unable to obtain loans when the *shemittah* year was approaching. Who would lend them money if the obligation to repay would soon be cancelled?

To mitigate this law, Hillel instituted the *perozbol*, derived from the Greek word meaning "official notice." The *perozbol* is a legal document in which the lender declares that he is turning over to the court for collection all loans that are due him (Mishnah *Shevi'it* 10:3ff. and *Gittin* 37a). The cancellation of debts during the *shemittah* year applies only to personal loans, not to public ones. By means of a legal fiction, the biblical law was interpreted in such a way to ensure that the poor could obtain loans even right before the *shemittah*. The *perozbol* thus protected the rich against monetary loss and made it possible for the poor to secure badly needed loans.

The view of the Rabbis of the Talmud with regard to the implementation of the death penalty is another expression of their compassion. Biblical law demands the death penalty for certain offenses, including abusing one's parents (*Exodus* 21:15,17), committing adultery (*Leviticus* 20:10) or incest (*Leviticus* 18:6–18), kidnapping (*Exodus* 21:16), violating the Sabbath (*Exodus* 35:2), and, of course, committing murder (*Exodus* 21:12). Yet the Rabbis acknowledged the fallibility of eyewitnesses and were wary of putting an innocent person to death by mistake. This is reflected in a statement in *Makkot* 7a: "Eli'ezer ben Azaryah said that a court that executes a person once in seventy years is a 'wicked court.' Rabbi Akiva and Rabbi Tarfon [went even further], declaring that 'capital punishment should never be carried out.'"

Such is the way in which the Talmudic masters exchanged views and interpreted the Bible text.

The Development of Aggadah

An Aramaic word meaning "narrative," *aggadah* (in Hebrew, *haggadah*) refers to the sections of the Talmud that contain stories, parables, and words of wisdom through which the Rabbis sought to teach a lesson. It includes discussions of ethics, philosophy, and theology, as well as popular tales, legends, and folklore. It also covers such topics as astronomy, astrology, medicine, magic, and mysticism. Note that the term *aggadah* is used by Palestinian scholars while *haggadah* is used by Babylonian scholars.

The *aggadah* is a window to Jewish life in the early centuries of the Common Era. From it we learn about the relationship between God and Jew, between fellow Jews, and between Jews and their environment. Above all, the *aggadah* inspires Jews to be loyal to their heritage and to face adversity with courage—in short, to be better human beings.

Leopold Zunz, the outstanding nineteenth-century German scholar, summarized the contents of the *aggadah* as follows: "Everything the imagination can conceive is found in the *aggadah* with one great exception: it contains no frivolity. It is there to teach love of God and fear of God."

The interconnection between *aggadah* and *halakhah* was once described by the poet Hayyim Nahman Bialik in this way: "The *halakhah* is the exemplification and crystallization of the *aggadah*, while the *aggadah* is the crucible of *halakhah*."

When the Romans decreed that it was forbidden for Jews to study Torah or practice its laws—and certainly to teach it—Pappus ben Yehudah found his colleague Akiva ben Yosef—Rabbi Akiva—assembling groups of Jews to whom he would teach Torah and asked him, "Aren't you afraid of the government?" Akiva replied, "Let me answer you with a parable." The parable follows:

> Once a fox was walking alongside a river and saw fish swimming by in schools, rushing from one place to another. Said the fox to the fish, "From whom are you fleeing?"
>
> The fish replied, "We are fleeing the fishermen's nets that are cast to entrap us."
>
> "Why don't you come up here on the dry land," said the fox, "so you and I can live together, just the way our ancestors once lived together?"
>
> To which the fish replied, "Aren't you the foolish one! You are called the most clever of animals, but you are the most foolish. If we are afraid here in the water, which is our element, how much more would we be afraid on dry land, which is a strange environment!"

"So it is with us," concluded Akiva. "If we are not safe when we study Torah, how much less safe would we be were we to neglect the Torah!" (*Berakhot* 61b)

Another famous *aggadah*, the story of a great Sage who experienced many miracles in his lifetime, demonstrates the length to which a man will go to atone for his religious and human failures.

Nachum of Gimzo, a learned tanna who taught Rabbi Akiva ben Yosef, was noted for his profound intellect, but especially for his courageous conduct in the face of misfortune. Whatever calamity befell him, he would say, *Gam zu le-tovah*, "This, too, is for the best" (*Sanhedrin* 108b).

Of this man of great faith the Talmud relates (*Ta'anit* 21a) that he was blind in both eyes, that his hands and legs had been amputated, that his entire body was covered with boils, and that he spent his days in a dilapidated house in a bed partially immersed in water.

> His disciples came to him and said, "Master, you have been such a completely religious person, why has this great calamity befallen you?"
>
> Nachum replied: "I deserved it all because I was a selfish, uncaring person. Once, when I was on my way to visit my father-in-law, I took along as gifts three donkeys laden with food and all kinds of delicacies. An emaciated man stopped me on the road and said: 'Master, give me something to eat.'
>
> "Instead of feeding him immediately, I said, 'Wait until I unload [my baggage], and I will find something for you.' While waiting, the man died."
>
> Filled with shame and remorse, Nachum threw himself upon the body of the dead man and exclaimed: "May my eyes that had no pity upon your eyes become blind. May my hands that had no pity on your hands be cut off. May my legs that had no pity on your legs be amputated."
>
> Nachum felt he had not done enough to atone for his sin, so he added, "And may my whole body be covered with boils."

The Babylonian Talmud

When a person speaks of the Talmud, he or she usually means the Babylonian Talmud. Referred to in Hebrew simply as the *Bavli* ("of Babylonia"), it was compiled and edited around 500 C.E., one hundred years after the Palestinian Talmud. Of the two, the *Bavli* is considered the more authoritative.

Life for the Jews of Babylonia under the Persians was far more secure and peaceful than life for the Jews of Palestine, who were under Roman rule. As long as the Babylonian Jewish community paid its taxes and was not a threat to the government, it enjoyed a high degree of autonomy.

One of the outstanding leaders of third-century Babylonian Jewry was Shemu'el (Samuel), a physician who headed the academy in Nehardea. Shemu'el was befriended by the Persian king Shapur and, in a famous ruling, he encouraged Jews to obey the king's laws. *Dina d'malkhuta dina*, "The law of the land is the law [by which Jews must abide]," he said.

In this atmosphere, Babylonian amora'im were free to think about and discuss matters that were more than halakhic in nature, devoting much of their attention to philosophical and theological questions. As a result, the *Bavli* is much broader in scope than the Palestinian Talmud, and it is more widely studied. In *Masters of the Talmud*, all Talmudic citations refer to the *Bavli*, unless otherwise noted.

The Babylonian Talmud is about three times the size of the Palestinian, filling six thousand folios and containing an estimated 2,500,000 words; approximately one-third of the *Bavli* is *halakhah* and two-thirds *aggadah*.

The language of the Babylonian Talmud is basically Hebrew and Eastern Aramaic, but it also contains a considerable number of Persian words that were used in the discussions and debates of scholars who studied in the academies of Sura, Pumbedita, Nehardea, Machoza, and other Babylonian towns. The opinions expressed in the text often reflect a restatement by a disciple of what he had been taught by his master. The verbal exchanges are far-reaching and do not follow any particular formula; hence, some material may seem out of place in a particular discussion.

The Babylonian Sages were noted for their dialectical discussions

40

BABYLONIA

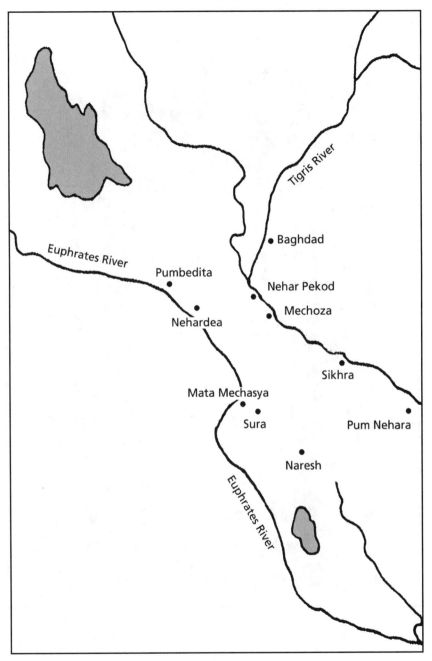

Major Jewish Centers of Learning During the Talmudic Period

The title page of the tractate *Berakhot* from an edition of the Babylonian Talmud published in the holy city of Jerusalem in the Hebrew calendar year 5733 (1973).

and hair-splitting analyses. *Bava Metzi'a* 38b says, "In Pumbedita, the students know how to pass an elephant through the eye of a needle," meaning that they could argue endlessly for the acceptance of statements or positions that were often illogical or untenable.

Particularly noteworthy is the extent to which the Babylonian Talmud was influenced by the esoteric teachings of the Persian religious leader Zoroaster (c. seventh century B.C.E.). Although the Rabbis did not subscribe to his doctrine of dualism, which maintains that light and righteousness are the motivating forces in the universe, they *were* influenced by Zoroaster's teachings about the power of angels, demons, and other supernatural forces. Hence, in many tractates of the *Bavli*, we find references to demonology, angelology, astronomy, and astrology. In *Chagigah* 16a, for example, the Rabbis discuss the attributes of angels, informing us that they walk upright, can fly in the air, and can foretell the future. Furthermore, the Rabbis caution us, since angels know only Hebrew, people should not pray to them in Aramaic, lest their prayers go unanswered.

The Babylonian Talmud does not comment on all six orders of the Mishnah. *Mo'ed, Nashim, Nezikin,* and *Kodashim* are covered almost completely. However, there is no *gemara* commentary for *Shekalim* in the orders *Mo'ed, Edduyot,* and *Avot* in *Nezikin,* or for *Middot* and *Kinnim* in the order *Kodashim.* With the exception of *Berakhot* and *Niddah,* the Babylonian Talmud has no *gemara* whatsoever for the orders *Zera'im* and *Tohorot,* respectively.

Ashi, the fourth/fifth-century amora and principal of the academy in Sura, began the work of redacting the Babylonian Talmud, which was completed by the fifth-century amora Ravina II.

• • •

When one opens a page of the Babylonian Talmud, one sees the Mishnah and *gemara* text surrounded by commentary in a different, smaller typeface. The commentary found closest to the inner margins (gutter) of two facing pages is that of Rashi (Rabbi Shelomoh Yitzchaki), the famous eleventh-century French scholar. The commentary in the outer columns is known as *tosafot,* meaning "additions," and consists mainly of the views of Rashi's grandchildren.

Also on the page, in very small type, are the commentaries of Rabbeinu Chananel, Rav Nissim Ga'on, and others.

The Palestinian Talmud

Compiled and redacted around 400 C.E., the Palestinian Talmud is also known as the Jerusalem Talmud or, in Hebrew, the *Yerushalmi* ("of Jerusalem"). In point of fact, after the destruction of the Second Temple and the city of Jerusalem by the Romans in 70 C.E., Jewish academies of learning were not permitted to operate there.

All of the main learning centers were situated in other parts of Palestine, including Tiberias, Lydda, Caesarea, and Sepphoris. Sa'adyah ben Yosef Ga'on (882–942), the Egyptian-born scholar who later settled in Babylonia and was appointed head of the academy in Sura, referred to the Palestinian Talmud as the "Talmud of Eretz Yisra'el [Land of Israel]." Still others called it the *Talmud ha-Ma'aravah* or *Talmud de-Venei Ma'aravah* ("Talmud of the West"), since Palestine was west of Babylonia.

It is estimated that one-sixth of the Palestinian Talmud is *aggadah*, while the *Bavli* consists of about one-third *aggadah*. The distinguished professor of Talmud Louis Ginzberg, in his *Commentary on the Palestinian Talmud*, explained the great difference in content between the two Talmuds by contrasting the comparative ease enjoyed by students in such Babylonian academies as Sura and Pumbedita with the harsh conditions imposed by the Romans on students in the great Palestinian academies. Not surprisingly, Palestinian scholars devoted themselves mostly to matters of practical law and practical living. Thus, when it comes to a discussion of angels and their influence, only Michael and Gabriel are mentioned in the *Yerushalmi*, whereas the *Bavli* cites the names of a host of others.

The Mishnah that appears in the *Yerushalmi* is not identical to that found in the *Bavli*. In many cases, the wording and phraseology are different, and sometimes there are substantive differences as well. Also in contrast to the *Bavli*, the language of the *Yerushalmi* is Western Aramaic and features many Greek words that were used in Syria and Palestine during the tannaitic period, which ended with the death of Yehudah ha-Nasi.

Unlike the Babylonians, the Palestinian Sages used a direct ana-

PALESTINE

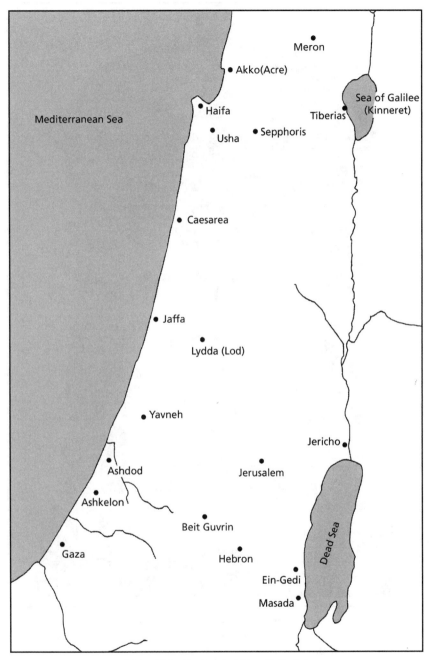

Major Cities During the Talmudic Period

The title page of the tractate *Berakhot* from an edition of the Palestinian (Jerusalem) Talmud published in Jerusalem in the Hebrew calendar year 5733 (1973).

The first page of *Pe'ah*, the second tractate in the order *Zera'im* ("Seeds"), as it appears in the Palestinian Talmud. Note that there is a *gemara* commentary following the *mishnah*, which is not the case in the Babylonian edition of this tractate. This is so because life in Babylonia was based on commerce rather than agriculture; hence, there was no need for the Babylonian masters to add commentary to the *mishnah*.

lytical approach, refraining from farfetched comparison and instead favoring concise discussion and logical deduction. What the *Yerushalmi* and the *Bavli* do have in common is the fact that neither expounds upon the complete Mishnah.

Palestinian *gemara* text can be found in the orders *Zera'im, Mo'ed, Nashim,* and *Nezikin* (except for tractates *Eduyyot* and *Avot,* as in the *Bavli*). *Gemara* commentary can also be found in the first three chapters of the tractate *Niddah* in the order *Tohorot.* The section "Talmudic Tractates," which begins on page 59, specifies in greater detail which parts of the Mishnah have *gemara* commentary.

Precisely who is responsible for compiling and editing the Palestinian Talmud around the year 400 A.D. is a matter of conjecture. As Professor Louis Ginzberg pointed out, the Talmud itself contains no internal evidence in that regard. Nonetheless, the traditional view is that Yochanan bar Yitzchak Nappacha, a brother-in-law of Reish Lakish, served as chief editor. Yochanan was a disciple of Oshaya Rabbah, also known as Hoshaya Rabbah, who had opened an academy in Caesarea that rivaled the prestigious academy in Tiberias.

The commentaries that appear in the Palestinian Talmud differ from those found in the Babylonian edition. Solomon Sirillo, who fled his native Spain as a consequence of the expulsion of 1492, eventually settling in Palestine, was the earliest commentator on the *Yerushalmi.* His work appeared in 1530. However, Joshua Benveniste of Turkey was the first to offer an extensive commentary on the *Yerushalmi,* and Moses Margalit (Margolies), who lived in Lithuania in the eighteenth century, was the first to publish a commentary on the entire Palestinian Talmud.

Talmudic Nomenclature

Students of the Talmud often encounter a great deal of difficulty in trying to ascertain the precise formulation of a Sage's name. In the Talmudic text, many of the most prominent and oft-quoted masters are mentioned by first name only. Rarely, if ever, is a patronymic appended to the first names of such celebrated scholars as Abbayei, Ashi, Chanina, Chiyya, Dimi, Elazar, Eli'ezer, Huna, Ya'akov, Yannai, Yehudah, Yishma'el, Yitzchak, or Yochanan.

Certain personalities under whom the earliest Sages studied were so prominent that it was unnecessary to identify them by more than their first name. When the name Yochanan was mentioned, for example, everyone knew that the reference was to the celebrated third-century Palestinian amora Yochanan bar Nappacha, but when the name Yehudah was uttered, it was unclear whether the person under discussion was the second-century Palestinian tanna Yehudah bar Ila'i or the third-century Babylonian amora Yehudah bar Yechezkel.

There are other masters for whom only a first name is often given. When the name Nachman is used, it is presumed to refer to Nachman bar Ya'akov; Eli'ezer, to Eli'ezer ben Hurkanos; Yehoshu'a, to Yehoshu'a ben Chananyah; Shimon, to Shimon bar Yochai; Elazar, to Elazar ben Pedat; and Yosei, to Yosei ben Chalafta. As mentioned earlier, third Yehudah, Yehudah ha-Nasi, is so outstanding that he usually is referred to simply as "Rabbi."

Of all the Talmudic scholars who were given nicknames, the second/third century Babylonian amora Shemu'el, Rav's colleague, stands out. He was referred to by four different names:

1. Shakud, meaning "the diligent one," because of the diligence he applied to his studies.
2. Aryokh, a variant form of *ari*, meaning "lion," because he pursued his studies with a lion's strength.
3. Shavur Malkah, the Aramaic form of the name of the Persian king Shapur, with whom Shemu'el was extremely friendly. *Sukkah* 53a states that Shemu'el would entertain King Shapur by juggling before him eight cups filled with wine.
4. Shemu'el Yarchina'a, because Shemu'el possessed an intimate knowledge of astronomy. *Yarchina'a* is an Aramaic term derived from the Hebrew *yarei'ach* and *yerach*, meaning "moon" and "month," respectively.

Shemu'el called his bright disciple Yehudah by the name Shinena, meaning "sharp one."

Another major difficulty confronting students of the Talmud is the question of *ben* versus *bar*. When should a scholar be listed as "so-and-so *ben* ['son of' in Hebrew] so-and-so," and when as "so-and-so *bar* ['son of' in Aramaic] so-and-so"?

The tanna'im in the Mishnah are always referred to as *ben*. Since all of the tannai'im were Palestinian, one might logically conclude that the proper designation for all Palestinian scholars was *ben*. However, the Palestinian scholar Yehudah son of Ila'i is referred to in the century-old *Jewish Encyclopedia* as Judah *ben* Ila'i, while in the more recent *Encyclopaedia Judaica* he is called Judah *bar* Ila'i. In only one instance (*Temurah* 15b) does the Talmud give this individual's name in full as Yehudah bar Ila'i; in hundreds of other references, the patronymic does not appear.

Some scholars maintain that the use of *ben* or *bar* varied with local custom, that no definitive rule was followed. Nonetheless, for consistency's sake, in this volume *ben* is usually used for the Palestinian masters and *bar* for the Babylonian. It is suggested that if readers cannot find a master's name under "so-and-so *bar* so-and-so," they look under "so-and-so *ben* so-and-so."

Yet another problem for Talmud students is that the Babylonian and Palestinian editions sometimes differ in their spelling of personal names. For example, in the *Bavli*, the third-century Babylonian tanna's name is spelled Oshaya, while in the *Yerushalmi* it is spelled Hoshaya. Yehudah in the Babylonian Talmud is Yudah in the Palestinian. Akiva and Chiyya both end with the letter *alef* in the Babylonian Talmud; in the Palestinian Talmud they end with the letter *hei*. The popular name Elazar in the Babylonian Talmud always appears as Lazar in the Palestinian.

In *Masters of the Talmud*, main entries primarily use Babylonian spellings. Alternative names and spellings, except for minor variations, are cross-referenced.

In both the Babylonian and Jerusalem Talmuds new names are sometimes created by combining two names or by shortening a name to make it easier to pronounce. Thus, in the Palestinian Talmud Avi Mari sometimes becomes Avmari, and in the Babylonian Talmud Rav Ammi sometimes is abbreviated as Rami and Rav Efrayim as Rafram. Shortened forms include Pas from Efes; Shimi, Simai, and Simi from Shimon; and Lazar from Elazar.

It is curious to note the absence in the Talmud of many important biblical names. There are no Talmudic masters named Avraham (Abraham), although there is an Avram; Yisra'el; Mosheh (Moses); David; or Shelomoh (Solomon). The names of some of Jacob's sons are used, but Dan, Gad, and Asher are not among them.

Except for Yirmeyahu (Jeremiah), none of the prophets' names are used. Not a single Talmudic master is named Yishayahu (Isaiah), Hoshei'a (Hosea), Yo'el (Joel), Amos, Ovadya (Obadiah), Micah, Habakkuk, Tzefanya (Zephaniah), or Malakhi (Malachi).

It is particularly difficult to explain why Yishmael (Ishma'el) was such a popular name during the Talmudic period, while the names of prominent biblical heroes and prophets were not commonly used. The Midrash (*Genesis Rabbah* 71:3) says of Yishmael, son of the patriarch Abraham, that his name is beautiful [it means "God will hear"], but his actions were ugly. However, *Berakhot* 56b says, "If one sees Ishmael in a dream, his prayer will be answered," which may explain why a parent would not hesitate to name a child Ishmael.

Honorific Titles

In both the Babylonian and Palestinian editions of the Talmud, honorific titles are used for masters deserving of great respect. The word *rabbi*, meaning "my master," was first used during the Talmudic period as a title for scholars who lived and studied in Palestine and received ordination. In the reference guide to the English edition of his Talmud translation, Adin Steinsaltz lists 186 of the most prominent tanna'im who were deemed deserving of the title "Rabbi." However, as mentioned above, the title "Rabbi" when appearing alone was reserved for the esteemed Yehudah ha-Nasi.

Babylonian scholars, regardless of how learned, were not called "Rabbi" because only scholars who lived and studied in Palestine received ordination. In place of "Rabbi," the titles "Rav" or "Mar," also meaning "master," were used by students to address their teachers or by teachers to address their colleagues. Palestinian luminaries so addressed were Rav Ashi, Rav Pappa, Rav Huna, Mar Shemu'el, Mar Ukba, and Mar Zutra.

Rabbinic Occupations

While many masters of the Talmud devoted their entire lives to Torah study and pedagogy, the academies encouraged their students to pursue an occupation so they would not be dependent on the community for support. Gamali'el III, Palestinian tanna and the eldest son of Yehudah ha-Nasi, said, "It is good to combine the study of Torah with an occupation, for the two together can keep one away from sin. . . ." (*Avot* 2:2).

Yochanan bar Nappacha said, "Whoever wishes to become rich should [avoid other difficult occupations and] get involved in the breeding of small cattle" (*Chullin* 84b).

A few tanna'im and amora'im were supported by their wealthy families, while others were engaged in profitable ventures of their own. Most scholars, however, earned a modest living as laborers or artisans. While even the most humble of occupations was not considered demeaning, Me'ir suggested, "One should always teach his son a clean and easy craft" (*Kiddushin* 82a).

Abba of Sidon, a disciple of Abba Guri'a, cautioned, "One should not teach his son to be an ass driver, camel driver, barber, sailor, shepherd, or shopkeeper because these are the occupations of thieves, lending themselves to fraud and deception" (*Kiddushin* 82a).

The first-century tanna Eli'ezer ben Hurkanos favored agriculture as an occupation. He predicted that "a time will come when all craftsmen will turn to agriculture" (*Yevamot* 63a). Other scholars recommended farming because it provided ample time to engage in Torah studies.

Below is a list of some of the many occupations in which tanna'im and amora'im were engaged:

- beer brewer—Chisda
- blacksmith—Yochanan bar Nappacha
- carpenter—Avin bar Nachman
- coin tester—Elazar ben Pedat
- coppersmith—Elazar ha-Kappar
- cupper—Abba Umana
- farmer—Huna
- gladiator—Shimon ben Lakish
- gravedigger—Abba Sha'ul
- manufacturer—Abbahu (women's veils), Huna bar Minyomi (*tzitzit*)
- needleworker—Yehoshu'a ben Chananyah
- physician—Shemu'el, Chanina bar Chama

- repairer of religious articles—Huna bar Chiyya in partnership with Levi bar Shemu'el Minyomi
- scribe—Efrayim Safra
- shoemaker—Yochanan ha-Sandelar, Chananyah
- wine merchant—Abba Sha'ul ben Botnit in partnership with Elazar ben Tzadok, Huna bar Yehoshu'a in partnership with Pappa
- tailor—Abba ben Zemina
- tradesman—Yochanan ben Zakkai
- wine taster—Karna

Ecclesiastes 3:10–11 says, "I have seen the task that God has given to the sons of men . . . God has made everything beautiful in its time . . ." This teaches us, the Rabbis concluded, that every occupation is suitable to those who engage in it (*Berakhot* 43b).

The Post-Talmudic Authorities

For five hundred years following the final editing of the Talmud—from about 500 to 1000 C.E.—great scholars, particularly in Babylonia, continued the process of interpreting the Bible and addressing legal questions that had not been resolved. The elucidations of these authorities appear in the form of commentaries in the back of many printed Talmud texts.

The first group of post-Talmudic commentators, those active primarily in the sixth century, were known as *savora'im* or *sabora'im* (singular, *savorah*), meaning "expositors." The first *savorah* of note was Rav Yosi, who expanded and commented upon the edited Talmud text. Generally speaking, little personal information is known about the *savora'im*.

The Talmudic expositors active between the seventh and eleventh centuries were known as *ge'onim* (singular, *ga'on*), meaning "[people of] grandeur, eminence." The most prominent of them were the Egyptian-born Sa'adya Ga'on (882–942), who became head of the Babylonian academy in Sura, and Sherira Ga'on (906–1006) and his son, Hai Ga'on (939–1038), who served as principals of the academy in Pumbedita. Sherira lived to the age of 100 and Hai to age 99.

Scholars from Europe and North Africa who emerged between the eleventh and sixteenth centuries are referred to as *rishonim*, meaning "early ones." In addition to analyzing the Talmud and writing commentaries on it, they prepared responsa to questions addressed to them by rabbis and teachers from many countries.

Among the most celebrated of the *rishonim* were Yitzchak Alfasi (1013–1103; Alfasi means "of Fez"), known as the Rif; Shelomoh Yitzchaki (1040–1105), better known as Rashi; his grandson Ya'akov ben Me'ir Tam (1100–1171), known as Rabbenu Tam; Moses Maimonides (1135–1204), known as Rambam; Moses Nahmanides (1194–1270), known as Ramban; and Meir ben Barukh of Rothenberg (c. 1215–1293). The commentators who followed the *rishonim* are referred to as *acharonim*, meaning "later ones."

Printed Editions of the Talmud

Medieval popes, convinced that the Talmud contained blasphemies against Christianity, consigned cartloads of Talmud manuscripts to flames; the only complete Talmud manuscript that remained dated back to 1334. Known as the Munich manuscript, it was kept in the possession of the Vatican.

In 1517 Christian merchant Daniel Bomberg, who lived in Venice, set up a Hebrew press and printed the first Hebrew Bible. In 1520 Bomberg received permission from Pope Leo X to issue a printing of both the Babylonian and Palestinian Talmuds (only certain tractates of the *Bavli* had been issued until then) based on the Munich manuscript.

However, the Church scrutinized Bomberg's effort. He was forced, for example, to replace the word *goy* (literally, "nation"), which was construed as a defamatory synonym for Christian, with the word *akum*, an acronym of the Hebrew words *oveid kokhavim u-mazalot*, "worshippers of stars and constellations," making clear that such references were not to Christians but to idolators.

Bomberg's format became the model for future editions of the Talmud. The numbering of pages in the *Bavli* began with page two (*bet*), the first being the title page. Rashi's commentary was placed next to the inner margins, to ensure that if the book became damaged his words would be the last to be affected; the *tosafot*

לְהַכְרָזָה – **for** the principle of **proclamation.** The verse teaches that the courts must publicly proclaim the punishment meted out to the offender for his sin, to serve as a warning to others. וְרַבִּי – **And R' Meir derives the** principle of **proclamation from** the verse's earlier phrase **they shall hear and they shall fear,** leaving the end of the verse – *and they shall not continue [to do] further* – to serve as the warning to *zomemin* witnesses.

מֵאִיר הַכְרָזָה מִ,,יִשְׁמְעוּ וְיִרָאוּ'' נָפְקָא

Mishnah

מְשַׁלְּשִׁין בְּמָמוֹן – They [the convicted *zomemin* witnesses] **divide a monetary [sentence]** among themselves, וְאֵין מְשַׁלְּשִׁין בְּמַכּוֹת – **but they do not divide the number of lashes.** כֵּיצַד – **How so?** הֵעִידוּהוּ שֶׁהוּא חַיָּיב לַחֲבֵרוֹ מָאתַיִם זוּז – **If they testified that he owed his fellow two hundred zuz,** וְנִמְצְאוּ זוֹמְמִין – **and were found to be *zomemin,* and were thus sentenced to pay two hundred *zuz* to their intended victim,** מְשַׁלְּשִׁין בֵּינֵיהֶן – **they divide** the payment **among themselves,** with each of the two witnesses paying one hundred *zuz.* [1] אֲבָל אִם הֵעִידוּהוּ שֶׁהוּא חַיָּיב מַלְקוּת אַרְבָּעִים – **But if they testified against him that he was liable to forty lashes** וְנִמְצְאוּ זוֹמְמִין – **and were found to be *zomemin,* and were thus sentenced to a reciprocal punishment of forty lashes,** כָּל אֶחָד וְאֶחָד לוֹקֶה אַרְבָּעִים – **each one receives forty lashes,** [2] and the lashes are not apportioned among the witnesses.

Gemara

The Gemara seeks the source for the law that each *zomem* witness receives the full set of lashes: מְנָא הָנֵי מִילֵּי – **From where is this derived?** אָמַר אַבַּיֵּי – **Abaye said:** נֶאֱמַר ,,רָשָׁע'' בְּחַיָּיבֵי מַלְקוּיוֹת – **The word** *rasha* [guilty one] **is stated concerning those who are liable to lashes,** [3] וְנֶאֱמַר ,,רָשָׁע'' בְּחַיָּיבֵי מִיתוֹת בֵּית דִּין – **and the word** *rasha* **is stated concerning those who are liable to execution by the courts.** [4] מַה לְהַלָּן אֵין מִיתָה לְמֶחֱצָה – **Just as there in the** case of the death sentence, **there is no execution by half,** אַף כָּאן – **so too, here,** אֵין מַלְקוּת לְמֶחֱצָה – **there are no lashes by half;** i.e. the punishment of lashes is not meted out by the courts in half measures. [5]

Another basis for the Mishnah's rule is offered:

רָבָא אָמַר – **Rava said:** ,,כַּאֲשֶׁר זָמַם לַעֲשׂוֹת לְאָחִיו'' – **To** בְּעֵינַן – properly carry out the reciprocal punishment, **we need** to do to each witness just **as he planned to do to his brother,** וְלֵיכָּא – **and this would be lacking** if we gave them each just a share of the lashes they sought to impose upon their intended victim.

The Gemara asks:

אִי הָכֵי מָמוֹן נַמִּי – **If so, a monetary [payment], too,** should be exacted in full from each of the witnesses?

The Gemara answers:

מָמוֹן מִצְטָרֵף – **Money can be combined** to form one joint reciprocal payment from all of the witnesses; מַלְקוּת לֹא מִצְטָרֵף – **lashes cannot be combined** to form one joint punishment, since each one's *malkus* has no link whatsoever to that of the other.**

Mishnah

אֵין הָעֵדִים נַעֲשִׂים זוֹמְמִין – **Witnesses do not become** *zomemin* עַד שֶׁיָּזוֹמּוּ אֶת עַצְמָן – **until** other witnesses discredit them **personally.** כֵּיצַד – **How so?** אָמְרוּ – **If they said** in their testimony: ,,מְעִידִין אָנוּ בְּאִישׁ פְּלוֹנִי – **'We testify against this man** שֶׁהָרַג אֶת הַנֶּפֶשׁ'' – **that he killed someone,'** אָמְרוּ לָהֶם – and the second set of witnesses **said to them,** הֵיאַךְ אַתֶּם מְעִידִין – **'How can you testify** to such a thing, שֶׁהֲרֵי – **was** הָיָה עִמָּנוּ אוֹתוֹ הַיּוֹם בְּמָקוֹם פְּלוֹנִי'' – **when this murder victim or the alleged murderer** נֶהֱרַג זֶה אוֹ הַהוֹרֵג זֶה – **with us that day in such-and-such a place?'** אֵין אֵלּוּ זוֹמְמִין – **These** first witnesses **are not rendered** *zomemin* by this form of refutation. [6] אֲבָל אִם אָמְרוּ לָהֶם – **But if they** [the second pair of witnesses] **said to them,** הֵיאַךְ אַתֶּם – ,,**when you were** מְעִידִין – **'How can you testify** about this event שֶׁהֲרֵי אַתֶּם הֱיִיתֶם עִמָּנוּ אוֹתוֹ הַיּוֹם בְּמָקוֹם פְּלוֹנִי'' – **with us on that day in such-and-such a place?'** הֲרֵי אֵלּוּ זוֹמְמִין – **These** first witnesses **are** *zomemin* וְנֶהֱרָגִין – **and are put to death by their word,** עַל פִּיהֶם – by the testimony of the second set of witnesses.** בָּאוּ אֲחֵרִים – **If other** witnesses came after the first set had already been discredited, and the new set testified to the same crime as did the first set, וַהֲזִימוּם – **and they** who discredited the first set **discredited them** [the

---

NOTES

1. This applies to a standard case of two witnesses. If there were more witnesses in the group, they would divide the punishment accordingly.

2. That is, thirty-nine lashes, as explained by the Mishnah 22a.

3. וְהָיָה אִם בִּן הַכּוֹת הָרָשָׁע – *And it shall be that if the* ***rasha*** (guilty one) *is liable to lashes* (Deut. 25:2).

4. אֲשֶׁר־הוּא רָשָׁע לָמוּת – *That he is a* ***rasha*** [sentenced] *to die* (Num. 35:31).

5. This type of derivation is known as a *gezeirah shavah.* This is one of the thirteen principles of hermeneutics by which the Torah is expounded. It allows the laws in one passage of the Torah to be applied to another by means of a code word which appears in both passages, and indicates that the laws stated in each of the two passages are considered as having been stated in the other passage as well. This cross-referencing is not arbitrary. The code words of a *gezeirah shavah* are designated as such in the Oral Tradition which goes back to Moses who received it at Sinai. There is a well-known Talmudic maxim: אֵין אָדָם דָּן גְּזֵרָה שָׁוָה אֶלָּא אִם כֵּן קִבְּלָהּ מֵרַבּוֹ – *One cannot infer a* gezeirah shavah *on his own, only if he received it from his teacher* (Niddah 19b).

6. This form of refutation is called הַכְחָשָׁה, *contradiction,* in which the court is left with contradictory testimonies without knowing which to believe. Thus, the matter remains in a state of legal doubt, and the court does not act upon the testimony of either set of witnesses.

INSIGHTS

* There is a conceptual difference between the *zomemin* punishments of *malkus* and money. In the case of a monetary payment, the purpose is to **compensate** the intended victim for the money which the *zomemin* sought to deprive him. Once the *zomemin* pool their separate funds to make up the required payment, the sum becomes a single unit of money, which belongs to the victim. In the case of *malkus,* however, the intended victim receives nothing as a compensation, but a penalty that the Torah imposes on the *zomemin* as a **punishment.** Since they are separate people, thirteen lashes imposed on each of three people, for example, would not add up to a single set of thirty-nine (see Rashi, Ritva, et al.).

** In the first example, the **contradiction** to the first witnesses is directed at the facts they have attempted to establish with their testimony. The murder did not take place at the time and place the first pair claimed for the event. This is הַכְחָשָׁה, contradictory testimony, and the court has no reason to believe one set of witnesses more than the other. In the second case, however, the facts of the event are not challenged directly; the murder may very well have occurred in the manner told by the first pair of witnesses. It is the **integrity** of the witnesses that is **being attacked.** Even if the event occurred as related by them, the testimony against them is that they **could not have seen it.** This is *hazamah,* and the Torah states that the second set of witnesses is believed (see introduction to Chapter 1).

In the ArtScroll edition of the Talmud, transliterations from Hebrew into English are rendered following the Ashkenazic system of pronunciation. Hence, the fifth tractate of the order *Nezikin* is spelled *Makkos* (circled), rather than *Makkot,* as the tractate's name would be pronounced by Sephardim. The various comments and insights offered on the above English page elucidate the Hebrew text, which appears on a facing page.

REALIA

קַלָּתָה **Her basket.** The source of this word is the Greek κάλαθος, *kalathos*, and it means a basket with a narrow base.

Illustration from a Greek drawing depicting such a basket of fruit.

CONCEPTS

פֵּאָה *Pe'ah.* One of the presents left for the poor (מַתְּנוֹת עֲנִיִּים). The Torah forbids harvesting "the corners of your field," so that the produce left standing may be harvested and kept by the poor (Leviticus 19:9).

The Torah did not specify a minimum amount of produce to be left as *pe'ah.* But the Sages maintained that it must be at least one-sixtieth of the crop.

Pe'ah is set aside only from crops that ripen at one time and are harvested at one time. The poor are allowed to use their own initiative to reap the *pe'ah* left in the fields. But the owner of an orchard must see to it that each of the poor gets a fixed share of the *pe'ah* from places that are difficult to reach. The poor come to collect *pe'ah* three times a day. The laws of *pe'ah* are discussed in detail in tractate *Pe'ah.*

TRANSLATION AND COMMENTARY

¹and her husband threw her a bill of divorce into her lap or into her basket, which she was carrying on her head, ²would you say not, too, that she would not be divorced? Surely we know that the law is that she is divorced in such a case, as the Mishnah (*Gittin* 77a) states explicitly!

³Rav Ashi **said** in reply to Ravina: The woman's basket is considered to be at rest, and it is she who walks beneath it. Thus the basket is considered to be a "stationary courtyard," and the woman acquires whatever is thrown into it.

MISHNAH ⁴If a person was riding on an animal and he saw an ownerless object lying on the ground, and he said to another person standing nearby, "Give that object to me," ⁵if the other person took the ownerless object and said, "I have acquired it for myself," ⁶he has acquired it by lifting it up, even though he was not the first to see it, and the rider has no claim to it. ⁷But if, after he gave the object to the rider, the person who picked it up said, "I acquired the object first," ⁸he in fact said nothing. His words are of no effect, and the rider may keep it. Since the person walking showed no intention of acquiring the object when he originally picked it up, he is not now believed when he claims that he acquired it first. Indeed, even if we maintain that when a person picks up an ownerless object on behalf of someone else, the latter does *not* acquire it automatically, here, by *giving* the object to the rider, he makes a gift of it to the rider.

GEMARA תְּנַן הָתָם ⁹We have learned elsewhere in a Mishnah in tractate *Pe'ah* (4:9): "Someone who gathered *pe'ah* — produce which by Torah law [Leviticus 23:22] is left unharvested in the corner of a field by the owner of the field, to be gleaned by the poor — **and said, 'Behold, this** *pe'ah* **which I have gleaned is intended for so-and-so the poor man,' **¹⁰Rabbi Eliezer says: The person who gathered the *pe'ah* has **acquired** it

---

LITERAL TRANSLATION

in a public thoroughfare ¹and [her husband] threw her a bill of divorce into her lap or into her basket, ²here, too, would she not be divorced?

³He said to him: Her basket is at rest, and it is she who walks beneath it.

MISHNAH ⁴[If a person] was riding on an animal, and he saw a found object, and he said to another person, "Give it to me," ⁵[and the other person] took it and said, "I have acquired it," ⁶he has acquired it. ⁷If, after he gave it to him, he said, "I acquired it first," ⁸he said nothing.

GEMARA ⁹We have learned there: "Someone who gathered *pe'ah* and said, 'Behold this is for so-and-so the poor man,' ¹⁰Rabbi Eliezer

---

¹בִּרְשׁוּת הָרַבִּים ²וְזָרַק לָהּ גֵּט
לְתוֹךְ חֵיקָהּ אוֹ לְתוֹךְ קַלָּתָהּ
— הָכָא נַמִי דְּלָא מְגָרְשָׁה?
³אֲמַר לֵיהּ: קַלָּתָהּ מֵינָח
נַיְיחָא, וְאִיהִי דְּקָא מְסַגְיָא
מִתּוּתָהּ.

מִשְׁנָה ⁴הָיָה רוֹכֵב עַל גַּבֵּי
בְהֵמָה וְרָאָה אֶת הַמְּצִיאָה,
וְאָמַר לַחֲבֵירוֹ ⁵"תְּנָה לִי",
⁶נְטָלָהּ וְאָמַר, "אֲנִי זָכִיתִי בָּהּ",
זָכָה בָּהּ. ⁷אִם, מִשֶּׁנְּתָנָהּ לוֹ,
אָמַר, "אֲנִי זָכִיתִי בָּהּ תְּחִלָּה",
⁸לֹא אָמַר כְּלוּם.

גְּמָרָא ⁹תְּנַן הָתָם: ¹⁰"מִי
שֶׁלִּיקֵּט אֶת הַפֵּאָה וְאָמַר, 'הֲרֵי
זוֹ לִפְלוֹנִי עָנִי', ¹⁰רַבִּי אֱלִיעֶזֶר

RASHI

קַלָּתָהּ — סַל שֶׁעַל רֹאשָׁהּ, שֶׁמַּנַּחַת בּוֹ
כְּלֵי מְלַאכְתָּהּ וְכוּ׳ וְעוֹד שָׁלֵב. הִכִי וְנִמֵי דְּלָא
הָוֵי גִּיטָּא — וְהֵלֹא מָן כְּמוּסְכָּת גִּיטִין
(עֶ,אְ): וְזַק לָהּ גִּיטָּה לְתוֹךְ חֵיקָהּ אוֹ
לְתוֹךְ קַלָּתָהּ — סַל זוֹ מְגֻרְשָׁת.

מִשְׁנָה לֹא אָמַר כְּלוּם — דְּאֵפִילוּ לְמַאן דְּאָמַר הַמַּגְבִּיהַ מְצִיאָה לַחֲבֵירוֹ
לֹא קָנָה חֲבֵירוֹ, כֵּיוָן דִּיהָבָהּ לֵיהּ — קַנְיֵיהּ מַמַּשׁ מִשּׁוּם. לֹא קַנְיֵיהּ
קָמָא דְּלָא מַכְּוִין לְמִקְנֵיהּ לַחֲבֵירוֹ — אֲבָל יַהֲבָה נְסָלֵיהּ בִּמְתָּנָה. וּמִי
לֹא קַנְיֵיהּ קָמָא מִשּׁוּם דְּלָא הָוֵי מְכַוֵין לְמִקְנֵיהּ — אַף הָכָא לֵיהּ הֶסְפֵּק
עַד דְּמָטַא לִידֵיהּ דְּהַאי, וְקַנְיֵיהּ הַאי כְּמֹתֵל דְּאִיכְּוַן מִידֵיהּ דְּקָמָא לְשֵׁם
קַנְיֵיהּ.

גְּמָרָא מִי שֶׁלִּיקֵּט אֶת הַפֵּאָה — אָדָם בְּעָלְמָא שֶׁאֵינוֹ בַּעַל שָׂדֶה.
דְּאִי בְּנֵעַל שָׂדֶה — לֹא אָמַר רַבִּי אֱלִיעֶזֶר וְכוּ׳. דְּלֵיכָא לְמֵימַר "מִגּוֹ
הֲוֵי לְנַפְשֵׁיהּ", דַּאֲפִילוּ הוּא עָנִי מַחֲזַר הוּא עָלָהּ לְנַפְשֵׁיהּ פֵּאָה מִשָּׂדֵהוּ
שֶׁלּוֹ, כִּדְאָמַר בִּשְׁמֹעַתָּא פוֹלִין (קִלָּח,ג): "לֹא תְלַקֵּט לַעֲנִי" — לְהַזְהִיר
עָנִי עַל שֶׁלּוֹ.

NOTES

מִי שֶׁלִּיקֵּט אֶת הַפֵּאָה **If a person gathered** *pe'ah.* According to *Rashi*, the Mishnah must be referring to someone other than the owner of the field. By Torah law

the owner of a field is required to separate part of his field as *pe'ah*, even if he himself is poor, and he may not take the *pe'ah* for himself. Therefore the "since" (מִגּוֹ) argument

---

HALAKHAH

קַלָּתָה **A woman's basket.** "If a man throws a bill of divorce into a container that his wife is holding, she thereby acquires the bill of divorce and the divorce takes effect." (*Shulhan Arukh, Even HaEzer* 139:10.)

הַמְלַקֵּט פֵּאָה מָּאָה עֲבוּר אַחֵר **A person who gathered** *pe'ah* **for someone else.** "If a poor person, who is himself entitled to collect *pe'ah,* gathered *pe'ah* for another poor person, and said, 'This *pe'ah* is for X, the poor person,' he acquires

the *pe'ah* on behalf of that other poor person. But if the person who collected the *peah* was wealthy, he does not acquire the *pe'ah* on behalf of the other poor person. He must give it instead to the first poor person who appears in the field," following the opinion of the Sages, as explained by Rabbi Yehoshua ben Levi. (*Rambam, Sefer Zeraim, Hilkhot Mattenot Aniyyim* 2:19.)

106

were placed next to the outer margins. The text of the first edition of the *Yerushalmi* begins on page one (*alef*).

In 1789, Baruch ben Joseph Romm founded a press in Grodno, Lithuania, and later opened a second plant in Vilna. Beginning in 1835, Joseph's son, Menahem Mannes, was instrumental in producing the acclaimed Vilna Talmud, also known as the Vilna Shas.

Recent Talmud Editions

During the twentieth century, commentaries on and translations of the Babylonian Talmud appeared in many languages, including English, French, Portuguese, and German. An eleven-volume French translation of the *Yerushalmi* was prepared by Moïse Schwab at the end of the nineteenth century.

For several decades, the thirty-five-volume English translation of the Talmud published in 1935 by the Soncino Press of London was widely used. In 1946, at the end of World War II, hardly a copy of the Talmud was to be found anywhere on the European continent. In 1948, Rabbi Philip Bernstein, special adviser on Jewish affairs to General Joseph McNarney, U.S. military commander in Germany, requested that the Army print fifty sets of the Talmud. The request was approved.

In 1967 a Hebrew edition of the Babylonian Talmud with accompanying commentary by Rabbi Adin Steinsaltz began to appear. In 1989 the first volumes of an English translation of this masterful work were issued, and by the year 2000 twenty-two volumes had been published, covering all or part of *Ta'anit*, *Ketubbot*, *Bava Metzi'a*, and *Sanhedrin*. Unfortunately, the English translation of the Steinsaltz Talmud was suspended. In 1990 Mesorah Publications (ArtScroll) began publication of the *Bavli*, with a new English translation and commentary.

An Eternal Legacy

Because of the devotion with which it has been studied, the Talmud has endured for more than fifteen hundred years. When a student and his *chavruta* ("study partner") complete a Talmudic tractate, they express their delight with the endearing Aramaic phrase, *Hadran alakh massekhta* such-and-such, "We will return to you, tractate such-and-such." In other words, "We will proceed to study the other sixty-two tractates, but will not forget to return and study you again."

If a person studies one *daf*, or "folio"—that is, two sides—of the *Bavli* each day for seven and a half years, he or she will have covered the entire Babylonian Talmud. Thousands of people dedicate themselves to the *daf yomi* ("daily page") program, whether through daily classes, compact disks, or the Internet. When the cycle is complete, it is begun again.

Students engaged in Talmud study find that their ability to analyze problems and understand complicated situations is greatly heightened. It is hoped that the biographical and other information presented in this volume will further enhance their ability to appreciate the contents of the Talmud and gain insight into the masters who shaped it.

The Talmudic Tractates and Their Contents

Seder Zera'im

Zera'im ("Seeds"), the first order (*seder* in Hebrew; plural, *sedarim*) of the Mishnah, deals with agricultural laws, blessings and daily prayers, and contributions made to Priests and Levites. The Palestinian Talmud contains *gemara* commentary to all eleven tractates (*massekhtot* in Hebrew) of this order, whereas the Babylonian Talmud contains *gemara* only to the tractate *Berakhot*. The following tractates are part of the *seder Zera'im*.

1. <u>*Berakhot*</u> ("Benedictions"). Consisting of nine chapters, *Berakhot* deals with laws and regulations of the liturgy, including the *Shema*. *Berakhot* also specifies the blessings to be recited over various foods, fragrances, and sights. Out of the eleven tractates in the order *Zera'im*, the Babylonian Talmud contains *gemara* only to the tractate *Berakhot*.

2. <u>*Pe'ah*</u> ("Corner"). Consisting of eight chapters, *Pe'ah* deals with gifts to the poor, in particular gifts of produce from the harvest (*Leviticus* 19:9–10, *Deuteronomy* 24:19–21). For example, the owner of a field is required to leave a corner of his property for the poor to harvest, as well as sheaves forgotten in the field for the poor to gather.

3. <u>*Demai*</u> ("Something Doubtful [Tithed Produce]"). Consisting of seven chapters, *Demai* analyzes the problems of produce—fruit, grain, etc.—from which tithes may not have been taken in accordance with Jewish law. Those who stringently observed the laws of tithing were considered trustworthy individuals.

4. <u>*Kilayim*</u> ("Mixtures"). Consisting of nine chapters, *Kilayim* deals with prohibited mixtures of seeds, animals, plants,

מסכת
ברכות
מן
תלמוד בבלי
עם כל המפרשים כאשר נדפס מקדם ועם הוספות
חדשות מבואר בשער השני.

כפי שנדפס
בווילנא
בדפוס והוצאות האלמנה והאחים ראם

הוצאת "אל המקורות" בע"מ
שנת התש"ח
עיה"ק ירושלם תובב"א

The title page of *Berakhot*, the first tractate in the order *Zera'im*. Published in Jerusalem in the Hebrew calendar year 5708 (1948), this is a reprint of an edition of the Talmud originally published by the widow and brothers Romm. The Romm family began to issue the Talmud in Vilna, Lithuania, in the mid-nineteenth century.

and cloth for garments. The tractate also discusses the laws prohibiting the grafting of different species of plants and the cross-breeding of animals. According to Jewish law, animals of different species may not be yoked together to work a field (*Leviticus* 19:19 and *Deuteronomy* 22:9–11).

5. *Shevi'it* ("Sabbatical Year"). Consisting of ten chapters, *Shevi'it* deals with laws that apply to the sabbatical year, which falls every seventh year and is a year of "rest" for the land (*Exodus* 23:10–11, *Leviticus* 25:2–7, and *Deuteronomy* 15:1–3).

6. *Terumot* ("Heave Offerings"). Consisting of eleven chapters, *Terumot* deals with the heave offerings that were given to the Priests (*Numbers* 18:8ff. and *Deuteronomy* 18:3–4).

7. *Ma'aserot* ("Tithes"). Consisting of five chapters, *Ma'aserot* deals with the regulations of produce subject to tithing. The Priests, the Levites, and the poor received several annual tithes (*Numbers* 18:21ff.).

8. *Ma'aser Sheni* ("Second Tithe"). Consisting of five chapters, *Ma'aser Sheni* deals with the second tithe—taken during the first, second, fourth, and fifth years of the seven-year cycle—which was to be consumed in Jerusalem. The tractate discusses how this tithe is to be brought and how it is to be redeemed, as prescribed in *Leviticus* 27:30–31 and *Deuteronomy* 14:22–29 and 26:12.

9. *Challah* ("Offering"). Consisting of four chapters, *Challah* deals with the commandment to separate as a heave offering a portion of the dough one is preparing, as prescribed in *Numbers* 15:17–21.

10. *Orlah* ("Uncircumcised [Fruit]"). Consisting of three chapters, *Orlah* deals with "uncircumcised [forbidden]" fruit—fruit produced during the first three years after a tree's planting, which may not be eaten as prescribed in *Leviticus* 19:23–25—as well as mixtures of food that are prohibited.

11. *Bikkurim* ("First Fruits"). Consisting of three chapters, *Bikkurim*, the last tractate of *Zera'im*, deals with the offer-

ing of first fruits (*Exodus* 23:19 and *Deuteronomy* 26:1–11), the seven species of the Land of Israel as enumerated in *Deuteronomy* 8:8: wheat, barley, grapes, figs, pomegranates, olives, and honey.

Seder Mo'ed

Mo'ed ("Appointed Time"), the second order of the Mishnah, deals with the laws of the Sabbath, festivals, and fast days. The Palestinian Talmud contains *gemara* commentary to all twelve *massekhtot* in this order, whereas the Babylonian Talmud contains *gemara* to eleven tractates only (all but *Shekalim*).

1. *Shabbat* ("Sabbath"). Consisting of twenty-four chapters, *Shabbat* deals with the laws of the Sabbath (*Exodus* 16:25–30, 20:8–11, and 23:12), including the thirty-nine categories of work prohibited on that day.

2. *Eruvin* ("Mergings"). Consisting of ten chapters, *Eruvin* deals with the laws relating to carrying objects from the private domain to the public domain on the Sabbath. Most scholars believe that *Eruvin* is a continuation of the tractate *Shabbat.*

3. *Pesachim* ("Paschal Lamb"). Consisting of ten chapters, *Pesachim* deals with the laws pertaining to paschal sacrifice and the Passover festival, as prescribed in *Exodus* 12:1–20, *Leviticus* 23:4–8, and *Numbers* 9:1–5.

4. *Shekalim* ("Shekels"). Consisting of eight chapters, *Shekalim* deals with the half-shekel tax collected for the maintenance of the Temple and communal sacrifices, based on the half-shekel tax called for in *Exodus* 30:11–16. There is no *gemara* for *Shekalim* in the Babylonian Talmud.

5. *Yoma* ("Day [of Atonement]"). Consisting of eight chapters, *Yoma* deals with the regulations pertaining to the Temple service on Yom Kippur, including the "scapegoat" and the High Priest's entry into the Holy of Holies (*Leviticus* 16 and *Numbers* 29:7–11), and with the laws of fasting and repentance.

6. *Sukkah* ("Booth"). Consisting of five chapters, *Sukkah* deals with the laws of the Sukkot festival, including the construction of a valid *sukkah* and the regulations concerning the *lulav* and *etrog* (*Leviticus* 23:34–36 and *Numbers* 29:12–38).

7. *Beitzah* ("Egg"). Consisting of five chapters, and deriving its name from the first word of the tractate, *Beitzah* deals with the types of work that are permitted and prohibited on the holidays, as prescribed in *Exodus* 12:16 and *Leviticus* 23:3–44. Tractate *Beitzah* sometimes is referred to as *Yom Tov* ("Holiday") and also as *Bei'a*, another word for egg.

8. *Rosh Hashanah* ("New Year"). Consisting of four chapters, *Rosh Hashanah* deals with the laws of Rosh Chodesh (the New Moon) and the laws of Rosh Hashanah (the New Year) as prescribed in *Leviticus* 23:23–25 and *Numbers* 29:1–6.

9. *Ta'anit* ("Fast [Day]"). Consisting of four chapters, *Ta'anit* deals with the laws governing public fasts, particularly fasts observed in times of drought, and the liturgy to be recited on such days. Chapter 4 concludes with a discussion of two fasts in commemoration of the destruction of the Temple, Shivah Asar b'Tammuz and Tishah b'Av.

10. *Megillah* ("Scroll [of Esther]"). Consisting of four chapters, *Megillah* deals with the reading of the book of *Esther* and the observance of the Purim holiday. It also deals with laws pertaining to the reading of the Torah and the holiness of the synagogue.

11. *Mo'ed Katan* ("Minor Festivals"; literally, "Minor Appointed Time"). Consisting of three chapters, *Mo'ed Katan* deals with the type of work permitted on the intermediate days (*chol ha-mo'ed*) of Pesach and Sukkot. It also details the rules pertaining to mourning. Originally, this tractate was named *Mashkin*, meaning "to irrigate," after the first word of the first *mishnah*.

12. *Chagigah* ("Festival Offering"). Consisting of three chapters, this last tractate of the order *Mo'ed* deals with the laws of pilgrimage to Jerusalem (*Exodus* 23:14–17 and *Deuteronomy* 16:16–17) and with the sacrifices to be brought by

מסכת

תענית

מן

תלמוד בבלי

עם כל המפרשים כאשר נדפס מקדם ועם
הוספות חדשות כמבואר בשער השני .

כפי שנדפס

בווילנא

בדפוס והוצאות האלמנה והאחים ר אם

הוצאת "אל המקורות" בע"מ
שנת התש"י
עיה"ק ירושלם תובב"א

The title page of *Ta'anit*, the ninth tractate in the order *Mo'ed*. Published in Jerusalem in the Hebrew calendar year 5710 (1950), this is a reprint of an edition of the Talmud originally published in Vilna by the Romm family.

pilgrims, particularly the *Chagigah* (festival) offering. This tractate also deals with laws governing ritual purity as it relates to the cleansing of the Temple vessels after a festival.

Seder Nashim

Nashim ("Women"), the third order of the Mishnah, deals with the laws of betrothal, marriage, and divorce. Both the Palestinian and Babylonian Talmuds contain *gemara* to all seven tractates in this order.

1. *Yevamot* ("Levirate Marriages"). Consisting of sixteen chapters, *Yevamot* deals with the concept of levirate marriage (*Deuteronomy* 25:5–10), in which the brother of a man who dies childless is required to marry his widow in order to provide an heir for him. This tractate is also the main source of laws pertaining to forbidden marriages (*Leviticus* 18).

2. *Ketubbot* ("Marriage Contracts"). Consisting of thirteen chapters, *Ketubbot* deals with the laws of marriage and the obligations and rights of husbands and wives, particularly those outlined in the *ketubbah*, the marriage contract. It also deals with laws pertaining to rape.

3. *Nedarim* ("Vows"). Consisting of eleven chapters, *Nedarim* deals with vows and oaths and their annulment. The discussion of vows and oaths made by women (*Numbers* 30) explains tractate *Nedarim*'s inclusion in this order.

4. *Nazir* ("Nazirite"). Consisting of nine chapters, *Nazir* deals with the laws pertaining to the Nazirite, a man or woman who vows not to cut his or her hair, drink wine, or touch a corpse, even that of a close relative, as prescribed in *Numbers* 6:1–21.

5. *Sotah* ("Suspected Woman"). Consisting of nine chapters, *Sotah* deals with laws pertaining to a wife suspected of adultery, as prescribed in *Numbers* 5:11–31.

6. *Gittin* ("Bills of Divorce"). Consisting of nine chapters, *Gittin* deals with the laws of divorce (*Deuteronomy* 24:1–

מסכת

גיטין

מן

תלמוד בבלי

עם כל המפרשים כאשר נדפס מקדם ועם
הוספות חדשות כמבואר בשער השני.

כפי שנדפס

בווילנא

בדפוס והוצאות האלמנה והאחים ר א ם

הוצאת "אל המקורות" בע"מ
שנת התשי"א
עיה"ק ירושלם תובב"א

The title page of *Gittin*, the sixth tractate in the order *Nashim*. Published in Jerusalem in the Hebrew calendar year 5711 (1951), this is a reprint of an edition of the Talmud originally published in Vilna by the Romm family.

4), which is effected under Jewish law by the husband delivering to his wife a *get*, a bill of divorce.

7. <u>*Kiddushin*</u> ("Betrothal"). Consisting of four chapters, *Kiddushin*, the last tractate of *Nashim*, deals with the subject of betrothal, the first of the two stages of marriage. This tractate also contains laws relating to the acquisition of slaves and property, and to the proper relationship between parents and children, including the importance of parents educating their children.

Seder Nezikin

Nezikin ("Damages"), the fourth order of the Mishnah, deals with civil law, criminal law, monetary damages, the judicial system, and ethical matters. Originally, the first tractate of this order also was called *Nezikin*. But because of its great length, it was split into three separate "gates": *Bava Kama*, the first gate; *Bava Metzi'a*, the second; and *Bava Batra*, the third. Both the Palestinian and the Babylonian Talmuds contain *gemara* to eight of the ten *massekhtot* in this order; there is no *gemara* in either Talmud to tractates *Eduyyot* and *Avot*.

1. <u>*Bava Kama*</u> ("First Gate"). Consisting of ten chapters, *Bava Kama* deals with the laws of torts: property damage, bodily injury, and theft, based on *Exodus* 21 and 22.

2. <u>*Bava Metzi'a*</u> ("Middle Gate"). Consisting of ten chapters, *Bava Metzi'a* deals with the laws of lost property, trusts, interest, relations between employers and employees, guardians, and real estate, as prescribed in *Exodus* 22 and 23; *Leviticus* 19:13; 25:14, 36; *Deuteronomy* 22:1–4; and other biblical passages.

3. <u>*Bava Batra*</u> ("Last Gate"). Consisting of ten chapters, *Bava Batra* deals with the possession of property, particularly real estate, the right of preemption, laws of partnership and inheritance, and laws regarding the execution of legal documents and deeds.

מסכת

בבא בתרא

מן

תלמוד בבלי

עם כל המפרשים באשר נדפס מקדם ועם
הוספות חדשות כמבואר בשער השני.

כפי שנדפס

בווילנא

בדפוס והוצאות האלמנה והאחים ראם

הוצאת "אל המקורות" בע"מ
שנת התשי"א
עיה"ק ירושלם תובב"א

The title page of *Bava Batra*, the ninth tractate in the order *Nezikin*. Published in Jerusalem in the Hebrew calendar year 5711 (1951), this is a reprint of an edition of the Talmud originally published in Vilna by the Romm family.

4. *Sanhedrin* ("High Court"). Consisting of eleven chapters, *Sanhedrin* deals with the composition of the courts, judicial procedures, examination of witnesses, the administration of civil and criminal law, and capital punishment. This tractate also digresses to discuss a person's place in the world to come.

5. *Makkot* ("Flogging"). Consisting of three chapters, *Makkot* originally was the end of the tractate *Sanhedrin* and continues *Sanhedrin's* discussion of capital punishment. It also deals with offenses punishable by flogging, the punishment of false witnesses (*Deuteronomy* 25:1–3), and laws relating to cities of refuge for those who killed another by mistake (*Numbers* 35:9–15 and *Deuteronomy* 19:1–10).

6. *Shevu'ot* ("Oaths"). Consisting of eight chapters, *Shevu'ot* deals with various categories of oaths (*Exodus* 22:6–10), as well as matters of ritual impurity relating to impure persons entering the Temple and offering sacrifices.

7. *Eduyyot* ("Testimonies"). Consisting of eight chapters and, unlike other tractates, revolving around no central theme, *Eduyyot* is a collection by later Sages of halakhic pronouncements made by earlier Sages. It records many of the conflicts between the schools of Hillel and Shammai. Sometimes referred to as *Bechirta* ("Chosen One"), *Eduyyot* does not contain *gemara* in either the Palestinian or Babylonian Talmud.

8. *Avodah Zarah* ("Idolatry"). Consisting of five chapters, *Avodah Zarah* contains prohibitions against idolaters and idolatry (*Deuteronomy* 4:25).

9. *Avot* ("Fathers"). Consisting of six chapters, *Avot* is more commonly referred to as *Pirkei Avot* or, in English, *Ethics of the Fathers.* A compendium of ethical maxims of the Sages, *Avot* is the only tractate that deals exclusively with moral rather than legal conduct. The tractate has no *gemara* in either Talmud.

10. *Horayot* ("Decisions"). Consisting of three chapters, *Horayot*, the last tractate of *Nezikin*, concerns erroneous rulings by

the High Priest or High Court (the Sanhedrin); sin offerings required of the community, High Priest (as prescribed in *Leviticus* 4 and 5), or king; and the conduct of courts.

Seder Kodashim

Kodashim ("Holy Things"), the fifth order of the Mishnah, deals with sacrifices, ritual slaughter and dietary laws, and Temple practices. The Babylonian Talmud contains *gemara* to nine of the eleven tractates in this order; it does not contain *gemara* for *Middot* or *Kinnim*. The Palestinian Talmud contains no *gemara* whatsoever to this order.

1. *Zevachim* ("Animal Sacrifices"). Consisting of fourteen chapters, *Zevachim* deals with the laws governing animal and bird sacrifices in the Temple, including the sprinkling of blood and the burning of fat, as prescribed in *Leviticus* 1 and 3–7.

2. *Menachot* ("Meal Offerings"). Consisting of thirteen chapters, *Menachot* deals with meal offerings, prescribed in *Leviticus* 2, as opposed to the animal sacrifices of tractate *Zevachim*. *Menachot* also discusses the laws pertaining to *tzitzit* and *tefillin*.

3. *Chullin* ("Profane [Secular] Things"). Consisting of twelve chapters, *Chullin* deals with the ritual slaughter of animals for general consumption, rather than sacrificial use. This tractate also focuses on the dietary laws, including the prohibition against eating meat and dairy together.

4. *Bekhorot* ("Firstborn"). Consisting of nine chapters, *Bekhorot* discusses the laws concerning firstborn male animals and human males (*Exodus* 13:2, 12–15; *Numbers* 18:15–19; and *Deuteronomy* 12:18–21). The tractate specifies which blemishes make a firstborn animal unfit for sacrifice and how long an owner can keep a firstborn animal before giving it to the Priest. It also details the laws of inheritance for a firstborn son: a father's firstborn son receives a double inheritance; a mother's firstborn son is consecrated to the Temple.

Page 29b from *Menachot*, the second tractate in the order *Kodashim*. On occasion, the Talmudic commentators known as *tosafot* used illustrations when discussing a *gemara* text. Here, the subject under discussion is the use of *tagin* (decorative crowns) on seven letters of the Hebrew alphabet when they appear in a Torah scroll. The *za'yin* (shaded area) is one of those letters.

מסכת

בכורות

מן

תלמוד בבלי

עם כל המפרשים כאשר נדפס מקדם ועם
הוספות חדשות במבואר בשער השני .

כפי שנדפס

בווילנא

בדפוס והוצאות האלמנה והאחים ראם

הוצאת "אלהמקורות" בע"מ
שנת התשי"א
עיה"ק ירושלם תובב"א

The title page of *Bekhorot*, the fourth tractate in the order *Kodashim*. Published in Jerusalem in the Hebrew calendar year 5711 (1951), this is a reprint of an edition of the Talmud originally published in Vilna by the Romm family.

5. *Arakhin* ("Valuations"). Consisting of nine chapters, *Arakhin* deals with the valuation of persons or land dedicated to the Temple, as prescribed in *Leviticus* 27.

6. *Temurah* ("Exchange"). Consisting of seven chapters, *Temurah* discusses the substitution of an ordinary animal for one already dedicated to the altar for sacrifice, as prescribed in *Leviticus* 27:10 and 27:33.

7. *Keritot* ("Excisions"). Consisting of six chapters, *Keritot* deals with sin offerings to be brought by those who may inadvertently have committed one of the thirty-six offenses punishable by *karet*—being cut off from God—as prescribed in *Genesis* 17:14 and *Exodus* 12:15.

8. *Me'ilah* ("Trespass"). Consisting of six chapters, *Me'ilah* deals with the sin of using for mundane purposes objects or property that have been consecrated to the Temple. A reparation offering must be made to atone for this offense (*Leviticus* 5:14–16).

9. *Tamid* ("Daily Sacrifice"). Consisting of seven chapters (originally there were six, but in printed editions of the tractate the sixth chapter was divided into two parts), *Tamid* deals with the daily Temple service, including the *tamid* sacrifice, which was offered every morning and evening (*Exodus* 29:38–42 and *Numbers* 28:1–8), and the division of labor among Priests.

10. *Middot* ("Measurements"). Consisting of five chapters, *Middot* deals with the size and shape of the Temple, describing its courts, halls, chambers, gates, and their usages. There is no *gemara* for *Middot* in either Talmud.

11. *Kinnim* ("Birds' Nests"). Consisting of three chapters, this last tractate of *Kodashim*, deals with the pigeons or turtledoves brought as sacrifices, as purification offerings after childbirth, or by the poor for certain sins, as prescribed in *Leviticus* 1:14, 12:8, 14:21–31, and 15:14–30. There is no *gemara* for *Kinnim* in either Talmud.

Seder Tohorot

Tohorot ("Ritual Purities"), the sixth and last order of the Mishnah, deals with laws of ritual purity and impurity and purification rites. Only one tractate of the twelve in this order, *Niddah*, has *gemara* in the Talmud (Babylonian and Palestinian).

1. *Keilim* ("Vessels"). Consisting of thirty chapters, *Keilim* deals with ritual impurity (*Leviticus* 11:33–36), including furniture, garments, and vessels of all types that have become impure. The highest level of impurity applies to a dead body.

2. *Ohalot* ("Tents"). Consisting of eighteen chapters, *Ohalot* deals with the laws of ritual impurity that apply to tents or other dwelling places that may have housed a dead body—human or animal—and the people or objects who may have come into contact with the corpse (*Numbers* 19:13–23).

3. *Nega'im* ("Plagues"). Consisting of fourteen chapters, *Nega'im* deals with the laws of contamination caused by the disease generally defined as leprosy and rituals of purification as prescribed in *Leviticus* 13 and 14.

4. *Parah* ("Heifer"). Consisting of twelve chapters, *Parah* deals with laws pertaining to the red heifer (*Numbers* 19), whose ashes were required for a ritual purification ceremony for those who had come into contact with a dead body.

5. *Tohorot* ("Purifications"). Consisting of ten chapters, *Tohorot* deals with laws pertaining to the uncleanness of food and liquids, the people who prepare them, and the vessels in which they are prepared, as prescribed in *Leviticus* 11:29–32.

6. *Mikva'ot* ("Ritual Baths"). Consisting of ten chapters, *Mikva'ot* deals with the construction of ritual baths, water sources, and the laws of ritual immersion, as prescribed in *Leviticus* 15.

7. *Niddah* ("Menstruating Woman"). Consisting of ten chapters, *Niddah* deals with ritual impurity among women as the result of menstruation or childbirth (*Leviticus* 12:2–8 and

מסכת

נדה

מן

תלמוד בבלי

עם כל המפרשים כאשר נדפס מקדם ועם הוספות
חדשות כמבואר בשער השני.

עיה"ק ירושלים תובב"א

שנת חמשת אלפים שבע מאות
שלושים ושלוש ליצירה

הוצאת
תורה לעם

The title page of *Niddah*, the seventh tractate in the order *Tohorot*, from an edition of the Babylonian Talmud published in Jerusalem in the Hebrew calendar year 5733 (1973).

15:19–31). There is *gemara* to this tractate in the Babylonian Talmud and partial *gemara* in the Palestinian Talmud.

8. *Makhshirin* ("Preparations"; literally, "Those Things That Render Pure"). Consisting of six chapters, *Makhshirin* deals with food that is rendered impure after coming into contact with liquid (*Leviticus* 11:34–38).

9. *Zavim* ("Discharges"; literally, "Persons With Impure Discharges"). Consisting of five chapters, *Zavim* deals with the defilement caused by genital discharges, as described in *Leviticus* 15.

10. *Tevul Yom* ("Daytime Immersions"; literally, "One Who Has Immersed That Day"). Consisting of four chapters, *Tevul Yom* deals with the specific problems of a person who has taken a ritual bath but who must wait until sunset before being regarded as completely cleansed.

11. *Yadayim* ("Hands"). Consisting of four chapters, *Yadayim* deals with the laws pertaining to the ritual washing of hands.

12. *Uktzin* ("Stalks"). Consisting of three chapters, *Uktzin*, the last tractate of *Tohorot*, deals with the ritual impurities of plants and fruit stems.

Minor Tractates

In addition to the sixty-three tractates that comprise the Talmud, there are fourteen tractates not included in the Talmudic canon. These are referred to as *massekhtot ketannot* ("minor tractates") or *massekhtot chitzoni'ot* ("extracanonical tractates"). In many editions of the Babylonian Talmud the minor tractates are appended to the fourth order, *Nezikin*. The minor tractates probably were not finalized until early ge'onic times, around the eighth or ninth century, three to four centuries after the main body of the Talmud was redacted.

1. *Avot de-Rabbi Natan* ("The Fathers According to Rabbi Nathan"). Consisting of forty-one chapters, *Avot de-Rabbi*

Natan serves as a supplement to and commentary on *Avot*. Some scholars attribute *Avot de-Rabbi Natan* to the second-century tanna Natan ha-Bavli.

2. *Soferim* ("Scribes"). Consisting of twenty-one chapters, *Soferim* details the rules for the writing of Torah scrolls and the public reading of Scripture. *Soferim* also contains laws pertaining to the liturgy of the Sabbath, holidays, and fast days.

3. *Eivel Rabbati* ("Great [Tractate of] Mourning"). Consisting of fourteen chapters, *Eivel Rabbati*, referred to euphemistically as *Semachot* ("Rejoicings"), details the laws of death and mourning.

4. *Kallah* ("Bride"). Consisting of one chapter, *Kallah* deals with betrothal, marriage, sexual relations, and moral purity.

5. *Kallah Rabbati* ("Great [Tractate] of Brides"). Consisting of ten chapters, the first two chapters of *Kallah Rabbati* are devoted to a discussion of betrothal and marriage. The following eight chapters enlarge upon the minor tractates *Derekh Eretz Rabbah* and *Derekh Eretz Zuta* (see below), which deal with questions of good manners and proper personal behavior.

6. *Derekh Eretz Rabbah* ("Great [Tractate on] Good Manners"; literally, "Way of the Land"). Consisting of eleven chapters, *Derekh Eretz Rabbah* deals with ethical conduct and etiquette.

7. *Derekh Eretz Zuta* ("Lesser [Tractate on] Good Manners"). Consisting of ten chapters, like *Derekh Eretz Rabbah*, *Derekh Eretz Zuta* also deals with moral and ethical behavior but is directed primarily at scholars. Appended to *Derekh Eretz Zuta* is *Perek ha-Shalom* ("Chapter on Peace"), which deals with the theme of peace, one of the pillars on which the world is said to stand. *Perek ha-Shalom* addresses the degeneracy that will prevail preceding the coming of the Messiah.

8. *Gerim* ("Strangers"). Consisting of four chapters, *Gerim* details how converts are to be admitted into the Jewish com-

munity and how they are to be treated—with love and kindness.

9. _Kutim_ ("Samaritans"). Consisting of two brief chapters, _Kutim_ addresses the question of how Samaritans are to be treated. A nonnative population that had been transferred by Sargon II from Cuthah (Babylonia) to Samaria, the Samaritans intermingled with the Jewish population and began observing Jewish practices, while maintaining their idolatrous beliefs.

10. _Avadim_ ("Slaves"). Consisting of three chapters, _Avadim_ discusses the treatment of Hebrew slaves and the method of their release from bondage.

11. _Sefer Torah_ ("Torah Scroll"). Consisting of five chapters, _Sefer Torah_ deals with the writing and reading of the Torah and the names of God. This minor tractate is quite similar to _Soferim_.

12. _Tefillin_ ("Phylacteries"). Consisting of one chapter, _Tefillin_ specifies the rules for the writing and wearing of phylacteries.

13. _Tzitzit_ ("Fringes"). Consisting of one chapter, _Tzitzit_ details the laws pertaining to the _tzitzit_—fringes—attached to the four corners of a garment.

14. _Mezuzah_ ("Doorpost"). Consisting of two chapters, _Mezuzot_ discusses the laws pertaining to the writing and placement of the parchment scroll (containing the first two paragraphs of the _Shema_) that is to be attached to the doorposts of Jewish homes.

A Note on Style

In an effort to be true to the original Talmud text, the names of the masters included in this volume are rendered as they are pronounced in the original Hebrew or Aramaic. Thus, the entry for the scholar Samuel will be found under "Shmu'el," the entry for the scholar Judah the Prince under "Yehuda ha-Nasi," and so on. For ease of use, a cross-reference will direct the reader from the anglicized form to the entry.

The task of transliterating Hebrew or Aramaic names and other foreign terms into English is not as simple as it might seem, owing to the fact that there are two styles of pronunciation. Of today's popular editions of the Talmud, the transliterations found in the Mesorah Publications (ArtScroll) edition of the *Talmud Bavli* follow the Ashkenazic dialect, while *The Steinsaltz Talmud* follows the Sephardic dialect. This volume basically follows the Sephardic pronunciation, although because of the range of accents found among speakers of any single dialect, it is impossible to achieve absolute consistency.

Key to Transliteration

- The gutteral *khaf* (כ) sound found in words such as *berakha* is represented by the letters *kh*.
- The gutteral *chet* (ח) sound found in words such as *chutzpah* is represented by the letters *ch*.
- The vowel sound in the English word *pique* and the Hebrew word *bimah* is represented by the letter *i*.
- The vowel sound in the English word *pin* and the Hebrew word *minchah* is also represented by the letter *i*.
- The dipthong sound in the English word *pie* and the Hebrew word *chai* is represented by the letters *ai*.

- The dipthong sound in the English word *eight* and the Hebrew word *eish* is represented by the letters *ei*.
- The vowel sound in the English word *far* and the Hebrew word *chag* is represented by the letter *a*.
- The vowel sound in the English word *met* and the Hebrew word *get* is represented by the letter *e*.
- The vowel sound in the English word *to* and the Hebrew word *zu* is represented by the letter *u*.
- Except for the letters *shin* and *tzadi*, consonants with a *dagesh forte* are represented by a double letter, as in *tefillin*.
- The final letter *hei* in such Hebrew words as *mishnah* or *chuppah* is represented by the letter *h*.

A

Aaron

See Aharon.

Abba

Four prominent scholars were known by this name:

1. A first-century tanna of noble character who, in tractate *Yevamot* 65b, advises that one should not reprimand a neighbor if he is certain the admonition will not be heeded. In *Rosh Hashanah* 35a, Abba agrees with Eli'ezer that before engaging in prayers on Rosh Hashanah and Yom Kippur, a person should review the prayers so that he will recite them fluently, without making mistakes.

2. A third-century Palestinian amora who, in *Ketubbot* 67b, reveals how considerate he was when offering charity to an indigent person, always making sure that he did not cause the individual embarrassment for having to receive help. In *Shabbat* 63b Abba says, quoting Shimon ben Lakish: "He who lends money [to a poor man] is greater than he who gives charity."

3. A third/fourth-century Babylonian amora who is widely quoted in tractate *Berakhot* (9a, 11b, and 19b). In *Berakhot* 14a he insists that it is improper to greet anyone in the morning before reciting the *tefillah* (the *Amidah* prayer). In *Eruvin* 13b Abba quotes his mentor Shemu'el, who commented on the three-year-long debate between Beit Hillel and Beit Shammai, each asserting that the law was according to its view. Finally, a divine voice was heard saying that the utterances of each were the words of the living God but that the law was according to Beit Hillel.

4. A fourth-century Babylonian amora who is quoted extensively in *Yevamot* (68b and 76b), *Nedarim* (7b and 11b), and *Sukkah* (3a and 20a).

Abba Ammi

See Avimi.

Abba Arikha

See Rav.

Abba Avuha de-Rabbi Simlai (second/third century)

Palestinian amora. Known in English as Abba, Father of Simlai, he is mentioned in *Rosh Hashanah* 20b as a contemporary of Shemu'el and comments on the veracity of witnesses' testimony.

Abba Avuha de-Rav (second/third century)

Babylonian amora. According to *Eruvin* 24a, Abba was the son of Mesharshya bar Rava.

Abba bar Abba (second century)

Also known as Avuha di-Shemu'el.

Berakhot 18b indicates that there were many scholars named Abba bar Abba, the most famous being Avuha di-Shemu'el, in English, the Father of Shemu'el, principal of the academy at Nehardea. The Midrash to the book of *Samuel*, quoted by Rashi for the first time in his commentary on *1 Samuel* 2:30, describes Samuel's [Shmuel's] father as a silk dealer. In *Berakhot* 18b Abba bar Abba is said to have been a wealthy, learned man who was entrusted with funds belonging to orphans. He is depicted in *Bava Metzi'a* 24b as very honorable and highly ethical. In one instance, he found some stray donkeys that had been roaming in the desert for more than a year, and, although according to the law he could have kept them, he found the owner and returned them.

Although he lived in Babylonia, he traveled to Palestine and was friends with Yehudah ha-Nasi, to whom he turned for guidance. In *Pesachim* 103a, Abba bar Abba asked Yehudah ha-Nasi for a ruling on the proper sequence of prayers to be recited at the *Havdalah* service. One of Abba bar Abba's closest friends was Levi ben Sisi (*Megillah* 29a), who taught Samuel.

Abba bar Acha (third/fourth century)

Palestinian amora. He is quoted in *Shekalim* 2b as saying: "It is difficult to determine the character of Israel. When asked to contribute to the erection of a golden calf, they do so, and when asked to contribute to the building of the Tabernacle, they also do so."

Abba bar Acha Karsela of Kafri (second century)
Babylonian amora. He is mentioned only once in the Talmud, in *Sanhedrin* 5a.

Abba bar Aivu (second century)
See Rav.

Abba bar Chana
See Rabbah bar Chana.

Abba bar Chanan (third/fourth century)
Babylonian amora. A contemporary of Chisda, Abba bar Chanan is quoted in *Avodah Zarah* 60b.

Abba bar Chanina (third century)
Babylonian amora. Son of the well-known Chanina, Abba bar Chanina is quoted in *Nedarim* 39b as having said: "He who visits the sick removes one-sixtieth of the patient's pain."

Abba bar Charina (third century)
Babylonian amora. A contemporary of Chisda, Abba bar Charina is quoted in *Avodah Zarah* 31a.

Abba bar Chisda (third/fourth century)
Babylonian amora. Son of the famous Chisda, Abba bar Chisda is quoted in *Avodah Zarah* 49b.

Abba bar Chiyya bar Abba (fourth century)
Palestinian amora. As noted in *Shabbat* 121b, he was a fellow student of Ze'eira in the academy run by Yannai. In *Chullin* 50a, *Berakhot* 61b, and *Ta'anit* 14b Abba bar Chiyya bar Abba is mentioned as a disciple of Yochanan bar Nappacha.

Abba bar Huna (third/fourth century)
See Rabbah bar Huna.

Abba bar Isaac (third century)
Babylonian amora. In *Menachot* 110a he is noted as a disciple of Chisda.

Abba bar Jeremiah
See Rava bar Yirmeyahu.

Abba bar Joseph
> *See* Abba bar Yosef.

Abba bar Joseph bar Abba
> *See* Abba bar Yosef bar Abba.

Abba bar Levi (third century)
> Babylonian amora. In *Ketubbot* 77b Abba bar Levi is named as a contemporary of Huna.

Abba bar Marta (third/fourth century)
> *Also known as* Abba bar Menyomi *and* Abba bar Minyamin bar Chiyya.
>
> Babylonian amora. According to *Yoma* 84a, he was named after his mother, who cured him after he had been bitten by a dog. A contemporary of Huna bar Chiyya, Abba bar Marta is mentioned in *Shabbat* 121b, *Mo'ed Katan* 120a, and many other tractates.

Abba bar Mateina (third/fourth century)
> Babylonian amora. He is mentioned in *Gittin* 8b as a colleague of Rava.

Abba bar Memel (third/fourth century)
> *Also known as* Rabbah bar Memel.
>
> Palestinian amora. Abba bar Memel belonged to a group of scholars in Tiberias that was headed by Ammi bar Natan (*Yevamot* 105a); Elazar ben Pedat refers to Abba as his teacher.
>
> Abba bar Memel probably spent time studying in Babylonia, for in *Bava Batra* 105a he quotes his teacher Rav, and in *Chullin* 129a he is mentioned as a colleague of Assi.

Abba bar Menyomi
> *See* Abba bar Marta.

Abba bar Minyamin bar Chiyya
> *See* Abba bar Marta.

Abba bar Pappa (third century)
> Palestinian amora. In *Bava Kamma* 80b Acha ben Pappa is named as Abba bar Pappa's disciple. In *Bava Metzi'a* 43b it is written that Ze'eira, colleague of Abba bar Pappa, spent much time with Abba bar Pappa in Babylonia.

Abba bar Rava (third century)
Babylonian amora. In *Chagigah* 61b he is said to have been a contemporary of Chisda.

Abba bar Samuel
See Abba bar Shemu'el *and* Rabbah bar Shemu'el.

Abba bar Shemu'el (second/third century)
Babylonian amora. Not to be confused with the third-century Babylonian amora known as Rabbah bar Shemu'el (who in *Zevachim* 105a is referred to as Abba bar Shemu'el), Abba bar Shemu'el considered the biblical Job to have been more generous with his money than Abraham. Abba bar Shemu'el is quoted in *Bava Batra* 15b.

Abba bar Shila (third century)
Babylonian amora. In *Gittin* 26b he is mentioned as the mentor of Ze'eira.

Abba bar Shumani (fourth century)
Babylonian amora. In *Eruvin* 64a he is named as a colleague of Menashya bar Yirmeyahu of Difti.

Abba bar Tachlifa (fourth century)
Palestinian amora. In *Eruvin* 63a he is said to have been a colleague of Elazar of Hagronia and Acha bar Ika.

Abba bar Yirmeyahu
See Rava bar Yirmeyahu.

Abba bar Yosef (fourth century)
Babylonian amora. He is referred to only once in the Talmud, in *Bava Metzi'a* 63b.

Abba bar Yosef bar Abba (third/fourth century)
Babylonian amora. According to *Chullin* 141a, Abba bar Yosef bar Abba is said to have been a contemporary of Kahana.

Abba bar Yosef bar Chama
See Rava.

Abba ben Abina
See Abba ben Avina.

Abba ben Adda (third century)
Palestinian amora. In *Shabbat* 130a he is named as a contemporary of Isaac, whom he quotes.

Abba ben Avina (third century)
Also spelled Abba ben Abina.
Palestinian amora. A pupil of Rav and a native of Babylonia, Abba ben Avina immigrated to Palestine where he established a reputation for creating aggadic sayings. The Palestinian Talmud records in *Yoma* 45a that he composed a confession for the Day of Atonement. It reads: "My God, I have sinned and done wicked things. I have persisted in my bad disposition and followed its direction. What I have done I will do no more. Be it Thy will, O everlasting God, that Thou mayest blot out my iniquities, forgive all my transgressions, and pardon my sins." In *Shabbat* 60b he is mentioned as a teacher of Abba ben Zavda.

Abba ben Benjamin ben Chiyya
See Abba ben Binyamin ben Chiyya.

Abba ben Binyamin ben Chiyya (third/fourth century)
Palestinian amora. His comment on the Priestly Benediction is mentioned in *Rosh Hashanah* 35a; he also is quoted in *Niddah* 13a.

Abba ben Ika (second century)
Palestinian tanna. He is mentioned in *Sanhedrin* 90a as a disciple of Yosei ben Chalafta.

Abba ben Jacob
See Abba ben Ya'akov.

Abba ben Kahana (third century)
Palestinian amora. It is thought that he was born in Babylonia but, like many scholars of his generation, moved to Palestine. In *Berakhot* 3b and 6a he states that one single individual "is equal in value to the whole world." *Shabbat* 122a lists his fellow students Ze'eira and Levi and his mentor Chanina.

Abba ben Mari
See Rabbah bar Mari.

Abba ben Memel
See Abba bar Memel.

Abba ben Ya'akov (second/third century)
Palestinian amora. In *Ketubbot* 77a and *Gittin* 59a Abba ben Ya'akov is mentioned as a disciple of Yochanan bar Nappacha.

Abba ben Zavda (third/fourth century)

Palestinian amora. He studied in Babylonia under Rav and Huna (*Shabbat* 111a), subsequently settling in Tiberias, where he occupied a respected academic position with his colleagues Ammi bar Natan, Assi, and Mari bar Mar (*Gittin* 86b). In *Sanhedrin* 44a Abba ben Zavda comments on the statement in *Joshua* 7:11, "Israel has sinned," saying: "Even though they sinned they are still called Israel . . . Though a myrtle stands among thorns, its name is still myrtle."

Abba ben Zemina (fourth century)

Also known as Abba ben Zevina.

Palestinian amora. A pupil of Ze'eira, Abba ben Zemina was employed in Rome as a tailor in the home of a Gentile who tried to force him, under threat of death, to violate the Jewish dietary laws. Abba refused, and the Roman so admired his courage that he exclaimed: "If you had eaten, I should have killed you. If you are a Jew, be a Jew; if a heathen, be a heathen."

Abba ben Zevid (third/fourth century)

Palestinian amora. He is mentioned in *Bava Batra* 24b.

Abba ben Zevina

See Abba ben Zemina.

Abba ben Zutra (third/fourth century)

Palestinian amora. He often is confused with Abba ben Zevid. In *Bava Batra* 25a and *Gittin* 38a reference is made to a female slave of Abba ben Zutra who was kidnapped.

Abba Benjamin

See Abba Binyamin.

Abba Binyamin (second century)

Palestinian tanna. He believed strongly that "A man's prayer is heard by God only in a synagogue" (*Berakhot* 6a). Like many of his contemporaries, Abba Binyamin was very superstitious. "If the eye had the power to see them, no creature could endure the sight of the demons," he remarked (ibid.).

Abba, Brother of Rav

See Abba Ahuva de-Rav.

Abba Chalafta (second century)

Palestinian tanna. He lived in Kefar Chananiah, a town situated in the Galilee. *Sanhedrin* 80a portrays Abba Chalafta as a pious scholar. In *Bava Metzi'a* 94a Abba Chalafta is said to have been a disciple of Me'ir. In *Bava Batra* 56b Abba's son Yosei ben Chalafta reports that his father studied Torah in the academy of Yochanan ben Nuri.

Abba Chalifa of Keruya (third/fourth century)

Palestinian amora. A disciple of Chiyya bar Abba, Abba Chalifa of Keruya is quoted in *Bava Batra* 123a.

Abba Chanan (third century)

Babylonian amora. In *Yoma* 3b and *Yevamot* 48b he is mentioned as a disciple of Eli'ezer. In *Niddah* 29a Abba Chanan is noted as a disciple of Yehoshu'a.

Abba Channin (second century)

Also known as Channin Abba.

Palestinian tanna. In *Zevachim* 4a and *Sanhedrin* 17a he is mentioned as a disciple of Eli'ezer.

Abba Chilkiah (third century)

Palestinian amora. Grandson of the well-known Choni ha-Me'aggel, Abba Chilkiah was highly praised for his righteousness.

Abba Elazar ben Dola'i (first century)

Palestinian tanna. He is quoted in Mishnah *Mikva'ot* 2:10.

Abba Elazar ben Gamala (first century)

Palestinian tanna. He is quoted in *Gittin* 30b.

Abba Elazar ben Gimal (second century)

Also known as Abba Eli'ezer ben Gomel.

Palestinian tanna. Mentioned in *Bekhorot* 58b as a contemporary of Yosei ben Judah, Abba Eli'ezer ben Gimal is quoted in *Menachot* 54b and *Beitzah* 13b.

Abba Eli'ezer ben Gomel

See Abba Elazar ben Gimal.

Abba, Father of Simlai

See Abba Avuha de-Rabbi Simlai.

Abba Guri'a (second century)

Palestinian tanna. *Kiddushin* 82a names Abba Guri'a as a teacher of Abba Guryon of Sidon.

Abba Guryon of Sidon (second century)

Palestinian tanna. *Kiddushin* 82a names Abba Guri'a as his teacher.

Abba ha-Kohen bar Pappa (first/second century)

Palestinian tanna. Known in English as Abba the Priest, he is mentioned in *Ta'anit* 13b and *Rosh Hashanah* 15b as a disciple of Yosei ha-Kohen.

Abba Immi

See Avimi.

Abba Joseph ben Channin

See Abba Yosef ben Channin.

Abba Judah of Sidon

See Abba Yehudah of Sidon.

Abba Kohen bar Dala (third century)

Also known as Abba Kohen Bardela.

Babylonian amora. In *Bava Metzi'a* 10a, Abba Kohen bar Dala is mentioned as a mentor of Shimon ben Lakish. Also known as Abba Kohen Bardela, it is not certain if *Bardela* is the name of a person or place, since a town near Lydda is so-named.

Abba Kohen Bardela

See Abba Kohen bar Dala.

Abba Mar ben Pappa (fourth century)

Palestinian amora. *Berakhot* 45b records a dispute between Abba Mar and his father. *Ketubbot* 8a notes that Abba Mar ben Pappa tended to the preparations for his son's wedding, and *Kiddushin* 32b notes that he served drinks at the celebration.

Abba Mari

Also known as Avi Mari *and* Avmari, *contractions of Abba Mari.* Babylonian amora. He is noted in *Gittin* 29b and *Berakhot* 29b as a disciple of Rav.

Abba of Akko (third century)

Palestinian amora. When a search was being conducted to find a successor to Yochanan bar Nappacha as principal of the academy in Tiberias, Abbahu withdrew in favor of Abba of the northern Palestinian city Akko. Abbahu used to say: "I once thought I was a humble man, but when Abba of Akko showed no annoyance when an interpreter did not express his decision on a particular issue correctly... I said to myself, 'I am not such a humble man after all.'" In *Ketubbot* 22a Abba of Akko is praised by his student Ze'eira.

Abba of Bira'ah (first/second century)

Palestinian amora. In *Menachot* 93b he is mentioned as a teacher in the academy of Eli'ezer ben Ya'akov II.

Abba of Caesarea (third/fourth century)

Palestinian amora. A contemporary of Adda I, Abba of Caesarea comments in *Ta'anit* 15b: "To humiliate oneself is not the same as being humiliated by others."

Abba of Haifa (third century)

Palestinian amora. He is mentioned in *Shabbat* 45b.

Abba of Sidon (second century)

Palestinian tanna. In *Kiddushin* 82a, where he is noted as a disciple of Abba Guri'a, he suggests a number of occupations a parent should advise his son to avoid, including camel driver, barber, sailor, and tavern keeper.

Abba of Sura (fourth century)

Babylonian amora. He was the father-in-law of the amora Pappa (*Ketubbot* 39b).

Abba Salla the Great (third/fourth century)

Palestinian amora. Mentioned only once in the Talmud, in *Ketubbot* 111a, he questions whether at the time of the resurrection it will not be painful for the righteous dead to roll underground to their resting place in the Holy Land.

Abba Saul

See Abba Sha'ul.

Abba Sha'ul (second century)

Palestinian tanna. According to *Avot* 2:12, Abba Sha'ul is

said to have been a disciple of Yochanan ben Zakkai. Abba Sha'ul was reputed to be the tallest man of his generation and earned a living as a gravedigger (*Niddah* 24b). He is best known for his interpretation of *Exodus* 15:2: "This is my God and I shall honor Him." To "honor" God, he says, means "to be like Him—to be gracious and compassionate just as He is gracious and compassionate" (*Shabbat* 133b). In *Avot* 2:12 Abba Sha'ul rates Eli'ezer ben Arakh as one of the greatest scholars.

Abba Sha'ul ben Batnit (first century B.C.E.)
Also known as Sha'ul ben Botnit.
Palestinian tanna. A Jerusalem shopkeeper, according to *Pesachim* 57a Abba Sha'ul ben Botnit was a disciple of Abba Yosef ben Channin. Abba Sha'ul also is mentioned in Mishnah *Shabbat* 24:5 and *Beitzah* 3:8.

Abba Sha'ul ben Imma Miryam (second century)
Palestinian tanna. In *Ketubbot* 88b he is mentioned as a contemporary of Shimon bar Yochai.

Abba Sha'ul of Nashor (third century)
Babylonian amora. Expressing his view on the sex of an embryo, Abba Sha'ul of Nashor is quoted in *Niddah* 25b.

Abba Sha'ul of Ramash (third century)
Babylonian amora. A contemporary of Abba Sha'ul of Nashor, Abba Sha'ul of Ramash is quoted in *Niddah* 25b.

Abba the Cupper
See Abba Umana.

Abba the Younger
See Abba Zuti.

Abba Umana (fourth century)
Babylonian amora. Known in English as Abba the Cupper, Abba Umana was a kindly, pious man whose specialty was cupping blood to relieve distress. He is quoted in *Ta'anit* 21b.

Abba Yehudah of Sidon (second century)
Palestinian tanna. He is quoted in *Yevamot* 122a.

Abba Yosef ben Channin (first century B.C.E.)
Also known as Abba Yosei ben Channin *and* Yosei ben Channin.
Palestinian tanna. In *Pesachim* 57a he is noted as a mentor of

Abba Sha'ul ben Batnit. According to Mishnah *Middot* 2:6, Abba Yosef ben Channin was a colleague of Eli'ezer ben Ya'akov.

Abba Yosei (third century)
Babylonian amora. In *Menachot* 33b he is named as a contemporary of Rechumi, with whom he disagreed on the proper placement of a *mezuzah*.

Abba Yosei bar Judah
See Abba Yosei bar Yehudah.

Abba Yosei bar Yehudah (third century)
Babylonian amora. He is quoted in *Zevachim* 96b and was the brother of Yitzchak bar Yehudah.

Abba Yosei ben Abba (second century)
Palestinian tanna. In *Zevachim* 97a he is said to have been a mentor of Yochanan bar Nappacha.

Abba Yosei ben Chanan
See Abba Yosei ben Yochanan.

Abba Yosei ben Channin
See Abba Yosef ben Channin.

Abba Yosei ben Dosai (second century)
Palestinian tanna. According to *Chagigah* 13b, Abba Yosei ben Dosai was a mentor of Yehudah ha-Nasi.

Abba Yosei ben Dostai (second century)
Also known as Yosei ben Dostai.
Palestinian tanna. In *Zevachim* 116b he is named as a mentor of Yehudah ha-Nasi and in *Bava Kamma* 13a and *Temurah* 8a as a contemporary of Simeon ben Azzai and Yosei ha-Gelili I.

Abba Yosei ben Johanan
See Abba Yosei ben Yochanan.

Abba Yosei ben Simai (second century)
Palestinian tanna. A contemporary of Yehudah ha-Nasi, *Yevamot* 115a reports that Abba Yosei ben Simai once traveled on a ship that sank. The two scholars who accompanied him were presumed to have drowned, raising the issue of an *agunah*, a woman who is not permitted to remarry either because her husband refuses to grant her a divorce or, in this case, because there is insufficient evidence of her husband's death.

Abba Yosei ben Yochanan (second century)
Also known as Abba Yosei ben Chanan.

Palestinian tanna. He is quoted in *Zevachim* 65a and *Sotah* 20b, and in *Yevamot* 53b he is mentioned as a disciple of Me'ir.

Abba Zuti (third century)

Babylonian amora. Known in English as Abba the Younger, according to *Menachot* 15b he was a contemporary of Eli'ezer and Rav.

Abbahu (third century)
Also spelled Avahu.

Palestinian amora. A wealthy, humble man whose business enterprises included the manufacture of women's veils, Abbahu also owned an orchard in partnership with Yosei ben Chanina II and Shimon ben Lakish. It was reported that Abbahu had seats made of ivory in his home and was served by Gothic slaves. When he visited Tiberias, where his sons Chanina ben Abbahu and Avimi ben Abbahu were studying (*Shabbat* 119b), he would bathe in its warm baths. A very heavyset man, it is said that he needed the help of two slaves to lower himself into the pool of water. He was exceptionally handsome: *Bava Metzi'a* 84a says that his beauty had "some of the quality of father Jacob's beauty."

Abbahu was a very religious man who accepted God's will without complaint. When a third son died while still young, two of Abbahu's colleagues, Yonah and Yosei II, came to comfort him, and he said to them:

> We are taught that after the execution of a person condemned by an earthly court, where deception, favoritism, and bribery may have existed, but whose judges are mortal beings, the kinsfolk of the executed person come and pleasantly greet the judges and witnesses, to demonstrate that they have no grievance in their heart against them because they have judged truthfully. How much more so, when a decree is issued from the Heavenly Tribunal, where no human defects and shortcomings exist, should we receive, with humility and submission, the verdict of Heaven.

Among the great teachers who influenced Abbahu was Yochanan ben Nappacha. References to their relationship are found in *Berakhot* 14a, *Bava Kamma* 20b, *Bava Metzi'a* 16b, *Eruvin* 78b, *Gittin* 44b, *Kiddushin* 9b, and a host of other places. In *Yoma* 80a and *Sotah* 32a Abbahu is mentioned as a disciple of Eli'ezer, and in *Beitzah* 13a, *Eruvin* 31b, and *Pesachim* 35b as a student of Shimon ben Lakish.

Among Abbahu's colleagues are numbered Tachlifa bar Ma'arava (*Bava Kamma* 33b), Ze'eira (*Sukkah* 44a), and Safra (*Avodah Zarah* 4a). Abbahu's students include Nachman bar Ya'akov, mentioned in *Sanhedrin* 22b, and his own son Avimi ben Abbahu, who is singled out in *Gittin* 29b and *Kiddushin* 31b. Abbahu praises his son for having fulfilled the *mitzvah* of honoring his parents.

In *Bava Batra* 51b, Abbahu is lauded as one of the chief legal authorities of his generation, even more so than Huna ben Avin. Abbahu is referred to in the Babylonian Talmud over 550 times and many times in the Palestinian Talmud. His expertise extended beyond the realm of *halakhah*, as detailed in *Sotah* 40a:

> Once Abbahu and his [Palestinian] colleague Chiyya ben Abba visited a town to deliver lectures. Abbahu was to expound on *aggadah* [popular lore] and Chiyya on *halakhah* [legal matters]. When the crowd went to hear Abbahu rather than Chiyya, Chiyya was terribly upset. Abbahu consoled him with a parable that compared two men, one of whom was selling expensive precious stones and the other selling various types of inexpensive items. To whom would the people turn? Would it not be to the seller of cheaper items?

But Abbahu's scholarship was not limited to Jewish studies. He was well versed in Greek literature and insisted that his daughter learn Greek as well. Because of his keen intellect, he was a popular lecturer and was able to carry on debates with Christian scholars as indicated in *Berakhot* 10a. His talks were always well attended because they were presented in an intelligible manner.

Abbahu's affable nature and great erudition made him a welcome guest in elite Roman society. The Talmud (*Ketubbot* 17a and *Sanhedrin* 14a) reports that when he would leave his academy in Caesarea to visit Caesar's palace, Roman noblewomen in the palace would greet him with the following words of welcome:

> Prince of thy people,
> Leader of thy nation,
> Lantern of light,
> Thy coming be blessed with peace.

Some of Abbahu's Talmudic colleagues frowned upon his association with non-Jews and Romans, but because of his contacts he was able to have several severe decrees against the Jews annulled. His attitude towards those who would oppress Jews was expressed in *Bava Kamma* 93a, where he said: "Always strive to be numbered among the persecuted rather than the persecutors, for among the fowl, none are more persecuted than doves and pigeons, yet only these were declared by Scripture as acceptable on the altar [for sacrifice]."

Abbahu was the last important personage in Judea of his generation. According to tradition, he died in 309. When his death occurred, legend tells us, "the pillars of Caesarea wept for him."

Abbahu bar Geniva (third/fourth century)

Also spelled Avahu bar Geniva.

Babylonian amora. In *Bava Batra* 139a he is mentioned as a disciple of Rava.

Abbahu bar Kahana (third century)

Also spelled Avahu bar Kahana.

Babylonian amora. He was a contemporary of Yehudah bar Yechezkel (*Menachot* 95b).

Abbahu bar Zutrati (third century)

Also spelled Avahu bar Zutrati.

Babylonian amora. In *Berakhot* 12b he is said to have been a contemporary of Yehudah ben Zevida.

Abbahu ben Ichi (second/third century)

Also spelled Avahu bar Ichi.

Babylonian amora. Brother of Binyamin ben Ichi, Abbahu is named in *Nazir* 24b as a teacher of Shemu'el.

Abbaya
See Abbayei.

Abbaye
See Abbayei.

Abbayei (c. 278–338)
Also spelled Abbaya *and* Abbaye.

Babylonian amora. One of the most frequently quoted scholars in the entire Babylonian Talmud (over 3,500 times), Abbayei was born into a Priestly family. According to *Zevachim* 118b and *Kiddushin* 31b, his father, Kaylil, died when Abbayei was conceived, and his mother died giving birth to him.

At birth, Abbayei was adopted by his father's brother, Rabbah bar Nachmani. Abbayei's given name was Nachmani, but to avoid confusion with his grandfather Nachmani, he was called Abbayei, an Aramaic endearment meaning "little father" or "my father."

Abbayei received his formal education in the prestigious academy in Pumbedita, a town located near the Euphrates River. His Uncle Rabbah not only was the principal of the school but Abbayei's teacher as well. To show his respect and admiration for Rabbah, *Sukkah* 53a describes how on Sukkot, at the water-drawing celebration, Abbayei would entertain him by juggling four or eight eggs without dropping them. Later, as a teacher, Abbayei showed the same respect and admiration for his accomplished students by juggling for them.

As noted in *Mo'ed Katan* 12a and 18b, and in *Yevamot* 25a, Rabbah and his wife were very caring adoptive parents. Rabbah's wife, whom Abbayei called *imma* ("mother"), had a loving relationship with the boy, and her influence was evident throughout his life.

Berakhot 62a records that as a young boy Abbayei was afraid to go to the privy by himself, so his adoptive mother trained a lamb to accompany him. She also engaged a nurse to help care for him, as noted in *Ketubbot* 50a. *Eruvin* 29b describes a remedy for heart trouble taught to Abbayei by his nurse.

That Abbayei's mother devoted time to his education and to building his character is evident from teachings she instilled in him as a youth that he recalled in later life. *Mo'ed Katan* 18b quotes his mother as explaining to him the difference between gossip and rumor: "Local gossip lasts for a day and a half and dies quickly, but a rumor can persist and be devastating to an individual."

Perhaps it was his mother who fostered Abbayei's interest in mysticism and susceptibility to superstitious beliefs. *Yoma* 84a offers Abbayei's prescription for the treatment of a bite by a mad dog; *Berakhot* 6a reveals clearly his belief in the reality and power of demons: "They are more numerous than we [humans], and they surround us like a hedge around a field."

The Talmud records the name of Abbayei's second wife, Choma, daughter of Isi bar Yitzchak bar Yehudah, who married three times (she was widowed by Rechavah of Pumbedita and Yitzchak bar Rabbah bar Chana before marrying Abbayei). Abbayei and Choma had several children. *Eruvin* 8a and 23b mention Abbayei's son Bivi ben Abbayei, and *Nedarim* 23a describes how Abbayei and Choma disagreed on whom their daughter should marry. Abbayei insisted that she marry one of his relatives, while Choma preferred that their daughter marry into her family. Choma ignored her husband's wishes, and their daughter married one of her relatives.

In *Yoma* 78b and *Kiddushin* 31b, Abbayei, after he had children of his own, recalled: "Mother told me the proper treatment for a child to improve his health is to bathe him in warm water and massage him with oil. If he is a bit older, massage him with a mixture of egg and *kutah* [a combination of sour milk, bread crusts, and salt]."

In *Sukkah* 56b Abbayei emphasizes the strength of a parent's influence upon his children. He says: "The talk of a child in the marketplace is a repetition of words he heard at home from his father and mother." In *Shabbat* 21b, after conceding an argument to his colleagues, Abbayei expressed regret over the fact that in his youth he had not studied more diligently. He realized that that which one learns in one's youth (*girsa de-yankusa*) is not quickly forgotten.

To earn a livelihood, Abbayei worked the land as a farmer. As he prospered, he purchased more land, which he leased out to tenant-farmers. So focused did he become on Torah study and performing charitable deeds that he failed to pay sufficient attention to his business affairs and inspect his properties regularly. *Chullin* 105a indicates that pilferage by his tenant-farmers brought him to near bankruptcy.

Before long, Abbayei was stricken with edema, and by the time he died at age sixty his property had lost most of its value. *Ketubbot* 65a reports that after his estate was liquidated there were insufficient funds to take care of the essential needs of his widow. The learned scholar Rava bar Yosef was appointed executor of Abbayei's estate, and Choma had to appeal to him for a food allowance.

Aside from Rabbah bar Nachmani, Abbayei's most important teachers and mentors included Yosef (*Berakhot* 28b, *Mo'ed Katan* 24a, and *Shabbat* 13b), Nachman bar Ya'akov (*Eruvin* 3b), and Ze'eira (*Eruvin* 59b).

Among Abbayei's fellow students at the academy, his best friend was Rava. The two were study-partners (*chavruta*) who often would engage in legal debates. It would appear that Rava was the superior scholar: with six exceptions, the rulings proposed by Rava were adopted as law.

Still, Abbayei was widely recognized as a competent scholar, and when Rabbah retired as principal of the Pumbedita academy, after twenty-two years of service, Abbayei was chosen as his successor. (Before Abbayei took office, Yosef served as interim principal for two and a half years. After Abbayei's death, Rava would succeed him.) Abbayei fulfilled his new role admirably and was overwhelmed with joy each time he saw a student succeed in his studies. *Shabbat* 118b quotes him as saying: "May I be rewarded for celebrating a day on which I saw that a disciple had completed a tractate of the Talmud as a festive day for scholars."

Abbayei's meritorious character also is evinced in *Kiddushin* 33a, which notes how considerate he was of others. In Abbayei's day it was customary for people to stand when a scholar passed by. So as not to inconvenience those around him, whenever

Abbayei saw a group of people in his path, he would change his route. In *Berakhot* 6b we find his famous comment: "When a person heads towards the synagogue he should take large steps, and when he leaves he should walk slowly."

Another favorite saying of Abbayei is noted in *Berakhot* 17a: "One should always strive to be on good terms with his brothers, and relatives, and all men—even with the heathen on the street—in order that he may be loved above [by God] and below [by his fellowman on earth]."

Abbayei also said: "The world has never less than thirty-six righteous men who are vouchsafed a sight of the Shekhinah [God's divine presence] every day" (*Sukkah* 45b).

Realizing that the Temple, which had been destroyed in 70 C.E., was unlikely to be rebuilt soon, if ever, Abbayei felt it important that it be remembered respectfully. Consequently, in *Avodah Zarah* 42a, he ruled that the Temple structure and its holy vessels should not be cheapened by having them duplicated by the masses: "A person may not construct a house after the design of the Temple, or a porch after the design of the Temple porch, or a courtyard duplicating the Temple courtyard, or a table after the design of its table, or a candelabrum after its design [with seven branches]. He may, however, make [a candelabrum] with five, six, or eight branches."

Abbayei bar Abin
See Abbayei bar Avin.

Abbayei bar Avin (fourth century)
Also spelled Abbayei bar Abin. *Also known as* Abbayei bar Rabin.

Babylonian amora. He and his brother, Chanina bar Avin (*Yevamot* 36a, *Pesachim* 34a), studied at the academy in Pumbedita under Rabbah bar Nachmani.

Abbayei bar Rabin
See Abbayei bar Avin.

Abbayei Kashisha (third century)
Babylonian amora. Known in English as Abbayei the Elder, he is quoted in *Shabbat* 54a, where he points out a contradiction in one of the statements of Rav. In *Yevamot* 24a, Abbayei

Kashisha states his view with regard to the obligation of brothers to perform the duty of levirate marriage.

Abbayei the Elder
See Abbayei Kashisha.

Abbuha
See Avuha.

Abbuha bar Ichi
See Avuha bar Ichi.

Abdimi
See Dimi.

Abidan
See Avdan.

Abimi
See Avimi.

Abin
See Avin.

Abina
See Avina.

Abram
See Avram.

Abtalyon
See Avtalyon.

Abudimi
See Dimi.

Abudma
See Dimi.

Acha
More than eighty scholars by this name are quoted in the Talmud, some of whom have been misnamed by copyists as Achai. Most prominent among them are:

1. A second-century Palestinian tanna who was a younger contemporary of Shimon bar Yochai (*Pesachim* 46a). In *Bava Kamma* 50a Acha is named as a colleague of Chanina ben Dosa.

2. A third-century Babylonian amora whose brother was Abba, father of Jeremiah III (*Shabbat* 56b). Acha's chief oppo-

nent was Ravina I, as indicated in a score of references including *Yevamot* 41b and *Eruvin* 24b. In *Berakhot* 47a Acha is presented as a highly respected contemporary of Rav and in *Sanhedrin* 20b as a contemporary of Abbayei. In *Yevamot* 37a Acha is noted as a colleague of Rafram I.

3. A third-century Palestinian amora who was also referred to as Berabbi ha-Gadol, which means "the great, esteemed rabbi." He systematized the *baraitot* at the academy of Chiyya and was a teacher of Shemu'el Sava (*Shabbat* 79b). According to *Berakhot* 3b, Acha was a disciple of Oshaya Rabbah; according to *Shabbat* 79b, he was a disciple of Achi ben Chanina.

4. A fourth-century Palestinian amora who was born in Lydda but settled in Tiberias. Thereafter, he became closely associated with Huna.

Acha Aricha ben Pappa
    See Acha bar Pappa.

Acha bar Abba (third century)
    Babylonian amora. In *Shabbat* 114a he is mentioned as a disciple of Yochanan bar Nappacha and in *Avodah Zarah* 19b as a disciple of Rav and Hamnuna. In *Zevachim* 4a Acha bar Abba is named as a colleague of Rava and in *Menachot* 5b as a colleague of Ashi. In *Chullin* 49a Acha is said to have been a student of Huna. *Kiddushin* 81b refers to Acha bar Abba as the father-in-law of Chisda, although a variant textual reading suggests that Chisda was married to the daughter of Chanan bar Rava.

Acha bar Abbayei (third/fourth century)
    Babylonian amora. In *Shabbat* 4a and *Bava Kamma* 39b he is mentioned as a colleague of Ravina I.

Acha bar Acha (fourth/fifth century)
    Babylonian amora. According to *Shabbat* 101a, he was a colleague of Ashi.

Acha bar Ammi (third century)
    Babylonian amora. In *Zevachim* 61b he is mentioned as a contemporary of Chisda and Rav.

Acha bar Ashi (third/fourth century)

Babylonian amora. According to *Zevachim* 91a, he was a colleague of Ravina I. In *Chullin* 97b Acha bar Ashi expresses views contrary to those of Ravina I regarding certain aspects of *kashrut*.

Acha bar Avira (fourth century)

Babylonian amora. A contemporary of Ashi (*Berakhot* 44a and *Pesachim* 44b), in *Shabbat* 74b and *Eruvin* 11b Acha bar Avira expresses his view on what constitutes a violation of the Sabbath.

Acha bar Aviya (fourth/fifth century)

Babylonian amora. He visited Palestine, where he attended the lectures of Assi (*Pesachim* 24b). Acha bar Aviya's principal Babylonian teacher was Ashi (*Chullin* 39b), with whom he often disagreed (*Nedarim* 35a and *Bava Batra* 3a). In *Yevamot* 117a Acha bar Aviya comments on a question of levirate marriage.

Acha bar Avya

See Acha bar Aviya.

Acha bar Azza (third century)

Babylonian amora. In *Temurah* 21a he is quoted by Nachman bar Yitzchak.

Acha bar Beivai Mar (third/fourth century)

Babylonian amora. In *Yevamot* 8a he is mentioned as a colleague of Ravina I.

Acha bar Bizna (third/fourth century)

Babylonian amora. Quoting Shimon ha-Tsadik in *Berakhot* 3b, he relates the legend of the harp that hung over King David's bed: "As soon as midnight struck, a north wind would blow across the harp and it would play by itself. Thereupon, David would rise and start studying Torah until daybreak."

Acha bar Chanina (third century)

Also known as Acha bar Chinena.

Palestinian amora. A disciple of Chanina, Acha bar Chanina collected rare *baraitot* from scholars in southern Palestine and transmitted them to his colleagues in Babylonia. In *Pesachim* 50a he argues that the world to come will be infinitely better than this world.

There is a dispute in *Bava Kamma* 55a over whether Shemu'el ben Nachum was Acha's uncle or grandfather.

Acha bar Chinena
See Acha bar Chanina.

Acha bar Difti
See Beivai Acha of Difti.

Acha bar Huna (fourth century)
Babylonian amora. In *Berakhot* 23a and 32a, *Eruvin* 20b, and *Bava Batra* 70a, he is mentioned as a disciple of Sheshet. Acha bar Huna's colleagues included Ashi (*Shabbat* 66b), Safra and Huna bar Chanina (*Bava Batra* 167a), and Chisda (*Yevamot* 89b).

Acha bar Ika (fourth century)
Babylonian amora. A contemporary of Ashi (*Bava Kamma* 47a) and a nephew of Acha bar Ya'akov, *Eruvin* 63a names Acha bar Ika as a colleague of Elazar of Hagronia and Abba bar Tachlifa. In *Gittin* 24a and 64b, and in *Bava Metzi'a* 71b, Acha bar Ika is said to have been a teacher of Huna bar Mano'ach.

Acha bar Isaac (fourth century)
Palestinian amora. He was a contemporary of Ze'eira and Ammi bar Natan.

Acha bar Jacob
See Acha bar Ya'akov.

Acha bar Joseph
See Acha bar Yosef.

Acha bar Minyomi (fourth century)
Babylonian amora. A contemporary of Abbayei, Acha bar Minyomi probably was the brother of Adda bar Minyomi. *Bava Batra* 148b lists Acha bar Minyomi as a disciple of Nachman bar Ya'akov.

Acha bar Pappa (third century)
Palestinian amora. As noted in *Shabbat* 111a and *Berakhot* 33a, his nickname was Aricha, meaning "tall." In *Bava Kamma* 80b he is said to have been a disciple of Abba bar Pappa.

Acha bar Rav (fourth century)

Babylonian amora. In *Kiddushin* 13a and *Bava Batra* 124b Acha bar Rav, the grandfather of Mesharshya, is said to have been a disciple of Ravina I.

Acha bar Rava (fourth/fifth century)

Babylonian amora. He served as head of the academy in Pumbedita for the last five years of his life. In *Pesachim* 29a he is mentioned as a disciple of Joseph and in *Ta'anit* 25a as a disciple of Yehudah ha-Nasi. His colleagues included Ravina I (*Shabbat* 120b and *Yevamot* 45b), Abbayei (*Pesachim* 48a), and Ashi (*Berakhot* 6a and 50a). In *Shabbat* 22a Acha bar Rava expresses his view on the proper placement of the Chanukkah *menorah*. He died in 419.

Acha bar Tachlifa (fourth/fifth century)

Babylonian amora. A friend of Acha bar Ika, according to *Eruvin* 63a Acha bar Tachlifa also was friendly with Elazar of Hagronia and Abba bar Tachlifa. *Gittin* 73a says that Acha bar Tachlifa was a colleague of Ravina II, and *Eruvin* 68b a disciple of Rava.

Acha bar Ulla (fourth century)

Babylonian amora. He would later immigrate to Palestine. In *Eruvin* 21b he is noted as a teacher of Pappa bar Acha bar Adda. According to *Shabbat* 54b, Acha bar Ulla was a student of Chisda.

Acha bar Ya'akov (third/fourth century)

Babylonian amora. He was the uncle of Nachman bar Yitzchak (*Shabbat* 140a). *Sotah* 49a notes that Acha bar Ya'akov raised his daughter's son, also named Ya'akov. *Bava Batra* 52a singles out Nachman bar Ya'akov as Acha bar Ya'akov's primary teacher. Acha bar Ya'akov also was a disciple of Huna, principal of the academy in Sura and an outspoken critic of Chama of Nehardea, headmaster of the academy at Pumbedita.

Eruvin 63a and *Bava Kamma* 40a extol Acha bar Ya'akov as a man of great distinction, perhaps because, in addition to his pursuit of Jewish learning, he studied philosophy and mysticism. Indeed, his study of the latter discipline led him to a strong belief in the efficacy of demons. *Sukkah* 38a reports that when he waved the *lulav* on Sukkot he would say, "This is an arrow in the eye of Satan."

On one occasion, a demon was said to have settled in the vicinity of Abbayei's academy and harassed the students even when they walked to school in a group during daylight hours, a time when demons are at their weakest. No one seemed to be able to dislodge the demon.

When Abbayei was informed that Acha bar Ya'akov was coming to visit Pumbedita, he arranged with its citizens that no one would provide him with accommodations: Acha bar Ya'akov would have to sleep at the academy, where he would expel the demon. No sooner had Acha bar Ya'akov settled down for the night than the demon made its appearance in the shape of a seven-headed hydra. Acha bar Ya'akov immediately began to pray. Each time he genuflected, one of the heads of the hydra fell off.

In the morning Abbayei said to Acha bar Ya'akov: "Had not heaven seen fit to work a miracle, my life would have been endangered."

Acha bar Yeva (fifth century)

Babylonian amora. In *Niddah* 61b he is said to have been a disciple of Zutra.

Acha bar Yosef (fourth/fifth century)

Babylonian amora. As a youth he attended Chisda's lectures (*Bava Metzi'a* 87a and *Chullin* 105a). In *Pesachim* 31b and *Yevamot* 31b Acha bar Yosef is mentioned as a colleague of Ashi. *Shabbat* 140a notes that Acha bar Yosef suffered from asthma; according to *Shabbat* 110b, during one especially severe attack, he was treated by Kahana. Acha bar Yosef recovered and lived to an old age. He died in 427.

Acha Bardela (third century)

Babylonian amora. He was a colleague of Sheshet (*Beitzah* 14a) and a disciple of Rav (*Sukkah* 26a).

Acha ben Abba ben Acha (third century)

Palestinian amora. He is quoted in *Berakhot* 25a.

Acha ben Adda (fourth century)

Babylonian amora. Born and educated in Palestine, he immigrated to Babylonia, where he frequently reported the decisions of his Palestinian teachers. In Babylonia he became a disciple of Yehudah bar Yechezkel, Yitzchak (*Shabbat* 17b and *Avodah Zarah* 36b), and Hamnuna (*Eruvin* 77b and *Kiddushin* 65a), who was a disciple of Rav.

A popular saying recorded in *Sukkah* 21b is ascribed to Acha ben Adda, namely that "Even the casual, everyday conversation of scholars is worthy of study."

Acha ben Ahava (second century)

Palestinian amora. In *Eruvin* 98a he is named as a contemporary of Shimon Ben Azzai.

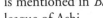

Acha ben bar Chana (third century)

Rabbi

Palestinian amora. According to *Menachot* 31b, he was a disciple of Yochanan bar Nappacha.

Acha ben Chana (third century)

Palestinian amora. He was a disciple of Sheshet (*Eruvin* 68b) and of Yochanan bar Nappacha (*Avodah Zarah* 38b).

Acha ben Chiyya ben Abba (fourth century)

Palestinian amora. In *Berakhot* 14a he is noted as a colleague of Yonah, a disciple of Ze'eira.

Acha of Bei-Chozai (fourth century)

Babylonian amora. Quoted in *Gittin* 7a. Bei-Chozai was in southern Babylonia, later called Khuzistan.

Acha of Difti

See Beiva Acha of Difti.

Acha, Governor of the Castle

See Acha Sar ha-Birah.

Acha of Hutzal (third/fourth century)

Babylonian amora. In *Beitzah* 32b and *Keritot* 13b he is mentioned as a colleague of Ravina I and Ashi.

Acha Sabba (fourth/fifth century)

Babylonian amora. Known in English as Acha the Elder, he is mentioned in *Bava Kamma* 36a and *Kiddushin* 21a as a colleague of Ashi.

Acha Sar ha-Birah (third/fourth century)

Palestinian amora. Known in English as Acha, Governor of the Castle, he is quoted in *Ketubbot* 88a and *Arakhin* 22b. His title reflected his high social standing. According to *Yevamot* 45a, he was a colleague of Tanchum bar Chiyya of Kefar Akko.

Acha the Elder

See Acha Sabba.

Achadvoi bar Ammi (fourth/fifth century)

Babylonian amora. He was a disciple of Chisda (*Pesachim* 75a), Rava (*Chullin* 113b), and Sheshet (*Bava Batra* 9b). On one occasion Achadvoi insulted his teacher Sheshet by speaking of him in a mocking manner when disagreeing with one of Sheshet's views. Soon thereafter, Achadvoi lost his power of speech and forgot his learning. Achadvoi's mother, who had been the nursemaid of Sheshet, appealed to Sheshet to pray for her son. Reluctantly, Sheshet agreed, and Achadvoi was healed (*Bava Batra* 9b).

In *Shabbat* 83b Achadvoi bar Ammi conjectures about how large an idol must be to be called an idol.

Achadvoi bar Mattnah (fourth/fifth century)

Babylonian amora. In *Bava Batra* 151a he is named as a colleague of Tavi bar Mattnah.

Achai

Several amora'im were known by this name. The two most prominent are:

1. A third-century Palestinian amora who was a contemporary of Chiyya bar Abba (*Berakhot* 14a) and Ashi (*Bava Metzi'a* 90b). In *Gittin* 5b Achai is referred to as Achi, a judge who presided over divorce cases.

2. A fifth/sixth-century Babylonian amora who was a distinguished teacher and whose halakhic authority was recognized even in Palestine. It was said of Achai when a dispute arose between him and Palestinian authorities: "Beware of the views of Achai, for he is the light of the Diaspora (*Chullin* 59b).

Berakhot 25b records that Achai tried to contract a marriage for his son with a daughter of Yitzchak bar Shemu'el bar Marta but was unsuccessful.

Some scholars identify Achai as Achai bar Chanilai, while others identify him with Achai bar Huna, who is not quoted in the Talmud. According to the *tosafot* on *Ketubbot* 2b, Shemu'el ben Me'ir (known as the Rashbam), one of Rashi's grandsons, identifies Achai with Achai of Shabcha, an eighth-century scholar, but Ya'akov ben Me'ir Tam (known as Rabbenu Tam), Shemu'el's brother, disagrees.

Achai bar Chanilai
See Achai.

Achai bar Chanina (third/fourth century)
Babylonian amora. In *Menachot* 32b he is mentioned as a teacher of Achai.

Achai bar Huna (fifth/sixth century)
Babylonian amora. A native of a small town near Nehardea, Achai bar Huna was one of the scholars who worked with Ravina II in the final editing of the Talmud. Achai bar Huna, who sometimes is identified as Achai, died in 506.

Achai ben Josiah
See Achai ben Yoshiyyahu.

Achai ben Yoshiyyahu (second century)
Also known as Achi ben Yoshiyyahu.

Palestinian tanna. His father, Yoshiyyahu, is thought to have been a well-known pupil of Yishma'el ben Elisha. In *Gittin* 14a–b, where Achai's name appears as Achi ben Yoshiyyahu, it is reported that while living in Palestine he commissioned Dostai ben Yannai and Yosei ben Kippar, who were traveling to Nehardea in Babylonia, where Achai had spent his last years, to bring back a silver goblet that he had left there. It appears that Achai ben Yoshiyyahu was preparing to put things in order before his death, which occurred sometime before the death of Yehudah ha-Nasi around 220 C.E.

In *Berakhot* 2b Achai comments on the proper time for the evening recitation of the *Shema* and, in *Eruvin* 13a, on the ritual to be performed when a woman is suspected of infidelity.

A highly moral man, Achai ben Yoshiyyahu cautioned in *Nedarim* 20a that "He who gazes at a woman will eventually come to sin, and he who looks even at a woman's heel will beget degenerate children. This applies even to one's wife when she is a *niddah* [menstruant]."

Acher

See Elisha ben Avuyah.

Achi

See also Achai.

Achi ben Chanina (third century)

Palestinian amora. In *Shabbat* 79b he is noted as a mentor of Acha.

Achi ben Josiah

See Achai ben Yoshiyyahu.

Achi ben Yoshiyyahu

See Achai ben Yoshiyyahu.

Achiyya (second century)

Babylonian leader who probably was a *reish galuta*—an exilarch. *Mo'ed Katan* 20a makes reference to the death of his son, who was living in Babylonia. In *Menachot* 56a Achiyya comments on the posture of a Priest when offering a sacrifice.

Achli (second century)

Babylonian amora. In *Eruvin* 12a he is mentioned as a colleague of Yechi'el.

Adda

Two scholars were known by this name:

1. A second-century Babylonian amora who in *Bava Metzi'a* 107b is described as a surveyor and a colleague of Yehudah bar Yechezkel. In *Yoma* 37a Adda is named as a teacher of Shemu'el bar Pappa, and in *Yevamot* 83b and *Makkot* 23b as a disciple of Rav.

2. A third-century Palestinian amora and a disciple of Simlai. Adda comments on the procedure to be followed during the recitation in synagogue of *Birkat ha-Kohanim* when all worshippers are *Kohanim*—Priests (*Sotah* 38b). In *Niddah* 60a Adda is said to have been a contemporary of Yehudah ha-Nasi and Shimon ben Gamli'el II.

Adda bar Abba (third/fourth century)

Babylonian amora. In *Bava Metzi'a* 63b and *Bava Batra* 22a he is named as a colleague of Rava.

Adda bar Abbahu (third/fourth century)

Babylonian amora. In *Ta'anit* 8a he is described as a diligent student of Rava.

Adda bar Abin

See Adda bar Avin.

Adda bar Acha

Babylonian amora. Of unknown date, he is quoted in *Zevachim* 22a.

Adda bar Ahava (third/fourth century)

Babylonian amora. He is quoted frequently in both the Babylonian and Palestinian Talmuds and, according to legend, was born on the day Yehuda ha-Nasi died in the year 220 (*Kiddushin* 72a–b). A disciple of Rav, it is said that at Rav's funeral Adda bar Ahava rent his garments twice as a sign of respect (*Berakhot* 42b). In *Ta'anit* 16a Adda insists that confession of sin without repentance is an exercise in futility.

For many years Adda bar Ahava taught at the famous academy in Pumbedita, where he attracted numerous students. Listed among his disciples are Hamnuna Sabba (*Gittin* 26b), Nachman bar Ya'akov (*Chagigah* 25a), and Beivai (*Eruvin* 75b). Adda's daughter, according to *Yevamot* 110b, married the amora Chana.

In *Pesachim* 75a his student Chinena bar Idi asks him whether it is permissible to use an oven that had once been fired by shells of an *orlah*, the fruit (or, in this case, the nuts) of newly planted trees, which is not to be used during its first three years. Idi permitted the eating of bread baked in such an oven.

Adda bar Ahava lived to old age. In *Ta'anit* 20b he ascribed his longevity to the following: "I have never displayed any impatience in my house, and I have never walked in front of anyone greater than myself, nor have I ever meditated [over the words of the Torah] in dirty alleys, nor have I ever walked four cubits without thinking about the Torah or without wearing *tefillin* . . . nor have I delighted over the disgrace of my friends, nor have I ever called my neighbor by a [disparaging] nickname."

Adda bar Avin

Babylonian amora. Of unknown date, he is quoted in *Keritot* 21a.

Adda bar Azza (third/fourth century)

Babylonian amora. A disciple of Assi, Adda bar Azza is quoted in *Kiddushin* 81b, where he discusses the ages of maturity for boys and girls.

Adda bar Chama (fourth century)

Babylonian amora. According to *Bava Metzi'a* 30a, he was a disciple of Sheshet.

Adda bar Chanina (third/fourth century)

Babylonian amora. He is quoted in *Nedarim* 22b.

Adda bar Ika (third/fourth century)

Babylonian amora. According to *Gittin* 84b, he was a colleague of Abbayei.

Adda bar Isaac

See Adda bar Yitzchak.

Adda bar Ivya (fourth/fifth century)

Babylonian amora. In *Bava Kamma* 62a he is said to have been a colleague of Ashi.

Adda bar Mari bar Isur (fourth/fifth century)

Babylonian amora. *Kiddushin* 65b describes how his two sons, Zutra bar Mari and Adda Sabba, turned to Ashi for advice.

Adda bar Matna (third/fourth century)

Babylonian amora. In *Ketubbot* 77b and *Shabbat* 48a he is listed as a student of Abbayei. In *Megillah* 28b he is named as a fellow student of Ravina I, who studied under Rav. According to *Berakhot* 30b and *Yoma* 4b, Adda bar Matna himself studied under Rav.

Adda bar Minyomi (third century)

Babylonian amora. Thought to be the brother of Acha bar Minyomi, in *Chullin* 5a and *Bava Kamma* 31b Adda bar Minyomi is mentioned as a colleague of Ravina I. *Sanhedrin* 17b notes that when the Talmud uses the expression "the court of Nehardea," it is referring to Adda bar Minyomi.

Adda bar Shimi (third century)

Babylonian amora. In *Chullin* 63a he is named as a colleague of Mar bar Idi.

Adda bar Yitzchak (third century)

Babylonian amora. He is quoted in *Gittin* 28a and *Yoma* 17a. In *Beitzah* 19b he is mentioned as a contemporary of Shemu'el bar Abba, in *Zevachim* 38a as a contemporary of Rava, and in *Niddah* 54a as a contemporary of Sheshet.

Adda ben Abimi (fourth/fifth century)

Also known as Adda ben Bimi.

Palestinian amora. In *Eruvin* 9b and 12a he is mentioned as a disciple of Chanina.

Adda ben Bimi

See Adda ben Abimi.

Adda Karchina (fourth century)

Babylonian amora. In *Sanhedrin* 92a he is listed as a colleague of Elazar and in *Yevamot* 10a as a disciple of Kahana and Rav.

Adda Mari (fourth century)

Babylonian amora. In *Shabbat* 66b he is mentioned as a disciple of Nachman bar Barukh, a disciple of Rav.

Adda of Caesarea (fourth century)

Also known as Adda of Kisrin.

Palestinian amora. In *Mo'ed Katan* 20b he is named as a disciple of Yochanan bar Nappacha.

Adda of Jaffa (second/third century)

Palestinian amora. A contemporary of Yochanan bar Nappacha, in *Megillah* 16b Adda of Jaffa explains why, when reading the *Book of Esther* on Purim, all of Haman's ten sons are recited in one breath—because "All their souls departed together."

Adda of Kisrin

See Adda of Caesarea.

Adda of Naresh (third century)

Babylonian amora. Naresh was a town located on the eastern bank of the Euphrates. According to *Shabbat* 60a and 140a, Adda of Naresh was a disciple of Yosef.

Adda of Sura (fifth century)
Babylonian amora. He is quoted in *Niddah* 67b.

Adda Sabba (fourth/fifth century)
Babylonian amora. In *Kiddushin* 65b he is listed as the son of Adda bar Mari bar Isur and the brother of Zutra bar Mari.

Admon ben Gadai (first century B.C.E.)
Palestinian tanna. In *Ketubbot* 105a he is described as one of three judges who administered justice in Jerusalem. In *Bava Batra* 30b he is referred to as Admon, without patronymic, and is quoted by Rava as the source of a ruling.

Afes
See Efes.

Aftoriki
See Aptoriki.

Aggara
See Agra.

Agra (fourth century)
Also known as Aggara.
Babylonian amora. In *Menachot* 29a he is mentioned as the father-in-law of Abba.

Aharon (fifth century)
Babylonian amora. He is noted in *Bava Kamma* 109b and *Menachot* 7b as a colleague of Ravina II.

Ahava ben Ze'eira (fourth century)
Palestinian amora. In *Nedarim* 32a he applauds persons who do not practice "enchantments." According to *Rosh Hashanah* 30b, Ahava ben Ze'eira's father was his teacher.

Aibu
See Aivu.

Aivu
Also spelled Aibu. *Also known as* Ivu.
Five scholars were known by the name Aivu. Three of them were members of Rav's family in Babylonia.
1. A second-century Babylonian amora and father of Rav. Aivu studied under the second-century Palestinian tanna Elazar ben Tzadok (*Sukkah* 44b).

2. A third-century Babylonian amora who, though he was a son of Rav, was not a good student. It was suggested he become a businessman (*Pesachim* 113a).

3. A third/fourth-century Palestinian amora who is noted in *Sanhedrin* 5a as the son of Chiyya bar Abba's sister.

4. A fourth-century Babylonian amora. He and his brother, Chizkiyyah, were the maternal grandsons of Rav (*Sukkah* 44b). In *Pesachim* 46a Aivu is mentioned as a colleague of Nachman bar Yitzchak.

5. A fourth-century Palestinian amora who, in *Ketubbot* 54b and 104b, is named as a disciple of Yannai.

Aivu ben Naggari (third/fourth century)

Also spelled Aibu ben Naggari. *Also known as* Aivu ben Nagri. Palestinian amora. In *Sotah* 10a and *Rosh Hashanah* 21a he is listed as a disciple and colleague of Chiyya bar Abba.

Aivu ben Nagri

See Aivu ben Naggari.

Akavyah ben Mahalalel (first/second century)

Palestinian tanna. Little is known of his association with individual rabbis, except for Me'ir (*Niddah* 19b). Mishnah *Eduyyot* 5:6 portrays Akavyah ben Mahalalel as a scholar of strong opinion, who is not willing to back down even when the majority of rabbis hold an opposite view. In fact, in one instance, when a majority of colleagues asked him to abandon his divergent stance, promising to appoint him *av beit din*—head of the Sanhedrin— he rejected the offer and said: "I would rather be called a fool all my lifetime than be a sinner for one moment [deviating from what I consider to be the truth]."

Sanhedrin 88a notes that when he does differ with the majority, he refrains from offering practical guidance as to how the ruling of the court should be carried out. However, continues *Sanhedrin* 88a, toward the end of his life, when he was on his deathbed, Akavyah had a change of heart and advised his son to submit to the views of the majority even in those cases in which Akavyah himself had disagreed.

Akavyah ben Mahalalel is best remembered for his comment in *Avot* 3:1: "Keep three things in mind and you will not be led to sin. Know where you came from, where you are going, and before Whom you will have to give a strict accounting of your actions."

Akiba ben Joseph
See Akiva ben Yosef.

Akiba ben Yosef
See Akiva ben Yosef.

Akiva ben Yosef (c. 40–135)
Also spelled Akiba ben Yosef.

Palestinian tanna. Known popularly as Rabbi Akiva and mentioned more than 2,300 times in the Babylonian Talmud, he developed from an unlettered child of humble parentage (*Berakhot* 27b) into the most prestigious, learned scholar of his generation.

Little is known of Akiva's formative years, but legends about his early adult years abound, many having to do with his romance and marriage to Rachel, the daughter of one of the three wealthiest men in Jerusalem. Rachel's father's name was Yehoshu'a, but he was more popularly known by the Aramaic name Kalba Savu'a (*Yadayim* 3:5).

Rachel first noticed Akiva when he was hired to tend her father's sheep, and she soon fell in love with him. Her father, while not a learned man, was a great patron of the scholars of Jerusalem and supported them generously. He felt that the young, ignorant Akiva was no match for his beautiful daughter.

Akiva resented the learned rabbis who called on Kalba Savu'a for funds to support their institutions and who never failed to deprecate unlettered individuals, whom they called *amei ha-aretz*, meaning "people of the earth," that is, uncultured people. At one point, Akiva is said to have exclaimed: "If I had a scholar in my grasp, I would beat him like an ass" (*Pesachim* 49b). It never entered Akiva's mind that one day he would be one of those scholars seeking support for his students.

Unwilling to countenance his daughter's association with Akiva, Kalba Savu'a warned her that if she married him, he would disown and disinherit her. But Kalba Savu'a's threat fell on deaf ears: Akiva and Rachel were married and resolved to live in poverty (*Nedarim* 50a).

After ten years of marriage, during which time Rachel bore Akiva eight children—seven sons and one daughter—she became frustrated by her husband's progress and convinced that they were destined to live in permanent penury. In the year 80 C.E., Rachel implored Akiva to "Go, and become a scholar" (*Nedarim* 50a). Together with his young son Shimon, Akiva went to Lydda to study, beginning with the basics—the letters of the Hebrew alphabet. *Pesachim* 112a notes that Yehoshu'a, another son, did not accompany them but later became a Talmudic scholar.

According to some sources, Akiva and Rachel's daughter married Shimon ben Azzai, a poor, ignorant boy much like Akiva. Rachel prevailed upon her daughter to encourage Shimon ben Azzai to go off and study as well, which he did. This led to the comment in *Ketubbot* 63a: "Ewe follows ewe; a daughter emulates her mother."

Avot de-Rabbi Natan 6 describes the metamorphosis in Akiva's thinking that took place when he stood at the mouth of a well with thick walls of heavy stone. "How could this stone have been hollowed so as to create a well?" he asked himself. He concluded that it was water dripping from the trees above, day after day, year after year, that pierced the stone and hollowed it. If that was so, he reasoned, "If water, which is soft, can wear away stone, which is hard, surely words of Torah, which are as hard as iron, will hollow out my heart, which is soft flesh and blood."

Shabbat 67b describes the banquet Akiva made to celebrate his son Shimon's scholarly accomplishments. After each glass of liquor raised to toast the young scholar, Akiva would cry out: "Wine and health to the mouths of our teachers and their disciples." This was quite a turnabout from the young shepherd who earlier could refer to scholars only with disdain.

Among the teachers of Akiva, when finally he was admitted to the academy of higher studies in Lydda, were Eli'ezer ben Hurkanos and Yehoshu'a ben Chananiah. But Nachum of Gimzo, a fine scholar who had endured much suffering in his lifetime, exerted a special influence on Akiva. Much more than teaching Akiva Mishnah, Nachum of Gimzo taught him to face life with resignation and to respond to every setback by saying, "*Gam zu le-tovah*"—"This, too, is for the best."

After twelve years of study (some say thirteen), during which Rachel had to fend for herself and her children, Akiva returned home with some of his students. According to an account in *Ketubbot* 62b, a poorly clad woman rushed up to embrace Akiva upon his return, but his students restrained her, not knowing who she was.

"Let her be," ordered Akiva. "I am what I am because of her. Let us bow and offer thanks to this noble woman."

According to another version, before he could greet his wife after returning home from his twelve-year absence, Akiva overheard a conversation between Rachel and her neighbors in which they criticized her for living alone in poverty for twelve long years while her husband was off studying. So infuriated was Rachel by the remarks of her neighbors that she replied, "I wouldn't mind if he stayed away for another twelve years so that he could immerse himself more deeply in Torah studies and increase his knowledge twofold" (*Nedarim* 50a). Akiva turned around and headed back to the academy in Lydda for twelve more years of study.

According to these various accounts, when Akiva finally returned to his wife, he was accompanied by a multitude of students, some say as many as twenty-four thousand. Kalba Savu'a, Rachel's father, was on hand to greet the great rabbi being feted. At first he didn't recognize Akiva, but when he realized that the celebrity was his son-in-law, he fell to the ground, kissed Akiva's feet, and begged forgiveness, pleading with Akiva to be released from the vow he had made to disinherit his daughter. Akiva acquiesced, and Kalba Savu'a gave Akiva half his fortune.

Akiva, now a wealthy man, returned with his family to Lydda, where he was appointed principal of the academy, succeeding his teacher Eli'ezer ben Hurkanos. Akiva also was appointed to the Sanhedrin, which met in Yavneh, the city near Ashdod in which Yochanan ben Zakkai had established an academy during the war with the Romans in the year 70.

Later, Akiva opened an academy in the city of Bene Berak, which was much closer to the seat of the Sanhedrin. It is reported that so influential and respected was Akiva that no dispute was ever resolved in the Sanhedrin without first considering Akiva's views.

Despite his ability to live in comfort and ease, Akiva devoted much time to traveling to cities with significant Jewish populations in order to raise funds for the poor students of his academy. In addition, he had been assigned by the *nasi* Gamli'el II the prestigious task of distributing charitable funds to the Jewish poor.

The Talmud affirms Akiva's affection for Rachel, who had managed to care for their family during the many lean years when he was off studying. To show his gratitude, Akiva commissioned a gold necklace for her known as the "Golden City." On it was engraved a picture of the holy city of Jerusalem (*Shabbat* 59b; Mishnah *Shabbat* 6:1 forbids a woman from wearing this type of accessory in public on the Sabbath). In another expression of affection for his wife, when asked, "Who is wealthy?" Akiva responded, "He who has a wife comely in deeds."

According to a legend recounted in *Yevamot* 62b, Akiva had twelve thousand "pairs of students" who lived in all parts of Palestine; all twenty-four thousand died in one day because "They did not treat each other with respect."

Among Akiva's more prominent students Yehoshu'a ha-Garsi stands out. He tended to Akiva's needs when he was imprisoned by the Romans (*Eruvin* 21b), bringing his master water each day. Also included among Akiva's disciples were Yochanan ha-Sandelar (*Berakhot* 22a), Bizna ben Zavda (*Berakhot* 55b), and Shimon ben Azzai (*Berakhot* 62a).

Yevamot 62b lists five celebrated scholars who were among Akiva's disciples. These were Me'ir, Yehudah bar Ila'I, Yosei ben Chalafta, Shimon bar Yochai, and Elazar ben Shammu'a. *Yevamot* 76b and 78a single out a proselyte by the name of Minyamin the Egyptian as one of Akiva's disciples.

During his career, Akiva engaged in disputes with a number of colleagues. Chief among them was Yishma'el ben Elisha, as is noted in many tractates, including *Nedarim* (87b), *Pesachim* (5a), and *Shabbat* (19b and 113a). On one issue they agreed, as indicated by Abbayei in *Shabbat* 128a: "All of Israel are royal children and deserve royal treatment."

In the year 132, Roman emperor Hadrian instituted a number of oppressive measures against the Jews of Judea, including forbidding the teaching of Torah. Shimon Bar Kokhba led a rebellion against Rome. Akiva adored Bar Kokhba and even regarded him as the Messiah. Akiva and nine other outstanding scholars defied the Roman edict and continued to teach Torah. Bar Kokhba's rebellion failed, and Akiva and his colleagues were all imprisoned and finally executed in a most merciless manner—they were flayed to death—which is recounted each year during the Yom Kippur *Musaf* service.

When it was Akiva's turn to be executed, he was taken out of his cell at the morning hour, when the *Shema* was to be recited. *Berakhot* 61b records that Akiva's disciples, who witnessed the event, expressed wonderment at his complacent and even cheerful demeanor. As the Romans were raking Akiva's flesh with iron combs, he was reciting the words *"Shema Yisra'el, Adonai Eloheinu, Adonai Echad"* ("Hear, O Israel, the Lord is our God, the Lord is One").

After pronouncing the final word, Akiva turned to his awe-struck disciples and said: "All my life I have interpreted the verse 'with all my soul' [*Deuteronomy* 6:5] to mean 'even if He takes your soul.' Now that the opportunity has arisen, shall I not fulfill that important precept." He then prolonged the concluding word of the *Shema*, the word *Echad* ("One"), until he expired. As life left him, a divine voice went forth and proclaimed: "Fortunate are you, Akiva, for you are destined for the world to come."

The Talmud says that after Akiva died, the glory of the Torah ceased and the fountains of wisdom were stifled (*Sotah* 49a–b).

Rabbi Yehudah ha-Nasi once characterized the merits of each of the important sages of the Talmud. He summed up the genius and scholarly ability of Rabbi Akiva in this story:

Akiva is a well-stocked storehouse—a treasury with compartments. To whom may Akiva be compared? To a laborer who took his basket and went forth to the field. When he found wheat, he put some into [the basket]; when he found barley, he put that in, likewise beans and lentils—they too went into the basket. Upon returning home, he sorted out the wheat by itself, the barley by itself, the beans by themselves, the lentils by themselves. This is how Akiva acted, arranging the whole Torah [systematically] "in rings upon rings." (*Avot de-Rabbi Natan* 18)

A number of Akiva's significant maxims are quoted in *Avot*. The following are among the most popular:

- The fence that protects wisdom is silence. (3:17)
- Beloved is a man, for he was created in the image of God. (3:18)
- Beloved is Israel, for it was given a precious instrument [the Torah]. (3:18)
- Everything is foreseen [by God], yet free will is granted [to man]. (3:19)
- Everything is given on pledge, and a net is spread for all living people; the store is open, and the storekeeper [God] offers credit; the ledger is open, and the hand writes; whoever wishes to borrow may come and borrow, but the collectors visit regularly to exact payment from man, whether he realizes it or not . . . (3:20)

Elsewhere in the Talmud are these aphorisms:

- Treat your Sabbath like a weekday [and eat sparingly] rather than becoming dependent upon your fellowman [for charity]. (*Pesachim* 112a)
- He who does not visit the sick is comparable to one who has shed blood. (*Nedarim* 40a)
- More than the calf wishes to suckle [its mother] does the cow wish to be suckled. (*Pesachim* 112a)

Kiddushin 72a quotes an unknown Sage as saying, "When Akiva died, Yehudah ha-Nasi was born," thus making the point that a righteous person does not depart this world until another righteous person is born.

Aleksa (third/fourth century)
Palestinian amora. In *Chagigah* 18a it is reported that when he died at Lod (Lydda) all Israel assembled to mourn for him.

Aleksander (second/third century)
Babylonian amora. In *Sotah* 10a he is named as a contemporary of Rav.

Aleksandri (third century)

Palestinian amora. In *Nedarim* 41a he is mentioned as a disciple of Chiyya bar Abba and in *Berakhot* 59a as a disciple of Yehoshu'a ben Levi. In *Sanhedrin* 22a Aleksandri reflects on the loss of a wife and comments: "The world has darkened for one whose wife has died in his lifetime." In *Sotah* 5a he remarks: "Every person who is haughty of spirit will be upset even by the slightest gust of wind."

Alexa

See Aleksa.

Alexander

See Aleksander.

Alexandri

See Aleksandri.

Ameimar

Two Babylonian amora'im were known by this name, which is a composite of *Ami* ("my nation") and *Mar* ("master"):

1. A fourth-century junior contemporary of Yehudah bar Yechezkel of Pumbedita (*Avodah Zarah* 48a) and Sheshet (*Chullin* 107a).

2. A fourth/fifth century judge who restored the once esteemed academy in Nehardea to prominence. More widely quoted in the Talmud than his namesake, he headed the academy at Nehardea for over thirty years (390–422), and was scrupulous in following the rules of impartiality. In one instance (*Yevamot* 105b), he was presiding as judge at a trial that was presumably being held out-of-doors (or perhaps it was during a recess), when a bird landed on his head. One of the litigants approached him and removed the bird. Whereupon Ameimar recused himself so that it might not be argued that his decision could have been influenced by the friendly action of the litigant.

Ameimar's legal decisions covered a wide range of issues. In *Kiddushin* 10a he quotes his teacher Rava on what constitutes "complete" sexual intercourse. In *Sukkah* 55a he introduces changes in the holiday Torah reading procedure, which differ from those of Ashi, who had been principal of the academy at Sura.

In *Mo'ed Katan* 20b reference is made to the death of Ameimar's grandson (his son's son) and the fact that he rent his garment while standing. Ashi asked Ameimar: "From what biblical verse do we learn that *keri'ah* [rending one's garment as a sign of mourning] must be done while standing?" Ameimar responded: "From the verse in *Job* [1:20] that reads: 'And Job rose and tore his mantle.'"

Along with his colleague Mar Zutra, Ameimar was highly respected by his students. *Beitzah* 25a reports that when the two men entered the synagogue to deliver a sermon on the Sabbath before Sukkot, they were carried on the shoulders of their disciples. Some say their disciples carried them so the congregants of the synagogue would not have to suffer the imposition of remaining standing while the two distinguished scholars made their way slowly through the crowded assembly.

Ameimar transmitted his teachings to his son Mar, who quotes him often (*Pesachim* 74b).

Ameimar bar Mar Yanuka (fifth century)
Babylonian amora. Mentioned in *Chullin* 18b as a colleague of Chiyya bar Aviyya, Ameimar bar Mar Yanuka was imprisoned and executed in 470 during the Persian persecution of Babylonian Jews.

Ammi
See Ammi bar Natan.

Ammi bar Abba (third/fourth century)
Babylonian amora. He is quoted in *Nedarim* 32a and *Niddah* 20a.

Ammi bar Abin
See Ammi bar Avin.

Ammi bar Adda of Harpania (third/fourth century)
Babylonian amora. In *Eruvin* 59b he is noted as a contemporary of Rabbah bar Nachmani.

Ammi bar Avin (fourth century)
Also spelled Ammi bar Abin.
Babylonian amora. In *Keritot* 20a he is mentioned as a colleague of, or possibly the brother of, Chanina bar Avin.

Ammi bar Chama (fourth century)

Babylonian amora. In *Ketubbot* 48b he is said to have been a colleague of Rava.

Ammi bar Matnah (third century)

Babylonian amora. According to *Berakhot* 63a he was a disciple of Shemu'el.

Ammi bar Natan (third/fourth century)

Also known as Immi bar Natan, Rabmi, Rabbammi, *and* Rami, *the last three being contractions of Rabbi Ammi.*

Two amora'im were known by this name, one Babylonian and one Palestinian, both of whom lived during the same period. In the Babylonian Talmud only the name Ammi is used, while all three forms of the name—Ammi, Aimi, Immi—appear in the Palestinian Talmud, with Immi predominating.

The Palestinian amora is by far the better known of the two. Born in Babylonia, he spent most of his life in Palestine. According to *Gittin* 44a, his father's family was of Priestly descent. Ammi's closest friend and associate was Assi, who has been identified as Assi ben Natan, also of Priestly descent. This led to speculation that the two were blood brothers, sons of the same father. They seem to have been inseparable, for their names appear in tandem in many Talmudic passages. To their Babylonian colleagues, Ammi and Assi were known as "the distinguished Priests of Palestine" and "the Palestine judges." *Sanhedrin* 17b notes that whenever the Talmud speaks of "the judges of Eretz Yisra'el" it is referring to Ammi and Assi.

So highly respected were Ammi and Assi that Yehudah Nesi'ah, patriarch of Palestine, appointed them, along with their colleague Chiyya, inspectors of the schools of Palestine, mandated to suggest improvements where needed.

In his youth, Ammi attended the academy in Caesarea but later transferred to the school in Tiberias, where he studied under Elazar ben Pedat and closely with the famous Yochanan bar Nappacha. Upon the death of Yochanan bar Nappacha, Ammi succeeded him as head of the academy.

Ammi was a highly moral person and insisted that his students be more stringent than others in following the law (*Shabbat*

51a). In *Niddah* 13b Ammi warns: "He who excites himself by lustful thoughts will not be allowed in the presence of the Holy One, blessed be He."

Ammi was wary of those who could not keep confidences. When, twenty-one years after being entrusted with a secret, a disciple finally revealed the confidence, Ammi remarked about him: "This man cannot keep a secret" (*Sanhedrin* 31a).

Ammi spent the last years of his life in Caesarea where he continued to associate with the younger rabbis of the academy (*Yoma* 78a).

Ammi bar Nathan
See Ammi bar Natan.

Ammi bar Samuel
See Ammi bar Shemu'el.

Ammi bar Shemu'el (second/third century)
Babylonian amora. In *Niddah* 25b he is mentioned as a disciple of Shemu'el.

Ammi bar Tabyomi
See Ammi bar Tavyomi.

Ammi bar Tavyomi (third/fourth century)
Also known as Ammi bar Tabyomi.
Babylonian amora. In *Sukkah* 15b he comments on the validity of particular coverings for a *sukkah*.

Ammi of Vardina'ah (third century)
Babylonian amora. He lived in a city on the eastern bank of the Tigris River near Baghdad but then settled in Palestine. In *Beitzah* 27a it is reported that he examined firstling animals for the house of Yehudah ha-Nasi.

Ammi Shapir Na'eh (second/third century)
Palestinian amora. In *Gittin* 41a Nachman bar Yitzchak comments on Ammi Shapir Na'eh's name, saying, "He makes pronouncements that are not commendable."

Amram (third/fourth century)
Babylonian amora. Usually referred to as Rav Amram, he studied under many prominent teachers including Rava (*Mo'ed Katan* 24a), Chisda (*Bava Batra* 70a and *Chullin* 52b), Nachman

bar Ya'akov (*Bava Batra* 162a), Yitzchak (*Kiddushin* 18b and 45a), and most notably Rav, who founded the academy at Sura.

In *Berakhot* 44a and *Eruvin* 102a Amram is presented as the teacher of the very popular amora, Rami bar Yechezkel. Amram also taught Idi bar Avin (*Berakhot* 49b), Chiyya bar Avin (*Yevamot* 25b), and Menashi'a bar Tachlifa (*Yoma* 78a).

In *Bava Metzi'a* 38b Amram is referred to as a colleague of Sheshet, with whom he often debated intricate and subtle legal issues. On one occasion, during an argument, Amram said to Sheshet: "Perhaps you are from the academy in Pumbedita where they draw an elephant through the eye of a needle."

Amram ben Shimon ben Abba (fourth century)
Palestinian amora. He was a disciple of Chanina (*Sanhedrin* 70a) and Shimon ben Abba (*Shabbat* 119b).

Amram ben Simeon ben Abba
See Amram ben Shimon ben Abba.

Amram Chasida (fourth century)
Babylonian amora. Known in English as Amram the Pious, he was so devout that he hung *tzitzit* even on the aprons of the women in his household (*Sukkah* 11a). *Gittin* 67b describes his feud with the *reish galuta*, and *Kiddushin* 81a describes his battle to overcome the evil inclination.

Amram the Pious
See Amram Chasida.

Anan (third century)
Babylonian amora. An especially prominent teacher of civil and ritual law, Anan is noted in *Yevamot* 83b, *Eruvin* 95a, *Ketubbot* 45a, and *Kiddushin* 39a as a disciple of Shemu'el; in *Berakhot* 30b and *Shabbat* 12b as a disciple of Rav; and in *Ketubbot* 79a as a disciple of Ukba. According to *Ketubbot* 69a, Anan was a colleague of the outstanding scholar Huna, but Huna deprecated him and did not consider Anan his equal. Among Anan's other colleagues were Abbahu (*Shabbat* 119a), with whom he shared meals, and Chanan (*Kiddushin* 39a). In *Kiddushin* 21b, Anan's colleague Nachman bar Ya'akov refers to Anan's tendency to have wasted time playing chess (some say checkers) when he was a student at Mar Shemu'el's academy; nevertheless,

Nachman bar Ya'akov respected Anan and called him Mar, "Master" (*Chullin* 56a).

Ketubbot 106a relates that Elijah the Prophet, who went up to heaven in a whirlwind, (*2 Kings* 2:11) frequently appeared to Anan, to whom he was teaching *Seder Eliyyahu*, a rabbinic work of mysterious origin and authorship.

Anan bar Chiyya (second century)

Babylonia amora. In *Ketubbot* 21a he is named as a colleague of Chanan bar Rabbah.

Anan bar Rav (third century)

Babylonian amora. He is quoted in *Eruvin* 74b.

Anan bar Rava (second/third century)

Babylonian amora. In *Rosh Hashanah* 31a he is mentioned as a disciple of Rav.

Anan bar Tachlifa (third century)

Babylonian amora. In *Pesachim* 101a he is said to have been a contemporary of Shemu'el.

Anani ben Sasson (third century)

Palestinian amora. According to *Shabbat* 64b, he was a disciple of Yishma'el ben Yosei.

Antigonus of Sokho (third century B.C.E.)

Pre-tannaitic teacher. He is mentioned in Mishnah *Avot* 1:3, where he is described as having been a disciple of Shimon ha-Tzadik. Antigonus lived during a period in which Hellenism had become a strong influence in Jewish life. His name, Antigonus, is Greek. Legend has it that he had two disciples: Zadok and Boethus, both of whom later rejected his teaching and became heretics.

Antigonus of Sokho is known for the following maxim: "Be not like servants who serve the Master [God] in order to receive a reward. Rather, be like servants who serve the Master without any thought of reward. And may the fear of Heaven be upon you!" (*Avot* 1:3).

Aptoriki

Two scholars were known by this name:

1. A first/second-century Palestinian tanna who, in *Zevachim* 12a, is said to have been a contemporary of Yishma'el.

2. A third-century Palestinian amora who is quoted in *Chullin* 81a.

Aptoriki, Father of
See Avuha de-Rabbi Aptoriki.

Aquila (second century)
Also known as Akilas *in Greek.*

Palestinian scholar. The Midrash *Tanchuma* ("*Mishpatim*" 5) refers to Aquila as a proselyte who was "the son of the sister of the Roman emperor Hadrian." He is, therefore, often confused with Onkelos the Proselyte, to whom *Gittin* 56b refers as the son of the sister of the Roman emperor Titus.

Aquila the Proselyte was a Gentile by birth who, for a short time, joined the Christian community, but then decided he wanted to be a Jew. He probably became attached to Judaism after being appointed by his uncle Hadrian in the year 128 to a commission that dealt with the rebuilding of Jerusalem, which had been laid to waste fifty-eight years earlier. As Aquila witnessed the devastation wrought upon the beautiful, ancient Jewish Temple, he was stirred to learn more about its history and the values of Judaism.

For a while, Aquila kept his attraction to Judaism secret, fearful of arousing the wrath of his uncle. Finally, he overcame his fear and told Hadrian that he was planning to convert to Judaism. "Why would you want to do that?" asked Hadrian. "Why would you want to join people that I have humiliated and persecuted?"

Aquila replied: "I want to join a group in which the least of them knows how God created the world, and what was created on each day . . . Besides, their Torah is truth!"

Hadrian responded: "Go ahead! Study their Torah, but do not become circumcised."

According to legend, Aquila was circumcised, converted to Judaism, and continued to study Torah under two of the great tanna'im of the second century: Eli'ezer ben Hurkanos and Yehoshu'a ben Chananyah. Aquila also became a disciple of the renowned Akiva ben Yosef (*Genesis Rabbah* 70:5, *Exodus Rabbah* 30:12, and *Numbers Rabbah* 8:9).

Aquila's great contribution was his translation of the Bible into Greek, of which very little is extant.

Aryokh
See Shemu'el.

Ashi (fourth/fifth century)
Babylonian amora. According to a tradition preserved in *Kiddushin* 72b, "when Rava died, Ashi was born." Rava had been an outstanding teacher at the academy at Machoza, and Ashi, a precocious child, became, at the age of twenty, head of the academy in Sura. Thanks to the income he derived from the many forests his wealthy family owned, Ashi was able to rebuild the academy in Sura, which had been in decline since Chisda's death around the year 310. (Mata Mechasya was later absorbed into the more prominent Sura.) During Ashi's fifty years of leadership, Sura attained a position unmatched by any other academy. A saying current during Ashi's lifetime, and attributed to Adda bar Abba, was that "from the days of Rabbi [Yehudah ha-Nasi] to Ashi, learning and political distinction [Torah and high office] were never combined in one person as in Ashi" (*Sanhedrin* 36a). In 427 his son Mar would succeed him as head of the academy.

Despite Ashi's affluence, he was a very modest and moral person who found favor in the eyes of the king of Persia, who ruled Babylonia at that time. *Berakhot* 31a reports that at the marriage feast made for Ashi's son, some of the invited Sages were overly boisterous. Ashi brought out an expensive, white crystal cup and smashed it before them—they immediately restrained themselves. Ashi's wife is mentioned in *Beitzah* 29a as being the daughter of Rami bar Chama, a very pious scholar.

Like Yehudah ha-Nasi, who edited the Mishnah, Ashi began the gigantic task of collecting and arranging the explanations, deductions, and amplifications of the Mishnah, which constitute the Gemara. The task was completed two generations later, under Ravina II, who died in 499.

Ashi is quoted more than two thousand times in the Babylonian Talmud. Among his most influential teachers were

Kahana, who became principal of the prestigious academy in Pumbedita (*Pesachim* 18b, *Megillah* 7b, and *Sukkah* 7a) and who sometimes referred to Ashi as "Mari," a title of distinction; Yehoshu'a bar Idi, for whom Ashi had great respect and admiration (*Shabbat* 11a); and Yannai ben Yishma'el (*Ta'anit* 14a).

Among Ashi's colleagues most frequently referred to in the Babylonian Talmud were Ameimar (*Berakhot* 30b and *Sukkah* 41b), Assi (*Eruvin* 64b), Ravina I (*Megillah* 32a), and Abbayei (*Sukkah* 55a).

Ketubbot 69a discusses the disposition of the estate of Ashi, who, besides Mar, had a son named Samma and a daughter whose name is unknown. Ravina was involved in settling the claim of the daughter, who was dissatisfied with her share of the estate.

Ashi bar Abin

See Ashi bar Avin.

Ashi bar Avin (fourth century)

Babylonian amora. In *Shabbat* 66b he is mentioned as a teacher of Nachman bar Barukh.

Ashi of Avirya (fourth/fifth century)

Babylonian amora. According to *Shevu'ot* 24b, Ashi of Avirya was a disciple of Ze'eira.

Ashi'an

Three Palestinian amora'im were known by this name:

1. A third-century disciple of Yochanan bar Nappacha, who is referred to as Ashi'an ha-Naggara (Ashi'an the Carpenter).

2. A fourth-century colleague of Ammi bar Nathan, quoted in *Berakhot* 14a. Ashi'an's task was to repeat and elaborate upon the lectures of his teachers.

3. A third-century colleague of Assi whose full name was Ashi'an bar Yakim. Ashi'an's father Yakim is mentioned in Mishnah *Eduyyot* 7:5 as a contemporary of Yehoshu'a ben Chananiah.

Ashi'an bar Nidbak (third century)

Babylonian amora. In *Menachot* 29a Ashi'an bar Nidbak is said to have been a son-in-law of Ye'iva and a disciple of Yehudah bar Yechezkel.

Assi

Two prominent third/fourth-century amora'im were known by this name. Both were born in Babylonia; however, the second studied with Shemu'el in Nehardea before immigrating to Palestine.

The name Assi appears in various forms, including Assa, Issi, and Yosei. When it does, it generally refers to the second Assi.

1. His many colleagues included Ashi (*Eruvin* 64b), Ze'eira (*Bava Metzi'a* 72b), and Yirmeyahu bar Abba (*Shabbat* 12b); his disciples included Aviyya (*Pesachim* 24b), Beivai (*Shabbat* 14a), and Rami bar Chama, who in *Eruvin* 100b quotes Assi as saying: "A man is forbidden to walk on the grass on the Sabbath," a conclusion he draws from a verse in *Proverbs* 9:2.

According to *Bava Kamma* 11a, Assi and Kahanai were disciples of Rav, but from a discussion found in *Bava Kamma* 80a–b as to who shall enter a room first, it appears that Assi had achieved status equal to that of Rav. In *Pesachim* 113a Rav advised Assi: "Do not live in a town where no horses neigh and where no dogs bark," presumably because when dogs bark they raise an alarm, and when horses neigh they are fired up to pursue marauders. Rav added: "Do not dwell in a town where the community leader is a physician," presumably because doctors would be too busy caring for patients and have little time to devote to communal matters.

2. Along with his close friend Ammi bar Natan, Assi moved from Babylonia to Palestine, where both men studied under Yochanan bar Nappacha and became brilliant scholars. Yochanan was head of the academy in Tiberias, and Assi turned to him often for legal advice and homiletical instruction (*Bava Kamma* 60b). Among Assi's contemporaries were Ze'eira and Yehoshu'a ben Levi (*Bava Metzi'a* 17a), Ze'iri ben Chama (*Yoma* 78a), and Ravah bar Natan (*Eruvin* 32b). When Yochanan died, Assi succeeded him as head of the academy in Tiberias. Later, when Assi died, it was said that "the gates of Tiberias collapsed" (*Gittin* 5b and 17a, *Kiddushin* 60b, *Sotah* 21b, and *Yoma* 24b).

Assi was a great believer in the power of *tzedakah*. In *Bava Batra* 9a he says: "Charity is equivalent to all the other commandments [*mitzvot*] in the Torah combined."

Assi bar Chama (third/fourth century)

Babylonian amora. In *Bava Kamma* 93a he is named as a disciple of Rabbah bar Nachmani.

Assi bar Chanina (fourth/fifth century)

Babylonian amora. In *Bava Batra* 56a he is mentioned as a disciple of Assi and a mentor of Acha bar Aviya.

Assi bar Chini (second/third century)

Also known as Issi bar Chini.

Babylonian amora. His academy was once visited by Ulla, who was asked whether it was permitted to create a *marzev*, a pocket fashioned by gathering up one's skirt, on the Sabbath, similar to capes worn by Babylonian women (*Shabbat* 147a). In Mishnah *Chullin* 137b, where Assi bar Chini is referred to as Issi bar Chini, it says that he spent time teaching in Palestine.

Assi bar Chiyya (fourth century)

Babylonian amora. In *Avodah Zarah* 51b Assi bar Chiyya is mentioned as a contemporary of Pappa.

Assi bar Natan (third century)

Babylonian amora. In *Shabbat* 53a Assi bar Natan is listed as a disciple of Chiyya bar Ashi.

Assi bar Nathan

See Assi bar Natan.

Assi ben Saul

See Assi ben Sha'ul.

Assi ben Sha'ul (fourth century)

Palestinian amora. Dimi and Assi ben Sha'ul often traveled to Babylonia to transmit teachings of the various Palestinian academies (*Shabbat* 50a).

Assi of Hozna'a (fourth/fifth century)

Babylonian amora. According to *Shabbat* 87b, Assi of Hozna'a was a colleague of Ashi.

Assi of Hutzal (third century)

Babylonian amora. He lived in Hutzal, a town located between Sura and Nehardea (*Kiddushin* 58b).

Assi of Nehar Bil (fourth century)

Also known as Yosei of Nehar Bil.

Babylonian amora. He probably was a colleague of Yirmeyahu of Difti and is mentioned in *Chullin* 87b. *Chullin* 136a makes mention of Yosei of Nehar Bil, who is thought to be identical with Assi. Bil was a town located east of Baghdad.

Avahu

See Abbahu.

Avdan (third century)

Also known as Avidan *or* Abidan.

Palestinian amora. The name Avdan may be a contraction of Abba Yudan. *Yevamot* 108a refers to Avdan as a disciple of Yehudah ha-Nasi.

Avdimi

See Dimi.

Avdimi bar Chama (fourth century)

Also known as Avdimi bar Chasa *and* Dimi bar Chama.

Palestinian amora. Avdimi bar Chama immigrated to Babylonia. In *Avodah Zarah* 19a he is quoted as saying: "He who occupies himself with Torah study will have his desires granted by God." *Shabbat* 88a and *Avodah Zarah* 2b record his famous comment on *Exodus* 19:17, which reads, "They [the Israelites] stood under the mountain." According to Avdimi, this "teaches us that God held the mountain over them like an inverted dome, declaring: 'If you accept the Torah, all will be well with you, and if not, there shall be your burial place.'"

Avdimi bar Chama bar Dosa (third/fourth century)

Babylonian amora. In *Eruvin* 55a Avdimi bar Chama bar Dosa is mentioned as a colleague of Rava.

Avdimi bar Chasa

See Avdimi bar Chama.

Avdimi ben Chasa (second/third century)

Palestinian amora. *Zevachim* 118a names Avdimi ben Chasa as a colleague of Yannai.

Avdimi ben Hamduri (third century)

Palestinian amora. He is quoted in *Sukkah* 20a.

Avdimi Malacha (fourth century)

Palestinian amora. A sailmaker by profession, Avdimi Malacha was a contemporary of Chiyya ben Abba.

Avdimi of Haifa (third/fourth century)

Also known as Dimi of Haifa.

Palestinian amora. A recognized halakhic authority, Avdimi of Haifa pronounced rules of etiquette and observations on proper personal living. He once said: "When a scholar passes to take his seat at the academy, one should rise in his honor." In *Bava Batra* 12a he is quoted as saying: "Since the day the Temple was destroyed, prophecy was taken away from the Prophets and given to the Sages." According to *Kiddushin* 33b, Abbahu was one of Avdimi of Haifa's disciples.

Avidan

See Avdan.

Avi Mari

See Abba Mari.

Avimi

Also spelled Abimi, *a contraction of* Abba Ammi *or* Abbi Immi.

Two Babylonian amora'im were known by this name:

1. A third-century amora whose teachings were reported by Chisda (*Menachot* 7a).

2. A fourth-century amora who, according to *Eruvin* 58b, was a disciple of Rabbah bar Nachman and Rami bar Yechezkel.

Avimi bar Nazi (third/fourth century)

Also spelled Abimi bar Nazi.

Babylonian amora. He was the father-in-law of Ravina (*Bava Kamma* 115a).

Avimi bar Pappi (fourth century)

Also spelled Abimi bar Pappi.

Babylonian Amora. In *Ketubbot* 43b he is mentioned as a contemporary of Ze'eira.

Avimi ben Abbahu (fourth century)

Also spelled Abimi ben Abbahu.

Babylonian amora. *Kiddushin* 31b records the words of Abbahu: "My son Avimi has fulfilled the precept of honoring parents." Avimi had five sons who were ordained in his father's lifetime, yet when Abbahu came to visit his son, Avimi would rush to be the first to open the door for him.

Avimi Nota'ah (fourth century)

Also spelled Abimi Nota'ah.

Babylonian amora. Known in English as Avimi the Nabatean, he was, according to *Avodah Zarah* 36a, a disciple of Rav.

Avimi of Bei-Chozai

Also spelled Abimi of Bei-Chozai.

Babylonian amora. An obscure scholar, he is quoted in *Niddah* 5b.

Avimi of Hagronia (fourth century)

Also spelled Abimi of Hagronia.

Babylonian amora. *Yevamot* 64b names Avimi of Hagronia as a disciple of Huna and *Ketubbot* 109b calls him a disciple of Rava.

Avimi of Senavta (fourth century)

Also spelled Abimi of Senavta.

Babylonian amora. *Avodah Zarah* 36a refers to his native town as Nivtei (Nabatea). In *Shabbat* 17b Avimi of Senavta is said to have been a teacher of Bali.

Avimi the Nabatean

See Avimi Nota'ah.

Avin

Also spelled Abin.

A number of scholars known by this name—a shortened form of Avina (other variants include Abun, Abuna, and Bun)—are mentioned in both the Jerusalem and Babylonian Talmuds. The most prominent are:

1. A third/fourth-century Babylonian amora whose teachings were preserved by Elazar ben Pedat. In the Babylonian Talmud Avin generally is referred to as Ravin (short for Rav Avin) Sabba—in English Ravin the Elder. Though he was born in Babylonia, Avin studied in Palestine. A disciple of Pappa, Abbahu, and Ze'eira, Avin is quoted in *Berakhot* 7a.

2. A third-century Palestinian amora who was a carpenter by

trade (*Shabbat* 23b). Highly regarded, Avin was complimented on his learning by Abbahu and Ze'eira. A disciple of Ila'i and Yochanan bar Nappacha and a colleague of Huna, Avin is quoted in *Shabbat* 5a–b and *Eruvin* 96a. In *Pesachim* 70b Abbayei mentions the fact that Avin was childless.

Avin bar Adda
Also spelled Abin bar Adda.
See Ravin bar Adda.

Avin bar Huna (third century)
Also spelled Abin bar Huna.
Babylonian amora. In *Zevachim* 62b Avin bar Huna is listed as a disciple of Chama bar Gurya.

Avin bar Nachman (third century)
Also spelled Abin bar Nachman. *Also known as* Avin ha-Naggar.
Babylonian amora. Sometimes referred to in English as Avin the Carpenter, noting how diligently Avin bar Nachman was engaged in study, Huna predicted that he would have two great scholars for sons. And so it was: Idi bar Avin and Chiyya bar Avin were his learned progeny (*Shabbat* 23b).

Avin ben Chisda (fourth century)
Also spelled Abin ben Chisda.
Palestinian amora. He was a disciple of the widely quoted Yochanan bar Nappacha.

Avin ben Chiyya (fourth century)
Also spelled Abin ben Chiyya.
Palestinian amora. He was a colleague of Yirmeyahu and a disciple of Ze'eira (*Kiddushin* 44a).

Avin ben Kahana (fourth century)
Also spelled Abin ben Kahana.
Palestinian amora. His teachings were transmitted by the Palestinian amora Yonah (*Kiddushin* 44a and *Zevachim* 9a).

Avin ben Shabba
Also spelled Abin ben Shabba.
An amora, probably Palestinian, of unknown date, he is mentioned only once in the Talmud (*Chullin* 86a). His name has been confused with Ravin ben Abba.

Avin, Father of
See Avuha de-Rabbi Avin.

Avin ha-Levi (fourth century)
Also spelled Abin ha-Levi.
Palestinian amora. Known in English as Avin the Levite and distinguished for his knowledge of *aggadah*, Avin ha-Levi is widely quoted in *Berakhot* 64a.

Avin ha-Naggar
See Avin bar Nachman.

Avin of Neshikya (third century)
Also spelled Abin of Neshikya.
Babylonian amora. In *Shabbat* 121a Avin of Neshikya is noted as a colleague of Yirmeyahu bar Abba and Chanan bar Raba.

Avin of Sepphoris (fifth century)
Also spelled Abin of Sepphoris.
Palestinian amora. In *Shabbat* 29b he is mentioned as a colleague of Yitzchak ben Elazar. Sepphoris was in the Galilee, in northern Palestine.

Avin of Toran (second/third century)
Also spelled Abin of Toran.
Babylonian amora. *Shabbat* 122b reports that Avin of Toran was visited by Shemu'el.

Avin the Carpenter
See Avin bar Nachman.

Avina (third/fourth century)
Also known as Abina *and* Bun.
Babylonian amora. In *Gittin* 65a he is named as a student of Huna and a colleague of Ganiva. In *Pesachim* 50a and *Kiddushin* 71a Avina comments on the rule regarding the treatment of God's name, namely that the Tetragrammaton, spelled *yud-hei-vav-hei* (Yehovah), is to be read as if spelled *alef-dalet-nun-yud* (Adonai).

In his later years Avina migrated to Palestine. There he was befriended by Ze'eira and Yirmeyahu ben Abba, through whom he was able to transmit decisions made by the scholars of Babylonia to the scholars of Palestine (*Shabbat* 137b).

Avira (fourth century)
Palestinian amora. He was a colleague of Chelbo and Yosei bar Chanina (*Berakhot* 20b and *Sotah* 5a).

Aviya (fourth century)
Also known as Ivya.
Babylonian amora. According to *Bava Batra* 100b, Aviya was married to the sister of Rami bar Pappa. Soon after their marriage, it was discovered that she had lost her *ketubbah*. She and Aviya appeared before Yosef for a ruling on whether it was proper for them to live together under these circumstances (*Ketubbot* 56b–57a). Yosef required that a new *ketubbah* be written before the couple could resume cohabitation.

Aviya was very scrupulous about following the letter of the law. Absent one day from Yosef's lectures because he was ill, Aviya explained that he was weak because he had not eaten and that one is not permitted to taste food until he has recited the *Musaf* prayer (*Berakhot* 28b).

Aviya Sabba (third/fourth century)
Babylonian amora. Known in English as Aviya the Elder, it is noted in *Beitzah* 21a that Aviya Sabba studied under the famous Huna, who considered him a great scholar.

Aviya the Elder
See Aviya Sabba.

Avmari
See Abba Mari.

Avram (third/fourth century)
Babylonian amora. A colleague of Rava, he is also known as Avram Choza, Choza being a town in southwest Persia later known as Khuzistan. In *Gittin* 50a he states that a claim made against the estate of orphans to compensate for damages may be collected only from their poorest land, not the most expensive.

Avtalyon (first century B.C.E.)
Also spelled Abtalyon.
A member of the Great Assembly, he, together with Shemayah, formed one of the famous *zugot*—"pairs." While Shemayah served as *nasi*—president—of the Sanhedrin in

Jerusalem, Avtalyon served as *av beit din*—"head of the court." Avtalyon, who was probably identical with Pollion, or Ptollion, mentioned by Josephus, was a leader of the Pharisees and a teacher of Hillel and Shammai, the last of the *zugot*. According to the Talmud, Avtalyon was the descendant of a proselyte, but this is doubtful. One of Avtalyon's popular maxims was this: "Wise men, heed your words lest you be condemned to exile" (*Avot* 1:11). Along with his colleague Shemayah, Avtalyon was considered one of the greatest men of his generation (*Pesachim* 66a).

Avtilos ben Reuben
See Avtilos ben Re'uven.

Avtilos ben Re'uven (second century)
Palestinian tanna. Because of his close contact with the Roman government, Avtilos ben Re'uven was permitted (as was the family of Rabban Gamaliel) to cut his hair in Gentile fashion, leaving a fringe on the forehead and letting curls hang down on his temples (*Bava Kamma* 83a).

Avtilos ben Yosei (second century)
Palestinian tanna. Noted in *Shabbat* 118b are the names of Avtilos ben Yosei's four brothers: Yishma'el, Elazar (Eli'ezer in some manuscripts), Chalafta, and Menachem ben Yosei.

Avtolemos (second century)
Palestinian tanna. He is quoted by Yosei ben Chalafta in *Rosh Hashanah* 15a.

Avudimi
See Dimi.

Avudma
See Dimi.

Avuha (second century)
Also spelled Abbuha.
Palestinian amora. According to *Yoma* 50b and *Temurah* 2b, Avuha was a disciple of Yochanan ben Nappacha. In *Arakhin* 6a, Avuha is listed as a mentor of Nachman bar Ya'akov.

Avuha bar Ichi (second/third century)
Also spelled Abbuha bar Ichi.

Babylonian amora. *Megillah* 28a and *Ketubbot* 61a record that he was a brother of Minyamin bar Ichi.

Avuha de-Rabbi Abin
See Avuha de-Rabbi Avin.

Avuha de-Rabbi Aptoriki (third century)
Babylonian amora. Known in English as the Father of Aptoriki, he is recorded in *Bava Metzi'a* 5a contradicting a ruling of Chiyya bar Abba.

Avuha de-Rabbi Avin (third century)
Also spelled Avuha de-Rabbi Abin.
Palestinian amora. Known in English as the Father of Avin, he is quoted in *Sanhedrin* 76a.

Avuha di-Shemu'el
See Abba bar Abba.

Avyatar (third century)
Palestinian amora. In *Gittin* 6b Avyatar is named as a colleague of Chisda.

Ayo (second century)
Palestinian tanna. In *Eruvin* 36b and 37b he is mentioned as a disciple of Yehudah bar Ila'i.

B

Bali (fourth century)

Babylonian amora. In *Berakhot* 25b he is noted as a disciple of Ya'akov, son of the daughter of Shemu'el. Bali also was a disciple of Avimi of Senavta (*Shabbat* 17b) and Chiyya bar Abba (*Ta'anit* 18a).

Bana'ah (third century)

Palestinian tanna. According to *Zevachim* 118a, *Bava Batra* 57b, and *Yevamot* 71b, his greatest student was Yochanan bar Nappacha. In *Ta'anit* 7a, Bana'ah is quoted as saying: "To one who studies Torah for its own sake, Torah becomes an elixir of life. To one who studies Torah for any other reason, it becomes a deadly poison."

Bana'ah bar Ulla (fourth century)

Babylonian amora. He is quoted in *Pesachim* 54a.

Bar Abubram (third/fourth century)

Babylonian amora. He is mentioned in *Chullin* 38a as a contemporary of Ravina I.

Bar Achina (third/fourth century)

Babylonian amora. According to *Kiddushin* 51a, he was a teacher of Rava.

Bar Hamduri (third century)

Also known as Mar bar Hamduri.

Babylonian amora. A teacher of Rava (*Yevamot* 83b), Bar Hamduri is referred to as Mar bar Hamduri in *Shabbat* 107b.

Bar Hedya (fourth century)

Palestinian amora. According to *Sukkah* 43b, Bar Hedya visited Babylonia to establish the date of Rosh Chodesh. A contemporary of Abbayei and Rava, Bar Hedya was reputed to be an interpreter of dreams. To those who paid him, the interpretation was positive; to those who did not pay him, he would render a negative interpretation of the same dream (*Berakhot* 56a). *Gittin* 5b recounts how Bar Hedya consulted Achi, Ammi bar Natan, and Assi to ask if he was permitted to deliver a *get* from Babylonia to Palestine.

Bar Kappara

See Elazar ha-Kappar.

Bar Kasha (second/third century)

Babylonian scholar. A contemporary of Rav, it was said that when Rav died, everyone except Bar Kasha mourned the loss. Most authorities do not grant Bar Kasha the status of amora.

Bar Levai (third century)

Babylonian amora. In *Niddah* 40a he is mentioned as a teacher of Shimon.

Bar Padda (third century)

Palestinian amora. He is quoted in *Chullin* 23a and 71a, and in *Nedarim* 28b.

Bar Tachlifa (second century)

Palestinian tanna. In *Zevachim* 63a he is mentioned as a colleague of Ya'akov bar Korshai and Yirmeyahu.

Bar Tutani (third century)

Palestinian amora. He is named in *Shabbat* 71a as a teacher of Shimon ben Lakish.

Bardela (third century)

Palestinian amora. In *Makkot* 14b he is said to have been a contemporary of Yochanan bar Nappacha and Shimon ben Lakish.

Bardela bar Tavyomi (third century)

Babylonian amora. He is mentioned in *Chagigah* 5a as a disciple of Rav, and in *Zevachim* 33b he is quoted by Yochanan bar Nappacha.

Bava ben Buta (first century B.C.E.)

Palestinian tanna. According to *Bava Batra* 3b–4a, Bava ben Buta was a blind teacher whom Herod tried to induce to curse him; when Herod later had members of the Sanhedrin executed,

Bava was spared. *Gittin* 57a names him as a disciple of Shammai, and in *Keritot* 25a Bava ben Buta is described as a pious Sage who brought a guilt offering to the Temple every day except on the day after Yom Kippur.

Beibai
See Beivai.

Bebai ben Gidal
See Beivai ben Gidal.

Beiha (third century)
Babylonian amora. A contemporary of Yochanan bar Nappacha, Beiha is quoted in *Temurah* 29a.

Beivai (fourth century)
Also spelled Beibai.

Babylonian amora. In *Kiddushin* 81a he is described as the best friend of the wife of his colleague Yosef. According to *Shabbat* 80b it is reported that he had a daughter and that he drank strong liquor; *Mo'ed Katan* 9b refers to his drinking beer, which leads to obesity, according to Rashi.

Among Beivai's many teachers were Yehoshu'a ben Levi (*Menachot* 103b), Assi (*Shabbat* 14a), Shimon ben Lakish (*Berakhot* 62b), Eleazar (*Pesachim* 72b), and Nachman bar Ya'akov (*Chagigah* 22b and *Nedarim* 35b). In *Niddah* 45a, Beivai lists three types of women who are permitted to use contraception (*mokh*)—a minor, a pregnant woman, and a nursing mother—and explains why.

Beivai Acha of Difti (fifth century)
Also known as Acha bar Difti.

Babylonian amora. He was in line to succeed Ashi as principal of the academy in Sura after Ashi's death in 427 but lost out to Ashi's son, Mar bar Rav Ashi. In *Yevamot* 54a and *Nedarim* 23a Beivai Acha of Difti is named as a disciple of Ravina II.

Beivai ben Gidal (second/third century)
Also spelled Beibai ben Gidal.

Palestinian tanna. In *Bava Batra* 113b he is mentioned as a contemporary of Shimon ha-Tzadik.

Ben Azzai
See Shimon ben Azzai.

Ben Bag Bag (first century B.C.E.)
Also known as Yochanan ben Bag Bag.
Palestinian tanna. A disciple of Hillel whose real name was Yochanan, Ben Bag Bag is believed by some authorities to have been a proselyte or the son of a proselyte. Ben Bag Bag is quoted in *Menachot* 49b and in *Avot* 5:22, where he is known for the popular saying about the Torah: "Turn it and turn it, for everything can be found in it."

Ben Bathyra
See Ben Beteira.

Ben Beteira (fourth century)
Also known as Shimon ben Beteira.
Babylonian amora. Known in English as Ben Bathyra, he is quoted in *Shabbat* 94a and *Menachot* 6b and 8b.

Ben Bokhri (first century)
Palestinian tanna. A contemporary of Yochanan ben Zakkai, Ben Bokhri is quoted in *Menachot* 21b and 46b.

Ben Dama (second century)
Also known as Elazar ben Dama.
Palestinian tanna. Referred to as Ben Dama in *Berakhot* 56b and *Menachot* 99b, elsewhere he is known as Elazar ben Dama. In *Avodah Zarah* 27b, he speaks of Yishma'el as his brother, though *Menachot* 99b reports that Ben Dama was the son of Yishma'el's sister. There he asks Yishma'el: "May one such as I, who has studied the whole of the Torah, learn Greek wisdom?" According to *Avodah Zarah* 27b, Elazar died after being bitten by a snake; Yishma'el eulogized him as one who was pure in body and soul.

Ben Elasa (second century)
Little regarded Palestinian scholar. He was the wealthy son-in-law of the illustrious Yehudah ha-Nasi.

Ben Hei Hei (first century B.C.E.)
Palestinian tanna. Like Ben Bag Bag, the scholar nicknamed Ben Hei Hei was a disciple of Hillel and a proselyte. Some authorities believe that the two tanna'im were one and the same

person. Ben Hei Hei's oft-quoted proverb appears in *Avot* 5:23: "According to one's pain [labor and effort] is his reward."

Ben Nannas

See Shimon ben Nannas.

Ben Pedat

See Elazar ben Pedat.

Ben Petora (second century)

Palestinian tanna. In *Bava Metzi'a* 62a Ben Petora comments that if two people are traveling through the desert and one has a flask with just enough water for himself, it is preferable that they share the water and die together, rather than that one witness the death of the other. Akiva ben Yosef disagrees. He quotes the biblical verse "That thy brother may live with thee" (*Leviticus* 25:36) to mean that the life of the person with the flask takes precedence over the other person's life.

Ben Rechumei (third/fourth century)

Babylonian amora. According to *Nazir* 13a, he was a disciple of Abbayei.

Ben Shelkot (first/second century)

Palestinian tanna. A contemporary of Akiva ben Yosef, Ben Shelkot discusses the degree of maturity a girl must reach before she is considered an adult, free to determine whom she shall marry (*Niddah* 52b).

Ben Zoma

See Shimon ben Zoma.

Benei, Achu'a d'Rabbi Chiyya bar Abba (third/fourth century)

Babylonian amora. Known in English as Benei, Brother of Chiyya bar Abba, in *Ketubbot* 50b he consults Shemu'el on a legal matter.

Benjamin

See Binyamin.

Berekhyah

Two Palestinian scholars were known by this name:

1. A third-century amora who, in *Leviticus Rabbah* 1:4, is

referred to as Berekhyah Sabba (Berekhyah the Elder) by Avin to distinguish him from his later, more prominent namesake.

2. A fourth-century Palestinian amora who probably was born in Babylonia. He is identified as a Palestinian scholar because most of his teachings are preserved in the Palestinian Talmud and in Palestinian *midrashim*. In the Midrash he often is referred to as Berekhyah ha-Kohen.

In a comment on the phrase in *Ecclesiastes* 3:2, "a time to be born and a time to die," Berekhyah says, "Fortunate is the man who at the time of his death is as pure and innocent as at the time of his birth" (Palestinian Talmud, *Megillah* 19).

Berekhyah's disciple, Yudan ben Channin, quotes Berekhyah as saying that God spoke these words to Israel: "My children, when you see the merit of the fathers [patriarchs] and the merit of the mothers [matriarchs] declining, go and beseech God's kindness directly" (Palestinian Talmud, *Sanhedrin* 1:1).

Berim
See Biryam.

Beroka Choza'i
Amora. Of unknown date and origin, Beroka Choza'i is described in *Ta'anit* 22a as a mystic who would frequent the marketplace of Bei Lapat in Khuzistan, where Elijah the Prophet would appear to him.

Berona (third century)
Also spelled Beruna.

Babylonian amora. In *Berakhot* 9b Berona is referred to as a brother of Ila'a and a contemporary of Ulla. In *Avodah Zarah* 38a, *Shabbat* 21a, and many other tractates, he is mentioned as a disciple of Rav. In *Eruvin* 60a, he is noted as a colleague of Yehudah bar Yechezkel, a disciple of Shemu'el.

Beruna
See Berona.

Beruri'ah
See Beruryah.

Beruryah (second century)
Scholarly daughter of Chananyah ben Teradyon, the very

courageous tanna who defied the Roman edict forbidding the teaching of Torah. One of the Ten Martyrs, Chananyah ben Teradyon was executed while holding a Torah scroll in his arms.

Beruryah, who lived in Tiberias, was a learned, saintly, and courageous woman, who followed in her father's footsteps. Her knowledge of Jewish law was prodigious. *Pesachim* 62b notes that she could master three hundred *halakhot* in one day. Her formidable knowledge of Jewish law is mentioned in numerous Midrashic and Talmudic sources including *Eruvin* 53b–54a and *Berakhot* 10a. She is the only woman documented in the Talmud to have participated in legal discussions with the Rabbis, and in two instances, her legal opinions were accepted as authoritative.

Wife of the tanna Me'ir, their faith was severely tested when, according to legend, their twin sons died suddenly on a Sabbath afternoon while Me'ir was delivering his weekly Sabbath lecture in the synagogue. Beruryah carried the boys to her room and covered them with a sheet. When Meir returned after evening services, he asked his wife about the boys, whom he had missed in the synagogue. Instead of replying, she asked him to recite *Havdalah* to mark the close of the Sabbath. Afterwards, she gave him his evening meal.

Beruryah then turned to Me'ir and said, "I have a question to ask. Not long ago, some precious jewels were entrusted to my care. Now the owner has come to reclaim them. Shall I return them?"

"Of course," said Meir. "You know the law. They must be returned."

Beruryah then took him by the hand, led him to the bedroom, and drew back the sheet. Me'ir burst into bitter weeping. "My sons! My sons!" he lamented. Then Beruryah reminded him tearfully, "Did you not say that we must restore to the owner that which was entrusted to our care? Our sons were the jewels given to us by God, and now their Master has taken back His very own."

Binyamin (third century)

Babylonian amora. In *Ketubbot* 84a he engages in a dispute

with Elazar ben Pedat about the rights of a woman as specified in her *ketubbah*.

Binyamin Asya (fourth century)

Also known as Minyomi Asya.

Babylonian amora. *Asya* is an Aramaic term meaning "physician," which Binyamin Asya was. He founded a school and named it after himself: De-bei Minyomi Asya.

Binyamin bar Gidal (fourth century)

Palestinian amora. In *Chullin* 125a he is listed as a disciple of Yochanan bar Nappacha.

Binyamin ben Ichi (second/third century)

Babylonian amora. He was the brother of Abbahu bar Ichi, who was a teacher of Shemu'el (*Chagigah* 24b).

Binyamin ben Levi (third/fourth century)

Palestinian amora. He was a younger contemporary of Ammi bar Natan.

Binyamin ben Yefet (third century)

Palestinian amora. According to *Yoma* 29a, he was a teacher of Elazar. In *Berakhot* 38b he is noted as a disciple of Yochanan bar Nappacha and a colleague of Chiyya bar Abba.

Binyamin Ginzakaya (third century)

Babylonian amora. A contemporary of Shemu'el, little else is known about him.

Bira (fourth century)

Palestinian amora. In *Sukkah* 27a he is said to have been a colleague of Ammi bar Natan.

Bira'a (fourth century)

Palestinian amora. According to *Sukkah* 34b, he was a disciple of Ammi bar Natan.

Biryam (second/third century)

Palestinian amora. He is quoted in *Chullin* 98a as well as in *Berakhot* 55b, where he is mentioned as a teacher of Nachum.

Bisa (third century)

Palestinian tanna. He was the father of Chama bar Bisa and the grandfather of Oshaya Rabbah (*Ketubbot* 62b and *Bava*

Batra 59a). Yehudah ha-Nasi once commended Chama bar Bisa to Yishma'el bar Yosei as a great man (*Niddah* 14b). In Midrash *Tanchuma* ("*Miketz*") Bisa is quoted as saying: "There is no man in the world who does not experience pain."

Bivi ben Abbayei (fourth century)
Babylonian amora. Son of the famous principal of the academy at Pumbedita, Bivi ben Abbayei was a judge in Pumbedita. In *Berakhot* 6b he is named as a colleague of Nachman bar Yitzchak.

Bizna ben Zavda (first century)
Palestinian tanna. In *Berakhot* 55b he is named as a disciple of Akiva ben Yosef.

Boni'as ben Noni'as (third century)
Palestinian tanna. According to *Gittin* 59a, he was a contemporary of Yehudah ha-Nasi.

Botnit ben Abba ben Botnit (second/third century)
Palestinian tanna. In *Nedarim* 23a he is mentioned as a colleague of Shimon ben Yehudah, the younger son of Yehudah ha-Nasi.

Bubi (fourth century)
Babylonian amora. In *Niddah* 27a he is said to have been a colleague of Pappa and a student of Hamnuna.

Budi'a (fifth century)
Babylonian amora. In *Gittin* 45b he is named as a colleague of Ashi.

Bun
See Avina.

C

Chagga

In addition to Chaggai of Sepphoris (see below), four other scholars were known by this name:

1. A first-century Palestinian tanna, who, in *Yoma* 41b, is mentioned as a colleague of Josiah I and, in *Bava Batra* 19b, as a disciple of Yosei ben Chalafta.

2. A third-century Palestinian amora who, in *Keritot* 28a, is mentioned as a disciple of Oshai'a Rabbah.

3. A third-century Babylonian amora, who, according to *Mo'ed Katan* 25a, was a disciple of Huna and, according to *Bava Metzi'a* 113b, a colleague of Rabbah bar Chana.

4. A fourth-century Babylonian amora who, in *Gittin* 23a, was named as a disciple of Ulla.

Chaggai (third century)

Palestinian amora. Like Chaggai of Sepphoris, he was born in Babylonia and immigrated to Palestine. Chaggai achieved greatness as a scholar and was given the honor of opening each study session. His colleague Yosei ben Chalafta respected him greatly and called him "rabbi." He and Yosei explained that the reason one should not look at the *Kohanim* when they recite the Priestly Benediction is in order not to distract them and ruin their concentration while they are blessing the congregation (Palestinian Talmud, *Ta'anit* 4:1).

Chaggai of Sepphoris (third century)

Also known as Chagga.

Palestinian amora. Born in Babylonia, he was one of the prominent pupils of the exilarch Huna. When Huna died, Chaggai of Sepphoris (in the Galilee, in northern Palestine) was given the honor of placing his teacher's coffin in a sepulcher (*Mo'ed Katan* 25a). Chaggai of Sepphoris eventually immigrated to

Palestine to attend the academy of Yochanan bar Nappacha. In *Mo'ed Katan* 25a Chaggai of Sepphoris is referred to as Chagga.

Chalafta (first/second century)

Palestinian tanna. A senior contemporary of Gamli'el II, Chalafta lived in Sepphoris during the Hadrianic persecutions, where he taught his famous son, Yosei ben Chalafta. Chalafta is quoted in *Rosh Hashanah* 27a and *Ta'anit* 16b concerning *shofar*-blowing procedures.

Chalafta ben Dosa of Kefar Chananyah
(second/third century)

Palestinian tanna. A contemporary of Akiva ben Yosef, Chalafta ben Dosa's famous quote, which appears in *Avot* (3:6), reads: "When ten [persons] sitting together are occupied with the study of Torah, God abides among them."

Chalafta ben Karuya

Two scholars were known by this name:

1. A second-century tanna (also known as Chalfa) who was a contemporary of Gamli'el.

2. A third-century Palestinian amora who was a contemporary of Chiyya bar Abba.

Chalafta ben Saul

See Chalafta ben Sha'ul.

Chalafta ben Sha'ul (second/third century)

Also known as Tachlifa ben Sha'ul.

Palestinian tanna. In *Zevachim* 93b he comments on whether the garment of a Priest on which the blood of a sacrifice has spurted needs washing, and in *Menachot* 7b he comments on the vessel in which the sacrificial blood is placed. In *Mo'ed Katan* 10a he is referred to as Tachlifa ben Sha'ul.

Chalafta of Huna (third century)

Palestinian amora. In *Gittin* 86b he is mentioned as a colleague of Yochanan bar Nappacha.

Chalfa ben Agra (second century)

Palestinian tanna. According to *Shabbat* 105b, he was a teacher of Shimon ben Elazar and a disciple of Yochanan ben Nuri.

Chama (fourth century)

Babylonian amora. A native of Nehardea (*Bava Batra* 7b), Chama succeeded Nachman bar Yitzchak as principal of the academy in Pumbedita. According to *Sanhedrin* 17b, Chama was such an outstanding scholar that whenever the Babylonian Talmud refers to "the amora'im of Nehardea" they mean specifically Chama.

Apparently, Chama was on good terms with King Shapur of Persia. When the king asked Chama (*Sanhedrin* 46b) which passage in the Torah required that Jewish dead be buried in the ground, Chama remained silent. Presumably, he was aware that Persians considered the earth holy ground and did not bury their dead in it so as not to defile it with decomposing bodies. Chama avoided upsetting the king by responding that in the Bible, the patriarchs, Moses, and others were buried in the earth.

Chama bar Adda (fourth century)

Babylonian amora. He is quoted in *Yevamot* 62b along with Chiyya bar Avin.

Chama bar Beratei de-Chasa (third/fourth century)

Babylonian amora. Known in English as Chama, Grandson of Chasa, he was the son of Chasa's daughter (*Bava Metzi'a* 86a).

Chama bar Bisa (third century)

Palestinian tanna. In *Niddah* 14b he is praised by Yehudah ha-Nasi in the presence of Yishma'el ben Yosei as being a great man. Chama is reported to have left his family for twelve years to devote time exclusively to Torah study. When Chama returned, his son, Oshaya Rabbah, went out to welcome him but did not recognize him at first. When Chama got to know his son and saw how learned he was, he regretted not having been at home to help educate him (*Ketubbot* 62b).

Chama bar Buzi (fourth century)

Babylonian amora. In *Bava Batra* 16b he and Ravina I are mentioned as students of Rava. *Berakhot* 50a refers to a dinner that Chama bar Buzi attended, along with Ravina I, at the home of the exilarch.

Chama bar Goryon
See Chama bar Gurya.

Chama bar Gurya (second/third century)
Also known as Chama bar Goryon *and* Chami bar Gurya.

Babylonian amora. *Shabbat* 37a lists him as a teacher of Chelbo and *Eruvin* 9a as a disciple of Rav.

Chama bar Kettina (third century)
Babylonian amora. He is quoted in *Kiddushin* 77b.

Chama bar Tobiah
See Chama bar Toviyyah.

Chama bar Toviyyah (sixth century)
Also spelled Chama bar Tuvyah.

Babylonian amora. *Sanhedrin* 52b recounts the harsh punishment Chama bar Toviyyah imposed on Imarta, the daughter of Tali, a Priest, because she committed adultery.

Chama bar Ukba (third century)
Palestinian amora. In *Kiddushin* 55a he is listed as a disciple of Yosei bar Chanina and is quoted in the Palestinian Talmud in *Shevi'it* 9:1.

Chama ben Anilai (third century)
A wealthy, charitable Babylonian Jew and a contemporary of Huna, Chama ben Anilai always opened his home to feed the needy. It was said that bread was baked day and night in his kitchen for the relief of the poor.

Chama ben Chanina (second/third century)
Palestinian amora. Chama ben Chanina was a disciple of Yitzchak (*Berakhot* 5b) and Chiyya (*Sanhedrin* 29a), and a contemporary of Yehudah ha-Nasi's grandson, Yehudah Nesi'ah. Like his father, Chanina bar Chama, before him, Chama was principal of the academy in Sepphoris. A very wealthy man, Chama built a synagogue there (Palestinian Talmud, *Pe'ah* 8:8). Much earlier one of Chama ben Chanina's ancestors had built a synagogue in Lydda, a fact that Chama bemoaned, for "There were not many people who could spare the time to study Torah there."

In *Sotah* 14a Chama asks: "What is the meaning of the text in *Deuteronomy* 13:5, 'You shall walk after your God'? Is it possible for one to walk after the Shekhinah?" Chama explains that "The text means that one should emulate the attributes of God. Just as He clothes the naked, so shall you clothe the naked; just as He visits the sick, so shall you visit the sick . . ."

Among Chama's notable sayings are:

- If a person sees his prayers are not answered, he should pray again. (*Berakhot* 32b)
- Great is penitence for it brings healing to the world. (*Yoma* 86a)
- Just as the hand can kill, so can the tongue [by uttering slanderous words]. (*Arakhin* 15b)

Chama ben Joseph

See Chama ben Yosef.

Chama ben Oshai'a (third century)

Palestinian amora. He is quoted in *Sanhedrin* 25a with regard to gambling on pigeon racing.

Chama ben Pappa (fifth century)

Palestinian amora. In *Sukkah* 49b he says: "Every man endowed with a loving and kind nature is without doubt a God-fearing man."

Chama ben Rabba ben Abbahu (fourth century)

Palestinian amora. He is mentioned in *Bava Metzi'a* 105b.

Chama ben Yosef (third century)

Also known as Chama ben Yosei.

Palestinian amora. In *Avodah Zarah* 14b he is mentioned as a teacher of Dimi and a contemporary of Abbayei. Chama ben Yosef is referred to as Chama ben Yosei in *Sanhedrin* 16a and 112a.

Chama ben Yosei

See Chama ben Yosef.

Chama, Grandson of Chasa

See Chama bar Beratei de-Chasa.

Chama of Nehardea (fourth century)

Babylonian amora. A pupil of Chisda, Chama of Nehardea served as principal of the academy at Pumbedita from 356 to 377; his long tenure in office was undistinguished.

Chami bar Gurya
See Chama bar Gurya.

Chana (third century)
Babylonian amora. In *Shabbat* 97a he is named as a disciple of Yehudah bar Yechezkel and Shemu'el. According to *Yevamot* 110b, Chana married the daughter of Adda bar Ahava.

Chana bar Abba (third/fourth century)
Babylonian amora. He is quoted in *Sukkah* 52b.

Chana bar Adda (fourth century)
Babylonian amora. In *Berakhot* 62b he is named as a disciple of Samma bar Mari and in *Beitzah* 25b as a contemporary of Nachman bar Ya'akov.

Chana bar Bizana
See Chana bar Bizna.

Chana bar Bizna (third/fourth century)
Also spelled Chana bar Bizana. *Also known as* Huna bar Bizna. Babylonian amora. In *Berakhot* 7a he quotes Shimon ha-Tzadik, who said that the verse in *Exodus* 33:23, ". . . and you shall see My back," teaches that "God showed Moses the knot of the *tefillin*." In *Sanhedrin* 22a, Chana bar Bizna quotes Shimon ha-Tzadik as saying: "He who prays should regard himself as if the Shekhinah were standing before him." Chama bar Bizna sat as a judge in Pumbedita.

Chana bar Chanilai (third/fourth century)
Babylonian amora. A prominent philanthropist as well as a scholar, Chana bar Chanilai is mentioned in *Megillah* 27a and 28a as a junior contemporary of Chisda and Huna.

Chana bar Chinena (third century)
Babylonian amora. In *Pesachim* 106b he is mentioned as a colleague of Huna.

Chana bar Judah
See Chana bar Yehudah.

Chana bar Kettina (third century)
Babylonian amora. In *Yevamot* 79a he is named as a contemporary of Huna.

Chana bar Livai

Amora of unknown date and location. He is quoted in *Sanhedrin* 108b as repeating a conversation between Shem, Noah's eldest son, and Abraham's servant Eli'ezer.

Chana bar Yehudah (fourth century)

Babylonian amora. In *Berakhot* 48a he is named as a disciple of Rava.

Chana ben She'ina

See Chana ben She'una.

Chana ben She'una (second/third century)

Also known as Chana ben She'ina.

Palestinian amora. In *Niddah* 65b he is mentioned as a disciple of Rabbah bar Chana, who was a disciple of Yochanan bar Nappacha. In *Avodah Zarah* 75a Chana ben She'una is referred to as Chana ben She'ina.

Chana of Baghdad (second/third century)

Babylonian amora. In *Ketubbot* 7b he is said to have been a contemporary of Shemu'el. According to *Berakhot* 54b, he and other rabbis visited Yehudah bar Yechezkel when he was ill and gave thanks for his survival.

Chana of Carthage

See Chana of Kartigna.

Chana of Kartigna (third century)

Palestinian amora. Known in English as Chana of Carthage, he is mentioned in *Bava Kamma* 114b as a contemporary of Yehoshu'a ben Levi and Yehudah ha-Nasi.

Chana of Sepphoris (third century)

Palestinian amora. According to *Rosh Hashanah* 35a, he was a disciple of Yochanan bar Nappacha.

Chanan

See also Channin.

Two prominent scholars were known by this name:

1. A second-century Palestinian tanna who was a contemporary of Yitzchak (*Berakhot* 41a). In *Berakhot* 56b Chanan distinguishes between three types of dreams that symbolize peace, one involving a river, another a bird, and a third a pot.

2. A third-century Palestinian amora, Babylonian by birth, who studied under Rav in his older years (*Yoma* 41b) and who associated with Rav's son, Anan bar Rav, who lived and died in Babylonia (*Kiddushin* 39a).

Chanan bar Abba (third century)

Babylonian amora. In *Berakhot* 45a he states that one should not respond "Amen" in a voice louder than that of the prayer leader. In *Shabbat* 112b he is noted as a disciple of Rav.

Chanan bar Ammi (third century)

Babylonian amora. In *Ketubbot* 6a he is mentioned as a disciple of Shemu'el.

Chanan bar Chisda (fourth century)

Babylonian amora. In *Avodah Zarah* 11b he is mentioned as a disciple of Rav.

Chanan bar Kettina (fourth century)

Babylonian amora. According to *Chullin* 19a, he was a disciple of Nachman bar Ya'akov.

Chanan bar Molada (third century)

Babylonian amora. In *Sanhedrin* 71a he is listed as a disciple of Huna.

Chanan bar Pinchas (third/fourth century)

Babylonian amora. In *Kiddushin* 72b he expressed his view on the boundaries of Babylonia.

Chanan bar Rabbah (second century)

Also known as Channin bar Rabbah.

Babylonian amora. In *Sukkah* 2b he is mentioned as a colleague of Yoshiyyahu, with whom he disagreed about the construction of a sukkah. Channin bar Rabbah also is mentioned in *Pesachim* 117a.

Chanan bar Rava (third century)

Babylonian amora. In *Shabbat* 66a he is listed as a colleague of Chiyya bar Rav of Difti and a disciple of Rav. According to *Shabbat* 121a, Chanan bar Rava was a colleague of Yehudah bar Yechezkel and Yirmeyahu bar Abba.

Chanan bar Tachlifa (fourth century)
Babylonian amora. In *Sanhedrin* 97b he discusses with his colleague Yosef the source of a scroll written in Assyrian.

Chanan ben Avishalom (first century)
Palestinian tanna. According to *Ketubbot* 105a, he was a colleague and fellow judge of Chanan ha-Mitzri.

Chanan ben Pitom (second century)
Palestinian tanna. In *Ta'anit* 22b he is mentioned as a disciple of Akiva ben Yosef.

Chanan ha-Mitzri (first century)
Palestinian tanna. Known in English as Chanan the Egyptian, he was a disciple of Akiva ben Yosef. According to *Ketubbot* 105a, Chanan ha-Mitzri was a colleague and fellow judge of Chanan ben Avishalom.

Chanan ha-Nechba (first century)
Palestinian tanna. Known in English as Chanan the Hidden One, so-called because, out of modesty, he would lock himself in a room and hide, he was the grandson of the famous Choni ha-Me'aggel. Following in his grandfather's footsteps, *Ta'anit* 23b relates that when the world was in need of rain the Rabbis would send children to plead with Chanan to pray for it. Chanan would then offer the following prayer: "Master of the Universe, [make it rain] for the sake of these [children] who are unable to distinguish between the Father who gives them rain and the Father who does not."

Chanan of Carthage (fourth century)
Babylonian amora. According to *Ketubbot* 27b, he was a contemporary of Dimi.

Chanan of Nehardea (third/fourth century)
Babylonian amora. In *Niddah* 66b he is noted as a colleague of Kahana.

Chanan the Egyptian
See Chanan ha-Mitzri.

Chanan the Hidden One
See Chanan ha-Nechba.

Chananel (third century)

Babylonian amora. In *Rosh Hashanah* 35a and *Pesachim* 68a he is noted as a disciple of Rav.

Chananel bar Pappa (fourth century)

Babylonian amora. In *Shabbat* 88b he answers the following question: "Why are the words of the Torah compared to a prince? Just as a prince has the power of life and death [over his subjects], so have the words of the Torah the power of life and death."

Chananiah

See Chananyah.

Chananyah

Among the scholars known by this popular name were:

1. A second-century Palestinian tanna who is noted in *Eruvin* 6b and 11b as subscribing to Hillel's teachings. In *Yoma* 59a Chananyah is mentioned as a colleague of Yosei ben Chalafta. Chananyah's uncle, the scholar Yehoshu'a ben Chananyah, sent his nephew to Babylonia to remove him from sectarian influences in Capernaum and to prevent him from being persecuted by the Roman emperor Hadrian. Chananyah eventually opened a school there and strove to make the communities of Babylonia independent of the Sanhedrin in Palestine. Finally, however, he submitted to its authority (*Sanhedrin* 32b).

2. A third/fourth-century Palestinian amora and a shoemaker by trade who migrated to Palestine from Babylonia. It is assumed that he was a brother of Rabbah bar Nachmani. In *Ketubbot* 45b Chananyah is noted as a colleague of Ila'i.

3. A third/fourth-century Babylonian amora who, in *Pesachim* 104a, is mentioned as a colleague of Shemu'el bar Idi and, in *Bava Metzi'a* 6b, as a colleague of Oshaya.

4. A fourth-century Babylonian amora and nephew of Oshaya and a contemporary of Yosei. In *Beitzah* 17b Chananyah is said to have been a colleague of Nachman bar Yitzchak.

Chananyah bar Avin

See Chanina bar Avin.

Chananyah bar Bebai
See Chananyah bar Beivai.

Chananyah bar Beivai (fourth/fifth century)
Babylonian amora. In *Pesachim* 110a he is noted as a colleague of Ashi.

Chananyah bar Idi (fifth century)
Babylonian amora. He is mentioned in *Pesachim* 104a as the brother of Shemu'el bar Idi.

Chananyah bar Shelemiah
See Chananyah bar Shelemya.

Chananyah bar Shelemya (third century)
Also known as Chanina bar Shelemya.
Babylonian amora. In *Chullin* 9a he is noted as a disciple of Rav. In *Sanhedrin* 24b he is referred to as Chanina bar Shelemya.

Chananyah bar Shila (second/third century)
Babylonian amora. In *Eruvin* 12a he is mentioned as a contemporary of Shemu'el.

Chananyah ben Achi [Nephew of] Yehoshu'a
(first/second century)
Palestinian tanna. In *Berakhot* 63a he is said to have visited Babylonia, where he assisted the Rabbis in establishing a correct calendar, as Akiva ben Yosef had done earlier.

Chananyah ben Akashia
See Chananyah ben Akashya.

Chananyah ben Akashya (first/second century)
Palestinian tanna. He is noted for his famous comment in *Makkot* 23b (which also appears as the closing passage of *Avot* 6): "The Holy One, blessed be He, desired to make Israel a worthy people and therefore imposed upon them many laws [to study] and commandments [to carry out]."

Chananyah ben Akavia
See Chananyah ben Akavya.

Chananyah ben Akavya (second century)
Also known as Chanina ben Akavya *and* Chanina ben Akabya.
Palestinian tanna. In *Eruvin* 86b he is mentioned as a colleague of Yehudah bar Ila'i.

Chananyah ben Antigonus
See Chanina ben Antigonus.

Chananyah ben Chakhinai (second century)
Also known as Chanina ben Chakhinai.

Palestinian tanna. In *Chagigah* 14b he discusses with his master, Akiva ben Yosef, the mysteries of the celestial chariot described in *Ezekiel. Ketubbot* 62b notes that Chananyah ben Chakhinai attended the wedding of Shimon bar Yochai. A famous maxim of Chananyah is quoted in *Avot* 3:4: "He who keeps awake at night, or walks alone on the road and turns his mind to idle thoughts, is guilty of harming his own life." In *Kiddushin* 55b he comments on the proper animal to sacrifice as a sin offering.

Chananyah ben Chizkiyyah (second century)
Palestinian tanna. According to *Chagigah* 13a, he was a contemporary of Yehudah bar Ila'i.

Chananyah ben Chizkiyyah ben Garon (first century)
Palestinian tanna. In *Shabbat* 12a he is referred to as a disciple of Hillel and Shammai.

Chananyah ben Hezekiah
See Chananyah ben Chizkiyyah.

Chananyah ben Hezekiah ben Garon
See Chananyah ben Chizkiyyah ben Garon.

Chananyah ben Judah
See Chananyah ben Yehudah.

Chananyah ben Minyomi (first/second century)
Palestinian tanna. According to *Yoma* 45b, he was a student in the school of Eli'ezer ben Ya'akov II.

Chananyah ben Shimon ben Gamli'el (second/third century)
Palestinian tanna. In *Yevamot* 48b he explains why proselytes of his day were oppressed and visited with afflictions: "Because they had not observed the Seven Noahide Laws."

Chananyah ben Simeon ben Gamaliel
See Chananyah ben Shimon ben Gamli'el.

Chananyah ben Teradyon (second century)

Also known as Chanina ben Teradyon.

Palestinian tanna. *Avodah Zarah* 18a relates that when Yosei ben Kisma died, all the great men of Rome came to his funeral and lamented his death. Upon returning from the funeral, they found Chananyah ben Teradyon, a colleague of Yosei, teaching Torah to the masses in violation of Roman law. The Romans promptly built a bonfire and burned Chananyah to death while he was holding a Torah scroll to his bosom. Chananyah is one of the Ten Martyrs who met their deaths following the failed Bar Kokhba Revolt; Chananyah's wife also was sentenced to death, and their daughter was condemned to degradation. A second daughter, Beruryah, became the wife of the tanna Me'ir (*Pesachim* 62b).

One of the popular maxims for which Chananyah is known appears in *Avot* 3:3: "If two people sit together and words of Torah are not exchanged between them, this is a meeting of scoffers. . . . But when two meet and there is a discussion about Torah between them, the Shekhinah abides with them."

Chananyah ben Yehudah (second century)

Palestinian tanna. He was a contemporary of Akiva ben Yosef.

Chananyah ben Yosei ha-Gelili (first century)

Also known as Chanina ben Yosei ha-Gelili.

Palestinian tanna. Known in English as Chananyah ben Yosei the Galilean, he is noted in *Bava Metzi'a* 24b as a colleague of Yehudah bar Ila'i. In *Rosh Hashanah* 32a Chananyah ben Yosei ha-Gelili is referred to as Chanina ben Yosei ha-Gelili.

Chananyah ben Yosei the Galilean

See Chananyah ben Yosei ha-Gelili.

Chananyah Kera

See Chanina Kera.

Chananyah, Nephew of Joshua

See Chananyah ben Achi Yehoshu'a.

Chananyah of Ono

See Chanina of Ono.

Chananyah of Sepphoris

See Chanina of Sepphoris.

Chananyah of Trita
>*See* Chanina of Torta.

Chananyah Segan ha-Kohanim
>*See* Chanina Segan ha-Kohanim.

Chananyah the Bible Teacher
>*See* Chanina Kera.

Chanilai (third century)
>Palestinian amora. He is best known for the popular maxim: "A man with no wife lives without joy, without blessing, and without goodness" (*Yevamot* 62b). In *Niddah* 43b he is referred to as a disciple of Eli'ezer ben Shimon.

Chanilai bar Idi (second/third century)
>Babylonian amora. In *Gittin* 52a he is mentioned as a disciple of Shemu'el.

Chanilai ben Chanilai (third/fourth century)
>Palestinian amora. In *Avodah Zarah* 18b he is quoted as saying: "He who scoffs brings destruction upon the world."

Chanilai of Choza'ah (fourth/fifth century)
>Babylonian amora. In *Eruvin* 57a he is noted as a colleague of Ashi.

Chanin of Choza'ah
>*See* Huna of Choza'ah.

Chanina
>*See also* Chananyah.
>
>In addition to Chanina bar Chama (see below), other scholars who share the name Chanina include:
>
>1. A second/third-century Babylonian amora who in *Shabbat* 9b is mentioned as a colleague of Rav.
>
>2. A third/fourth-century Palestinian amora of whom it was said that at age eighty he was able to stand on one foot and take off his shoe (*Chullin* 55a). In *Shabbat* 52a he is listed as a teacher of Dimi and Shemu'el ben Yehudah, and in *Chullin* 24b as a teacher of Ila'i.
>
>In *Shabbat* 55a he proclaimed, "The seal of God is truth," and in *Chullin* 7b he said, "No man bruises a finger here on earth unless it has been proclaimed from above."

Chanina bar Adda (third century)

Also spelled Chanina bar Idda. *Also known as* Chanina bar Idi.

Babylonian amora. Chanina bar Adda was a pupil of Adda bar Ahava (*Pesachim* 75a). In *Ta'anit* 7a, where Chanina bar Adda is referred to as Chanina bar Idi, he compares the words of the Torah to water, based on a verse in *Isaiah* 55:1.

Chanina bar Agil (third century)

Also known as Chanina bar Agul.

Palestinian amora. In *Bava Kamma* 54b–55a Chanina bar Agil poses the following question to Chiyya bar Abba: Why in the giving of the Decalogue recorded in *Exodus* 20:12 is there no mention of a reward of well-being for honoring one's parents, while in the account in *Deuteronomy* 5:16 there is such a reward? Chiyya bar Abba was unable to provide an answer.

Chanina bar Agul

See Chanina bar Agil.

Chanina bar Avdimi (second/third century)

Babylonian amora. In *Kiddushin* 64b he is mentioned is a disciple of Rav.

Chanina bar Avin (fourth century)

Also known as Chananyah bar Avin *and* Chinena bar Avin.

Babylonian amora. According to *Eruvin* 62a and *Yevamot* 36a, he was a colleague of Abbayei. In *Berakhot* 29b Chanina bar Avin and his brother Abbayei bar Avin emphasize the importance of reciting the morning and afternoon prayers at their fixed times; both Chanina bar Avin and his brother studied at the academy in Pumbedita under Rabbah bar Nachmani. In *Keritot* 20a Chanina bar Avin is mentioned as a colleague of, or possibly the brother of, Ammi bar Avin.

Chanina bar Chama (second/third century)

Also known as Chanina ha-Gadol.

Palestinian amora. Most often referred to as Chanina without patronymic, it is believed that he was born in Babylonia and migrated to Palestine at an early age. He sometimes is referred to as Chanina ha-Gadol (*Ta'anit* 27b)—"Chanina the

Great"—an indication of how highly he was regarded by his fellow scholars as well as by the elite of Roman society. Known in English as Chanina the Elder, he was descended from an old and noble family and was a physician by training. According to one report, Chanina became wealthy as a honey trader.

In *Bava Metzi'a* 107b he says, "Everything is in the hands of Heaven except for the blowing of the cold winds," believing that diseases were caused by changes in the weather and that certain illnesses were caused by catching cold. In *Chullin* 7b he says: "No man bruises his finger here on earth unless it was so decreed against him in heaven."

Chanina had one son who died young (*Bava Kamma* 91b) and another, named Chama, who inherited his father's talents. One of Chanina's daughters married her father's disciple, Shemu'el bar Nadav (*Arakhin* 16b); another daughter died during Chanina's lifetime (*Shabbat* 151b).

Chanina lived a long, healthy, and fruitful life, eventually assuming leadership of the academy at Sepphoris and witnessing the accession of three patriarchs: Yehudah ha-Nasi, who was his teacher; Gamli'el III, Yehudah ha-Nasi's son; and Yehudah Nesi'ah, Yehudah ha-Nasi's grandson (*Chullin* 24b). Chanina attributed his good health and longevity to the hot baths and oil treatments his mother had given him in his youth.

In *Yevamot* 43a, the great scholar Elazar ben Pedat refers to Chanina bar Chama's ruling on what constitutes the three-month period a woman must wait before remarrying, following divorce or the death of her husband. Elazar was one of Chanina bar Chama's disciples.

It would appear that Chanina bar Chama was a bit of a mystic. In *Shabbat* 119a it is reported that on the Sabbath eve, he would wrap himself in a special robe, rise, and say: "Come let us go forth to welcome the Sabbath Queen."

Berakhot 5b reports that when Chanina went to visit his ailing disciple Yochanan bar Nappacha, he attempted to cure Yochanan by the touch of his hand. And when Chanina fell ill, Yochanan came from Tiberias to visit him. On the way, Yochanan learned that Chanina had died. He immediately dismounted from his donkey, rent his clothes, and said: "The man in whose presence I stood in awe is gone" (*Mo'ed Katan* 24a).

One of Chanina bar Chama's favorite sayings was: "Charity may be compared to a garment. Just as a garment is woven out of single threads, so is charity made up of single coins, slowly gathered, until they add up to a great sum" (*Bava Batra* 9b).

Chanina bar Chama died around the year 250.

Chanina bar Idda
See Chanina bar Adda.

Chanina bar Idi
See Chanina bar Adda.

Chanina bar Ika (fourth century)
Also known as Chinena bar Ika.

Babylonian amora. According to *Berakhot* 58b, he was a contemporary of Huna bar Yehoshu'a. In *Niddah* 8b Chanina bar Ika is listed as a contemporary of Sheshet bar Idi and in *Niddah* 47b as a contemporary of Pappa.

Chanina bar Kahana (third century)
Babylonian amora. In *Avodah Zarah* 20b he quotes Rav's students as saying: "If one wants to keep a corpse from deteriorating, he should turn it on its face."

Chanina bar Shelemya
See Chananyah bar Shelemya.

Chanina ben Abbahu (fourth century)
Also spelled Chanina ben Avahu. *Also known as* Chanina of Caesarea.

Palestinian amora. One of Abbahu's two promising sons (his other was Avimi), Chanina ben Abbahu was sent by his father from Caesarea to Tiberias to continue his education. Instead of studying, Chanina spent his time performing pious deeds and burying the dead. Upon learning of this, Abbahu wrote his son: "Has Caesarea no graves that I should be obliged to send you for this purpose to Tiberias? Study must precede practical works" (Palestinian Talmud, *Pesachim* 3:7). In *Kiddushin* 33b Chanina ben Abbahu is quoted as saying: "When a Sage passes by, one must rise before him as he approaches at a distance of four cubits [six feet]."

Chanina ben Akabya
See Chananyah ben Akavya.

Chanina ben Akavya
See Chananyah ben Akavya.

Chanina ben Akiba
See Chanina ben Akiva.

Chanina ben Akiva (second century)
Also spelled Chanina ben Akiba.
Palestinian tanna. In *Shabbat* 50a he is noted as a colleague of Shimon ben Gamli'el.

Chanina ben Antigonus (second century)
Also known as Chananyah ben Antigonus.
Palestinian tanna. A scholar of Priestly descent, he was a contemporary of Akiva ben Yosef and Yishma'el. Although others were permitted to perform on instruments in the Temple, in *Arakhin* 10a and *Sukkah* 51a Chanina ben Antigonus claims that the musicians who played instruments in the Temple were Levites.

Chanina ben Avahu
See Chanina ben Abbahu.

Chanina ben Chakhinai
See Chananyah ben Chakhinai.

Chanina ben Chizkiyyah (second century)
Palestinian tanna. In *Menachot* 45a he is noted as a colleague of Yehudah bar Ila'i.

Chanina ben Choza'ah (third/fourth century)
Also known as Chanina of Choza'ei *and* Chanina of Choza'i.
Babylonian amora. He is quoted in *Eruvin* 32a and *Avodah Zarah* 41b on the subject of tithing produce.

Chanina ben Dosa (first century)
Palestinian tanna. Well noted for the extreme poverty in which he lived in the Galilee (*Ta'anit* 24b–25a), Chanina ben Dosa was blessed with a pious and patient wife who is described in *Bava Batra* 74b as laying away in her treasure chest purple-blue *tallit* threads to be used by the righteous in the world to come. In *Avot* 3:9 Chanina ben Dosa teaches that the performance of

good deeds is far more important than acquiring knowledge; in *Avot* 3:10 he teaches that God is pleased with a person when his fellow human beings are pleased with him.

Chanina ben Dosa was celebrated for his ability to perform miracles. Numerous legends recall the many wondrous acts performed by Chanina ben Dosa or on his behalf: the sick were healed, rains fell, and his own needs, or those of others, were fulfilled in answer to his prayers. *Sotah* 49a notes that when Chanina ben Dosa died, "Men capable of performing miracles ceased to be."

Chanina was a highly admired student of Yochanan ben Zakkai during the tragic period of the fall of Jerusalem (70 C.E.), when Israel lost its independence as a sovereign nation (*Berakhot* 34b).

Chanina ben Gamli'el (first/second century)

Palestinian tanna. In *Berakhot* 22a he is mentioned as a teacher of Yehudah ben Gamli'el. A contemporary of Akiva ben Yosef, Chanina ben Gamli'el witnessed, and perhaps was the victim of, the Roman persecutions of thousands of students at Betar, famous as the last stronghold of the Bar Kokhba Revolt against the Romans.

Chanina ben Idi (second/third century)

Babylonian amora. In *Shevu'ot* 38b he is noted as a colleague of Ravina I.

Chanina ben Joseph

See Chanina ben Yosef.

Chanina ben Kettina (third century)

Palestinian amora. In *Gittin* 38a he is noted as a disciple of Yitzchak.

Chanina ben Minyomi (third/fourth century)

Palestinian amora. In *Menachot* 70a he is listed as a colleague of Abbayei, and in *Zevachim* 83b he is described as the son of Eli'ezer ben Ya'akov II.

Chanina ben Pappa (third/fourth century)

Also known as Chinena ben Pappa.

Palestinian amora. In *Berakhot* 35b he is quoted as saying: "To enjoy this world without reciting a blessing is like robbing the Holy One, blessed be He." In *Berakhot* 51a he is referred to as Chinena ben Pappa.

Chanina ben Pappi (fourth century)
Palestinian amora. According to *Eruvin* 12a, he was a contemporary of Adda ben Abimi. In *Yevamot* 48b Chanina ben Pappi is mentioned as a colleague of Ammi bar Natan and Yitzchak Nappacha.

Chanina ben Teradyon
See Chananyah ben Teradyon.

Chanina ben Yosef (third century)
Palestinian amora. According to *Eruvin* 65b, Chanina ben Yosef was a colleague of Chiyya and Assi.

Chanina ben Yosei ha-Gelili
See Chananyah ben Yosei ha-Gelili.

Chanina ben Yosei the Galilean
See Chananyah ben Yosei ha-Gelili.

Chanina Choza'ah (third/fourth century)
Also known as Chanina of Choza'i.
Babylonian amora. In *Bava Metzi'a* 88a and *Eruvin* 32a he is referred to as Chanina Choza'ah, and in *Avodah Zarah* 41b and *Niddah* 15b he is called Chanina of Choza'ei. Choza'ah was a district in southwest Persia, in which the small Jewish settlement was known as Bei Choza'ei. Chanina left the settlement to study in Babylonia under the tutelage of Chisda and Nachman bar Ya'akov.

Chanina ha-Gadol
See Chanina bar Chama.

Chanina Katova (third century)
Palestinian scribe. He studied under Acha.

Chanina Kera (second/third century)
Also known as Chananyah Kera.
Palestinian amora. Known in English as Chanina the Bible Teacher, he is referred to in *Megillah* 22a as Chananyah Kera, a contemporary of Chanina ha-Gadol (Chanina bar Chama), and in *Berakhot* 30b as a student of Yannai. Bible teachers often were professional Torah readers, reading the Torah in front of worshippers.

Chanina of Caesarea
See Chanina ben Abbahu.

Chanina of Choza'i
See Chanina ben Choza'ah.

Chanina of Ono (second century)
Also known as Chananyah of Ono.

Palestinian tanna. In *Gittin* 66b he is mentioned as a disciple of Akiva ben Yosef. In *Sanhedrin* 11b he is referred to as Chananyah of Ono.

Chanina of Sepphoris (fifth century)
Also known as Chananyah of Sepphoris.

Palestinian amora. Educated in Palestine, where he was known as Chananyah, Chanina eventually settled in Sepphoris, becoming head of the religious community there. When his teacher, Mani, moved to Sepphoris, Chanina resigned as religious leader in favor of his master.

In the face of escalating Roman persecutions in Palestine, Chanina and his family immigrated to Babylonia, where he formed an association with Ashi (*Bava Batra* 25a). It was there that Chanina's daughter married the son of Ravina II (*Niddah* 66a), one of the editors of the Babylonian Talmud.

Chanina of Sura (fifth century)
Babylonian amora. He is mentioned as a younger contemporary of Mar Zutra in *Ketubbot* 63b, where it is reported that at one point Chanina's mother had such an aversion to her husband that she could not live with him. Mar Zutra effected a reconciliation, and Chanina was the offspring of that reconciliation.

Chanina of Tirna'a
See Chanina of Torta.

Chanina of Tirta
See Chanina of Torta.

Chanina of Torata
See Chanina of Torta.

Chanina of Torta (second/third century)
Also known as Chananyah of Trita, Chanina of Tereita'ah,

Chanina of Tirna'a, Chanina of Tirta, Chanina of Tirta'ah, *and* Chanina of Trita.

Palestinian tanna. It is not certain whether Chanina of Torta was born in Palestine or immigrated to Palestine from Babylonia, though most scholars believe he was born in Palestine. Known by a variety of names, he is noted in *Nedarim* 57b and 59b as a disciple of Yannai and Yochanan bar Nappacha.

In *Temurah* 29a and 31a, he is identified, respectively, as Chananyah of Trita and Chanina of Trita, a town in Babylonia. In *Nedarim* 57b and 59b he is identified respectively as Chanina of Tereita'ah and Chanina of Tirta'ah. In *Keritot* 9a he is referred to as Chanina of Tirna'a, a pupil of Yochanan bar Nappacha, and in *Menachot* 48a he is referred to as Chanina of Tirta, which has been identified by some scholars as Tirastan, near Machoza in Babylonia.

Chanina of Trita
See Chanina of Torta.

Chanina Segan ha-Kohanim (first/second century)
Palestinian tanna. Deputy (*segan*) to the High Priest, Chanina Segan ha-Kohanim stood beside the High Priest on the Day of Atonement, ready to take over for him should the need arise. In *Berakhot* 2b and 24a Chanina Segan ha-Kohanim is noted as a colleague of Me'ir and Eli'ezer ben Hurkanos, and as a contemporary of Yehudah ha-Nasi; in *Pesachim* 14b he is mentioned as a colleague of Akiva ben Yosef and Me'ir.

A disciple of Yochanan ben Zakkai, Chanina Segan ha-Kohanim expressed his belief in *Berakhot* 33b that "Everything is in the hands of heaven except the fear of heaven." In *Avot* 3:2 he is quoted as saying: "Pray for the welfare of the [ruling Roman] government, for if no fear of them existed, one man would swallow another alive."

Chanina the Bible Teacher
See Chanina Kera.

Chanina the Elder (second/third century)
See Chanina bar Chama.

Chanina the Great
See Chanina bar Chama.

Channin (fourth century)

Also known as Chanan.

Palestinian amora. *Mo'ed Katan* 25b notes that his father died on the day Channin was born and that Channin was named after him. He was a scholar of great faith, and *Berakhot* 32b records Channin's conviction that "If one prays long, his prayer will not go unanswered." In *Eruvin* 65a he is quoted as saying: "Wine was created for the sole purpose of comforting mourners and rewarding the wicked [for the little good they may have done in this world]."

Channin Abba

See Abba Channin.

Channin bar Abba (third century)

Babylonian amora. In *Niddah* 24a he is mentioned as a contemporary of Rav.

Channin bar Ammi (second/third century)

Babylonian amora. In *Shabbat* 13a he is noted as a disciple of Shemu'el.

Channin bar Ashi (third century)

Babylonian amora. In *Berakhot* 34a he is cited as a disciple of Shemu'el.

Channin bar Chisda (third/fourth century)

Babylonian amora. He is quoted in *Avodah Zarah* 16a.

Channin bar Rabbah

See Chanan bar Rabbah.

Channin bar Yeiva (third/fourth century)

Babylonian amora. A brother of Rami bar Yeiva and Safra bar Yeiva, Rava praises Channin bar Yeiva in *Bava Batra* 174a as a wise judge.

Channin ben Abbayei (third century)

Palestinian amora. In *Pesachim* 10a he is listed as a disciple of Yochanan bar Nappacha and Pedat.

Channin ben Bizna (second/third century)

Palestinian tanna. He is mentioned in *Sotah* 10b.

Channin ben Phinehas

See Channin ben Pinchas.

Channin ben Pinchas (first century)

Palestinian tanna. He is quoted in *Sotah* 4a.

Channin of Chuzna'a (fourth/fifth century)

Babylonian amora. He is mentioned in *Gittin* 85b as a colleague of Ashi. Chuzna'a was located in southwest Persia.

Chasa (third century)

Babylonian amora. He is noted in *Bava Metzi'a* 57a and *Niddah* 23b as a teacher of Rava. Chasa drowned and died intestate (*Ketubbot* 85b).

Chavina (fifth century)

Babylonian amora. In *Ketubbot* 20a he is noted as a contemporary of Mar bar Rav Ashi.

Chaviva

Three scholars were known by this name:

1. A second/third-century Palestinian tanna who is quoted in *Eruvin* 79b. In *Shabbat* 54b he is listed as a colleague of Yochanan bar Nappacha.

2. A fourth-century Babylonian amora who, in *Ketubbot* 8a, is noted as a friend of Ravina.

3. A fifth-century Babylonian amora who is mentioned in *Chullin* 51a, where his colleague, Yeimar, comments on a hip disease that had affected Chaviva's ewe.

Chaviva bar Joseph bar Rabbah

See Chaviva bar Yosef bar Rabbah.

Chaviva bar Rava (fourth century)

Babylonian amora. In *Avodah Zarah* 34a he is listed as a contemporary of Zevid.

Chaviva bar Yosef bar Rabbah (fourth century)

Babylonian amora. According to *Bava Batra* 143b, he was a disciple of Rava.

Chaviva ben Surmaki (fourth century)

Palestinian amora. Originally from Babylonia, he immigrated to Palestine. In *Yoma* 10a he renders an interpretation of *Daniel* 8:20.

Chaviva of Sura (sixth century)
Babylonian amora. When, according to *Bava Metzi'a* 106b, he was asked to rule on a difficult matter, he sent the question to Ravina II, his teacher.

Chavivi (second/third century)
Palestinian amora. In *Zevachim* 3b he is listed as a contemporary of Rav.

Chavivi of Choza'ah (third/fourth century)
Babylonian amora. According to *Eruvin* 57a, he was a colleague of Ashi. In *Bava Kamma* 72a he is referred to as Chavivi of Chuzna'a.

Chavivi of Chuzna'a
See Chavivi of Choza'ah.

Chelbo (third/fourth century)
Palestinian amora. Although born and educated in Babylonia, Chelbo would later settle in Palestine. Among the sayings for which he is known are: "A man must always honor his wife because blessings enter his home only on account of her" (*Bava Metzi'a* 59a) and "Proselytes are as troublesome to Israel as skin sores" (*Yevamot* 109b and *Niddah* 13b). He believed that many proselytes were insincere and would not live up to the commandments.

In *Berakhot* 6b he quotes his teacher Huna, under whom he studied at the academy in Sura, as saying, "When a man leaves the synagogue, he should not take long steps [which may be misunderstood as a sign of relief for having gotten rid of an obligation]."

It was reported that when Chelbo fell ill, Kahana announced it, but no one went to visit Chelbo because he kept an untidy house. Upon orders from Akiva ben Yosef, the house and grounds were "swept and sprinkled," and Akiva then went to visit him (*Nedarim* 40a).

Chenak (fourth century)
Babylonian amora. In *Pesachim* 101b he is noted as the principal of an academy.

Chidka (second century)

Palestinian tanna. In *Ta'anit* 11a he says, "A man's own soul testifies against him," meaning that a man can be his own worst enemy. In *Shabbat* 117b Chidka comments on how many meals one must eat on the Sabbath. He says four; the other Rabbis say three. In *Bava Metzi'a* 90b Chidka rules that non-Jews who have accepted the Seven Noahide Laws are forbidden, like Jews, to practice castration, despite the fact that castration is not one of the Noahide Laws.

Chilkiyah (first/second century)

Palestinian tanna. In *Kiddushin* 33b he joins his colleagues Shimon ben Elazar and Elazar ben Azaryah in declaring that one must rise when a Torah scroll is in view, "just as one must rise before those who study it."

Chilkiyah bar Aviya (third/fourth century)

Babylonian amora. In *Bava Metzi'a* 96b he participates in a discussion about whether a person who borrows an animal and works the animal so hard that it loses weight is liable to reimburse the owner additional money.

Chilkiyah bar Tavi (third century)

Babylonian amora. He is noted in *Gittin* 57a as a colleague of Minyomi bar Chilkiyah and Huna bar Chiyya.

Chilkiyah of Hagronia (third century)

Babylonian amora. He is quoted in *Yevamot* 9a and *Horayot* 8a.

Chinena (third/fourth century)

Palestinian amora. In *Nedarim* 28a he is noted as a disciple of Kahana.

Chinena bar Avin

See Chanina bar Avin.

Chinena bar Bisna (third century)

Palestinian amora. In *Beitzah* 22a he discusses whether it is permissible for one to handle a candlestick on a holiday.

Chinena bar Idi (third century)

Babylonian amora. In *Avodah Zarah* 40a and *Pesachim* 75a

he is noted as a disciple of Adda bar Ahava. In *Shabbat* 63a Chinena bar Idi is quoted as saying: "Whoever fulfills a *mitzvah* as commanded, no evil will befall him."

Chinena bar Ika
See Chanina bar Ika.

Chinena bar Joshua
See Chinena bar Yehoshu'a.

Chinena bar Judah
See Chinena bar Yehudah.

Chinena bar Kahana (third century)
Babylonian amora. In *Beitzah* 6a he is noted as a disciple of Rav.

Chinena bar Rabbah of Pashruni'a (fourth century)
Babylonian amora. Resident of a town near Sura, Chinena bar Rabbah of Pashruni'a is mentioned as a contemporary of Rava in *Pesachim* 76a and *Chullin* 112a.

Chinena bar Shelemya (second century)
Babylonian amora. In *Shabbat* 123a he is noted as a disciple of Rav and in *Eruvin* 98b as the teacher of Chiyya bar Rav.

Chinena bar Shila (third century)
Babylonian amora. In *Shabbat* 58a he is noted as a contemporary of Shemu'el.

Chinena bar Yehoshu'a (third century)
Babylonian amora. In *Pesachim* 110b he comments on the third cup of wine that is drunk at the *Seder* in connection with the Grace After Meals.

Chinena bar Yehudah (third century)
Babylonian amora. According to *Sanhedrin* 77b, he was a disciple of Rav.

Chinena ben Chiyya (second century)
Palestinian tanna. In *Ketubbot* 21a he is mentioned as a colleague of Yehudah bar Ila'i.

Chinena ben Pappa
See Chanina ben Pappa.

Chinena of Tora
See Chanina of Torta.

Chinena of Vardan (third century)

Palestinian amora. According to *Gittin* 64b, he was a contemporary of Chisda. Vardan was a town on the eastern bank of the Tigris River.

Chinena Sabba (third/fourth century)

Babylonian amora. Known in English as Chinena the Elder, he is mentioned in *Pesachim* 75a as a disciple of both Assi and Yochanan bar Nappacha. Chinena Sabba's son Kahana also was an amora.

Chinena the Elder

See Chinena Sabba.

Chisda (third/fourth century)

Babylonian amora. In *Sukkah* 33a, Chisda refers to his teacher Rav as "our great master." After conducting his own school in Kafri, Chisda succeeded Huna as principal of the academy in Sura, over which he presided for ten years. Their contemporaries usually referred to Huna and Chisda as "the Elders of Sura."

In *Avodah Zarah* 19a–b Chisda offered this advice to his young students: "I am about to tell you something even though it may encourage you to leave me and go elsewhere to study: he who studies under only one teacher will never see a sign of blessing."

A man of great integrity, Chisda's attitude toward a slanderer was expressed in these words: "I [God] and he [the slanderer] cannot live together in the world" (*Sotah* 5a). A favorite maxim of Chisda was: "If a man finds himself plagued by great pain, let him examine his conduct" (*Berakhot* 5a).

In *Zevachim* 7a and *Pesachim* 10b he is noted as a colleague of Rabbah bar Rav Huna and in *Eruvin* 8a as a teacher of Rami bar Chama. There are over fifteen hundred references to Chisda in the Babylonian Talmud.

Like Huna, Chisda was of humble origins. He would later attain great wealth as a brewer of beer (*Pesachim* 113a). Chisda married at age sixteen (*Kiddushin* 29b) and fathered seven or more sons and two daughters; he once remarked that daughters were preferable to sons. According to *Kiddushin* 81b, Chisda married the daughter of Acha bar Abba, although a variant textual reading suggests that he married the daughter of Chanan bar Rava. *Berakhot* 44a reports that one of Chisda's daughters married Chisda's disciple Rami bar Chama; after Rami bar Chama died, she would marry Rava (*Bava Batra* 12b), also a disciple of Chisda. Chisda's other daughter married Ukba bar Chama, Rami bar Chama's brother.

Chisda lived a long life and is said, between those of his children and grandchildren, to have attended sixty weddings.

Chisda devoted his entire life to study. Legend has it that when the time came for him to depart from this world, the Angel of Death could not touch him—Chisda never left his studies for a moment, and the Angel of Death is said to be powerless when a person is studying. It was only when a tree fell and crashed that Chisda left his studies to see what had happened, and the Angel of Death attacked him (*Makkot* 10a). Chisda died in the year 310, at the age of ninety-two.

Chisda bar Avdimi (c. third century)
Babylonian amora. He is quoted in *Berakhot* 53b.

Chiyya (second/third century)
Also known as Chiyya Rabbah.

Palestinian tanna. Sometimes referred to as Chiyya Rabbah—in English, Chiyya the Great—he was born in Kafri, Babylonia, spent his early years in study, and probably earned a living as a physician. In *Niddah* 25a he describes the development of the fetus in the womb.

During his years in Babylonia he married a woman named Yehudit (Judith) who bore him twin sons, Yehudah and Chizkiyyah, both of whom became great scholars, and twin daughters, Pazi and Tavi (*Yevamot* 65b).

Although Chiyya's wife refused to have any more children and took drugs that rendered her barren, Chiyya showered her with gifts, believing that men should show gratitude toward their wives for rearing the children and keeping their husbands from sin (*Yevamot* 63a).

Chiyya eventually migrated with his family to Palestine, settling in Tiberias, where he established a silk business, exporting goods to Tyre. His reputation as an outstanding scholar in Babylonia preceded him, and he was quickly accepted by the

Rabbis of Palestine as an authority. He was especially welcomed by the illustrious Yehudah ha-Nasi, the patriarch of Palestine, who considered Chiyya not only a pupil but a respected colleague. Whenever Chiyya visited Sepphoris, seat of the patriarchate, Yehudah ha-Nasi received him in his home as an honored guest.

Yevamot 65b recounts an occasion on which Yehudah ha-Nasi invited Chiyya and his two sons to dinner. The boys, though learned, were shy. In order to loosen their tongues, Yehudah ha-Nasi poured an extra serving of wine into each of their cups. Their talk then so displeased Yehudah ha-Nasi that Chiyya felt impelled to apologize, saying: "Master be not angered, for the numerical value of the letters of *yayin* ["wine"] is seventy; likewise the letters of *sod* ["secret"]. When *yayin* goes in, *sod* comes out" (*Sanhedrin* 38a).

In *Shabbat* 114a Chiyya quotes his teacher Yochanan bar Nappacha who said: "Any disciple of the wise on whose garment a stain is found deserves death." Scholars clearly were expected not to neglect their appearance.

Chullin 86a records a belief popular among the Rabbis of Palestine: from the time Chiyya and his sons came to live there, "There ceased to be shooting stars, earthquakes, storms and thunder; their wines never turned sour, and their flax was never blighted."

Chiyya demonstrated his compassionate nature (*Sanhedrin* 11a) by his willingness to sacrifice his own dignity rather than allow a colleague to be embarrassed. During a lecture by Yehudah ha-Nasi, the patriarch became aware of the odor of garlic. Having been in a bad mood that day, he exclaimed: "Whoever has eaten garlic should leave the academy!" So as not to embarrass the offender, Chiyya rose and left the room. The other students saw him leave and, knowing that he could not have been guilty of the offense, followed suit. When asked later from whom he had learned to be so sensitive, Chiyya replied, "From Rabbi Me'ir."

Bava Metzi'a 85b records a dispute between Chanina and Chiyya in which Chiyya summed up his contribution to the furtherance of Torah learning in Israel:

What did I do? I went and sowed flax, made nets [from the flax cords], trapped deer whose flesh I gave to orphans, and prepared scrolls [from the skins], upon which I wrote the five books [of Moses]. Then I went to a town that had no teachers and taught the five books to five children, and the six orders [of the Mishnah] to six children. And I said to them: "Until I return, teach each other the Torah and the Mishnah," thus preventing the Torah from being forgotten in Israel.

The Talmud adds: "This is what Rabbi [Yehudah ha-Nasi] meant when he said: 'How great are the works of Chiyya!'"

An imposing man, Chiyya was characterized in *Niddah* 25a as having been the tallest man of his generation; it is said that Rav (his nephew, also known for his height) reached only up to his shoulder (*Pesachim* 3b).

Chiyya Arikha (fourth century)

Babylonian amora. So-named because of his tall stature (*arikha* meaning "tall"), it is reported in *Ketubbot* 104b that Chiyya Arikha's brother died childless. Chiyya inherited his brother's estate and supported his sister-in-law for twenty-five years.

Chiyya bar Abba (third century)

Also known as Chiyya bar Va.

Palestinian amora. In the Palestinian Talmud he also is called Chiyya bar Va (Palestinian Talmud, *Berakhot* 3:1 [22b]). In both Talmuds, when the name Chiyya appears without cognomen, it refers to Chiyya bar Abba.

Though born in Babylonia of Priestly descent, Chiyya bar Abba immigrated to Palestine at a very young age and is considered Palestinian. In Palestine he studied under Chanina and Yehoshu'a ben Levi, was associated with Shimon ben Lakish, and studied under Yochanan bar Nappacha.

In *Ketubbot* 21b Rabbanai is listed as the brother of Chiyya bar Abba.

Berakhot 32b and 38b note that although Chiyya bar Abba was the author of many *aggadot*, he was averse to commiting them to writing.

Chiyya bar Abba was very poor and was compelled to take time away from his studies to go from town to town to lecture for a small fee. He finally accepted an offer from the patriarch Yehudah Nesi'ah to collect money from the public to help defray the expenses of the patriarchate. Chiyya had several children, including sons named Abba, Kahana, and Nechemyah.

Chiyya bar Adda (third century)

Palestinian amora. Son of Bar Kappara's sister, Chiyya bar Adda is noted in *Ketubbot* 11b as a tutor to Shimon ben Lakish's young children. The Midrashic anthology *Genesis Rabbah* 20:6 describes Chiyya bar Adda as a farmer and a disciple of Rav who could not concentrate on the lesson being taught because his mind was on his she-ass about to give birth to a foal.

Chiyya bar Ammi (fourth century)

Babylonian amora. A disciple of Ulla, Chiyya bar Ammi quotes him in *Berakhot* 8a as saying: "A man who lives from the labor of his hands is far greater than one who fears [God in] heaven." Chiyya bar Ammi also is quoted in *Bava Batra* 163a, *Sanhedrin* 28b, and *Ketubbot* 53a.

Chiyya bar Ashi (third century)

Babylonian amora. In *Eruvin* 4a and *Pesachim* 27a he is listed as a disciple of Yochanan bar Nappacha and Rav; in *Pesachim* 30b Chiyya is noted as a disciple of Shemu'el. In *Ketubbot* 112b Chiyya bar Ashi quotes Rav as saying: "In the time to come [in the days of the Messiah] all the wild trees in the Land of Israel will bear fruit," a statement based on *Joel* 2:22.

Chiyya bar Assi (third/fourth century)

Babylonian amora. In *Eruvin* 59b he expresses his view on whether an *eruv* must enclose an entire town in order to be considered ritually acceptable.

Chiyya bar Avin (third century)

Babylonian amora. The son of Avin bar Nachman (*Shabbat* 23b) and the brother of Idi bar Avin, Chiyya bar Avin is mentioned in *Megillah* 14a as a disciple of Yehoshu'a ben Karchah.

Chiyya bar Aviyya

See Chiyya bar Avuyah.

Chiyya bar Avuyah (fourth century)
Also spelled Chiyya bar Aviyya.
Babylonian amora. In *Sanhedrin* 82a he is quoted as saying: "He who is sexually intimate with a heathen is like one who has entered into a marriage with an idol." In *Yevamot* 39b he is mentioned as a disciple of Yehudah bar Yechezkel.

Chiyya bar Chinena (third century)
Babylonian amora. In *Menachot* 53b he is noted as a colleague of Chanina ben Pappa.

Chiyya bar Chiyya bar Nachmani (third century)
Babylonian amora. In *Avodah Zarah* 31a he is mentioned as a disciple of Chisda.

Chiyya bar Gamda (third/fourth century)
Palestinian amora. In *Rosh Hashanah* 24a and *Ketubbot* 104a he is listed as a disciple of Yosei ben Sha'ul, who was a disciple of Yehudah ha-Nasi.

Chiyya bar Giyyora (second/third century)
Babylonian amora. In *Niddah* 55b he is named as a contemporary of Rav.

Chiyya bar Huna (fourth century)
Babylonian amora. In *Niddah* 40a he is noted as a disciple of Rava.

Chiyya bar Ika (third century)
Babylonian amora. In *Niddah* 45a he comments on the unattributed statement in the Mishnah that "a girl of three years and one day may be betrothed by intercourse."

Chiyya bar Isaac
See Chiyya bar Yitzchak.

Chiyya bar Joseph
See Chiyya bar Yosef.

Chiyya bar Judah
See Chiyya bar Yehudah.

Chiyya bar Mattena (third century)
Babylonian amora. According to *Niddah* 60b, he was a disciple of Rav.

Chiyya bar Nachmani (second century)
Palestinian tanna. In *Berakhot* 48b he is noted as a disciple of Yishma'el.

Chiyya bar Natan (fourth century)
Babylonian amora. In *Pesachim* 41a and *Menachot* 39a he is mentioned as a disciple of Chisda.

Chiyya bar Nathan
See Chiyya bar Natan.

Chiyya bar Rabbah bar Nachmani (fourth century)
Babylonian amora. According to *Sanhedrin* 69b and *Avodah Zarah* 49b he was a disciple of Chisda.

Chiyya bar Rav (third century)
Babylonian amora. In *Shabbat* 61a he is noted as a colleague of Huna and in *Ketubbot* 21b as a disciple of Rav, who was his father.

Chiyya bar Rav of Difti (third century)
Babylonian amora. According to *Shabbat* 10a, he was a colleague of Chisda and Rabbah bar Huna. In *Bava Batra* 10a Chiyya bar Rav of Difti comments on the reason why Pappa's foot slipped when he was climbing: "Perhaps it was because a beggar appealed to you for alms and you were being punished for not assisting him."

Chiyya bar Va
See Chiyya bar Abba.

Chiyya bar Yehudah (third century)
Babylonian amora. According to *Ketubbot* 21a, he was a colleague of Chinena ben Chiyya.

Chiyya bar Yitzchak (third/fourth century)
Babylonian amora. In *Avodah Zarah* 33b he is listed as a contemporary of Ravina I and Rava.

Chiyya bar Yosef (second/third century)
Babylonian amora. Though he is noted in *Shabbat* 7b and 53a as a disciple of Rav, and in *Shabbat* 7a as a teacher of Giddal, Chiyya bar Yosef eventually would immigrate to Palestine. It was there that he differed with Yochanan bar Nappacha and

Shimon ben Lakish over the *kashrut* of an animal that had been attacked by a beast of prey (*Chullin* 54a).

Chiyya ben Luli'ani (fifth century)
Palestinian amora. He is quoted in *Ta'anit* 25a and *Bava Batra* 80b.

Chiyya ben Pappa (third century)
Palestinian amora. In *Bava Kamma* 80b he is noted as a mentor of Abba bar Pappa.

Chiyya ben Yeiva (third century)
Palestinian amora. In *Sukkah* 42b he is listed as a contemporary of Chisda.

Chiyya ben Zarnuki (second century)
Palestinian amora. In *Sanhedrin* 26a he is noted as a colleague of Shimon ben Yehotzadak. Both scholars were colleagues of Shimon ben Lakish.

Chiyya of Evel Arav (second century)
Palestinian tanna. He is noted in *Pesachim* 74a as a disciple of Me'ir. Evel Arav was a city in the Galilee.

Chiyya of Hormiz Ardeshir (fourth century)
Babylonian amora. In *Bava Batra* 52a he is mentioned as a colleague of Nachman bar Yitzchak.

Chiyya of Katospe'ah (third century)
Babylonian amora. He lived in a town on the banks of the Tigris River; in *Beitzah* 38b he is referred to as a disciple of Rav.

Chiyya of Parva'a (fourth century)
Palestinian amora. In *Avodah Zarah* 38b he is mentioned as a colleague of Zevid.

Chiyya of Vastanya (fifth century)
Babylonian amora. Resident of a small town near Pumbedita, according to *Ta'anit* 9a, he was a colleague of Huna bar Mano'ach and Shemu'el bar Idi. The three of them went regularly to study with Rava. When Rava died, they studied with Pappa but felt he was of lesser stature as a teacher.

Chiyyah Rabbah
See Chiyyah.

Chiyya the Great
See Chiyya.

Chizkiyyah
Also known as Hezekiah.

Three scholars were known by this name:

1. A second-century Palestinian tanna who, in *Eruvin* 50a, is named as a contemporary of Yochanan and, in *Bava Kamma* 59b, as a teacher of Shimon ben Lakish.

2. A third-century Palestinian amora who in *Bava Kamma* 10b is noted as a contemporary of Ammi bar Natan and Kahana (of Palestine).

3. A fourth-century Palestinian amora who was a disciple of Abbayei (*Shabbat* 38b) and Yirmeyahu (*Sukkah* 45b). In *Pesachim* 83b, where Chizkiyyah is noted as the principal of an academy, he discusses the question of using any form of leaven on Passover.

A number of popular maxims are quoted in Chizkiyyah's name. In *Sotah* 5a he says, "A man's prayer is not heard unless he makes his heart [soft] like flesh"; in *Kiddushin* 30b he says, "A father is obligated to find a wife for his son and to teach him a craft."

Chizkiyyah Avi Ikesh (first/second century)
Palestinian tanna. In *Bekhorot* 38a he is mentioned as a contemporary of Gamli'el II.

Chizkiyyah ben Biloto (third/fourth century)
Palestinian amora. In *Arakhin* 28b he is listed as a disciple of Chiyya bar Avin.

Chizkiyyah ben Chiyya (third century)
Palestinian amora. He was the son of Chiyya and the twin brother of Yehudah (*Mo'ed Katan* 25a). *Sanhedrin* 38a recounts a visit the brothers paid to Yehudah ha-Nasi: they were so quiet, Yehudah ha-Nasi had to serve them strong wine to loosen their tongues.

Although Chizkiyyah ben Chiyya was actually born in Babylonia, he left for Palestine to study under Yehudah ha-Nasi. Chizkiyyah never returned to Babylonia and died in the Galilee, where he was greatly revered.

One of Chizkiyyah's most famous sayings was: "Peace is more important than everything else. . . . Where peace is concerned, one must go out of his way to pursue it."

Chizkiyyah ben Parnak (third/fourth century)

Palestinian amora. The only mention of him is in *Berakhot* 63a, where he is noted as a disciple of Yochanan bar Nappacha and the person who transmitted his teacher's views concerning the unfaithful wife of *Numbers* 5:11–31.

Choni ha-Me'aggel (first century B.C.E.)

Palestinian tanna. Known in English as Choni the Circle Maker, or by the Greek name Onias, he was a contemporary of Shimon ben Shetach and famed for his great piety.

Ta'anit 19a recounts how, during a time of drought, the Jewish community implored him to pray to God to make it rain. The first time he prayed, nothing happened. So Choni drew a circle around himself—hence the name "Me'aggel"—and swore that he would not step outside it until God brought rain.

A light rain began to fall. "It is not for this that I have prayed," said Choni, "but for rain to fill pits, ditches, and caves." A tremendous downpour ensued. Again Choni said, "It is not for this that I have prayed, but for rain of benevolence, blessing, generosity." God adjusted the rain again—this time to a normal level. Shimon ben Shetach is said to have exclaimed to Choni that were it not for his religious devotion, "I would have excommunicated you [because you troubled God so many times] . . . but you act before God like a son who importunes his father, [who] fulfills his requests."

A famous legend regarding Choni's death tells how Choni, walking along the road, saw a man planting a carob tree and asked him, "How long must one wait until this tree bears fruit?" "It will take seventy years," the man replied. "Are you certain that you will live another seventy years?" mused Choni. "The whole world is like a carob tree," said the man. "Just as my forefathers planted a tree for me, I am planting a tree for my children."

Choni sat down to eat some bread. A deep sleep overtook him, so deep that he slept there for seventy years.

When he awoke, he saw a man picking the fruit of the carob tree. "Are you the man who planted the tree?" Choni asked. "No, I am not," he replied. "The man who planted the tree was my grandfather." Choni realized then that he had been sleeping for many decades. He went to his home to inquire about his son but was told that his son was no longer alive. "I am Choni," he told the people in his house, but they would not believe him. He then went to the academy where he heard the scholars invoking his name. "I am Choni," he told them, but they, too, refused to believe him. This pained Choni so much that he said, "A man who does not enjoy the society of his fellows is as if he were dead" (*Ta'anit* 23a). Choni prayed to God to take away his soul. God heard Choni's prayer, and Choni died.

However, according to other sources, Choni became caught up in the conflict between the Hasmonean rulers John Hyrcanus and Aristobulus. Choni refused to place a curse on Aristobulus at Hyrcanus's urging, and John Hyrcanus had Choni stoned to death in 65 B.C.E.

Choni the Circle Maker
See Choni ha-Me'aggel.

Chulfana (fourth century)
Babylonian amora. In *Arakhin* 28b he is listed as a teacher of Chiyya bar Ammi.

Chutzpit ha-Meturgeman (second century)
Palestinian tanna. Known in English as Chutzpit the Interpreter, he is listed in *Chullin* 142a and *Kiddushin* 39b as one of the Ten Martyrs murdered by the Romans during the Hadrianic persecution.

Chutzpit the Interpreter
See Chutzpit ha-Meturgeman.

Daniyyel bar Rav Kettina (third century)

Babylonian amora. Highly regarded as pious and saintly, he is noted in *Bava Kamma* 97a and *Bava Metzi'a* 64b as a disciple of Rav, and in *Ketubbot* 97a as a disciple of Huna.

Daru bar Pappa (second/third century)

Babylonian amora. In *Avodah Zarah* 27a he is mentioned as a disciple of Rav.

Dimi (third/fourth century)

Also known as Avdimi (Abdimi), Avudimi (Abudimi), *and* Avudma (Abudma).

Palestinian amora. The Palestinian Talmud refers to him as Avdimi Nechuta. *Nechuta*, literally "one who goes down," refers to those Sages who visited Babylonia often, transmitting to Babylonian scholars the teachings of their Palestinian counterparts and bringing back the teachings of their Babylonian colleagues to Palestine. Other Palestinian scholars who transmitted such teachings were Yochanan bar Nappacha and Elazar ben Pedat (*Yoma* 3b and 12b; *Bava Metzi'a* 75b and 105b).

In his later years Dimi settled permanently in Babylonia to escape the persecutions in Palestine by Constantine. Dimi served as principal of the academy in Pumbedita and was succeeded upon his death by Rafram bar Pappa.

Dimi Achuha de-Rav Safra (fourth century)

Babylonian amora. Known in English as Dimi, Brother of Rav Safra, he teaches in *Bava Batra* 164b: "One should never speak in praise of his friend, lest, by praising him, he brings about his blame [by inadvertently also pointing out his misdeeds]." He considered the mere taking of a vow to be improper and said, "He who vows, even though he fulfills it, is considered a sinner" (*Nedarim* 77b). According to *Ketubbot*

85b, Dimi was not endowed with worldly goods and died intestate.

Dimi bar Abba (fourth century)

Babylonian amora. In *Avodah Zarah* 15b he is quoted as saying: "Just as it is forbidden to sell to an idolator, so is it forbidden to sell to a robber who is an Israelite."

Dimi bar Chama

See Avdimi bar Chama.

Dimi bar Chanina

See Dimi bar Chinena.

Dimi bar Chinena (third/fourth century)

Also known as Dimi bar Chanina.

Babylonian amora. In *Rosh Hashanah* 34b he is said to have
been a teacher of Chiyya bar Rabbah bar Nachmani. In *Bava
Kamma* 98b he is known as Dimi bar Chanina. *Bava Batra* 13b
recounts a case that Dimi and his brother, Rava bar Chinena,
brought before Rava. The brothers were left two servants by
their father, one of whom knew how to bake and cook and the
other who knew how to spin and weave. One servant was more
valuable than the other. Could one brother receive the more
valuable servant and pay his brother compensation? No, Rava
ruled. One partner cannot say to another, "You name a price or
let me name a price."

Dimi bar Huna of Damharya (sixth century)

Babylonian amora. He lived in a small town near Sura and,
according to *Sanhedrin* 29b, was visited there by Ravina II.

Dimi bar Isaac

See Dimi bar Yitzchak.

Dimi bar Joseph

See Dimi bar Yosef.

Dimi bar Liva'i (fourth century)

Babylonian amora. He is mentioned in *Berakhot* 27b as a
contemporary of Abbayei.

Dimi bar Nachman bar Joseph

See Dimi bar Nachman bar Yosef.

Dimi bar Nachman bar Yosef (fifth century)
Babylonian amora. In *Sanhedrin* 23b he expresses his view with regard to acceptable judges in a litigation.

Dimi bar Shishna (third century)
Babylonian amora. In *Gittin* 62a he advises against offering a double greeting (such as saying "Shalom, shalom") to a heathen. In *Menachot* 90a he is mentioned as a disciple of Rav.

Dimi bar Yitzchak (fourth/fifth century)
Babylonian amora. In *Chullin* 45b he is named as a disciple of Yehudah, who instructed him about the anatomy of animals, specifically their spinal cords.

Dimi bar Yosef (third century)
Babylonian amora. In *Berakhot* 45b he is listed as a disciple of Rav and in *Ketubbot* 59b as a disciple of Shemu'el. In *Ketubbot* 60a Dimi bar Yosef solves a problem involving a divorced woman who denies that a particular child is her son.

Dimi, Brother of Rav Safra
See Dimi Achuha de-Rav Safra.

Dimi of Haifa
See Avdimi of Haifa.

Dimi of Nehardea (fourth century)
Babylonian amora. A produce merchant by trade, he served as principal of the academy in Pumbedita from 385 to 388. In *Shabbat* 127a he indicates that it is more important to extend hospitality to one in need than to engage in Torah study. In *Bava Batra* 21a he comments that it is better for children to have a teacher who goes slowly and makes no mistakes than to have a teacher who goes fast and errs.

Dosa (second century)
Palestinian tanna. In *Ketubbot* 36b he is noted as a colleague of Yehudah bar Ila'i and in *Eruvin* 83a as a colleague of Natan.

Dosa ben Harkinas (first century)
Palestinian tanna. A contemporary of Yochanan ben Zakkai and Gamli'el, he numbered among his students the distinguished Akiva ben Yosef, Elazar ben Azaryah, and Yehoshu'a ben Chananyah.

Dosa ben Harkinas believed that the authority of the president of the Sanhedrin must be upheld even when his opinions were erroneous. In a maxim quoted in *Avot* 3:10, he warns against the sin of wasting time that could be used for study: "Morning sleep, midday wine, children's talk, and sitting in the company of the ignorant remove a man from the world."

Akiva appears to have been one of his favorite students. "May there be many like you in Israel," Dosa said to him. The names Dosa and Harkinas are both of Greek origin.

Dosetai
See Dostai.

Dostai (second/third century)
Palestinian tanna. In *Kiddushin* 12a he is noted as a contemporary of Ravin and a colleague of both Yannai and Oshaya Rabbah.

Dostai Avuha de-Rabbi Aptoriki (fourth century)
Palestinian amora. Known in English as Dostai, Father of Aptoriki, he discusses in *Chullin* 64b, where he is noted as a contemporary of Yirmeyahu, whether an egg with a blood spot may be eaten. He concludes, as Rashi explains, that if the blood spot is on the yolk, it must have spread from the white; hence, the decay has penetrated the entire egg and it may not be eaten.

Dostai ben Mattan (second century)
Palestinian tanna. According to *Yoma* 30b, he was a disciple of Yochanan bar Nappacha.

Dostai ben Yannai (second century)
Palestinian tanna. According to *Eruvin* 35b, he was a disciple of Me'ir and a senior contemporary of Yehudah ha-Nasi. In *Avot* 3:10 Dostai ben Yannai quotes Me'ir, who taught: "Whoever forgets a single word of his studies is considered as having committed a capital offense." Little is known of Dostai ben Yannai's life except that he migrated to Babylonia from Palestine with his colleague Yosei ben Kippar (*Gittin* 14b).

Dostai, Father of Aptoriki
See Dostai Avuha de-Rabbi Aptoriki.

Dostai of Biri (fourth century)

Palestinian amora. Biri, properly known as Biriyyah, was a small town in the Galilee. In *Eruvin* 45a Dostai of Biri comments on *1 Samuel* 23:1, which describes a battle waged against the Philistines.

Dostai of Kefar Yatmah (first century)

Palestinian tanna. A pupil of Shammai, he is mentioned only once in the Talmud (*Orlah* 2:5).

$\mathcal{E}$

$\sim$

Efes (second/third century)

Also spelled Ephraim Maksha'ah.

Palestinian tanna. A contemporary of Yehudah ha-Nasi, Efes was his secretary and succeeded him upon his death as principal of the academy in Sepphoris (*Ketubbot* 103b). In the Palestinian Talmud Efes is referred to as Pas. Efes was one of the last tanna'im.

Efrayim Maksha'ah (second century)

Also spelled Ephraim Maksha'ah.

Palestinian tanna. *Maksha'ah* means "objector"; Efrayim was so-called because he often disagreed with the opinions of his colleagues. A disciple of Me'ir, Efrayim Maksha'ah is best known for his pithy remarks for which he credits his teacher. In *Sanhedrin* 39b he says: "From the very forest itself comes the [handle of the] ax [that fells it]."

Efrayim Safra (third century)

Also spelled Ephraim Safra.

Palestinian amora. Efrayim was a scribe (*safra* in Aramaic). *Bava Metzi'a* 119a lists him as a disciple of Shimon ben Lakish.

Eifah (third century)

Palestinian amora. According to *Shabbat* 60b, he was a colleague of Rabbah bar Bar Chana.

Eifah ben Rachavah of Pumbedita (fourth century)

Babylonian amora. In *Sanhedrin* 17b he and his brother are praised as being "keen intellects" from the academy in Pumbedita.

Eina (third/fourth century)

Babylonian amora. A contemporary of Yehudah bar Yechezkel, the two became known as *Sabbei de-Pumbedita*, "the Elders of Pumbedita" (*Sanhedrin* 17b).

Eina's views on blowing the *shofar* are stated in several tractates. In *Rosh Hashanah* 27a he disagrees with Eli'ezer ben Hurkanos on the blowing of the *shofar* in jubilee years, and in *Sukkah* 48b he states that the *shofar* is to be sounded at the Simchat Beit ha-Sho'eivah ceremony—the "Festival of Water Drawing"—on Sukkot. *Mo'ed Katan* 21a records a discussion in which Eina participated about the wearing of *tefillin* by a mourner.

Elazar

Also known as Lazar.

The name Elazar, sometimes abbreviated to Lazar, appears over three thousand times in the Babylonian Talmud without patronymic. In addition to Elazar ben Pedat (see below) and Elazar ben Shammu'a (also see below), three other scholars were known by this name:

1. A second-century Palestinian tanna who was a contemporary of Yochanan bar Nappacha (*Shabbat* 59a, *Beitzah* 10b, and *Chagigah* 13a). In *Mo'ed Katan* 6a and *Eruvin* 103a Elazar is noted as a colleague of Yosei bar Chanina. According to *Kiddushin* 6a, *Beitzah* 9a, and *Shabbat* 65a, his father's name was Shimon.

Among the many sayings for which he is known are: "Disciples of the wise increase peace in the world" (*Berakhot* 64a) and "When a man divorces his first wife, even the altar sheds tears" (*Gittin* 9b).

Based on the verse *Proverbs* 21:3, which reads, "To do charity and justice is more acceptable to the Lord than sacrifice," Elazar says: "Greater is he who [performs acts of] charity than he who offers all the sacrifices" (*Sukkah* 49b) and "He who inspires others to do good is greater than he who does good" (*Bava Batra* 90a).

2. A third-century amora who moved from Babylonia to Palestine (*Eruvin* 89b). In *Shabbat* 38b he is named as a contemporary of Shemu'el bar Yehudah and in *Yoma* 27a as a colleague of Hamnuna Sabba. Among Elazar's students were Abba Chanan (*Yoma* 3b) and Dimi (*Sukkah* 21a).

In *Yevamot* 63a Elazar says: "A man who does not own a

parcel of land is not a man." In the same source he says: "There will be a time when all craftsmen will take up agriculture."

3. A third/fourth-century Palestinian amora who, in *Pesachim* 103b and 115a, is listed as a disciple of Oshaya Rabbah. In *Eruvin* 21b he is noted as a teacher of Ulla and in *Sukkah* 45a as a teacher of Abbahu.

Elazar bar Chanina (third century)
Babylonian amora. According to *Megillah* 15a, he was a scholar who showed great respect for ordinary people.

Elazar bar Minyomi (third century)
Babylonian amora. In *Chullin* 19b he is listed as a contemporary of Nachman bar Ya'akov.

Elazar ben Abina
See Elazar ben Avina.

Elazar ben Antigonus (second century)
Also known as Eli'ezer ben Antigonus.
Palestinian tanna. In *Beitzah* 34a he is referred to as the teacher of Elazar ben Yannai, and in *Gittin* 9a as his disciple. In *Chullin* 9a he is referred to as Eli'ezer ben Antigonus.

Elazar ben Arakh (first century)
Palestinian tanna. He is noted in *Avot* 2:8 as one of Yochanan ben Zakkai's five favorite students; the other four were Yosei ha-Kohen, Eli'ezer ben Hurkanos, Yehoshu'a ben Chananyah, and Shimon ben Netanel. When Yochanan ben Zakkai asked these five disciples to state the best quality one should cultivate in life, Elazar ben Arakh responded, "a joyous heart" (*Avot* 2:9). He also said: "Be eager to study the Torah; know how to answer a disbeliever; and know before Whom you toil, Who is your Employer, and Who will reward you for your labor" (*Avot* 2:14).

According to *Shabbat* 147b, Elazar ben Arakh enjoyed a luxurious lifestyle, and he and his wife lived in Emmaus, a town located between Jerusalem and Jaffa that was famous for its untainted water supply.

Elazar ben Avina (fourth century)
Also spelled Elazar ben Abina.
Palestinian amora. He is quoted in *Berakhot* 4b and *Yevamot*

63a as saying: "Punishment descends upon the world only because Israel misbehaves."

Elazar ben Azariah

See Elazar ben Azaryah.

Elazar ben Azaryah (first/second century)

Palestinian tanna. Mentioned more than 150 times in the Babylonian Talmud, Elazar ben Azaryah came from a wealthy family that owned considerable property in Sepphoris and claimed descent from the biblical Ezra; even as a teenager, Elazar ben Azaryah was an acknowledged scholar. *Berakhot* 27b recounts that he was chosen to temporarily replace the deposed president of the Sanhedrin in Yavneh, Gamli'el II, because of Gamli'el's acerbic manner. Elazar ben Azaryah also won the respect of the Romans, who had occupied Palestine, as much for his learning as his humanity. In *Avot* 3:18 he is quoted as saying: "Where there is no Torah, there is no proper behavior [*derekh eretz*]; where there is no good breeding, there is no Torah."

In *Yoma* 85b Elazar says: "Sins committed against a fellow human being are not forgiven [by God] until one makes amends with the person against whom one sinned."

Colleagues and friends, Elazar ben Azaryah and Akiva ben Yosef socialized frequently (*Shabbat* 40a), and both would go on trips to raise funds for the support of needy students (*Eruvin* 41b and 43a, and *Yoma* 85a).

In *Chagigah* 3b Yehoshu'a ben Chananyah praises Elazar for his love of his fellowman: "It is not an orphan generation if Elazar ben Azaryah is one of its members." In *Sotah* 49b Elazar's learned colleagues said of him when he died: "With the death of Elazar ben Azaryah the crown of the Sages has been removed."

Elazar ben Chanokh (first/second century)

Also known as Elazar ben Enoch.

Palestinian tanna. According to a statement by Yehudah bar Ila'i, Elazar was excommunicated by the Sanhedrin because he quibbled about the rabbinic regulation concerning the cleansing of one's hands (Mishnah *Eduyyot* 5:6 and *Berakhot* 19a).

Elazar ben Charsom (second century)

Also spelled Elazar ben Charsum.

Palestinian tanna. Member of a wealthy, Priestly family, Elazar ben Charsom is quoted in *Yoma* 9a and 35b, and in *Kiddushin* 49b.

Elazar ben Charsum

See Elazar ben Charsom.

Elazar ben Chisma (second century)

Palestinian tanna. According to *Gittin* 62a, Elazar ben Chisma was a teacher of Yosei ben ha-Meshulam. In *Yoma* 19b Elazar says that "one who blinks his eyes, or gesticulates with his lips, or points with his fingers" when reciting the *Shema* has not fulfilled his biblical obligation.

A disciple of Akiva ben Yosef, Yehoshu'a ben Chananyah, and Gamli'el II (*Chagigah* 3a), Elazar ben Chisma was a poverty-stricken scholar who possessed a profound knowledge of the sciences. Later in life, at the request of Yehoshu'a ben Chananyah, Elazar was given a lucrative position in patriarch Gamli'el II's academy.

Mishnah *Bava Metzi'a* 7:5 ascribes to Elazar ben Chisma the rule that an employee is not entitled to a proportion of his employer's produce greater than the amount of his wages. Chisma is actually a place name rather than a personal name.

Elazar ben Dama

See Ben Dama.

Elazar ben Digla'i (second century)

Palestinian tanna. He is mentioned in Mishnah *Tamid* 3:8.

Elazar ben Dola'i

See Abba Elazar ben Dola'i.

Elazar ben Enoch

See Elazar ben Chanokh.

Elazar ben Isaac of Kefar Darom

See Elazar ben Yitzchak of Kefar Darom.

Elazar ben Jacob I

See Eli'ezer ben Ya'akov I.

Elazar ben Jeremiah
See Elazar ben Yirmeyahu.

Elazar ben Judah
See Elazar ben Yehudah.

Elazar ben Judah of Avlas
See Elazar ben Yehudah of Avlas.

Elazar ben Judah of Bartota
See Elazar ben Yehudah of Bartota.

Elazar ben Mahabai
See Eli'ezer ben Mahabai.

Elazar ben Malai (third century)
Also spelled Elazar ben Melai.
Palestinian amora. In *Shabbat* 139a he is mentioned as a disciple of Elazar ben Shimon.

Elazar ben Mattya (second century)
Palestinian tanna. Noted in *Sotah* 34a as a contemporary of Abba Chalafta and Chananyah ben Chakhinai, Elazar ben Matya states in *Kiddushin* 32a the lengths to which a child may not go to honor his parents. Thus, he says, "If my father orders me to give him a drink of water when I have a *mitzvah* to perform, I disregard my father's honor and perform the *mitzvah*, so we are both bound to fulfill the commandments."

Elazar ben Melai
See Elazar ben Malai.

Elazar ben Oshaya (second century)
Palestinian tanna. A contemporary of Eli'ezer ben Ya'akov II and Me'ir, Elazar ben Oshaya is quoted in *Rosh Hashanah* 4b.

Elazar ben Pedat (third century)
Palestinian amora. Most often referred to simply as Elazar, without patronymic, Elazar ben Pedat was born in Babylonia, where he studied under Rav and Shemu'el. *Ta'anit* 25a notes that although he was of Priestly descent, he was a very poor man who earned a modest living as a tester of coins (making sure they were not clipped), but who always was willing to share what he had with those who were less fortunate. According to

the same source, he was a pious man who engaged in conversation with God.

Although a serious scholar, he had a keen sense of humor: When asked "Why did God create human fingers shaped as they are?" Elazar ben Pedat answered, "It was done so that a man might plug his ears when he hears improper words."

At one point he left Babylonia and settled in Palestine, where he studied under Yochanan bar Nappacha in his academy in Tiberias. *Ketubbot* 111a notes that Elazar fell in love with "the Land of Israel" because he found it to be a superior place to enhance one's spiritual life.

In *Yevamot* 72b, Yochanan bar Nappacha is reported to have said to Shimon ben Lakish: "I notice that whenever Ben Pedat occupies the teacher's chair and expounds Torah, he is like Moses, expounding from the mouth of the Almighty."

Elazar often was consulted by Babylonian scholars on questions of Jewish law. One important issue that arose concerned whether Babylonian Jews were required to observe Jewish holidays for one day or two. The custom of celebrating an extra day had been introduced during the Roman occupation of Palestine, when messengers of the Sanhedrin had been unable to inform the Jewish community of Babylonia of the beginning of a new month in a timely fashion. Although Babylonian Jews could have determined the beginning of the new month themselves because they also followed the lunar calendar, the Babylonian exilarch nevertheless added an extra day to all holidays for fear that his calculations might differ from his Palestinian counterpart. Even when the Romans relaxed their vigilance and messengers were free to travel to Babylonia from Palestine, Elazar ben Pedat advised all Jews who lived outside of Palestine to continue to observe the second day of holidays. The tradition continues to this day among many Jews; although even in Israel, Rosh Hashanah is observed for two days.

Elazar ben Perata (second century)
Also known as Eli'ezer ben Parta.

Palestinian tanna. In *Pesachim* 119b and *Sukkah* 39a he is described as a colleague of Yehudah ha-Nasi. Elazar ben Perata's grandson, also a tanna, bore the same name as his grandfather, as noted in *Ketubbot* 100a. In *Sanhedrin* 22a Elazar ben Perata is referred to as Eli'ezer ben Parta.

Elazar ben Phinehas

See Elazar ben Pinchas.

Elazar ben Pila (second century)

Palestinian tanna. In *Tohorot* 7:9 he is mentioned as a colleague of Akiva ben Yosef. Elazar's father's name, Pila, is sometimes rendered as Piabi and is considered to be a variant of Philo.

Elazar ben Pinchas (first century)

Palestinian tanna. In *Yoma* 18a he is noted as a disciple of Yehudah ben Beteira.

Elazar ben Shammu'a (second century)

Also known as Lazar.

Palestinian tanna. Of Priestly descent, Elazar ben Shammu'a sometimes is referred to simply as Lazar or Elazar, without patronymic. In *Yevamot* 62b he, Me'ir, Yosei ben Chalafta, Yehudah bar Ila'i, and Shimon bar Yochai are listed as pupils of Akiva ben Yosef. In *Eruvin* 53a Yehudah ha-Nasi said, "When we studied Torah at the home of Elazar ben Shammu'a [so eager were the students to learn that] six of us used to sit [crowded] within the space of one cubit." In *Ketubbot* 40a Rav speaks of Elazar ben Shammu'a as being the most satisfied among the Sages because his rulings were accepted as reliable.

In *Avot* 4:12 the following maxim is quoted in Elazar ben Shammu'a's name: "Let the honor of your student be as dear to you as your own, the honor of your colleague like the fear of your teacher, and your reverence for your teacher like the reverence you have for God."

Elazar ben Shimon (second/third century)

Also known as Eli'ezer ben Shimon.

Palestinian tanna. Son of Shimon bar Yochai, he and his father hid in a cave for thirteen years to avoid persecution by the Romans. In *Shabbat* 136a Elazar ben Shimon is noted as a colleague of Yosei ben Yehudah and in *Shabbat* 32b as a contemporary of Rabbi Yehudah ha-Nasi, with whom he once engaged in a dispute about the type of girdle a *Kohen* should wear (*Yoma* 12b). *Bava Metzi'a* 84a notes that Elazar ben Shimon was extremely obese.

Elazar's rulings are quoted throughout the Talmud, including *Nedarim* 76b, *Sukkah* 33b, *Ta'anit* 12a, *Mo'ed Katan* 4a, and *Pesachim* 107a, where he notes—contrary to the view of others—that one may recite *Kiddush* over beer. In *Shabbat* 32b he rules on the type of sandals one may wear on the Sabbath and there he is quoted as saying that "Children die as punishment for unfulfilled vows of parents." *Bava Metzi'a* 83b–85a relates how Elazar had been appointed by the Roman authorities to track down thieves. Because he feared that he might have been responsible for the execution of an innocent man, he submitted himself to afflictions to atone for his error. His body was covered with painful sores that he accepted willingly, referring to them as his "friends."

In *Eruvin* 38b and *Sukkot* 33b he is referred to as Eli'ezer ben Shimon.

Elazar ben Simeon

See Elazar ben Shimon.

Elazar ben Taddai (second century)

Palestinian tanna. His legal rulings appear in *Shabbat* 123a and *Eruvin* 71b.

Elazar ben Tzadok

Two scholars were known by this name:

1. A first-century Palestinian tanna, sometimes referred to as Eli'ezer ben Tzadok, who was famous for his piety and admired by Yochanan ben Zakkai. A wine merchant by trade, Elazar is mentioned in Mishnah *Middot* 3:8 as a disciple of Yochanan ben he-Choranit. Son of the well-known tanna Tzadok, Elazar saw the Temple in all its glory during his youth (*Sukkah* 49a; *Sanhedrin* 52b) but also witnessed its destruction by the Romans.

Beitzah 22b relates that Elazar and his father were once guests in the home of Gamli'el I. Later, Elazar went to Yavneh where he became a friend of the patriarch Gamli'el II and a member of the Sanhedrin (*Shabbat* 11a and *Niddah* 48b).

In *Berakhot* 29b Elazar ben Tzadok proposes a prayer that one should recite when passing through a place infested by wild beasts or robbers.

2. A second-century Palestinian tanna and grandson of the first-century Elazar ben Tzadok. He spent many years in Babylonia, where Rav's father, Aibu, studied under him (*Sukkah* 44b).

Elazar ben Ya'akov I
See Eli'ezer ben Ya'akov I.

Elazar ben Ya'akov II
See Eli'ezer ben Ya'akov II.

Elazar ben Yannai (second century)
Also known as Eli'ezer ben Yannai.
Palestinian tanna. In *Beitzah* 34a he is mentioned as a disciple of Elazar ben Antigonus and in *Gittin* 31a as his teacher. In *Chullin* 9a Elazar ben Yannai is referred to as Eli'ezer ben Yannai.

Elazar ben Yehudah (second century)
Palestinian tanna. He is quoted in *Shabbat* 32b.

Elazar ben Yehudah of Avlas (second century)
Palestinian tanna. In *Zevachim* 28a he is noted as a disciple of Ya'akov bar Korshai.

Elazar ben Yehudah of Bartota (first/second century)
Also known as Elazar ben Yehudah of Kefar Bertota *and* Eli'ezer ben Yehudah.
Palestinian tanna. According to *Pesachim* 13a, he was a disciple of Yehoshu'a ben Chananyah; *Bekhorot* 57a records a dispute in which Elazar engaged with Akiva ben Yosef. In addition to being a great scholar, Elazar ben Yehudah of Bartota was extremely philanthropic. His motto, stated in *Avot* 3:7, was: "Render to God that which is His, for you and what you have are His."

The Palestinian Talmud illustrates Elazar ben Yehudah's kindliness by relating how he treated a blind man who came to his town. Elazar offered him a seat of honor above his own. The blind man then offered a prayer on behalf of Elazar in which he said: "You have dealt kindly with one who is seen but sees not.

May He who sees but is unseen accept your prayers and deal kindly with you."

Bartota was a small town in Upper Galilee.

Elazar ben Yirmeyahu (first century)

Palestinian tanna. In *Sotah* 4a he is listed as a contemporary of Shimon ben Azzai and Akiva ben Yosef.

Elazar ben Yitzchak of Kefar Darom

(first/second century)

Palestinian tanna. In *Sotah* 20b he is named as a contemporary of Yishma'el and Abba Yosei ben Yochanan.

Elazar ben Yosei

Two scholars were known by this name:

1. A first-century Palestinian tanna, also known as Eli'ezer ben Yosei and Lazar ben Yosei, who was the second oldest of Yosei ben Chalafta's five learned sons (*Shabbat* 118b and, in the Palestinian Talmud, *Yevamot* 1b). There is no mention of Elazar in the Mishnah, but he is mentioned often in the Tosefta.

Sanhedrin 111a describes a visit Elazar made to Alexandria, Egypt, where he met an old Egyptian who invited him to see all the places where the Egyptians had wreaked terrible tragedies upon the Israelites, Elazar's ancestors, during their sojourn in Egypt.

In *Ketubbot* 28b Elazar ben Yosei is quoted as saying: "In all my days, I have never been called upon to testify [in a court case]. Only on one occasion did I testify, and my testimony was disastrous because it was misunderstood. As a result, on the basis of my very evidence they elevated a slave to the Priesthood [with all the dire consequences that ensued]."

One of Elazar's well-known aphorisms appears in *Avot de-Rabbi Natan* (chapter 40): "If one sins and repents and proceeds to live an upright life, he is forgiven immediately."

2. A fourth-century Palestinian amora who also was known as Lazar ben Yosei. His father, who was his primary teacher, often chided him for not being sufficiently industrious. The remarks made in Elazar ben Yosei's name, which are quoted in the Palestinian Talmud, often were statements that he had heard made by other amoraim, such as Abbahu.

Elazar ben Zadok

See Elazar ben Tzadok.

Elazar ha-Kappar

Also known as Bar Kappara, Eli'ezer ha-Kappar, *and* Lazar ha-Kappar.

Palestinian tanna. Known in English as Elazar the Coppersmith, he is referred to in *Ta'anit* 11a as Elazar ha-Kappar Berabbi. Some scholars believe that the title "Berabbi" was added to distinguish him from his father, who bore the same name. Others are of the opinion that "Berabbi" signifies that he was a member of the school of "Rabbi"—Rabbi Yehudah ha-Nasi. In addition to Yehudah ha-Nasi, Elazar ha-Kappar was a disciple of Shemu'el (*Shabbat* 125a and *Yoma* 87b).

Among Elazar ha-Kappar's disciples were Huna ben Berekhyah, mentioned in *Berakhot* 63a, and Nachum ben Pappa, noted in *Yoma* 67a. Other disciples include Shimon bar Pazzi, Yehoshu'a ben Levi, and Shimon ben Lakish (*Shabbat* 75a, *Sukkah* 38b, and *Pesachim* 15a).

In *Megillah* 29a Elazar ha-Kappar expresses the belief that sometime in the future all the academies of learning in Babylonia will move to Eretz Yisra'el.

In *Berakhot* 63a Elazar advises: "A man should always teach his son a clean and easy trade." Chisda explains that the type of trade to which Elazar refers is one such as needlework.

Elazar ha-Kappar is credited with a number of popular maxims recorded in *Avot* 4:21–22: "Envy, lust, and ambition shorten a man's life"; "Know that all that happens is in accordance with a plan. Do not be deceived into thinking that the grave is a place of refuge for you. Contrary to your wishes you were born, contrary to your wishes you will die, and contrary to your wishes you will have to give an accounting of your life before the King of Kings, the Holy One, blessed be He." In *Kiddushin* 40b–41a he says: "A man who is bad-tempered achieves nothing but his bad temper." In *Shabbat* 105b, the Sages quote Elazar as saying: "When one sheds tears upon the demise of a virtuous man, God counts them and stores them in His treasury."

In *Nazir* 3a and *Shabbat* 135a Elazar ha-Kappar is referred to as Eli'ezer ha-Kappar. In the Palestinian Talmud (*Yevamot* 15:3), where he is called Lazar, Elazar ruled that "one may not purchase an animal or a fowl unless he is able to feed it properly."

Elazar ha-Kappar Berabbi
See Elazar ha-Kappar.

Elazar ha-Moda'i
See Elazar of Modi'in.

Elazar of Berekhyah (second century)
Palestinian tanna. He is quoted in *Sanhedrin* 94b.

Elazar of Hagronia (fourth-century)
Babylonian amora. In *Eruvin* 63a he is named as a colleague of Abba bar Tachlifa.

Elazar of Modi'in (first/second century)
Also known as Elazar ha-Moda'i.

Palestinian tanna. A contemporary of Yehoshu'a ben Chananyah, Elazar of Modi'in is mentioned in *Yoma* 76a as part of a study group that included Tarfon and Yishma'el ben Elisha. According to *Bava Batra* 10b, Elazar of Modi'in was highly respected by the patriarch Gamli'el II as an authority on *aggadah*. Elazar delivered many strictures, among them, "[H]e who embarrasses a fellow human being publicly . . . has no share in the world to come" (*Avot* 3:12). Elazar of Modi'in met his death in 135 C.E., during the Bar Kokhba Revolt.

Elazar of Ruma (second/third century)
Palestinian amora. In *Gittin* 67b he is noted as a teacher of Yochanan bar Nappacha. Ruma was a small town in the vicinity of Sepphoris.

Elazar the Coppersmith
See Elazar ha-Kappar.

Elazar Ze'eira (second/third century)
Also known as Eli'ezer Ze'eira.

Babylonian amora. *Bava Kamma* 59a reports that Elazar was a contemporary of Shemu'el, who agreed with his interpretation of a question of law concerning how much compensation one has to pay for damaging flowering buds on another person's date tree. Elazar once appeared in public wearing black shoes and, when questioned by deputies of the exilarch, claimed that he was mourning the destruction of Jerusalem.

Eleazar
See Elazar.

Eli'ezer
See Eli'ezer ben Hurkanos.

Eli'ezer ben Antigonus
See Elazar ben Antigonus.

Eli'ezer ben Hurkanos (first/second century)
Also known as Eli'ezer, Eli'ezer ha-Gadol *and* Eli'ezer Rabbah. *Also spelled* Eli'ezer ben Hyrcanus.

Palestinian tanna. Whenever the name Eli'ezer appears in the Talmud without patronymic, it refers to Eli'ezer ben Hurkanos. Occasionally he is referred to as Eli'ezer Rabbah or Eli'ezer ha-Gadol (*Berakhot* 32a); in English, Eli'ezer the Great.

Along with Elazar ben Arakh, Yosei ha-Kohen, Yehoshu'a ben Chananyah, and Shimon ben Netanel, Eli'ezer ben Hurkanos was one of the five most distinguished students of Yochanan ben Zakkai. Born into a wealthy family of Levites, it is said that Eli'ezer ben Hurkanos worked on his father's estates until he was in his early twenties; then, in the year 65, much to his father's displeasure, he decided to go to Jerusalem to study under Yochanan ben Zakkai. Despite Eli'ezer's utter ignorance, Yochanan ben Zakkai encouraged Eli'ezer and before long, because of his phenomenal memory, described him as a "plastered cistern that never loses a drop."

Sometime later Eli'ezer's father came to Jerusalem intending to disinherit his son, but when he witnessed the adoration Yochanan bestowed on Eli'ezer after listening to one of his lectures—Yochanan exclaimed, "Rabbi Eli'ezer, master, you have taught me Torah!"—Eli'ezer's father changed his mind and bequeathed his entire fortune to Eli'ezer. According to the minor tractate *Avot de-Rabbi Natan* (6:31), Eli'ezer refused the offer and agreed only to accept a share equal to that of his siblings. In further praise of Eli'ezer, Yochanan said: "If all the Sages of Israel were on one scale, and Eli'ezer on the other, he would outweigh them all" (*Avot* 2:8).

Despite the poor treatment Eli'ezer received from his father during his youth, Eli'ezer always acted respectfully toward him. Eli'ezer's attitude is reflected in the following story (*Avodah Zarah* 23b; the story, it should be noted, is attributed to Ulla as well in *Kiddushin* 31a):

> A Gentile named Dama ben Netina owned a diamond worth 600,000 shekels. The High Priest wanted it for his *ephod* [vestment] and sent some *Kohanim* to purchase it. When they arrived, Dama's father was asleep, the key to the safe beneath his pillow. Dama refused to wake his father, despite the fact that it would result in great monetary loss.

From Dama, Eli'ezer learned that the duty to honor one's father is so great that even if a man's father were to throw a bag of gold into the sea, his son should not question his actions. In *Kiddushin* 32a Eli'ezer discusses whether more respect is due a mother or a father and concludes that more honor should be given a father since "both you and your mother are bound to honor your father."

Gittin 56a reports that during the siege of Jerusalem by the Romans, which would end in the destruction of the Temple in 70 C.E., Eli'ezer ben Hurkanos and Yehoshu'a ben Chananyah smuggled Yochanan ben Zakkai out of the city in a coffin, in order for Yochanan to meet with Vespasian, the Roman commander. Since Yochanan was opposed to waging war against the Romans, Vespasian acceded to Yochanan's request to allow him to reestablish his academy in Yavneh. (According to a legend, Yochanan predicted that Vespasian would one day be emperor of Rome, and that is why Vespasian agreed to Yochanan's request to establish his academy in Yavneh.)

In *Shabbat* 116a and *Nedarim* 20b we learn of Eli'ezer's marriage to Imma Shalom, the learned sister of the patriarch Gamli'el II. After accompanying Yochanan ben Zakkai to Yavneh, where he became a member of the Sanhedrin, Eli'ezer left his mentor and went to Lydda, where he established his own academy (*Sanhedrin* 36b).

Eli'ezer's legal views are found in many tractates of the Talmud. In *Ketubbot* 4b he offers an opinion that the mourning period does not begin until the body has been taken out of the house where the death occurred. In *Yevamot* 26a he comments on levirate marriages and in *Eruvin* 23b on the specifications of an *eruv*. In *Sanhedrin* 97b Eli'ezer discusses issues of repentance and in *Shabbat* 104 what constitutes writing on the Sabbath.

Eli'ezer is quoted in *Avot* 2:15 as the author of the following three maxims:

• Let your friend's reputation be as dear to you as your own.
• Be not provoked to anger.
• Repent one day before your death [that is, today], since tomorrow may be your last day on earth.

In *Sotah* 48b Eli'ezer sums up his philosophy of life: "Whoever has a piece of bread in his basket and complains by saying 'What shall I eat tomorrow?' is one of little faith."

Because Eli'ezer firmly believed his interpretation of law was based on tradition, he was unwilling to accept the majority view of his colleagues. This led to his excommunication by his brother-in-law Gamli'el II. The ban was lifted after Eli'ezer's death.

Despite the ban, according to *Sanhedrin* 101a, when Eli'ezer took sick, some of the most illustrious scholars came to visit him at his bedside in Caesarea. These included Akiva ben Yosef, Tarfon, and Elazar ben Azaryah.

Eli'ezer ben Hyrcanus
See Eli'ezer ben Hurkanos.

Eli'ezer ben Jacob I
See Eli'ezer ben Ya'akov I.

Eli'ezer ben Jacob II
See Eli'ezer ben Ya'akov II.

Eli'ezer ben Judah
See Elazar ben Yehudah of Bartota.

Eli'ezer ben Mahabai (second century)
Also known as Elazar ben Mahabai.

Palestinian tanna. In *Shabbat* 106b he rules that if locusts and other insects "advance in thick swarms," they are easily gathered up without violating the Sabbath prohibition against "catching." In the Tosefta (*Yevamot* 14:4) Eli'ezer ben Mahabai is referred to as Elazar ben Mahabai.

Eli'ezer ben Parta
See Elazar ben Perata.

Eli'ezer ben Shimon
See Elazar ben Shimon.

Eli'ezer ben Simeon
See Elazar ben Shimon.

Eli'ezer ben Taddai (second century)
Palestinian tanna. He was a contemporary of Shimon ben Elazar.

Eli'ezer ben Tzadok
See Elazar ben Tzadok.

Eli'ezer ben Ya'akov I (first century)
Also known as Elazar ben Ya'akov I.

Palestinian tanna. A contemporary of Eli'ezer ben Hurkanos (*Perachim* 32a), Eli'ezer ben Ya'akov I was alive while the Temple in Jerusalem still stood and experienced its destruction in the year 70 C.E. In *Berakhot* 10b he is mentioned as a teacher of Yosei bar Chanina.

Eli'ezer ben Ya'akov II (second century)
Also known as Elazar ben Ya'akov II.

Palestinian tanna. A pupil of Akiva ben Yosef, Eli'ezer ben Ya'akov II was one of the Sages who assembled at Usha to revive the study of Torah after the Romans suppressed the Bar Kokhba Revolt in 135 C.E. (*Ketubbot* 49b–50a). Among Eli'ezer's colleagues were Me'ir, Yehudah bar Ila'i, Yosei ben Chalafta, Shimon bar Yochai, and Elazar ben Shammu'a.

In *Berakhot* 10b Eli'ezer ben Ya'akov II is reported as saying: "Whoever provides lodging in his home for a scholar, and shares with him his wealth, is as meritorious as one who offers up a daily sacrifice."

Eli'ezer ben Yannai
See Elazar ben Yannai.

Eli'ezer ben Yehudah
See Elazar ben Yehudah of Bartota.

Eli'ezer ben Yosei

See Elazar ben Yosei.

Eli'ezer ben Yosei ha-Gelili (second century)

Palestinian tanna. Son of the great scholar Yosei ha-Gelili, Eli'ezer, whose expertise was in the field of *aggadah*, was one of Akiva ben Yosef's principal disciples.

Eli'ezer expanded upon the thirteen hermeneutical principles that had been set forth by Yishma'el ben Elisha. Yochanan bar Nappacha and Elazar ben Shimon said that when Eli'ezer lectures one is advised to "make your ear [cupped] like a funnel [so you will not fail to hear every word he utters]" (*Chullin* 89a).

In *Berakhot* 63b, Eli'ezer ben Yosei ha-Gelili is listed as one of the teachers in the great academy of Yochanan ben Zakkai in Yavneh.

According to *Me'ilah* 17a, Eli'ezer and his colleague Shimon bar Yochai visited Rome, where, with the aid of their clever colleague Re'uven ben Itztrobili, they were successful in reversing several harsh decrees imposed by Hadrian upon the Jews of Jerusalem. These included a ban on Sabbath observance and a ban on circumcision. *Sukkah* 5a notes that while in Rome the two scholars saw the ritual objects that Titus had carried off after destroying the Second Temple in Jerusalem in 70 C.E.

In *Sanhedrin* 92b Eli'ezer ben Yosei ha-Gelili is quoted as saying: "The dead whom Ezekiel brought back to life [*Ezekiel* 37:11ff.] went up to the Land of Israel, married, and begot sons and daughters," intimating that just as the dry bones came back to life, so, too, the Jews would one day return from exile to the Land of Israel.

In *Shabbat* 32a Eli'ezer holds out hope for man's redemption, claiming that it can be accomplished through the performance of good deeds.

Eli'ezer ha-Gadol

See Eli'ezer ben Hurkanos.

Eli'ezer ha-Kappar

See Elazar ha-Kappar.

Eli'ezer Rabbah

See Eli'ezer ben Hurkanos.

Eli'ezer the Great
See Eli'ezer ben Hurkanos.

Eli'ezer Ze'eira
See Elazar Ze'eira.

Elisha ben Avuyah (first/second century)
Palestinian tanna. The son of a wealthy citizen of Jerusalem, Elisha ben Avuyah was a teacher of Me'ir and a colleague of Akiva ben Yosef, Shimon ben Azzai, and Shimon ben Zoma, all of whom dabbled in mystical speculation. Elisha fell under the influence of the Gnostics. Eventually, he came to despise Jewish law and used his knowledge of it to persecute those who adhered to it by informing on them to the Roman authorities. Because of his disloyalty to his faith, people called him Acher, meaning "the Other" (*Chagigah* 14b, *Kiddushin* 39b, and *Chullin* 142a).

Elisha ben Avuyah is mentioned only once in the Mishnah (*Avot* 4:25), as the author of the following maxim: "He who learns when he is young, to what may he be compared? To ink used on new paper. He who learns when he is old, to what may he be compared? To ink used on blotted paper."

In the Talmud several of Elisha's legal views are presented. In one instance, Tzadok consults him on how many days of mourning he is required to observe since he hadn't learned about the death of his father until three years after it had taken place (*Mo'ed Katan* 20a).

Elyakim (fourth century)
Babylonian amora. A student at Rava's academy in Machoza, Elyakim was a contemporary of Huna bar Nachman (*Avodah Zarah* 57b).

Elyeho'enai ben ha-Kof (first century)
Palestinian tanna. In Mishnah *Parah* 3:5 he is noted as a colleague of Chanan ha-Mitzri.

Ephraim
See Efrayim Maksha'ah *and* Efrayim Safra.

Ezekiel
See Yechezkel.

Ezra berei Avtolas (third/fourth century)
Palestinian amora. Known in English as Ezra, Son of Avtolas, he was a contemporary of Perida and Ammi bar Natan, and is quoted in *Menachot* 53a.

Ezra, Son of Avtolas
See Ezra berei Avtolas.

G

Gadda (fourth century)

Babylonian amora. In *Eruvin* 11b he is noted as an attendant of Sheshet. Sheshet disagreed with his fellow rabbis about the shape of a doorway leading from the private domain to the public domain. When Sheshet ordered Gadda to tear down a particular doorway, the exilarch's deputies arrested Gadda, but Sheshet freed him immediately.

Gamli'el I (first century)

Also known as Gamli'el ha-Zaken.

Palestinian tanna. Known in English as Gamli'el the Elder, or sometimes just as Gamli'el, without patronymic, he was the son of Shimon and the grandson of Hillel, six of whose descendants filled the office of *nasi*—"patriarch"—in ancient Israel. Gamli'el I was the first rabbi who was given the title "Rabban," meaning "master," and like his grandfather, he also bore the title "Zaken," meaning "elder."

Gamali'el I is mentioned in the New Testament (*Acts* 22:3) as being the teacher of Paul. For his tolerance toward the early Christians, Gamli'el was held in high esteem by all people.

Although Gamali'el I was a wealthy man, he requested of his disciples that he be buried in a plain linen shroud. Following his example, the custom of luxurious burial for the affluent was abandoned, and rich and poor were buried in like manner.

Sotah 9:15 states that when Gamli'el I died, "the glory of the Law [Torah] ceased, and purity and self-denial died." *Megillah* 21a notes:

> From the days of Moses to the time of Rabban Gamli'el, the Torah was studied only while one was in a standing position. When Rabban Gamli'el died, feebleness descended upon the world, and they studied Torah sitting.

And so, it has come to be said that from the time that Rabban Gamli'el died [full] honor ceased to be accorded to the Torah.

After Gamli'el's death, his son, Shimon ben Gamli'el I, who, as one of the Ten Martyrs, would die at the hands of the Romans, became *nasi* and Yochanan ben Zakkai became *av beit din.*

Gamli'el II (first/second century)
Also known as Gamli'el of Yavneh.

Palestinian tanna. Grandson of Gamli'el I and son of Shimon ben Gamli'el, *nasi* of the Sanhedrin, Gamli'el II was too young to succeed his father as *nasi* when Shimon died in the years immediately preceding the destruction of the Second Temple. Yochanan ben Zakkai was elevated to *nasi* instead, but relinquished the position in favor of Gamli'el II; thus, the mantle of leadership was restored to the house of Hillel.

When Gamli'el II assumed the presidency of the Sanhedrin, he became principal of the academy established by Yochanan ben Zakkai in Yavneh. Gamli'el's insistence upon exercising strict authority provoked his colleagues. Perhaps what upset them more was his proclamation, recorded in *Berakhot* 28a, that "No student whose inner character does not correspond to his exterior appearance may enter the house of study." *Bava Metzi'a* 59b reports that Eli'ezer ben Hurkanos, who was married to Imma Shalom, the sister of Gamli'el II, was excommunicated during Gamli'el II's tenure as patriarch because he refused to accept a decision of the Sages.

Gamli'el II was temporarily deposed for publicly humiliating the esteemed Yehoshu'a ben Chananyah; Gamli'el apologized and was reinstated. It is possible that the difference of opinion between Gamli'el and his colleagues centered on whether the academy should be merely a forum for discussion or whether its members had the power to make binding decisions.

During Gamli'el's tenure a number of additions to the liturgy were instituted. In particular, Gamli'el is noted (*Berakhot* 28b and *Megillah* 17b) for appointing Shemu'el ha-Katan to compose a prayer to be added to the *Amidah* that condemned the *minim* ("heretics") for undermining Judaism. Additionally,

Gamali'el made it mandatory to recite the *Amidah* three times a day.

In the spirit of his grandfather, Gamli'el ha-Zaken, Gamli'el II furthered the practice of inexpensive and less ornate funerals, and the custom of burying the dead in simple dress. In *Berakhot* 16b he is presented as a bit of a maverick: When it was reported that his disciples found him bathing on the night after the death of his wife, which was contrary to established law, he explained: "I am not like other men. I am very delicate."

Gamli'el taught that it was inappropriate for a master to accept condolences upon the death of a slave. Having done so upon the death of Tavi, his beloved Gentile slave, and having been reminded by his students of the prohibition, Gamli'el replied: "My slave Tavi was unlike other slaves. He was a good man" (*Berakhot* 16b). In fact, in *Sukkah* 20b and *Yoma* 87a, Gamli'el asserts that his slave Tavi was a Talmudic scholar worthy of ordination.

Despite Gamli'el's occasional departure from established practice, he was a highly respected and beloved leader. Upon his death in 110, Onkelos, a close friend, paid for his funeral, and Gamli'el II was mourned by the entire community, who called him "father." He was succeeded by his son, Shimon ben Gamli'el II.

Gamli'el III (second/third century)

Palestinian tanna. Noted in *Ketubbot* 10a as the eldest son of Yehudah ha-Nasi, popularly known throughout the Talmud simply as "Rabbi," Gamli'el III helped his father complete the awesome project of compiling and editing the Mishnah. Before his death, Yehudah ha-Nasi appointed Gamli'el III as his successor (*Ketubbot* 103a). The Babylonian amora Shemu'el reported that there were many differences of opinion between Gamli'el III and other scholars (*Niddah* 63b and *Bava Batra* 139b).

One of Gamli'el III's famous maxims, recorded in *Avot* 2:2, states, "It is good to combine the study of Torah with an occupation, for the two together can keep one away from sin. Torah study without an occupation will eventually lead one to transgress . . . Let all who work for the welfare of the community do so out of pure, unselfish motives."

When Yehudah ha-Nasi died in the year 220, Gamli'el succeeded him as president of the Sanhedrin and patriarch of the Jewish people. Gamli'el III was recognized, even by the Romans, as the political leader of the Jewish nation. His accession was in accordance with instructions willed by "Rabbi" (*Ketubbot* 103b), as was the appointment of Gamli'el III's brother, Shimon ben Yehudah ha-Nasi, to the position of *chakham*, which ranked third in title following *nasi* and *av beit din*.

Before Gamli'el III's death, he appointed his son, Yehudah Nesi'ah, to succeed him.

Gamli'el IV (third century)

Palestinian amora. As successor to his father, Yehudah Nesi'ah, grandson of Yehudah ha-Nasi, Gamli'el IV was head of the Sanhedrin from 250 to 265. He was succeeded as patriarch in 265 by his son Yehudah III.

Gamli'el V (fourth century)

Palestinian amora. Gamli'el V succeeded his father, Hillel II, to the patriarchate in the year 365. Upon the death of Hillel II, however, the office of patriarch became ineffectual. A direct descendant of Hillel ha-Zaken, Gamli'el V is best known for completing a permanent Jewish calendar, a project begun by his father. Gamli'el V died in 380 and was succeeded by his son, Yehudah IV.

Gamli'el VI (fourth/fifth century)

Palestinian amora. A direct descendant of Hillel, Gamli'el VI succeeded his father, Yehudah IV, as *nasi* in 400, and was the last of the patriarchs, the office having been stripped of all power by the Romans in 415. He died in 426, leaving no heirs, and the house of Hillel, which had been founded approximately 400 years earlier, came to an end.

Gamli'el ha-Zaken

See Gamli'el I.

Gamli'el of Yavneh

See Gamli'el II.

Gamli'el the Elder

See Gamli'el I.

Ganiva (third century)

Babylonian amora. In *Gittin* 65a–b he is noted as a student of Huna and a colleague of Avina. While Ganiva was respected for his erudition by Huna and Chisda, he was deprecated by them for his quarrelsomeness (*Gittin* 62a). In *Chullin* 44a Ravina I is mentioned as one of Ganiva's disciples.

Gebiha of Argiza (fifth century)

Babylonian amora. He is famous for the following saying: "God will praise the man who has reason to be upset over the conduct of his neighbor, yet who restrains himself and holds his peace" (*Gittin* 7a).

Gebiha of Bei Katil (fourth/fifth century)

Babylonian amora. A disciple of Abbayei and Rava, it is evident from *Yevamot* 60a and *Chullin* 26b that Gebiha of Bei Katil assisted Ashi in completing the editing of the Babylonian Talmud by reporting to him rulings that had come to his attention. Gebiha of Bei Katil served as principal of the academy in Pumbedita until his death in 433, when he was succeeded by Rafram.

Giddal (third century)

Also known as Giddul.

Babylonian amora. A devoted disciple of Rav, Giddal quotes his master's teachings in many tractates, including *Yoma* 18b, *Sukkah* 13a, *Yevamot* 20a, and *Mo'ed Katan* 17a. In *Shabbat* 7b and *Pesachim* 21b Giddal quotes Chiyya bar Yosef, also a disciple of Rav.

Giddal bar Menasheh (third/fourth century)

Babylonian amora. He lived in a town called Bairi of Naresh, located north of Sura. In *Bava Batra* 155a Giddal bar Menasheh is noted as a disciple of Rava and in *Mo'ed Katan* 24a as a disciple of Shemu'el.

Giddal bar Minyomi (third century)

Babylonian amora. In *Bava Batra* 39b he is listed as a contemporary of Huna, Chiyya bar Rav, and Chilkiyah bar Tovi.

Giddul

See Giddal.

Gursak bar Dari (third century)
Babylonian amora. In *Eruvin* 29a he is noted as a disciple of Menashya bar Shegovli, a contemporary of Yosef.

Guryon (fourth century)
Palestinian amora. In *Shabbat* 33b he is listed as a contemporary of Yosef bar Shemaya.

Guryon ben Astyon (second/third century)
Babylonian amora. In *Bava Metzi'a* 86b, he is mentioned as a disciple of Rav.

Guryon of Isporak (third century)
Babylonian amora. In *Bava Kamma* 65b and 93b–94a he is named as a colleague of Yosef.

H

Names that begin with the Hebrew letter chet *can be found under the letter* C.

Haggai
See Chaggai.

Hamnuna (third/fourth century)
Babylonian amora. Hamnuna was a disciple of Rav, from whom he received instruction over many years in *halakhah* (*Bava Kamma* 106a) as well as *aggadah* (*Eruvin* 54a). Scholars assume that when the Talmud uses the expression *bei Rav* ("the school of Rav"), it refers to a statement of Hamnuna. Contrary to statements in some sources, Hamnuna did not succeed Rav as head of the academy in Sura. His successor was Huna.

Hamnuna bar Joseph
See Hamnuna bar Yosef.

Hamnuna bar Yosef (fourth century)
Babylonian amora. In *Berakhot* 24a he is mentioned as a pupil of Rava.

Hamnuna ben Rava Pashruni'a (second century)
Palestinian tanna. In *Gittin* 45b he is quoted as ruling that a Torah scroll, *tefillin*, or a *mezuzah* written by an informer, a slave, a minor, or a woman is invalid.

Hamnuna Sabba (third century)
Babylonian amora. Known in English as Hamnuna the Elder (though he was younger than Hamnuna, he often is referred to in the Talmud as Hamnuna Sabba to distinguish him from younger scholars by the same name), Hamnuna Sabba had many distinguished teachers, including Chisda, with whom he was very close and whose colleague he eventually would become (*Shabbat* 97a and *Eruvin* 63a).

Shabbat 119a records that the *reish galuta* called upon Hamnuna Sabba for advice.

Kiddushin 29b recounts what transpired when Chisda spoke in praise of Hamnuna to the illustrious Huna, describing Hamnuna as "a great man."

"When he visits you," said Huna to Chisda, "bring him to me."

When Chisda arrived with Hamnuna, Hamnuna was bareheaded.

"Why have you no head covering," asked Huna?

"Because I am not married," replied Hamnuna.

"See to it that you do not appear before me again until you are married," responded Huna. And with that, he "turned his face away" from the young scholar.

Deeply concerned with the education of the young, Hamnuna proposed that as soon as a child is able to speak, his father must teach him to say: "The Torah that Moses has given us is the heritage of the congregation of Jacob (*Sukkah* 42a). In *Shabbat* 119b Hamnuna Sabba is quoted as saying, "Jerusalem was destroyed only because [the inhabitants] neglected the teaching of schoolchildren."

Hamnuna the Elder

See Hamnuna Sabba.

Henach (fourth century)

Babylonian amora. In *Pesachim* 101b he is noted as principal of an academy.

Hezekiah

See Chizkiyyah.

Hillel (first century B.C.E.)

Also known as Hillel I *or* Hillel ha-Zaken.

One of the greatest Torah scholars, known in English as Hillel the Elder, he was born in Babylonia toward the end of the first century B.C.E. *Sotah* 21a indicates that Hillel had a brother named Shevnah who was engaged in business while Hillel devoted himself to study and, as a consequence, lived in poverty. Shevnah offered to take him in as a partner, but Hillel refused and left Babylonia to study under great teachers such as Shemayah and Avtalyon in Palestine.

Hillel had great difficulty supporting his family and paying for his studies. One Friday in midwinter, it is written in *Yoma* 35b, short on funds to pay the gatekeeper of the academy to attend a lecture, Hillel climbed to the roof of the academy and lay near the skylight, where he could hear the discussion inside. Even though it had begun to snow, Hillel lay there all night long.

The following morning—the Sabbath—the lecture hall seemed darker than usual. The skylight was covered with snow, but when the worshippers looked up they could see the body of a man underneath. They rushed up to the roof, brushed away the snow, and saw that it was Hillel. Immediately they washed him, anointed his body with oil, and warmed him before the fire. Although such work is prohibited on Shabbat, the scholars declared that Hillel was worthy, even of the desecration of the Sabbath.

Before long Hillel was appointed a member of the *beit din*; later, he would be appointed *nasi*—president of the Sanhedrin. He founded the great school known as Beit Hillel. For the next four centuries Hillel's descendants would serve as leaders of Palestinian Jewry; the Hillel dynasty would not end until the death of Hillel II in 365 C.E.

Hillel and his chief intellectual adversary, Shammai, lived during a very oppressive period in Jewish history—the Roman occupation of Palestine. Shammai was concerned that if Jews had too much contact with the Roman heathens, the Jewish community would be weakened. He also felt that liberalizing Jewish law would be harmful and, therefore, favored a very strict interpretation of *halakhah*. Hillel did not share Shammai's fear and was more liberal in his approach to Jewish law. It was as the more popular of the two scholars that Hillel had been chosen to serve as president of the Sanhedrin.

Respected for his scholarship as well as his compassion, Hillel is credited with the popular saying, "What is hateful to you, do not do to your neighbor" (*Shabbat* 31a), an extension of the golden rule's declaration, "Love your neighbor as yourself" (*Leviticus* 19:18).

While Hillel and Shammai themselves did not differ on a great many basic issues of Jewish law, their disciples were often in conflict. The Rabbis of the Talmud generally sided with Beit Hillel—although they were quick to concede that the views of both schools were valid and inspired (*Eruvin* 13b)—believing that a lenient approach to the law would in no way lessen or weaken its observance.

Hillel's liberal attitude, which was based on a deep concern for the welfare of the individual, can be seen in his approach to three important issues facing the Jewish community of the first century B.C.E. Probably the most famous of these was the decision of Hillel to institute the *perozbol*, a legal instrument making it possible for poor landowners to obtain loans immediately prior to a sabbatical year (*Gittin* 37a), when all loans were to be annulled.

The second matter on which Hillel issued an important ruling was with regard to the remarriage of an *agunah*, a woman whose husband had disappeared and it was not known with certainty whether he was alive or dead. Hillel (and most of his colleagues) permitted the *agunah* to remarry even on the basis of indirect evidence of the husband's death. Beit Shammai, on the other hand, required actual witnesses to come forth with direct testimony.

Hillel's regard for the individual can be seen in his attitude toward potential converts, a third issue of great consequence to the Jewish community of his time. Hillel favored the admission of proselytes even when they made unreasonable demands. One heathen, a prospective proselyte, insisted that he be taught the whole Torah "while standing on one foot"; Shammai rejected him, but Hillel responded kindly, saying: "What is hateful to you, do not do to your neighbor." Another heathen approached Hillel and Shammai, offering to become a proselyte if he could become High Priest. Shammai dismissed him promptly, while Hillel responded benevolently (*Shabbat* 31a).

Patient and gentle, Hillel was a seeker of peace. One of the most interesting legends concerns a man who wagered a large sum of money that he could make Hillel angry:

On a Friday, at the very time that Hillel was bathing in preparation for the Sabbath, this man ran up and down in front of Hillel's house, shouting in a loud voice: "Who is Hillel and where is he?" Hillel wrapped himself in a cloak, stepped outside, and said, "I am Hillel. What do you want, my son?"

"I want to ask you a question," the man said.

"Ask," Hillel replied, "and whatever I know I will tell you."

"I want to know," the man said, "why the Babylonians have round heads."

"You have asked a proper question," Hillel answered. "It is because the Babylonians do not have skilled midwives; therefore the heads of the newborn children become rounded in their hands."

A moment later the man shouted again, "Hillel, where is Hillel?"

Again Hillel wrapped himself in a cloak, came out, and said, "I am Hillel. What do you want, my son?"

"Can you tell me," the man asked, "why the eyes of the people of Tadmor are weak?"

"You have asked well," Hillel replied. "It is because Tadmor is located in a sandy region, and dust gets into people's eyes."

Once more the man shouted, "Hillel, where is Hillel?"

For the third time, Hillel wrapped himself in a cloak and came out to answer the man: "Here I am. What to you want, my son?"

"I want to know," the man said, "why the feet of the Africans are so wide."

"It is a good question," Hillel answered. "It is a result of their going barefoot in swampy land."

Thereupon the man said, "I wish to ask you other questions but I fear that you will be angry."

"You may ask as many questions as you want, and I shall answer them to the best of my knowledge," Hillel replied.

"Are you Hillel, the *nasi* among Jews?" the man cried out.

"I am he," Hillel replied.

"Then I hope there are no more like you among the Jews."

"Why do you wish that?" Hillel asked.

"Because through you I have lost a large sum of money. I wagered that I could make you angry and now I do not know what to do to anger you."

To this Hillel replied, "Even if you were to lose twice that sum, still you could not anger me."

Hillel left many outstanding disciples, the youngest of all—Yochanan ben Zakkai—the most important. Yochanan summarized Hillel's brilliance in these words: "If all the heavens were parchments, and all the trees were quills, and all the seas were ink, it still would be impossible for me to write down even a small part of all that I have learned from my teacher. And if I could, all this would be only as much as a fly might absorb when plunging into the sea."

Many popular maxims attributed to Hillel are quoted in *Avot*. Among them are:

- Be of the disciples of Aaron, one who loves peace, loves mankind, and brings them close to the Torah. (1:12)
- If I am not for myself, who will be for me? If I care only for myself, what am I? If not now, when? (1:14)
- Do not keep aloof from the community; don't be too sure of yourself until the day of your death. (2:5)
- Do not judge your fellowman until you have been in his place. (2:4)
- Do not say, "When I have leisure, I will study." You may never have leisure. (2:4)

Hillel was succeeded as head of the Sanhedrin by his son Shimon.

Hillel I

See Hillel.

Hillel II (fourth century)

Palestinian amora. Hillel II succeeded his father, Yehudah III, as patriarch and president of the Sanhedrin in 320 C.E. Hillel II is best known for certain calendar reforms instituted during his term of office to equalize the solar and lunar years so that the holidays would be celebrated on the days called for in the Torah.

Despite the fact that Hillel II was on friendly terms with the Roman emperor Julian, during Hillel's term of office Babylonia overshadowed Palestine as the center of Jewish learning, and the role of patriarch lost its importance.

Chullin 53a records that Hillel II and Ashi had studied together in the academy run by Kahana. In *Beitzah* 36b, Hillel II is noted as a disciple of Rava and in *Shabbat* 109a and *Beitzah* 40a as a contemporary of Ravina. In *Pesachim* 115a Hillel comments on the practice of eating a sandwich of *matzah* and *maror* (bitter herb) at the Passover *Seder*.

Though Hillel II's son, Gamli'el V, succeeded his father as patriarch upon Hillel II's death in 365, the patriarchal legacy of Hillel the Elder effectively came to an end.

Hillel ben Samuel ben Nachman

See Hillel ben Shemu'el ben Nachman.

Hillel ben Shemu'el ben Nachman (fourth century)

Palestinian amora. He studied under his father, Levi ben Chama, and was, according to *Bava Batra* 98a, a colleague of Ashi. Hillel ben Shemu'el ben Nachman is quoted as saying: "There will be no Messiah for Israel because they have enjoyed him during the reign of Hezekiah" (*Sanhedrin* 98b).

Hillel ben Valess (third century)

Palestinian amora. In *Sanhedrin* 36a and *Gittin* 59a he is quoted as saying: "From Moses until Rabbi [Yehuda ha-Nasi] we do not find Torah and high office combined in one place [person]."

Hillel ha-Zaken

See Hillel.

Hon ben Nachman (fourth century)

Babylonian amora. In *Yevamot* 34b and 112a he is noted as a colleague of Nachman (bar Ya'akov).

Hosea

See Hoshe'a.

Hoshaya bar Idi (fourth/fifth century)

Also spelled Oshaya bar Idi.

Babylonian amora. In *Yevamot* 36b he is mentioned as a colleague of Ashi.

Hoshe'a (fourth century)

Palestinian amora. In *Yoma* 39b he comments on how Lebanon got its name.

Huna (third century)

Babylonian amora. He succeeded Rav as principal of the academy at Sura and served in that capacity for forty years, until his death in 297. Huna was regarded by Babylonian and Palestinian scholars alike as an important legal authority. He served as exilarch between the years 170 and 210.

Huna was not born into wealth. A farmer who owned a palm grove, he was not ashamed of getting his hands dirty (*Megillah* 28a and *Ketubbot* 105a). Later, when Huna attained great wealth, he shared his riches with his employees. It is said that when Huna sat down to dinner, he opened the door of his house and invited anyone who was hungry to join him (*Ta'anit* 20b). He supported scholars for months at a time while they studied at his school, and legend has it that as many as eight hundred students attended his lectures and ate in his home at one time.

Numbered among Huna's teachers were Rav (*Kiddushin* 3b and *Pesachim* 3b) and Chiya bar Avin (*Ta'anit* 8a). Among Huna's disciples were Abba (*Shabbat* 41a), Zerika (*Sotah* 21b), and Rava and Chelbo (*Berakhot* 5a). Shemu'el (*Gittin* 5a) and Ashi (*Shabbat* 37b) were among his prominent colleagues.

Huna's legal opinions and observations covered a broad spectrum:

- The proper height of an *eruv* (*Eruvin* 84a and 88a)
- The proper time to search for leaven on the day preceding Pesach, 14 Nisan (*Pesachim* 2a and 3a)
- Who may and who may not blow the *shofar* for others (*Rosh Hashanah* 29a)
- Proper conduct in synagogue (*Berakhot* 24b)

Huna respected those Jews who fasted every Monday and Thursday, referring to them as *yechidim*—singularly pious people. On the other hand, Huna said, "When a man sins once and once again [and there are no repercussions], he begins to believe his conduct is acceptable" (*Yoma* 86b).

When Huna died suddenly in his eighties, his son, Rabbah bar Huna, took his father's body to Palestine, where he had asked to be buried. Rabbah was met there by distinguished scholars who placed Huna's body in the vault of Chiyya, a fellow Babylonian.

Huna's reputation was so great that his successors often prayed to God to grant them the wisdom of Huna. His wisdom is exemplified in the famous remark he made that "He who occupies himself *only* with Torah study acts as if he had no God" (*Avodah Zarah* 17b).

For four decades Huna led Babylonian Jewry, and by reason of his undisputed authority, the Jewish community of Babylonia became completely independent of Judea.

Huna bar Acha (third century)
Babylonian amora. According to *Keritot* 8a, he was a disciple of Elazar.

Huna bar Ashi (third century)
Babylonian amora. In *Sotah* 16b he is mentioned as a disciple of Rav.

Huna bar Aviya (fourth century)
Babylonian amora. In *Bava Batra* 143a he is listed as a colleague of Mordekhai and Ashi.

Huna bar Bizna
See Chana bar Bizna.

Huna bar Chaluv (fourth century)
Babylonian amora. In *Shabbat* 115b he asks his colleague Nachman bar Ya'akov about the *kashrut* of a Torah scroll in which letters are missing.

Huna bar Chanina (fourth century)
Also known as Huna bar Chinena.
Babylonian amora. In *Berakhot* 30a Huna bar Chanina is

noted as a disciple of Chiyya bar Rav, in *Kiddushin* 20b and 21a as a disciple of Sheshet, and in *Kiddushin* 42a as a disciple of Nachman bar Yitzchak. Huna bar Chanina also studied under Abbayei and Rava, and in *Ketubbot* 100a is mentioned as a disciple of Nachman bar Ya'akov. Among Huna bar Chanina's colleagues were Ze'eira (*Berakhot* 39a), Yosef (*Eruvin* 14b), Safra and Acha bar Huna (*Shabbat* 124a), and Pappa (*Pesachim* 16a).

According to *Eruvin* 25b, the exilarch consulted with Huna bar Chanina as to whether it was permissible for him to hold a banquet on the Sabbath in his orchard and to carry food from his house to the garden area. The question was whether this would violate the Sabbath prohibition against carrying from the private domain to the public domain. Huna proceeded to erect a passageway—a reed fence—uniting the two areas and making the carrying of food from one to the other permissible.

Huna bar Chinena

See Huna bar Chanina.

Huna bar Chivan (sixth century)

Babylonian amora. He is referred to in *Shabbat* 139b.

Huna bar Chiyya (third/fourth century)

Babylonian amora. In his youth he attended Huna's academy in Sura, where he studied under Shemu'el (*Ta'anit* 10a). In *Shabbat* 47a and *Mo'ed Katan* 26a Huna bar Chiyya is named as a colleague of Levi bar Shemu'el. *Sanhedrin* 100a relates that the two of them repaired Torah mantles. In *Bava Kamma* 116b Huna bar Chiyya is listed as a colleague of Nachman bar Ya'akov.

Huna bar Diskarta (third/fourth century)

Babylonian amora. In *Bava Metzi'a* 47a he is mentioned as a colleague of Rava.

Huna bar Hoshaya (third century)

Also known as Huna bar Oshaya.

Babylonian amora. In *Horayot* 3b he is noted as a contemporary of Yonatan.

Huna bar Idi (third/fourth century)

Babylonian amora. According to *Rosh Hashanah* 24b, Huna bar Idi learned from a discourse given by Abbayei that since man is made in the image of God (*Genesis* 1:27), it is forbidden to make likenesses of the human face.

Huna bar Ika (fourth century)

Babylonian amora. In *Berakhot* 43b he is noted as a colleague of Pappa and in *Pesachim* 52b as a traveling companion of Safra and Kahana. In Talmudic times, *tefillin* were worn all day long, even on the street, and not merely at morning services as is the practice today. According to *Beitzah* 15a, Huna bar Ika objected to Abbayei's comment on what one is to do if he is on his way home as the Sabbath approaches and he is wearing his *tefillin*. Abbayei said: "He must place his hand over the *tefillin* on his head until he reaches home," rather than leave them in the academy where he had been wearing them, lest they be lost.

Huna bar Ila'i (third century)

Babylonian amora. In *Yoma* 35b he is noted as a contemporary of Shemu'el bar Yehudah.

Huna bar Jeremiah

See Huna bar Yirmeyahu.

Huna bar Joshua

See Huna bar Yehoshu'a.

Huna bar Judah

See Huna bar Yehudah.

Huna bar Kettina (third century)

Babylonian amora. Apparently he studied in Palestine, where he was a disciple of Shimon ben Lakish (*Chullin* 17b). In *Zevachim* 115b Huna bar Kettina is mentioned as a disciple of Chisda.

Huna bar Mano'ach (fourth century)

Babylonian amora. He was a disciple of Rava (*Ta'anit* 9a), Acha bar Ika (*Megillah* 25b and *Gittin* 24a), and Idi bar Ika (*Yevamot* 43a), about whom nothing more is known.

Huna bar Mar Zutra

See Huna bar Zutra.

Huna bar Minyomi (third century)

Babylonian amora. In *Avodah Zarah* 39a he is listed as a colleague of Amram Chasida, from whose wife he bought blue wool to make *tzitzit*, which he did to earn a livelihood.

Huna bar Mosheh (fourth century)

Babylonian amora. He was a *Kohen* and a contemporary of Abbayei. According to *Bava Batra* 174b, Huna's father, Mosheh bar Atzri, was named as guarantor in the *ketubbah* of Huna's wife, since Huna was but a poor scholar. This is the only place in the Talmud where Mosheh is used as a personal name.

Huna bar Nachman (fourth century)

Babylonian amora. In *Chullin* 49b he is noted as a colleague of Huna ben Chinena, in *Avodah Zarah* 57b as a contemporary of Elyakim, and in *Bava Metzi'a* 47a as a contemporary of Ashi. In *Avodah Zarah* 57b Huna bar Nachman comments on the sale of wine to Gentiles.

Huna bar Natan (fourth century)

Babylonian amora. In *Berakhot* 42a he is mentioned as a friend of Pappa and in *Eruvin* 58b as a disciple of Rava. Although he served as exilarch, *Gittin* 59a says that he deferred to the more learned scholar Ashi, and *Berakhot* 46b reveals that he engaged in a dispute with the blind amora Sheshet as to the proper etiquette to be followed at mealtime.

Although Huna bar Natan was not regarded as an outstanding teacher, he was invited to dine at the home of the great scholar Nachman bar Yitzchak. When some of the guests asked him his name, he replied "Rav Huna," using the rabbinic title.

When he was invited to sit on the couch, he sat, although it was common practice for only distinguished persons to sit on a couch, while ordinary persons sat on stools.

When Nachman's distinguished visitors offered Huna some wine, he accepted it at the first offering and helped himself to a second serving, thus displaying poor breeding.

When asked to explain his actions, Huna said he was following the popular precept that "Whatever your host tells you to do, you should do" (*Pesachim* 86b).

In some texts of the Talmud, Huna's comment has been changed to read: "Everything that a host tells you to do, do, except [leave his premises]." This bit of humor makes the point that one should not overstay a visit.

Huna bar Nathan
See Huna bar Natan.

Huna bar Nechemyah (fifth/sixth century)
Babylonian amora. In *Chullin* 17b he questioned his teacher, Ashi, about the type of knife a *shochet* may use.

Huna bar Nehemiah
See Huna bar Nechemyah.

Huna bar Oshaya
See Huna bar Hoshaya.

Huna bar Phinehas
See Huna bar Pinchas.

Huna bar Pinchas (third century)
Babylonian amora. In *Mo'ed Katan* 15b he is noted as a disciple of Yosef.

Huna bar Rava (fifth century)
Babylonian amora. In *Bava Kamma* 72a he is listed as a colleague of Ashi.

Huna bar Sechorah (third/fourth century)
Babylonian amora. In *Chullin* 107b he is noted a colleague of Hamnuna.

Huna bar Tachlifa (fourth century)
Babylonian amora. In *Kiddushin* 71a he is listed as a disciple of Rav, and in *Yevamot* 8b as a disciple of Rava.

Huna bar Yehoshu'a (fourth/fifth century)
Babylonian amora. In *Yoma* 49a and *Berakhot* 22b he is noted as a good friend of Pappa, with whom he later entered into partnership in the beer business. When Pappa became principal of the academy in Naresh, Huna was appointed *reish kallah*, head of the general assembly. Their friendship continued throughout their lives, and when Huna became ill, *Rosh Hashanah* 17a reports that Pappa came to visit him.

Huna bar Yehoshu'a was concerned with many aspects of Jewish life. In *Shabbat* 22b he discusses the law regarding lighting one lamp from another on the Sabbath, and in *Mo'ed Katan* 19b he rules on how mourning is to be observed on a festival.

One of the sayings for which he is best known is found in

Kiddushin 31a: "May I be helped [by God] for never having walked more than four cubits bareheaded," one of the reasons always given for wearing a *kippah.*

Huna bar Yehoshu'a died in 410.

Huna bar Yehudah (fourth/fifth century)

Babylonian amora. In *Berakhot* 52b and *Nedarim* 19b he is listed as a colleague and disciple of Rava, whose academy he attended (*Shabbat* 24a). Huna bar Yehudah also studied under Menachem (*Berakhot* 8a) and Sheshet (*Eruvin* 89a and *Ketubbot* 63b).

Huna bar Yirmeyahu (fifth century)

Babylonian amora. In *Pesachim* 43a he defines the term "oil of myrrh," which is mentioned in the *Book of Esther* (2:12), as *satkat,* identified by some scholars as cinnamon.

Huna bar Zavdi (third century)

Babylonian amora. In *Arakhin* 13b he is listed as a disciple of Huna.

Huna bar Zutra (third/fourth century)

Also known as Huna bar Mar Zutra.

Babylonian amora. In *Bava Batra* 86a he is mentioned as a colleague of Ravina I, with whom he discusses at which point a sale may be considered final. Huna's son, Zutra, served as exilarch, was imprisoned during the Persian persecution of Babylonian Jewry, and was executed in 470.

Huna ben Ammi (third century)

Palestinian amora. In *Berakhot* 55b he is noted as a disciple of Pedat, whom he quotes as saying, "If one has a dream that makes him sad, he should go and have it interpreted [by an expert] in the presence of three persons."

Huna ben Avin (fourth/fifth century)

Also known as Hunya.

Palestinian amora. Babylonian by birth, Huna ben Avin studied in Palestine with Yirmeyahu ben Abba, a fellow Babylonian who had migrated to Palestine. *Nedarim* 77b points out that when Huna ben Avin lived in Babylonia, he was well acquainted with Rava, principal of the academy in Machoza.

Huna ben Berekhyah (second century)

Palestinian tanna. In *Berakhot* 63a he is noted as a disciple of Elazar ha-Kappar. Huna ben Berekhyah taught that whoever praises God, even when he suffers evil, will have his sustenance doubled.

Huna ben Torta (second/third century)

Palestinian tanna. In *Chullin* 127a he is mentioned as a disciple of Shimon ha-Tsadik.

Huna Mar bar Aviya (fifth century)

Babylonian amora. *Chullin* 47a records a dispute between Huna Mar bar Aviya and Ashi about the *kashrut* of an animal with unusually formed lungs.

Huna Mar bar Chiyya (fourth/fifth century)

Babylonian amora. In *Chullin* 58b, he questions the ruling Ashi was about to pronounce declaring an animal to be *tereifah*.

Huna Mar bar Idi (third century)

Babylonian amora. In *Chullin* 49a he discusses whether an animal is kosher if a needle is found in its portal vein.

Huna Mar bar Mareimar (third/fourth century)

Babylonian amora. In *Bava Metzi'a* 81a he is noted as a student of Ravina I.

Huna Mar bar Nechemyah (fourth/fifth century)

Babylonian amora. In *Gittin* 14a, *Kiddushin* 6b, and *Chullin* 51b he is mentioned as a disciple of Ashi.

Huna Mar bar Nehemiah

See Huna Mar bar Nechemyah.

Huna Mar bar Rava of Parzikya (fourth/fifth century)

Babylonian amora. Son of the Babylonian amora Rava of Parzikya, Huna is noted in *Ketubbot* 10a as a colleague of Ashi.

Huna of Choza'ah (fourth/fifth century)

Also known as Chanin of Choza'ah.

Babylonian amora. In *Kiddushin* 6b he is listed as a colleague of Ashi.

Huna of Sepphoris (third/fourth century)

Palestinian tanna. According to *Rosh Hashanah* 34b, Huna of Sepphoris was a pupil of Yochanan bar Nappacha, whose sayings he transmitted, and in *Chullin* 51a Huna is noted as a colleague of Yosei Mada'ah.

Huna of Sura (third century)

Babylonian amora. In *Zevachim* 91a and *Keritot* 10a he is noted as a contemporary of Yehudah bar Yechezkel.

Hunya

See Huna ben Avin.

Hurkanos of Kefar Eitam (first/second century)

Palestinian tanna. In *Yevamot* 106b he comments on the *chalitzah* procedure.

Hyrcanus of Kefar Eitam

See Hurkanos of Kefar Eitam.

I

Ibu

See Aivu.

Idi (third century)

Babylonian amora. In *Shabbat* 120a, Abba ben Zavda is listed as Idi's disciple, as is Rabbah bar Nachmani in *Eruvin* 57b. In *Avodah Zarah* 25b Idi is quoted as saying: "Every woman has her weapons on her," implying that her physical weakness is her protection against being murdered.

Idi Avuha de-Rabbi Ya'akov (third century)

Also known as Idi, Father of Jacob ben Idi.

Palestinian amora. A disciple of the illustrious Yochanan bar Nappacha, Idi often traveled six months at a time to raise funds for Yochanan's academy. *Chagigah* 5b notes, however, that Idi would always return home to be with his family for Pesach and Sukkot.

Idi bar Avin (fourth century)

Babylonian amora. His father, Avin bar Nachman, was a carpenter, as noted in *Shabbat* 23b. Idi's brother, Chiyya bar Avin, also was a scholar. The family lived in Naresh, a small Babylonian town that housed an important academy.

Pesachim 49a records that Idi married a *Kohen*'s daughter and fathered two sons, Sheshet and Yehoshu'a, who also became scholars. In *Pesachim* 35a Idi is noted as a teacher of Pappa and Huna bar Yehoshu'a, and in *Kiddushin* 30b as a disciple of Rav.

Idi bar Ika

Of unknown date and origin, he is mentioned only once in the Talmud, in *Yevamot* 43a, as a teacher of Huna bar Mano'ach.

Idi bar Shisha (fifth century)

Babylonian amora. In *Pesachim* 106a he is noted as a colleague of Mar bar Rav Ashi.

Idi ben Idi ben Gershom (second century)
Palestinian amora. In *Chullin* 98a he is mentioned as a disciple of Levi ben Perata.

Idi, Father of Ya'akov ben Idi
See Idi Avuha de-Rabbi Ya'akov.

Idra (third century)
Babylonian amora. In *Rosh Hashanah* 23a he is mentioned as a member of Shila's academy.

Ika (second/third century)
Babylonian amora. According to *Megillah* 3a, he was a disciple of Rav; *Bava Kamma* 22a lists him as a teacher of Huna bar Mano'ach.

Ika bar Ammi (third/fourth century)
Babylonian amora. In *Bava Batra* 149a he is noted as a contemporary of Rava. In *Bava Kamma* 12a–b Ika bar Ammi expresses his attitude toward slaves, whom he considered personal property and not real estate.

Ika bar Avin (third century)
Babylonian amora. In *Kiddushin* 72a and *Nedarim* 37b he is said to have been a disciple of Chananel.

Ika bar Chanina (third century)
Babylonian amora. In *Chullin* 90b he is mentioned as a contemporary of Chisda. In *Eruvin* 100b Ika comments on the commandment "be fruitful and multiply," bringing proof from Scripture that a man may not compel his wife to have intercourse, and in *Shabbat* 39b voices his opinion on whether heated water may be used for personal washing on holidays.

Ika of Pashruniya (third/fourth century)
Babylonian amora. According to *Eruvin* 104a, he was a colleague of Rava.

Ila'a
See Ila'i II.

Ila'i I (second century)
Also known as Ila'i the Elder.
Palestinian tanna. A disciple of Eli'ezer ben Hurkanos, it is reported in *Sukkah* 27b that Ila'i I traveled to Lydda to pay his respects

to his master when Eli'ezer ben Hurkanos became principal of the academy there. In *Gittin* 6b Ila'i is noted as a contemporary of Yishma'el and in *Eruvin* 64b as a contemporary of Gamli'el II.

Ila'i is best remembered for the following saying: "A person's character is revealed in three ways: by his cup [*koso*, meaning his consumption of liquor], his pocket [*kiso*, meaning his charitable donations]; and his temper [*ka'aso*] (*Eruvin* 65b).

Another one of Ila'i I's famous sayings, reported in *Chagigah* 16a, *Kiddushin* 40a, and *Mo'ed Katan* 17a, reads: "When a man sees that his evil inclination [*yetzer ha-ra*] is gaining mastery over him [and he is unable to control his sexual urge], let him go to a place where he is unknown, dress in black garments [so that he will not be recognized], and do what his heart desires, rather than profane the name of God openly."

Ila'i II (third/fourth century)
Also known as Ila'a.
Palestinian amora. In *Eruvin* 14a and *Berakhot* 13b he is noted as a disciple of Rav, and in *Chullin* 50a as a disciple of Yochanan bar Nappacha. In *Chullin* 24b, where Ila'i II's name appears as Ila'a, he quotes his teacher Chanina on the question of when a *Kohen* is no longer eligible to serve in the Sanctuary, and until what age one is considered youthful and healthy. Chanina said: "Until he begins to tremble."

Ila'i reveals his understanding of the human condition when he states: "The world exists on the merit of those who control themselves in confrontational situations" (*Chullin* 89a). In *Yevamot* 65b he quotes his mentor, Elazar ben Shimon, asserting that one may tell a white lie for the sake of peace. As an example, Ila'i cites *Genesis* 50:16–17, in which his brothers say to Joseph: "Thy father did command before he died . . . So shall you say to Joseph: 'Forgive, I pray you now the transgressions of your brothers . . . ,'" when in fact Jacob never said any such thing. The brothers, however, attributed this statement to Jacob for the sake of establishing peace between themselves and Joseph.

Ila'i bar Elazar (second/third century)
Babylonian amora. In *Shabbat* 60a he is mentioned as a contemporary of Shemu'el.

Ila'i the Elder
See Ila'i I.

Ilfa (second/third century)
Also known as Ilfi.

Palestinian amora. According to *Ta'anit* 24a, where his name is rendered Ilfi, Ilfa was a contemporary of Yehudah ha-Nasi. *Ta'anit* 21a relates that Yochanan bar Nappacha and Ilfa studied together, but when they found themselves without funds, they decided to become partners in business. Before long, Yochanan had a change of heart and returned to the academy, while Ilfa, who had an extremely sharp mind, continued to pursue his business interests. When Yochanan became head of the academy in Tiberias, he said to Ilfa: "Had you returned to your studies, you might have been head of the academy."

Ilfi
See Ilfa.

Ilish (fourth century)
Babylonian amora. In *Bava Batra* 133b and *Gittin* 77b, Ilish is mentioned as a disciple of Rava. According to *Bava Metzi'a* 68b, Rava said of him that he was "a great man" who was very honest in arranging a business deal.

Imma Shalom (first/second century)
Shabbat 116a–b paints her as a highly gifted woman who, along with Me'ir's wife, Beruryah, was one of the most prominent women in Talmudic times. The wife of Eli'ezer ben Hurkanos and sister of Gamli'el II, Imma Shalom exerted considerable influence on both of them, although *Bava Metzi'a* 59b records that Eli'ezer ben Hurkanos was excommunicated during Gamli'el II's patriarchate because he refused to accept a decision of the Sages.

In *Nedarim* 20b Imma Shalom explains why her children are so handsome: "My husband is intimate with me neither at the beginning of the night nor at the end of the night, only at midnight [when his thoughts are pure and only of me]."

Immi
See Ammi.

Ina (third century)
Babylonian amora. In *Sukkah* 50b he is noted as a colleague of Yehudah bar Yechezkel.

Inyani ben Sasson (second century)
Palestinian tanna. In *Zevachim* 88b he is listed as a disciple of Dosa ben Harkinas.

Isaac
See Yitzchak.

Ishmael
See Yishma'el.

Isi bar Chini
See Assi bar Chini.

Isi bar Isaac bar Judah
See Isi bar Yitzchak bar Yehudah.

Isi bar Natan (third/fourth century)
Also known as Yosei bar Natan.
Babylonian amora. In *Berakhot* 62a he discusses proper etiquette for using the privy. In *Bava Batra* 121a, where he is mentioned as a pupil of Sheshet, Isi is referred to as Yosei bar Natan.

Isi bar Nathan
See Isi bar Natan.

Isi bar Yitzchak bar Yehudah (third/fourth century)
Babylonian amora. Isi was the son of amora Yitzchak bar Yehudah. According to *Yoma* 64b, Isi's daughter Choma was married three times: to Rechavah of Pumbedita, to Yitzchak bar Rabbah bar Chana, and to Abbayei.

Isi ben Gamali'el
See Isi ben Yehudah.

Isi ben Gamli'el
See Isi ben Yehudah.

Isi ben Judah
See Isi ben Yehudah.

Isi ben Menachem (second century)
Also known as Yosei ben Menachem.
Palestinian tanna. He is quoted in *Sotah* 16a.

Isi ben Yehudah (second century)

Also known as Isi ben Gamli'el, Isi ha-Bavli, *and* Yosei Ketanta.

Palestinian tanna. Born in Hutzal, Babylonia, an important center of Jewish learning, Isi ben Yehudah was known by many names, among them Isi ha-Bavli, in English, Isi the Babylonian. Isi is a short Aramaic form of Yosef.

When Isi moved to Palestine to pursue his studies, he changed his name to Isi ben Gamli'el. He also was known there as Yosei Ketanta, which means "youngest," and is described as "the youngest of the pious men" (*Sotah* 49a). In Palestine he studied with some of the disciples of Akiva ben Yosef, in particular Elazar ben Shammu'a (*Menachot* 18a).

In *Chullin* 63b, where there is a discussion as to how many unclean birds is meant by the words in *Leviticus* 11:14, "after its kind," Isi comments: "In the East [Babylonia] there are one hundred unclean birds all of the *ayyah* species."

Isi ha-Bavli

See Isi ben Yehudah.

Isi the Babylonian

See Isi ben Yehudah.

Ivu

See Aivu.

Ivya

See Aviya.

J

Names that begin with the Hebrew letter yud *can be found under the letter* Y.

Jacob
> *See* Ya'akov.

Jeremiah
> *See* Yirmeyahu.

Johanan
> *See* Yochanan ben Nappacha.

Jonah
> *See* Yonah.

Jonathan
> *See* Yonatan.

Jose
> *See* Yosei.

Joseph
> *See* Yosef.

Joshua
> *See* Yehoshu'a.

Josiah
> *See* Yoshiyyahu.

Judah
> See Yehudah.

Kahana

Eruvin 8b lists five scholars named Kahana who were active in different generations. The two most prominent are:

1. A third/fourth-century Palestinian amora who is described in *Bava Metzi'a* 84a as a very sensitive scholar. In *Nedarim* 39b–40a Kahana reprimanded his fellow scholars for not visiting their colleague Chelbo when he was sick.

Among Kahana's teachers were Ulla (*Ketubbot* 74a) and Yochanan bar Nappacha (*Bava Kamma* 20b and *Ketubbot* 46b). Once, when Yochanan was lecturing, Kahana challenged him on a matter of law. Yochanan's face was distorted because of an accident, and Kahana thought Yochanan was laughing at him. When Yochanan was told that Kahana was insulted, he made every effort to placate Kahana (*Bava Kamma* 117a–b).

2. A third/fourth century Babylonian amora who is described in *Bava Batra* 58a as being as handsome as his teacher Rav.

In *Shabbat* 63a Kahana says: "By the time I was eighteen years old, I had studied the whole *shas* [an acronym for *shishah sedarim*, the "six orders" of the Mishnah]."

In *Sukkah* 7a and 19a, as well as in many other tractates, Kahana is mentioned as a teacher of Ashi. Despite Ashi's youth, Kahana respected him greatly and sometimes referred to him as "Mari," a title of distinction. *Ketubbot* 8a refers to a wedding held in Ashi's house that was attended by Kahana.

Kahana served as head of the yeshiva in Pumbedita for twenty years. When Kahana fell ill, the Rabbis sent Yehoshu'a bar Idi to determine Kahana's condition. Idi arrived to find that Kahana had already died and immediately rent his garment (*Pesachim* 3b).

Kahana Achuha de-Rav Yehudah (third century)

Babylonian amora. Known in English as Kahana, brother of Judah, he is mentioned in *Chullin* 111b as a student of Huna.

Kahana bar Chinena Sabba (fifth century)

Also known as Kahana bar Chinena the Elder.

Babylonian amora. In *Pesachim* 76b he is noted as a contemporary of Rava of Parzikya and Mar bar Rav Ashi. Kahana's father, Chinena Sabba, also was an amora.

Kahana bar Chinena the Elder

See Kahana bar Chinena Sabba.

Kahana bar Malkiyyah (third century)

Babylonian amora. In *Eruvin* 8b he is named as a teacher of Kahana bar Minyomi.

Kahana bar Minyomi (third century)

Babylonian amora. In *Eruvin* 8b he is noted as a disciple of Kahana bar Malkiyyah and a teacher of Kahana bar Tachlifa.

Kahana bar Natan (fourth/fifth century)

Babylonian amora. In *Yevamot* 60b he is named as a contemporary of Ashi.

Kahana bar Nathan

See Kahana bar Natan.

Kahana bar Nechemyah (third/fourth century)

Babylonian amora. According to *Yevamot* 71b, he was a contemporary of Rava.

Kahana bar Nechunya (third century)

Babylonian amora. He is quoted in *Ta'anit* 24b, where he is listed as the personal attendant of Yehudah bar Yechezkel.

Kahana bar Nehemiah

See Kahana bar Nechemyah.

Kahana bar Tachlifa (third century)

Babylonian amora. In *Eruvin* 8b he is noted as a disciple of Kahana bar Minyomi.

Kahana, Brother of Yehudah

See Kahana Achuha de-Rav Yehudah.

Kahana Chamuha de-Rav Mesharshya
(third/fourth century)

Babylonian amora. Known in English as Kahana, Father-in-law of Rabbi Mesharshya, he is mentioned in *Bava Batra* 97b as a disciple of Rava.

Kahana, Father-in-law of Rabbi Mesharshya
See Kahana Chamuha de-Rav Mesharshya.

Kailil (third/fourth century)
Babylonian amora. He was a younger brother of Rabba bar Nachmani.

Kalba Savu'a (first century)
One of the wealthiest Jerusalemites of his time, he was the father-in-law of Akiva ben Yosef.

Karna (second/third century)
Babylonian amora. To earn a living, he worked in a wine store sampling the aroma of the goods to determine whether it was safe to store them. Among Karna's friends and colleagues were Shemu'el and Rav. In *Kiddushin* 44b he disagrees with Shemu'el on the status of a minor betrothed by her father without her consent. If the girl does not wish to go through with the marriage, she requires a *get*, according to Shemu'el; Karna says it is an open question. According to *Bava Kamma* 47b, Karna founded a school known as the School of Karna.

Kashisha bar Chisda (fourth/fifth century)
Also known as Mar Kashisha bar Chisda.

Babylonian amora. The brother of Yanuka, Kashisha is noted in *Menachot* 109b as a student of Abbayei and in *Sukkah* 8a, *Sanhedrin* 45b, and *Avodah Zarah* 71b as a student of Ashi.

Kashisha and Yanuka told Ashi that once, when Ameimar visited their town, he refused to recite *Havdalah* because they had no wine. This story is recounted in *Pesachim* 107a.

Kashisha bar Rava (third/fourth century)
Also known as Mar Kashisha bar Rava.

Babylonian amora. According to *Shabbat* 95a, he was a disciple of Ashi.

Kattina

See Kettina.

Kedi (third century)

Babylonian amora. Scholars believe this may have been a fictitious name. In *Yoma* 44a he is noted as a contemporary of Adda bar Ahava.

Keruspedai bar Shabbetai (second/third century)

Palestinian amora. According to *Rosh Hashanah* 16b he was a disciple of Yochanan bar Nappacha and according to *Niddah* 46a a contemporary of Yosei ben Yehudah.

Kettina (third century)

Also spelled Kattina.

Babylonian amora. Though little is known about his personal life, the Talmud refers to him as a holy man to whom the prophet Elijah appeared several times. According to *Bava Metzi'a* 55a, Kettina was a colleague of Rava and, according to *Bava Metzi'a* 79a, a teacher of Chisda.

Kettina's comments on a variety of subjects are quite unusual. In *Berakhot* 59a he expresses an opinion on the nature of earthquakes. He explains the rumbling of the earth as being caused by God clasping his hands together, as noted in *Ezekiel* 21:22: "I will also strike my hands together, and I will satisfy my fury . . ." In *Niddah* 31b Kettina says that he has it in his power to father only male children by controlling himself and allowing his wife to emit her "semen" first, a common understanding in Talmudic times.

In *Rosh Hashanah* 31a and *Sanhedrin* 97a Kettina predicts that the world will exist for six thousand years, and then, in the seventh millennium, be utterly destroyed. His view is based on an interpretation of *Isaiah* 11:11, in which the word *day* is said to be reckoned by God as one thousand years. *Psalms* 90:4 uses a similar metaphor.

Kohen (third/fourth century)

Babylonian amora. In *Bava Kamma* 115a he is mentioned as a contemporary of Ravina I.

L

Lazar

See Elazar.

Leili bar Memel (third century)

Babylonian amora. According to *Yevamot* 12a, he was a disciple of Ukba and Shemu'el.

Levi (third century)

See also Levi ben Lachma.

Palestinian amora. He always is referred to as Levi without patronymic and is sometimes confused with Levi ben Lachma, as in *Rosh Hashanah* 29b. In some Midrashic sources the title "Berabbi" has been added to his name.

In *Shabbat* 59b, Rav describes Levi as "a great, tall, lame man." Levi was a very respectful scholar and in *Eruvin* 63a has harsh words for anybody who would answer a question in the presence of his teacher rather than defer to him. Levi's teacher, Yehudah ha-Nasi, thought so highly of him that he sent him to be a teacher and judge in an outlying town (*Yevamot* 9a). Chama ben Chanina also was a primary influence in Levi's life, and Levi quotes him frequently.

While Levi handed down halakhic decisions, his principal interest was in the field of *aggadah*. He once said that aggadists can be divided into two categories: those who can string pearls (that is, penetrate the depths of Scripture), and those who can perforate but cannot string them.

One of Levi's most popular parables is found in *Yalkut Shimoni* ("Noach" 59):

> When God commanded Noah to include two of each kind of animal in the ark, Falsehood tried to enter, but Noah said, "You cannot, for you have no mate." Falsehood

searched for a mate and met Sin. Falsehood asked whether Sin would accompany him into the ark. Sin asked what the reward would be for doing so, and Falsehood promised that everything that he would earn, he would give to Sin. When they left the ark, Sin took everything that Falsehood had gained. When Falsehood protested, Sin reminded him of their pact. Falsehood thereupon replied: "How could you ever believe that I meant to do as I promised?"

Another of Levi's teachers was Pappi, who studied under Yehoshu'a of Sikhnin (*Bava Batra* 75b). Sheshet was a disciple of Levi (*Chullin* 134b). Levi is quoted as saying in *Bava Batra* 75b: "In the future there will be three Jerusalems [meaning a Temple in Jerusalem three times as large as the original], and [the Temple] will contain thirty buildings, one on top of another."

Levi bar Chama (third century)
See Levi ben Lachma.

Levi bar Chita (fourth century)
Palestinian amora. He is quoted in *Mo'ed Katan* 29a as saying: "In bidding farewell to the dead, one should not say, 'Go unto peace' [*lekh le-shalom*], but rather 'Go in peace' [*lekh be-shalom*]. And in bidding farewell to a [living] friend, one should not say, 'Go in peace' but rather 'Go unto peace.'"

Levi bar Huna bar Chiyya (fourth century)
Babylonian amora. According to *Chullin* 93a, he was a colleague of Yehudah bar Oshaya; *Shabbat* 51b describes him as a traveling mate of Rabbah bar Huna.

Levi bar Samuel
See Levi bar Shemu'el.

Levi bar Shemu'el (third/fourth century)
Babylonian amora. In *Chullin* 141b he is noted is a colleague of Yehudah bar Yechezkel and a disciple of Shemu'el. According to *Shabbat* 47a, Levi attended Huna's academy with Huna bar Chiyya; *Sanhedrin* 100a reports that Levi and Huna bar Chiyya repaired Torah mantles.

Levi bar Sisi
See Levi ben Sisi.

Levi ben Chiyya (second century)
Palestinian tanna. A colleague of Shimon bar Yochai, Levi ben Chiyya is quoted in *Berakhot* 64a as saying: "If one goes into the house of study immediately after leaving the house of prayer, the Shekhinah considers him worthy of being welcomed."

Levi ben Lachma (third century)
Also known as Levi bar Chama.

Palestinian amora. Usually referred to as Levi without patronymic, some scholars believe he is identical with Levi, a disciple of Yehudah ha-Nasi. Levi ben Lachma was a disciple of Shimon ben Lakish (*Berakhot* 5a) and Chama ben Chanina, whom he quotes frequently (*Rosh Hashanah* 29b).

In *Rosh Hashanah* 29b Levi comments on the ruling that the *shofar* is not to be sounded on the Sabbath but that we should memorialize the *shofar* blasts on Shabbat. The Talmud explains that when Rosh Hashanah falls on a Sabbath, we remember the *shofar* blasts in our prayers but do not actually blow the *shofar*.

Where the name Levi bar Chama appears, as in *Ta'anit* 16a, in which the placing of ashes on a person's head as a sign of mourning is discussed, the variant reading in some editions of the Talmud is Levi ben Lachma.

Levi ben Perata (third century)
Palestinian amora. In *Chullin* 98a he is mentioned as a disciple of Nachum and as a teacher of Idi ben Idi ben Gershom.

Levi ben Sisi (second/third century)
Also known as Levi bar Sisi.

Palestinian tanna. Referred to in the Babylonian Talmud without patronymic, he is known as Levi bar Sisi in the Palestinian Talmud, having been active in the transition period between the tanna'im and amora'im. Levi assisted his teacher, Yehudah ha-Nasi, in compiling and editing the Mishnah. Levi also was involved in collecting the *mishnayyot* that Yehudah ha-Nasi did not include in his collection. These were called *baraitot*, meaning "outside" the official Mishnah.

At the request of the community of Simonias, which lay south of Sepphoris, Yehudah ha-Nasi sent Levi to lecture, to decide questions of law, and to supervise the synagogue, but the congregation rejected Levi as unfit when he was unable to answer all of their questions. Levi also traveled continually between Palestine and Babylonia and served as an adviser to the patriarch Yehudah Nesi'ah on dealings with the Persian conqueror.

After the death of Yehudah ha-Nasi, Levi moved to Babylonia, where he was highly respected. There he joined the school of Rav, with whom he was often in dispute, and became friends with Abba bar Abba and taught his son, Shemu'el. At Levi's funeral Abba bar Abba delivered the eulogy and said that Levi alone was worth as much as the whole of humanity (Palestinian Talmud, *Berakhot* 2).

Levi ha-Sadar (first/second century)

Palestinian tanna. Known as a collator of texts of the Mishnah (his name comes from the Hebrew word *seder*, meaning "order" or "arrange"), *Yoma* 85a describes a journey that Levi took with Yishma'el ben Elisha, Akiva ben Yosef, and Elazar ben Azaryah, during which the scholars were asked, "How do we know that in case of danger to human life one can violate the laws of the Sabbath?" Yishma'el quotes *Exodus* 22:1 and says that if a thief breaks into a home and the owner is sure he will be attacked, he may violate the Sabbath by attacking the intruder. Akiva offers a similar answer, using the text in *Exodus* 21:14 as the basis for his opinion. Elazar responds that, "If circumcision, which applies only to one of the 248 parts of a body, suspends the Sabbath, how much more so should saving the entire body suspend Sabbath laws." Levi ha-Sadar does not offer an answer.

Levi Sabba (third century)

Palestinian amora. Known in English as Levi the Elder, he is noted in *Eruvin* 97b and *Bava Kamma* 72a as a teacher of the celebrated Shimon ben Lakish.

Levi the Elder

See Levi Sabba.

Levitas of Yavneh (second century)

Palestinian tanna. He is quoted in *Avot* 4:4 as saying: "Be exceedingly humble, for the destiny of man is the worm [the grave]."

Luda

See Luda'ah.

Luda'ah (second/third century)

Also known as Luda.

Babylonian amora. In *Yevamot* 71b and *Shabbat* 137a he is noted as a contemporary of Shemu'el.

M

Mabog (second/third century)
Babylonian amora. In *Zevachim* 9b he is noted as a teacher of Rav.

Malkiyya (third/fourth century)
Palestinian amora. In *Avodah Zarah* 29a and *Makkot* 21a he is listed as a disciple of Adda bar Ahava.

Mallukh of Arabia (third century)
Palestinian amora. In *Chullin* 49a he is noted as a disciple of Yehoshu'a ben Levi.

Mana (third century)
Also known as Mana I.
Babylonian amora. According to *Shabbat* 114b, he was a contemporary of Huna.

Mana I
See Mana.

Mana II
See Mani.

Manasseh
See Menasheh.

Manasseh bar Zevid
See Menashya bar Zevid.

Mani (fourth century)
Also known as Mana II.
Palestinian amora. Son and disciple of Yonah, Mani attended the discourses of Yitzchak ben Elyashiv, according to *Ta'anit* 23b. In *Megillah* 29b Mani argues for the opinion of Yitzchak Nappacha on Chanukkah Torah readings when Rosh Chodesh Tevet falls on a weekday; Yitzchak Nappacha said that the Rosh

Chodesh portion is read for three *aliyyot*, while one additional portion is read for Chanukkah.

In *Mo'ed Katan* 20b Mani rules that if one learns on the Sabbath that a close relative has died within the previous thirty days, when the Sabbath ends he is to observe *shivah* fully. But if thirty days have passed since the death by the time the Sabbath is over, the mourner need not tear his garment (*keri'ah*) or sit *shivah*. Mani believed that *keri'ah* was not required when one did not have to sit *shivah*.

In *Kiddushin* 13a Ya'akov refers to Assi as a disciple of Mani; according to *Chullin* 56b, Shemu'el ben Chiyya was another of Mani's disciples. When Mani moved to Sepphoris, his disciple Chanina of Sepphoris resigned as the town's religious leader in deference to him.

Mani bar Pattish (third century)
Palestinian amora. In *Pesachim* 66b, Mani bar Pattish predicts the downfall of anyone who cannot control his temper: "Whoever becomes angry, even if greatness has been decreed for him by Heaven, will be cast down." Mani concurs with Shimon ben Lakish in *Chullin* 48b that an animal whose lung has been penetrated with a needle is *tereifah*.

Mani ben Yonah (fourth century)
Palestinian amora. In *Ta'anit* 23b he is noted as one of the great men of Palestine who could successfully pray for rain.

Mani of Tyre (third/fourth century)
Palestinian amora. In *Sanhedrin* 5b he is noted as a contemporary of Tanchum ben Ammi.

Mar Acha (third/fourth century)
Babylonian amora. In *Bava Kamma* 112b he is noted as a contemporary of Ravina I.

Mar bar Acha bar Rava (fourth/fifth century)
Babylonian amora. In *Mo'ed Katan* 11b he is listed as an associate of Maryon bar Rabin. The two men together owned a yoke of oxen.

Mar bar Ameimar (third/fourth century)
Babylonian amora. According to *Beitzah* 27b and *Shabbat* 45b,

he was a disciple of Rava; in *Sukkah* 32b and 41b, and in *Bava Metzi'a* 68a, he is mentioned as a colleague of Ashi.

Mar bar Chiyya (second/third century)

Babylonian amora. In *Bava Batra* 165b he is noted as a colleague of Natan and in *Chullin* 45b as a contemporary of Rav and Shemu'el.

Mar bar Hamduri

See Bar Hamduri.

Mar bar Huna (third century)

Palestinian amora. In *Shabbat* 63a he is listed as a colleague of Kahana.

Mar bar Idi (third century)

Babylonian amora. In *Chullin* 63a he is named as a colleague of Adda bar Shimi.

Mar bar Joseph

See Mar bar Yosef.

Mar bar Pumbedita (third/fourth century)

Babylonian amora. In *Eruvin* 60a he is listed as a contemporary of Abbayei.

Mar bar Rabbana (third/fourth century)

Babylonian amora. In *Keritot* 15a he is named as a colleague of Nachumi bar Zekharyah. Mar's brother is referred to as Yochanan Achuha de-Mar bar Rabbana.

Mar bar Rav Ashi (fifth century)

Also known as Tavyomi.

Babylonian amora. Son of the famous amora Ashi, Mar, whose real name was Tavyomi, studied under his father and succeeded him as principal of the academy in Mata Mechasya. Although Mar would continue his father's work of editing the Talmud and was considered one of the greatest later amora'im, whose opinions became law, he was unable to restore the academy to its prestige of old.

Mar's mentors were Shimon ben Lakish (*Bava Batra* 5b) and Abbayei (*Kiddushin* 4a), with whom Mar disagreed about recovering a debt from the property of orphans. In *Ketubbot* 69a Ravina rules that Mar's sister may collect a portion of their father's estate.

In *Sanhedrin* 77b Mar questioned Pappa's ruling that a man who throws a stone in the air is liable if the stone falls back to the ground at an angle and kills a person. "Why," Mar asked, "should he be liable if he did not intentionally cause the accident?" Pappa insisted the stone-thrower was, nevertheless, responsible.

In *Ketubbot* 19b Mar bar Rav Ashi agrees with Nachman on the question of the reliability of witnesses who had attested to a promissory note. Though their signatures on the document were authentic, they claimed not to have seen the actual loan transaction take place.

Mar bar Ravina (fourth century)

Babylonian amora. *Eruvin* 65a recounts that his mother, in order to save him time so that he could concentrate on his studies, prepared seven garments for him, one for each day of the week.

According to *Shabbat* 108a, Mar bar Ravina was a disciple of Nachman bar Yitzchak, of whom he asked whether *tefillin* may be written upon the skin of a kosher fish. "Only if Elijah comes and rules on it," replied Nachman. We learn from *Menachot* 35b and 42a that Mar bar Ravina also was concerned about the manner in which the *tefillin* knot and the fringes of a *tallit* were made.

Berakhot 17a reports that when Mar bar Ravina concluded his formal prayers, he would add the following lines:

> My God, keep my tongue from evil and my lips from speaking guile. May my soul be silent to those who curse me, and may my soul be as dust to all. Open Thou my heart in Thy law, and may my soul pursue Thy commandments. Deliver me from evil happenings, from the evil impulse, from an evil woman, and from all evils that threaten to come upon the world. As for all who design evil against me, speedily annul their counsel and frustrate their designs! May the words of my mouth and the meditation of my heart be acceptable before Thee, O Lord, my rock and my redeemer!

To this day, Mar bar Ravina's prayer, though in a slightly modified form, is added at the end of the *Amidah*.

In *Berakhot* 30b it is said that Mar bar Ravina made a wedding feast for his son (*Sandedrin* 106b indicates that Mar had several sons). When the Rabbis in attendance grew overly merry, Ravina smashed an expensive vase in front of them; startled, they toned down their high spirits.

Mar bar Yosef (third/fourth century)

Babylonian amora. In *Beitzah* 27b, *Bava Metzi'a* 67a, and *Shabbat* 45b he is noted as a disciple of Rava. According to *Chullin* 48b, he was a colleague of Ashi.

Mar Judah

See Mar Yehudah.

Mar Kashisha bar Chisda

See Kashisha bar Chisda.

Mar Kashisha bar Rava

See Kashisha bar Rava.

Mar of Moshkei (third/fourth century)

Babylonian amora. In *Menachot* 43a he is named as a contemporary of Achai. Moshkei was a small town in Babylonia.

Mar Samuel

See Shemu'el.

Mar Shemu'el

See Shemu'el.

Mar Ukba

See Ukba *and* Ukba bar Chama.

Mar Yanuka bar Chisda

See Yanuka bar Chisda.

Mar Yehudah (third century)

Babylonian amora. In *Eruvin* 24a he is noted as a colleague of Huna bar Yehudah and in *Avodah Zarah* 16b as a contemporary of Abbayei. According to *Chullin* 48a, Mar Yehudah was a disciple of Avimi.

Mar Yochana bar Chana bar Adda

See Yochana bar Chana bar Adda.

Mar Yochana bar Chana bar Bizna
See Yochana bar Chana bar Bizna.

Mar Yochani (second/third century)
Babylonian amora. In *Avodah Zarah* 16b he is mentioned as a contemporary of Mar Yehudah and in *Mo'ed Katan* 23b as a disciple of Shemu'el.

Mar Zutra
See Zutra.

Mar Zutra bar Mari (fourth/fifth century)
Babylonian amora. According to *Kiddushin* 65b, he was the son of Adda bar Mari bar Isur and the brother of Adda Sabba. Mar Zutra bar Mari and Adda Sabba consulted Ashi on the division of their father's estate.

In *Bava Kamma* 29a, *Chullin* 108a, *Menachot* 56a, and *Zevachim* 22a Mar Zutra bar Mari is listed as a colleague of Ravina II.

Mar Zutra bar Nachman
See Zutra bar Nachman.

Mar Zutra bar Toviyyah
See Zutra bar Toviyyah.

Mar Zutra Chasida
See Zutra Chasida.

Mar Zutra of Darishba
See Zutra of Darishba.

Mar Zutra Rabbah
See Zutra Rabbah.

Mar Zutra the Great
See Zutra Rabbah.

Mar Zutra the Pious
See Zutra Chasida.

Mari
Two scholars are referred to as Mari, without patronymic:
1. A second/third-century Palestinian tanna who, in *Berakhot* 40a, is mentioned as a disciple of Yochanan bar Nappacha. In *Shabbat* 152b Mari is quoted as saying: "Even the righteous are destined to end up as dust."

2. A third/fourth-century Babylonian amora who was of modest disposition. In *Bava Batra* 98a he says: "One who is proud is not acceptable even to his own household."

In *Berakhot* 24a he is noted as a disciple of Pappa. Numbered among Mari's colleagues were Elazar (*Gittin* 34b); Rava, Pappa, and Huna bar Yehoshu'a (*Kiddushin* 32b); and Zevid (*Chullin* 117a). In *Sotah* 40a and *Bava Batra* 96a Mari disputes Zevid on the question of the point at which wine turns to vinegar.

Mari bar Abbahu (third century)

Palestinian amora. In *Chullin* 125a and *Pesachim* 83a he is noted as a disciple of Yitzchak.

Mari bar berei de-Rav Huna (fourth century)

Babylonian amora. Known in English as Mari, Grandson of Huna, he is mentioned in *Berakhot* 31a as the son of Yirmeyahu ben Abba.

Mari bar Bizna (third century)

Babylonian amora. In *Beitzah* 28b he is noted as a contemporary of Yosef.

Mari bar Chisda (third/fourth century)

Babylonian amora. In *Ketubbot* 61a he is mentioned as a brother of Pinchas bar Chisda.

Mari bar Huna bar Yirmeyahu bar Abba

(third/fourth century)

Babylonian amora. Mari, grandson of the fourth-century Babylonian amora Yirmeyahu bar Abba, is quoted in *Berakhot* 31a as saying, "Before departing from a friend, one should always offer a halakhic teaching so that he will not be forgotten." In *Eruvin* 21a Chisda questions Mari, who customarily walks a distance on the Sabbath that appears to exceed the two-thousand-cubit limit.

Mari bar Isak of Bei-Chozai (third century)

Babylonian amora. According to *Bava Metzi'a* 39b, a man came forward claiming to be Mari bar Isak's brother, demanding a share of his father's estate. The case was adjudicated by Chisda, who ruled that the estate must be shared.

Mari bar Kahana (third/fourth century)
Babylonian amora. In *Zevachim* 55a Mari bar Kahana is noted as a colleague of Rava.

Mari bar Mar (third/fourth century)
Babylonian amora. In *Gittin* 86b and *Bava Kamma* 21a he is listed as a colleague of Abba ben Zavda and in *Yevamot* 76a as a disciple of Mar Ukba.

Mar bar Phinehas
See Mar bar Pinchas.

Mar bar Pinchas (third century)
Babylonian amora. He is referred to in *Bava Kamma* 117a as a son of Chisda.

Mari bar Rachel (fourth century)
Babylonian amora. In this unusual case, Mari is identified by his mother's name—Mari, Son of Rachel—rather than his father's name. *Yevamot* 45b explains that this is because he was the son of a Jewish woman and a proselyte, and that he was conceived before his father's conversion and born after it. In *Bava Batra* 61b, where Mari is mentioned as a disciple of Abbayei, he is referred to as Mari de-vat Shemu'el—Mari, Son of the Daughter of Shemu'el. *Berakhot* 16a also states that Mari was the son of a daughter of Shemu'el.

It is noted in *Bava Metzi'a* 73b and *Shabbat* 124b that Mari was a colleague of Rava. *Shabbat* 154a asserts that some scholars believe he was Rava's brother.

Mari bar Ukba (second/third century)
Babylonian amora. He is listed in *Chullin* 43b as a disciple of Shemu'el.

Mari, Grandson of Huna
See Mari bar berei de-Rav Huna.

Mari, Son of the Daughter of Samuel
See Mari bar Rachel.

Mari, Son of the Daughter of Shemu'el
See Mari bar Rachel.

Mari Tavi (third century)

Babylonian amora. A disciple of Ukba, he is quoted in *Rosh Hashanah* 22a by his disciple, Tavi.

Marinos (third century)

Babylonian amora. In *Bava Batra* 56a he is mentioned as a disciple of Eli'ezer; according to *Ketubbot* 60a, he was highly respected by Yosef.

Maryon (third century)

Palestinian amora. In *Eruvin* 19a he is noted as the father of Rabbah ben Maryon and in *Sukkah* 32b as a disciple of Yehoshu'a ben Levi. Rabbah ben Maryon also was a disciple of Yehoshu'a ben Levi.

Maryon bar Rabin (third/fourth century)

Babylonian amora. According to *Mo'ed Katan* 11b, he and Mar bar Acha bar Rava owned a yoke of oxen in partnership.

Mattityah ben Judah

See Mattityah ben Yehudah.

Mattityah ben Samuel

See Mattityah ben Shemu'el.

Mattityah ben Shemu'el (first century)

Palestinian tanna. In *Menachot* 100a he is listed as a Temple officer.

Mattityah ben Yehudah (first century)

Palestinian tanna. He is quoted in *Menachot* 79b and *Chullin* 67a.

Mattnah I (third century)

Babylonian amora. In *Shabbat* 60b he is mentioned as the father of Achadvoi. Among Mattnah's teachers were Shemu'el (*Sukkah* 11b and *Niddah* 27a), Ze'eira (*Berakhot* 36a), and the Palestinian amora Yehoshu'a ben Levi (*Yoma* 69b).

Mattnah II (third/fourth century)

Babylonian amora. In *Mo'ed Katan* 26a he asks advice from Huna bar Chiyya but receives none. Mattnah II is noted in *Bava Metzi'a* 37a as a disciple of Rav.

Mattya ben Charash

See Mattya ben Cheresh.

Mattya ben Cheresh (second century)

Also spelled Mattya ben Charash.

Palestinian tanna. Mattya, short for Mattitya, lived and studied in Palestine in his youth. After his ordination he moved to the small Jewish community in Rome, where he often associated with visiting Palestinian scholars such as Shimon bar Yochai and Eli'ezer ben Yosei ha-Gelili, who came to raise funds for their academies. In *Yoma* 53b Mattya is listed as a contemporary of Shimon bar Yochai and in *Yoma* 84a as a contemporary of Yochanan bar Nappacha.

Having lived in a small Jewish community in Rome and a large Jewish community in Palestine, Mattya understood well the strengths and weaknesses of each. He preferred the small congenial community that was part of the leonine Roman Empire to the larger Jewish community of Palestine composed of many learned and clever scholars. He is quoted in *Avot* 4:15 as saying: "It is better to be the tail among the lions, than the head among foxes."

In the spirit of Yochanan ben Zakkai, Mattya was the first to welcome every person with a friendly greeting.

Matun (third century)

Palestinian amora. In *Bava Kamma* 96a he quotes Yehoshu'a ben Levi on the *kashrut* of a *lulav.* Yehoshu'a ben Levi contends that if the blade of the spine of the *lulav* is split, the *lulav* may not be used. Even today those who are very particular examine the *lulav* carefully to make sure there is no split.

Mechasya bar Idi (third century)

Babylonian amora. In *Yoma* 2a and 3b he is mentioned as a teacher of Minyomi bar Chilkiyah.

Mei'asha

Also known as Meisha *and* Misha.

Three scholars were known by this name:

1. A first/second-century Palestinian tanna who is noted in *Nazir* 65b as a teacher of Nachum ha-Livlar. Mei'asha studied

under his father, who had studied under members of the *zugot.*
Mishnah *Pe'ah* 2:6 mentions that Mei'asha's father was a contemporary of Yochanan ben Zakkai. In *Nedarim* 8b Mei'ashah
subscribes to the authority of Yehudah bar Ila'i.

2. A third/fourth-century Palestinian amora who was the
grandson and pupil of Yehoshu'a ben Levi. Mei'asha quotes his
grandfather in *Ketubbot* 75a. In *Bava Metzi'a* 142b and *Bava
Batra* 142b Mei'asha is listed as a colleague of Avin and Yirmeyahu, and in *Sanhedrin* 56a and *Shabbat* 99b as a contemporary of Yitzchak Nappacha.

3. The second-century Palestinian tanna Me'ir (see below) is
sometimes referred to as Mei'asha.

Me'ir (second century)
Also known as Mei'asha *and* Nehorai.
Palestinian tanna. Although he is mentioned over three thousand times in the Babylonian Talmud, little is actually known
about Me'ir's birth, parentage, or place of origin; according to
legend, he probably was born in Caesarea and was a descendant
of a family of converts. Much, however, is known about his
scholarly career, for he assumed the role of Akiva ben Yosef in
systematizing the teachings of the tanna'im, which were finalized in the Mishnah of which Yehudah ha-Nasi was the chief
editor. Following the Bar Kokhba Revolt, Me'ir was secretly
ordained by Yehudah ben Bava and became a member of the
Sanhedrin established at Usha.

From *Eruvin* 13a and *Sotah* 20a we learn that when he came
to Yishma'el ben Elisha to study Torah, Yishma'el asked him,
"What trade do you ply?" When Me'ir answered, "I am a scribe,"
Yishma'el said, "Be careful in carrying out your work, for yours
is the work of heaven. Should you omit one letter or add one
letter [when writing a Torah scroll] you may find yourself destroying the whole world." Yishma'el emphasized the sacred-
ness of the text by noting that if a scribe were to omit the *alef*
when writing the word *emet,* which means "truth," the word
would end up as *met,* meaning "death"; so, too, by adding a *vav*
at the end of the word *va-yedaber,* which means "He [God]
spoke," so that the word reads *va-yedabru,* meaning "and they

spoke," it would appear that instead of one God, there were many gods. As indicated in *Megillah* 18b, Me'ir was able to write out the entire book of *Esther* from memory and read it publicly on Purim.

According to some authorities, the real name of Me'ir was Mi'ashah, Mi'asa, or Moise (Greek for Moses). In *Eruvin* 13b it is said that Me'ir's original name was Nehorai, which means "light" or "enlightenment," because Me'ir enlightened the Sages through his wisdom.

After studying under Yishma'el ben Elisha, Akiva ben Yosef became Me'ir's primary teacher. Me'ir was one of Akiva's five outstanding students. In addition to Me'ir, these included Yehudah bar Ila'i, Yosei ben Chalafta, Shimon bar Yochai, and Elazar ben Shammu'a (*Yevamot* 62b). In *Eruvin* 13a Me'ir says: "When I studied under Yishma'el, I used to put vitriol in my ink [the addition of vitriol to the ink used to write sacred texts makes the letters written hard and indelible], and he did not object. Later, when I studied under Akiva, he forbade it." Apparently, Akiva was of greater influence on Me'ir than Yishma'el.

Me'ir's courage to go against accepted practice is revealed in several instances. Though greeting mourners on the Sabbath was generally prohibited—in fact, it was discouraged on weekdays as well—Me'ir was not averse to doing so. To justify his conduct, he quoted the verse in *Proverbs* 10:22: "The blessing of the Lord maketh rich . . ."

One of Me'ir's teachers was the heretic Elisha ben Avuyah, more popularly known in the Talmud as Acher, meaning "Other." Although Acher was shunned by his fellow scholars, Me'ir clung to him and revered him as a teacher, despite his rebellious views and actions. *Chagigah* 15b reports that one Sabbath day, Acher was riding on a horse, an activity forbidden on the Sabbath, while Me'ir walked behind to learn the Torah being spouted by Acher. When they reached the maximum of two thousand cubits that one may walk from his residence without violating Sabbath law, Me'ir urged Acher to stop and go back. Acher refused. When asked how he could learn Torah from a heretic such as Acher, Me'ir replied that when he finds a juicy pomegranate he eats the seeds and throws away the peel.

Many of Me'ir's views were unconventional and often revealed the mystic in him. In *Sotah* 17a, when asked why a *tallit* must have a blue thread in its fringes, he responded, "because blue resembles the color of the sea, and the sea resembles the color of heaven, and heaven resembles the color of the throne of God." He quoted the verses *Exodus* 24:10 and *Ezekiel* 1:26 to make his case.

In *Ketubbot* 10b Me'ir states that a woman who has an abundance of blood when menstruating will have many children. In *Megillah* 20a his disciple Yehudah bar Simon reveals his master's thinking on the question of whether the *Shema* must be recited aloud or whether it may be recited inaudibly. Me'ir replied: "In accordance with the concentration of the mind, so the value of the words." In other words, it doesn't matter whether it is said silently or aloud; what matters is the sincerity with which it is recited.

On the subject of study, in *Berakhot* 17a Me'ir attributes these words to God: "Study with all your heart and with all your soul to know My ways and to watch at the doors of My law. Keep My law in your heart and let My fear be before your eyes. Keep your mouth from all sin and purify and sanctify yourself from all trespass and iniquity, and I will be with you in every place."

Me'ir was married to Beruryah, daughter of Chananyah ben Teradyon and a scholar in her own right. When Beruryah and Me'ir's twin sons died suddenly one Sabbath afternoon, Beruryah postponed telling her husband until the Sabbath was over and gently broke the news to him with the following question:

"Not long ago, some precious jewels were entrusted to my care. Now the owner has come to reclaim them. Shall I return them?"

"Of course," said Me'ir. "You know the law. They must be returned."

Beruryah then took him by the hand, led him to the bedroom, and drew back the sheet, under which lay their sons. Me'ir burst into bitter weeping. "My sons! My sons!" he lamented. Then Beruryah reminded him tearfully, "Did you not say that we must restore to the owner that which was entrusted to our care? Our sons were the jewels given to us by God, and now their Master has taken back His very own."

Like Akiva and other rabbis who traveled to distant cities to raise funds for the support of their academies, Me'ir, too, devoted himself to fundraising. *Yevamot* 121a reports a story related by Akiva who said that once, while sailing on the stormy seas, he saw another ship about to capsize. He was distressed because one of the disciples of the wise was on the ship. And who was the scholar? None other than Me'ir.

It appears from a reference in *Sanhedrin* 90b that during his travels Me'ir had become acquainted with Cleopatra, queen of Egypt (scholars note that this was not the queen of Anthony and Cleopatra fame). On one occasion she asked him facetiously, "I know that the dead will come back to life, but will they arise nude or clad in their garments?" Me'ir replied that if a grain of wheat that is buried naked can sprout covered with leaves, so can the righteous dead, who are buried in their garments, come alive again fully clad. As noted in *Sanhedrin* 59a, Me'ir believed that even a Gentile who studied Torah was like a High Priest.

The Palestinian Talmud relates that when Me'ir's time came to die he was teaching in Asia Minor. He wanted to be buried in Israel and notified the people that it was their obligation to see to it that his wish was carried out. This, despite the fact that he used to say, "Adam—the earth from which he was created was gathered from the four corners of the entire world" (*Sanhedrin* 38b).

Meisha

See Mei'asha.

Menachem

Two scholars were known by this name:

1. A second-century Palestinian Tanna quoted in *Yoma* 43b and *Sanhedrin* 33a.

2. A third/fourth-century Babylonian amora who, in *Berakhot* 8a, is noted as a teacher of Huna bar Yehudah and, in *Ketubbot* 74a, as a teacher of Yosef bar Abba.

Menachem bar Simai (fifth century)

Babylonian amora. In *Pesachim* 104a Menachem is noted as a colleague of Shemu'el bar Idi.

Menachem ben Signai (first century)
Palestinian tanna. He is mentioned only once, in Mishnah *Eduyyot* 7:8.

Menachem ben Yosei (second century)
Palestinian tanna. In *Ketubbot* 22b, Yochanan ben Nuri agrees with Menachem on a question involving a woman who has married after two witnesses say her husband has died and two say he has not died. Both Menachem ben Yosei and Yochanan ben Nuri conclude that once the woman has remarried, she should stay married. Menachem was one of five sons of Yosei ben Chalafta (*Shabbat* 118b).

Menachem Jotapata
See Menachem Yotapata.

Menachem of Kefar She'arim (fourth century)
Babylonian amora. In *Niddah* 27a he is mentioned as a disciple of Ravin bar Adda.

Menachem Yodapah
See Menachem Yotapata.

Menachem Yodpa'ah
See Menachem Yotapata.

Menachem Yotapata (second/third century)
Also spelled Menachem Yodapah *and* Menachem Yodpa'ah.
Palestinian amora. According to *Zevachim* 110b, in which his name appears as Menachem Yodpa'ah, and *Me'ilah* 13b, in which his name appears as Menachem Yodapah, he was the teacher of Yochanan bar Nappacha. Yotapata, spelled in English as Jotapata, is the name of the Galilean fortress town held for forty-seven days by Josephus against the Romans in 67 C.E.

Menasheh (third/fourth century)
Palestinian amora. In *Eruvin* 104a he is noted as a colleague and friend of Ulla.

Menasheh bar Zevid
See Menashya bar Zevid.

Menashya (third century)
Babylonian amora. In *Shabbat* 139a he is noted as a disciple

of Shemu'el; in *Beitzah* 30b he is mentioned as a contemporary of Yehudah; and in *Shabbat* 156a he is referred to as a contemporary of Yosef.

Menashya bar Avat

Babylonian amora. A scholar of unknown date. In *Sanhedrin* 19a Menashya bar Avat states that in the graveyard of Huzal, his teacher, Yoshiyyah Rabbah, told him that a row (for condolences) must not consist of less than ten persons, excluding the mourners, and that it is immaterial whether the mourners stand still and the public passes by or vice versa.

Menashya bar Gadda (third/fourth century)

Also known as Menashya bar Gaddi.

Babylonian amora. According to *Menachot* 17a, he was a student of Abbayei. In *Sukkah* 13b he is noted as a disciple of Huna.

Menashya bar Gaddi

See Menashya bar Gadda.

Menashya bar Jeremiah

See Menashya bar Yirmeyahu.

Menashya bar Menachem (third century)

Babylonian amora. He is quoted in *Shabbat* 144b.

Menashya bar Rava (third century)

Babylonian amora. He is quoted in *Beitzah* 30b.

Menashya bar Shegovli (third century)

Babylonian amora. In *Eruvin* 29a he is noted as a colleague of Yosef.

Menashya bar Tachlifa (fourth century)

Babylonian amora. In *Pesachim* 6b and *Berakhot* 49b he is described as a disciple of Rav, and in *Berakhot* 47b as an adversary of Rami bar Chama. In *Pesachim* 6b, regarding the dating of events in the Torah, Menashya bar Tachlifa proclaims in the name of Rav: "There is no chronological order in the Torah."

Menashya bar Yirmeyahu (second century)

Babylonian amora. He is listed in *Nazir* 65b as a disciple of Rav.

Menashya bar Yirmeyahu of Difti (fourth/fifth century)

Babylonian amora. In *Eruvin* 64a he is mentioned as a colleague of Abba bar Shumani and a disciple of Mari bar Huna bar Yirmeyahu bar Abba.

Menashya bar Zevid (second/third century)

Also known as Menasheh bar Zevid.

Babylonian amora. In *Yevamot* 19b he is listed as a student of Huna and in *Menachot* 108b and *Shevu'ot* 45b as a disciple of Rav.

Menashya ben Jacob

See Menashya ben Ya'akov.

Menashya ben Ya'akov (second/third century)

Palestinian tanna. *Bava Metzi'a* 26a lists him as a contemporary of Shimon ben Elazar.

Mereimar (fifth century)

Babylonian amora. In *Gittin* 19b he is noted as a disciple of Dimi and in *Niddah* 36a as a strong believer in the rulings of Rav. In *Eruvin* 100a Mereimar is said to have been a colleague of Zutra, and, according to *Bava Metzi'a* 72b and *Nedarim* 60b, he was associated with Ravina II.

Mereimar bar Chanina (third/fourth century)

Babylonian amora. In *Bava Metzi'a* 97a he is listed as a contemporary of Rava.

Mesharshya (fourth/fifth century)

Babylonian amora. In *Chullin* 50a he is identified as the father of Rava, while in *Zevachim* 9b and *Bava Batra* 100a he is said to have been Rava's disciple. Mesharshya's colleagues included Yehudah bar Ila'i (*Sukkah* 26a), Ulla (*Sukkah* 53b), and Pappa (*Eruvin* 48a).

Among Mesharshya's more interesting rulings and comments are those found in *Chullin* 101b, in which he discusses whether the landlord or tenant must provide the *mezuzah* for a house; *Shabbat* 14a, in which he explains why the Rabbis considered scrolls of the Bible to be ritually unclean (originally, the food of *terumah* was stored near the Torah scrolls. The food attracted mice, who also ate away at the scrolls. To put an end to the practice, the Rabbis ruled that the scrolls were unclean and that *terumah* could no longer be stored near them); and *Gittin* 42b, in which he rules that if a child of a *Kohen* has become mixed up with the child of a female slave of the family, and it is unclear which child is which, both may eat *terumah*, usually the prerogative only of members of a Priestly family.

Mesharshya bar Acha (third/fourth century)
Babylonian amora. In *Chullin* 67b he is mentioned as a student of Ravina I.

Mesharshya bar Chilkai (third/fourth century)
Babylonian amora. It is reported in *Ketubbot* 100b that Kahana had in his possession, as trustee, some beer that belonged to the orphan Mesharshya bar Chilkai. Kahana kept the beer unduly long, even though there was the possibility it would sour, hoping to sell it at a later date, for a higher cash price, rather than selling it on credit.

Mesharshya bar Chiyya (fourth/fifth century)
Babylonian amora. According to *Bava Batra* 82a, he was a contemporary of Ashi.

Mesharshya bar Dimi (third/fourth century)
Babylonian amora. He is noted in *Gittin* 78a as a contemporary of Adda bar Ahava.

Mesharshya bar Idi (third century)
Babylonian amora. He is mentioned in *Avodah Zarah* 13a as a contemporary of Shimon ben Lakish.

Mesharshya bar Natan (fourth century)
Babylonian amora. In *Pesachim* 115a he is said to have been a colleague of Ravina I and a contemporary of Hillel II.

Mesharshya bar Nathan
See Mesharshya bar Natan.

Mesharshya bar Pakod (fifth century)
Babylonian amora. A resident of Sura, he was imprisoned during the Persian persecution of Babylonian Jews and was executed in 470, together with Ameimar bar Mar Yanuka and Zutra, son of amora Huna bar Zutra.

Mesharshya bar Rava (second/third century)
Babylonian amora. It is noted in *Eruvin* 24a that Abba, Avuha de-Rav, is the son of Mesharshya bar Rava.

Mesharshya ben Ammi (third/fourth century)
Palestinian amora. In *Kiddushin* 60a he is noted as a colleague of Assi.

Mesharshya of Tusaneya (third/fourth century)
Babylonian amora. According to *Yevamot* 21b, he was a disciple of Pappi.

Minyamin bar Ichi (second/third century)
Babylonian amora. *Ketubbot* 61a notes that he was a brother of Avuha bar Ichi and that both were very generous to their waiter at mealtime.

Minyamin Ger ha-Mitzri (second century)
Palestinian tanna. Known in English as Minyamin the Egyptian Proselyte, Yehudah bar Ila'i is quoted in *Sotah* 9a as saying: "Minyamin, an Egyptian proselyte, was a colleague of mine and one of the disciples of Akiva [ben Yosef]."

Minyamin of Saksana (second/third century)
Babylonian amora. According to *Niddah* 65a, he was a disciple of Rav.

Minyamin the Egyptian Proselyte
See Minyamin Ger ha-Mitzri.

Minyomi (fourth century)
Babylonian amora. In *Bava Metzi'a* 66a he is named as a contemporary of Rava and Nachman.

Minyomi Asya
See Binyamin Asya.

Minyomi bar Chilkiyah (third century)
Babylonian amora. In *Yoma* 2a and 3b he is listed as a disciple of Mechasya bar Idi and in *Menachot* 32b as a disciple of Chama bar Gurya.

Minyomi bar Nichumi (fourth/fifth century)
Babylonian amora. In *Bava Metzi'a* 109b he is listed as a contemporary of Ashi. In *Ketubbot* 81b Minyomi bar Nichumi quotes Yosef bar Minyomi, who was a disciple of Nachman.

Misha
See Mei'asha.

Mona
See Monbaz.

Monbaz (second century)
Also known as Mona.
Palestinian tanna. In *Shabbat* 68b he is noted as a disciple of
Akiva ben Yosef and Yehudah bar Ila'i. In *Shabbat* 108b Monbaz
is referred to as Mona.

Mordecai
See Mordekhai.

Mordekhai (third/fourth century)
Babylonian amora. In *Yevamot* 64b and *Chullin* 115b he is
identified as a colleague of Ashi, and in *Berakhot* 31a as a colleague of Shimi bar Abba. Among Mordekhai's disciples were
Zutra (*Shabbat* 50b), Rabbah bar Nachmani (*Shabbat* 99b),
and Ravina I (*Beitzah* 6a).

N

Nachman
See Nachman bar Ya'akov.

Nachman bar Abba (second/third century)
Babylonian amora. In *Avodah Zarah* 39a he is listed as a disciple of Rav.

Nachman bar Adda (second/third century)
Babylonian amora. In *Eruvin* 34b he is mentioned as a disciple of Shemu'el.

Nachman bar Barukh (fourth century)
Babylonian amora. In *Shabbat* 66b he is noted as a disciple of Ashi bar Avin.

Nachman bar Chisda (fourth century)
Babylonian amora. Son of the renowned amora Chisda, Nachman was head of the community of Daraukart. In *Bava Batra* 8a, he is reported to have levied a poll tax on rabbis who lived there. Among his teachers were Chisda (*Shabbat* 147a) and Rabbah bar Nachmani (*Gittin* 80b).

In *Berakhot* 61a and *Ketubbot* 104b Nachman bar Rav Chisda is noted as a teacher of Nachman bar Yitzchak; *Shevu'ot* 12b lists Rava as one of Nachman bar Rav Chisda's colleagues. According to *Sukkah* 56a, Nachman disputed the view of Rav on the order in which benedictions are to be recited upon entering a *sukkah*.

Bava Batra 36b recounts how the people of Pum Nahara turned to Nachman with a question about whether a plowed, fallow field helps to confer the right of possession (*chazakah*).

Commenting in *Berakhot* 61a on the odd spelling of the word *va-yyitzer* ("and He created") in *Genesis* 2:7, which reads, "And God created man of the dust of the earth . . . ," Nachman says the word *va-yyitzer* is spelled with two *yuds* instead of one to indicate that man was created with two inclinations, a *yetzer tov* ("a good inclination") and a *yetzer ra* ("an evil inclination").

In *Horayot* 10b Nachman declares that righteous people are most fortunate even when they suffer in this world because they will be rewarded in the world to come, something the wicked cannot look forward to.

Nachman bar Gurya (third century)
Babylonian amora. He is quoted in *Shabbat* 95a.

Nachman bar Isaac
See Nachman bar Yitzchak.

Nachman bar Jacob
See Nachman bar Ya'akov.

Nachman bar Kohen (fourth century)
Palestinian amora. According to *Ketubbot* 105b and *Sanhedrin* 7b, he was a contemporary of Dimi of Nehardea.

Nachman bar Pappa (third/fourth century)
Babylonian amora. In *Bava Metzi'a* 80b he is mentioned as a colleague of Rafram bar Pappa. It is related in *Chullin* 60b that Nachman bar Pappa planted seeds in his garden that did not sprout. He prayed for rain, rain fell, and the plants began to grow.

Nachman bar Rava (second/third century)
Babylonian amora. He is noted in *Shabbat* 25b as a disciple of Rav.

Nachman bar Samuel bar Marta
See Nachman bar Shemu'el bar Marta.

Nachman bar Shemu'el bar Marta (fourth century)
Babylonian amora. In *Chullin* 30b he is listed as a teacher of Ze'eira.

Nachman bar Ushpazti (fourth century)
Babylonian amora. In *Ta'anit* 24b he advises Pappa on how to induce rain to fall. Some scholars believe Ushpazti was the name of Nachman's mother rather than that of his father.

Nachman bar Ya'akov (third/fourth century)
Babylonian amora. A pupil of Shemu'el (*Eruvin* 47a, *Beitzah* 25b, and *Ketubbot* 108b) and Rav (*Sotah* 12b and *Pesachim* 13a), and a teacher of Nachman bar Yitzchak, Abbayei (*Eruvin* 3b),

Rava (*Nedarim* 22b and *Yevamot* 22a), Yosef bar Minyomi (*Yevamot* 107b), and Beivai (*Chagigah* 22b and *Nedarim* 35b), Nachman bar Ya'akov became widely know simply as Nachman, without patronymic.

During Nachman's youth the *reish galuta* was the wealthy Rabbah bar Avuha. Nachman married his daugther, Yalta, and was able to live in luxury, entertaining esteemed scholars as well as strangers. From a reference in *Shabbat* 12a we know that Nachman and his wife had several daughters and from *Sotah* 9a that they had a son named Zutra bar Nachman.

Commenting in *Yoma* 82a about at what age young boys and girls should start fasting on Yom Kippur, Nachman says: "Between the ages of nine and ten they are to be trained to fast for a few hours; between eleven and twelve to fast for the full day."

Although Nachman was an accomplished scholar, his colleagues frowned upon his haughtiness. With the exception of his devoted slave Daru, mentioned in *Shabbat* 51a, whom he regarded as a family member, Nachman treated slaves harshly. Yet, despite a reputation for being stern and demanding, there are stories that reflect Nachman's kindness.

A visiting scholar from Palestine named Yitzchak was invited by Nachman to join him for dinner. After dinner, Nachman asked Yitzchak for his blessing. In response, Yitzchak told Nachman the following story:

Once a traveler had lost his way in a desert and was wandering around tired, starving, and thirsty. Unexpectedly, he came upon a tree with sweet fruit and pleasant shade. It was watered by a stream that flowed under it. The wanderer ate the tree's fruit, sat in its shade, and drank from its spring. When he was ready to leave, the wanderer turned to the tree and said, "With what shall I bless thee, thou excellent tree? Shall I say, 'May your fruits be sweet?' They are already sweet. Shall I say, 'May your shade be pleasant?' It is already pleasant. 'Shall I ask for a stream to flow beneath you?' There is such a stream already. Then I will merely wish that all the plants that emerge from you may grow to be like you."

"It is the same with you," Yitzchak continued. "How shall I bless you? Shall I bless you with learning? You have sufficient learning already. Shall I bless you with riches? You already have riches. Shall I bless you with children? You have children. Then I will merely wish that all of your descendants may be like you."

According to one view, Nachman bar Ya'akov died around 320 C.E. Others estimate that he died around 329 C.E.

Nachman bar Yitzchak (fourth century)

Babylonian amora. Though little is known about his personal life, we do know that his mother influenced him to live a life of piety. In *Shabbat* 156b it is reported that she was told by astrologers that her son would be a thief. She would not let Nachman go bareheaded, as was the common practice in Talmudic times, admonishing him to cover his head "so the fear of heaven may be upon you." In *Shabbat* 33a Nachman condemns anyone who speaks lewdly and predicts that they will go to hell.

Like his colleague Rava, he studied under Nachman bar Ya'akov in Sura. As a young student Nachman bar Yitzchak was recognized for his scholarly ability and was appointed *reish kallah*. Nachman bar Yitzchak also studied under Nachman bar Rav Chisda, who praised his scholarship and often quoted him in his lectures (*Ta'anit* 21b). Rava later became headmaster of the academy in Pumbedita, and Nachman bar Yitzchak succeeded Rava as head of the academy when Rava died, moving the academy from Pumbedita to Machoza. Nachman held the position as head of the academy for only four years.

Nachman was a modest man. Once, when Nachman bar Rav Chisda was giving a lecture, he invited Nachman bar Yitzchak to come sit on the podium. Nachman refused, saying, "It is not the place that honors the man, it is the man who honors the place" (*Ta'anit* 21b).

Nachman was quite sensitive to the feelings of his fellowmen. In *Bava Metzi'a* 58b he comments that anyone who publicly shames a neighbor, causing his face to turn red from embarrassment, is to be compared to one who has shed blood. Nachman notes that he, himself, had witnessed such a case of extreme embarrassment.

To emphasize how important it is that Torah scholars respect their younger colleagues, Nachman bar Yitzchak asked, "Why are the words of the Torah likened to a tree?" Quoting *Proverbs* 3:18, "It [the Torah] is a tree of life to all who take hold of it," Nachman comments that this teaches us that just as a small piece of wood can kindle a large piece of wood, so can a younger scholar sharpen the minds of older ones." Nachman went on to say: "Much have I learned from my teachers, and from my colleagues more than from all" (*Ta'anit* 7a).

Nachman bar Yitzchak is believed to have died in the year 356.

Nachman bar Zavda (second/third century)
Babylonian amora. In *Shabbat* 25b he is noted as a disciple of Rav.

Nachman bar Zechariah
See Nachman bar Zekharyah.

Nachman bar Zekharyah (third/fourth century)
Babylonian amora. In *Bava Kamma* 25b he is listed as a disciple of Abbayei.

Nachman ben Ammi (third/fourth century)
Palestinian amora. He is quoted in *Eruvin* 67a.

Nachman ben Ika (third century)
Palestinian amora. According to *Makkot* 21a, he was a contemporary of Malkiyya.

Nachman ben Oshaya (third century)
Palestinian amora. In *Shabbat* 65a Nachman ben Oshaya is listed as a disciple of Yochanan bar Nappacha.

Nachman of Parhatya (fourth/fifth century)
Also known as Nachman of Parzakya.
Babylonian amora. In *Kiddushin* 81a he is mentioned as a contemporary of Ashi.

Nachman of Parzakya
See Nachman of Parhatya.

Nachmani
See Abbayei.

Nachum (second century)

Palestinian tanna. According to *Berakhot* 55b, he was a disciple of Biryam and a teacher of Panda.

Nachum, Attendant of Abbahu (third/fourth century)

Palestinian amora. In *Yevamot* 42b he is characterized as an attendant and disciple of Abbahu.

Nachum ben Pappa (second century)

Palestinian tanna. In *Yoma* 67a he is noted as a disciple of Elazar ha-Kappar.

Nachum ha-Livlar (fourth century)

Palestinian amora. Known in English as Nachum the Scribe, he is quoted in *Nazir* 56b on the amount of harvest that must be left in the field for the poor: If a man has sown his field with two varieties of wheat but harvests and threshes them together, he need leave only one corner of his field for the poor. However, if the farmer harvests and threshes the two varieties separately, he must leave two corners of his field unharvested for the poor.

Nachum ha-Midi (first century)

Palestinian tanna. Known in English as Nachum the Mede, he was a contemporary of Yochanan ben Zakkai and is described in *Ketubbot* 105a as a civil-law judge in Jerusalem. According to Oshaya, there were 394 courts in the city.

Nachum Ish Galya (third century)

Babylonian amora. Known in English as Nachum the Galatian, he was a mentor to Yosef and is quoted in *Ketubbot* 60a.

Nachum of Gimzo (first/second century)

Palestinian tanna. Well-known in Jewish folklore as a scholar to whom many disagreeable experiences occurred, Nachum always responded with the words: *Gam zu le-tovah*, "This, too, is for the best." His name is a pun on this famous phrase and the name of his city.

Ta'anit 21a and *Sanhedrin* 108b–109a both contain a fabulous legend involving Nachum of Gimzo and the Roman emperor. Once, when the emperor was angry and threatened to impose harsh, new decrees upon the Jews, the Jews decided to appease his anger with a gift. No one, however, was willing to act as messenger, fearing that he might lose his life should the emperor refuse the gift. The community decided to send the gift with Nachum, feeling certain that if he was the bearer of the gift it would be accepted and the king would make the desired concessions.

The Jews of the city filled a coffer with diamonds and pearls for the emperor. On his way to deliver the coffer, Nachum stopped overnight in a hostelry. During the night, thieves removed the diamonds and pearls and filled the box with sand. When Nachum awoke and saw what had happened, he said, "It is for the best." He felt certain that God would induce the king to accept the sand instead of the diamonds.

Nachum proceeded on his way until he arrived in the royal city. When the populace discovered that the gift he was carrying was ordinary sand, they became angry and felt that the Jews were mocking the emperor.

Suddenly, the prophet Elijah appeared in the guise of a courier and calmed the assembly by saying, "I think that the Jews have sent a very valuable gift to the emperor. The sand in this box is the same sand that was used by Abraham, who shot it from his bow at the kings who had captured his nephew, Lot."

It so happened that the emperor was then engaged in a war with a neighboring country. Unable to conquer it, the emperor tried the sand; its effects were so marvelous that the enemy was immediately routed. When the emperor realized the value of the sand that the Jews had sent him, he repaid them by filling a box with diamonds and pearls from his treasury, and Nachum was sent home in great honor.

On his return trip, Nachum lodged in the same hostelry, and everyone marveled that he was still alive. When asked what happened, he told them about the wondrous nature of the sand.

The people immediately filled large boxes with the same sand and took these to the emperor. They told the emperor that Nachum had been carrying diamonds and pearls as a gift for him but that when these had been stolen, sand from their houses had been substituted. As proof, they had brought boxes filled with the same sand as a gift for the emperor.

The emperor demanded an investigation. When the sand

was proven not to possess the same powers as the sand that Nachum had brought, the villagers were accused of trying to deceive the king and sentenced to death.

In later life Nachum of Gimzo suffered from many bodily afflictions, including blindness. Among Nachum's closest disciples was Akiva ben Yosef (*Shevu'ot* 26a and *Berakhot* 22a), who ministered to his teacher.

Nachum Sabba (first century)
Palestinian tanna. Known in English as Nachum the Elder, he is quoted in *Berakhot* 48b.

Nachum the Elder
See Nachum Sabba.

Nachum the Galatian
See Nachum Ish Galya.

Nachum the Mede
See Nachum ha-Midi.

Nachum the Scribe
See Nachum ha-Livlar.

Nachuma ben Afkashyon (second century)
Palestinian tanna. He is mentioned in *Yoma* 28b as a contemporary of Akiva ben Yosef.

Nachumi bar Adda (third century)
Also spelled Nechumi bar Adda.
Babylonian amora. In *Beitzah* 31b he is listed as a disciple of Shemu'el.

Nachumi bar Zechariah
See Nachumi bar Zekharyah.

Nachumi bar Zekharyah (third/fourth century)
Also spelled Nechumi bar Zechariah.
Palestinian amora. According to *Shabbat* 127a, *Eruvin* 102a, and *Beitzah* 16a, he was a disciple of Abbayei; *Shabbat* 136a lists Nachumi as a colleague of Mar bar Ravina.

Nannai bar Joseph bar Rabbah
See Nannai bar Yosef bar Rabbah.

Nannai bar Yosef bar Rabbah (fourth century)

Babylonian amora. He is mentioned in *Yevamot* 66b he as a colleague of Kahana.

Natan

Two scholars were known by this name:

1. A second-century Palestinian tanna widely quoted in the Babylonian Talmud, who sometimes is known as Natan ha-Bavli or, in English, as Natan the Babylonian. According to one tradition, Natan's father was the *reish galuta* who left Babylonia and settled in Palestine.

In *Bava Metzi'a* 50b–51a Natan is noted as a contemporary of Yehudah ha-Nasi. Though the two men were legal adversaries, they respected each other, and Natan assisted Yehudah ha-Nasi in the compilation of the Mishnah. Among Natan's other colleagues were Shimon ben Gamli'el II (*Shabbat* 128a), Dosa (*Eruvin* 83a), and Ya'akov (*Gittin* 14b and *Kiddushin* 79b). In *Sukkah* 19b and *Beitzah* 35a Natan is listed as a contemporary of Eli'ezer. Natan's principal disciple was Yishma'el (*Pesachim* 67b).

Natan was particularly concerned with the observance of Jewish rituals and considered anyone who did not have a *mezuzah* on his doorpost to be an *am ha-aretz*, an "ignoramus." In *Shabbat* 109a Natan expressed the belief that evil spirits cleave to one's hands during the night and must be gotten rid of by washing the hands three times each morning.

Some scholars attribute *Avot de-Rabbi Natan* to him. Among his moralistic teachings in this work is the following evocative statement:

> There is no greater love than the love of the Torah; there is no greater wisdom than the wisdom of the Land of Israel; there is no greater beauty than the beauty of Jerusalem; there is no greater wealth than the wealth of Rome; there is no greater valor than the valor of the Persians; there is no greater immorality than the immorality of the Arabs; there is no greater rudeness than the rudeness of the Land of Elam; there is no greater flattery than the flattery of Babylonia; there is no greater witchcraft than the witchcraft of Egypt. (Chapter 28)

2. A third/fourth-century Babylonian amora whose two major colleagues were Rabbah bar Nachmani (*Yevamot* 56a) and Rava (*Shabbat* 141b). In *Beitzah* 35b Natan disagrees with Yehudah bar Yechezkel about the word *mashilin* or *mashkilin*, used to describe the letting down of fruit from a roof, where it often was placed to dry, on a Sabbath or holiday.

In *Ketubbot* 55a Natan and Rav disagree on a ruling by Elazar ben Azaryah regarding a deed of land.

Natan Avuha de-Rav Huna bar Natan (fourth century)
Also known as Natan, Father of Huna bar Natan.
Babylonian amora. *Pesachim* 117b records his visit to Pappa.

Natan bar Abba (third century)
Babylonian amora. In *Bava Metzi'a* 41a he is noted as a disciple of Rav and a colleague of Ya'akov bar Abba.

Natan bar Abbayei (third/fourth century)
Palestinian amora. He is mentioned in *Chullin* 95a as a disciple of Chisda.

Natan bar Ammi (fourth century)
Babylonian amora. In *Shabbat* 150b and *Kiddushin* 30a he is listed as a disciple of Rava. *Bava Batra* 8b and *Ketubbot* 49b both note that Rava compelled Natan bar Ammi to contribute four hundred *zuzim* to charity.

Natan bar Asya (third century)
Babylonian amora. It is recorded in *Pesachim* 52a that Natan bar Asya was placed under a ban by his fellow rabbis for traveling on the second day of Shavu'ot from Rav's academy in Sura to Pumbedita. Jews who live outside of Israel were expected to observe festivals for an additional day, meaning, in the case of Natan bar Asya, that he was expected to keep Shavu'ot for two days instead of one.

Natan bar Avin (second/third century)
Babylonian amora. In *Chullin* 45b he is noted as a disciple of Rav.

Natan bar Mar Ukba (third century)
Babylonian amora. In *Berakhot* 13b he is noted as a disciple of Yehudah bar Yechezkel.

Natan bar Mar Zutra (fourth/fifth century)

Babylonian amora. In *Sanhedrin* 29a he is noted as an instructor of Ashi.

Natan bar Minyomi (third/fourth century)

Palestinian amora. In *Shabbat* 21b and *Chagigah* 3a he is mentioned as a disciple of Tanchum.

Natan bar Tavi (third century)

Palestinian amora. According to *Berakhot* 28a, he was a student of Ze'eira.

Natan ben Amram (second century)

Palestinian tanna. According to *Avodah Zarah* 37a, he was a contemporary of Yehudah ha-Nasi.

Natan ben Avishalom (second century)

Palestinian tanna. *Berakhot* 22a records a disagreement between Natan ben Avishalom and his colleague Yonatan ben Yosef about what holy books may be studied by one who is ritually impure.

Natan ben Avtolemos (second/third century)

Palestinian tanna. According to *Sanhedrin* 87b and *Zevachim* 49b, Natan ben Avtolemos disagreed with his fellow rabbis about whether leprosy can be spread through clothing.

Natan ben Isaac

See Natan ben Yitzchak.

Natan ben Oshaya (third century)

Palestinian amora. In *Shabbat* 81b and 102b he is listed as a colleague of Yochanan bar Nappacha, and in *Nazir* 44b as a contemporary of Abbayei. According to *Eruvin* 52a, Yehudah ben Ishtita brought Natan a basket of fruit one Sabbath eve, and Natan ben Oshaya invited him to spend the night in his home.

Natan ben Yitzchak (third century)

Palestinian amora. He is quoted in *Ta'anit* 3a.

Natan ben Yosei (second century)

Palestinian tanna. In *Sukkah* 26b he says that a man who has an emission of semen may not don *tefillin*.

Natan, Father of Huna bar Natan
See Natan Avuha de-Rav Huna bar Natan.

Natan ha-Bavli
See Natan.

Natan of Beit Guvrin
See Yonatan of Beit Guvrin.

Natan of Bira (fourth/fifth century)
Babylonian amora. In *Ketubbot* 75a Natan of Bira comments that the space of one handbreadth between a woman's breasts is considered a bodily defect. Abbayei believed that a space of three fingers was normal.

Natan the Babylonian
See Natan.

Nechemyah (second century)
Palestinian tanna. Always referred to without patronymic, little is known about his personal life except that he was a potter by trade. Extremely poor, he was a student in the academy of Yochanan ben Zakkai in Yavneh. *Berakhot* 63b lists Yehudah bar Ila'i, Yosei ben Chalafta, and Eli'ezer ben Yosei ha-Gelili as fellow students of Nechemyah. *Sanhedrin* 14a records that Yehudah ben Bava, contrary to Roman edict, ordained five rabbis; according to Aviya, Nechemyah was one of those rabbis.

In *Yevamot* 47b Nechemyah asserts that he will accept converts only if their motive is a pure love of Judaism. In *Kiddushin* 30a he differs with his colleague Yehudah bar Ila'i as to the parameters of youth: "One maintains that a youth is a person between the ages of sixteen and twenty-two, and the other, between the ages of eighteen and twenty-four." The text does not specify which is Nechemyah's view.

Nechemyah bar Barukh (third century)
Babylonian amora. In *Mo'ed Katan* 16a he is listed as a disciple of Chiyya bar Avin.

Nechemyah bar Chanilai (fourth century)
Babylonian amora. In *Eruvin* 43b he is noted as a disciple of Nachman bar Ya'akov and a contemporary of Chisda.

Nechemyah bar Joseph
See Nechemyah bar Yosef.

Nechemyah bar Joshua
See Nechemyah bar Yehoshu'a.

Nechemyah bar Yehoshu'a (fourth century)
Babylonian amora. In *Mo'ed Katan* 19b he is noted as a contemporary of Pappa.

Nechemyah bar Yosef (fourth century)
Babylonian amora. In *Mo'ed Katan* 19b Nechemyah is noted as a contemporary of Pappa and in *Bava Batra* 66b as a contemporary of Rabbah bar Huna Zuti. Nechemyah was named executor of the estate of Yosef bar Rabba, and *Ketubbot* 65a records that Yosef bar Rabba's wife requested "an allowance for board" from Nechemyah and that he granted it.

Nechemyah ben brei de-Rav (third century)
Babylonian amora. Known in English as Nechemyah, Grandson of Rav, Nechemyah served as *reish galuta*. According to *Chullin* 92a, he and Ukba were the sons of Rav's daughter.

Nechemyah, Grandson of Rav
See Nechemyah ben brei de-Rav.

Nechemyah ha-Imsoni (first century)
Also known as Nechemyah the Imsoni.

Palestinian tanna. A predecessor of Akiva ben Yosef, Nechemyah ha-Imsoni offers different interpretations of the word *et* wherever it appears in the Torah (*Bava Kamma* 41b).

Nechemyah of Beit Choron (third century)
Palestinian amora. A pious scholar who was highly respected and whose advice was sought on matters concerning the regulating of the calendar, he lived in the small town of Beit Choron, northwest of Jerusalem. Nechemyah's son also was a respected scholar.

Nechemyah of Beit Deli (first/second century)
Palestinian tanna. Nechemya was a teacher in the academy in Nehardea. Akiva ben Yosef quotes one of his rulings in *Yevamot* 115a and 122a on the issue of whether a woman may remarry if only one witness appears to testify that her husband is dead.

Nechemyah the Imsoni
See Nechemyah ha-Imsoni.

Nechumi
See Rechumi I.

Nechumi bar Adda
See Nachumi bar Adda.

Nechumi bar Zechariah
See Nachumi bar Zekharyah.

Nechumi bar Zekharyah
See Nachumi bar Zekharyah.

Nechunya (first century)
Palestinian tanna. Nechunya was an alternate name for Ne-chemyah. According to *Zevachim* 121b, Nechunya was a well digger whose daughter fell into a large cistern; the accident was reported to Chanina ben Dosa. In *Niddah* 25b Beivai ben Ab-bayei expresses respect for Nechunya's view on the viability of a fetus born without facial features, called a *sandal*, and which Shimon ben Gamli'el I described as resembling the tongue of a large ox.

Nechunya ben Elinatan (first/second century)
Palestinian tanna. He is quoted in Mishnah *Eduyyot* 6:2–3.

Nechunya ben Gudggada (first century)
Palestinian tanna. A *Levi* in charge of monitoring the Temple gates, he was a colleague of Yochanan ben Zakkai and is quoted in *Eduyyot* 7:9.

Nechunya ben ha-Kanah (first/second century)
Palestinian tanna. He is thought to have been a disciple of Yochanan ben Zakkai and sometimes is referred to as Nechunya ha-Gadol; in English, Nechunya the Great. His father probably was a grain dealer.

A very spiritual teacher, the brief prayers Nechunya would recite before entering and leaving the academy are recorded in *Berakhot* 28b. When he entered, he would pray: "Save me from error that I should have no occasion to be angered at my comrades, nor that they should be angry with me. I pray that in my teachings I should not declare the clean to be unclean nor the unclean to be clean and that I should not be put to shame, either in this world or in the world to come."

Upon leaving the academy after delivering his lecture, Nechunya would pray: "I thank the Creator for all that happened to me during the day; especially do I thank Him for this: that it is my share to sit in a house of learning and not among the sinful, the idle, and the scornful, for my way leads to eternal life and their way leads to hell."

Although he was wealthy and had many servants, Nechunya was modest and forgiving. In *Megillah* 28a, when asked by a student how he could account for having reached such an advanced age, Nechunya responded: "I have never sought respect by degrading my fellowman . . . and I have been generous with my money."

In *Megillah* 7b he equates damage done by an act of transgression on Yom Kippur to that done on the Sabbath.

Nechunya ha-Gadol
   See Nechunya ben ha-Kanah.

Nechunya of the Plain of Beit Churtan (third century)
   Palestinian amora. Noted in *Zevachim* 110b as an authority whom Yochanan bar Nappacha respected, Nechunya lived in a town southeast of Damascus, sometimes called Beit Chavarta.

Nechunya the Great
   See Nechunya ben ha-Kanah.

Nehemiah
   See Nechemyah.

Nehilai bar Iddi (third century)
   Babylonian amora. In *Yoma* 22b and *Ta'anit* 6a Nehilai is mentioned as a disciple of Shemu'el.

Nehorai
   See Me'ir.

Nimos ha-Gardi (first/second century)
   Palestinian tanna. Known in English as Nimos the Weaver, he was, according to *Chagigah* 15b, a contemporary of Me'ir.

Nimos the Weaver
   See Nimos ha-Gardi.

Nittai (third century)

Babylonian amora. According to *Bava Batra* 111a, he was a colleague of Shemu'el.

Nittai of Arbela (first/second century B.C.E.)

Pre-tannaitic Palestinian teacher. A member of the *zugot*, he was the partner of Yehoshu'a ben Perachyah. Nittai served as *av beit din* of the Sanhedrin.

According to *Chagigah* 16a, Nittai and Shimon ben Shetach agreed that the "laying on of hands" was permissible when offering a sacrifice. The laying of hands on an animal to be sacrificed required great strength, and some authorities considered this "work," in violation of the laws; Nittai did not agree with this interpretation. In *Avot* 1:7, Nittai of Arbela warns: "Maintain distance between yourself and an evil neighbor, and do not become a partner with a wicked person."

Nivli (third century)

Babylonian amora. He is listed in *Chullin* 45b as a disciple of Huna.

O

Onias the Circle Maker

See Choni ha-Me'aggel.

Onkelos (first/second century)

Palestinian scholar. Popularly known as Onkelos the Proselyte, he translated the Bible into Aramaic and frequently is
confused in the Talmud and Tosefta with Aquila, also a proselyte, who translated the Bible into Greek.

In *Avodah Zarah* 11a Onkelos is referred to as Onkelos, Son
of Klonimos, and in *Gittin* 56b as Onkelos, Son of Klonikos,
who was the son of Emperor Titus's sister. According to one
legend, Titus sent a contingent of Roman soldiers to induce
Onkelos to forsake Judaism, but instead, all of the soldiers converted to Judaism. This story is recounted in *Avodah Zarah* 11a.

The relationship between the *nasi* Gamli'el II and Onkelos
seems to have been a close one, for Onkelos is always mentioned as being associated with him. Upon Gamli'el's death,
Onkelos arranged a very lavish funeral for him.

Onkelos's translation of the Bible has been preserved in its
entirety, while very little of Aquila's translation survived.

Oshaya (third century)

Also spelled Hoyasha. *Also known as* Oshaya of Nehardea.

Babylonian tanna. One of Oshaya's primary teachers was Rav,
whom he quotes as saying that when Adam was created, God
assembled "his torso from Babylonia, his head from the land of
Israel, his limbs from other lands, and his private parts from
Akra di Agma [a town near Pumbedita in Babylonia that was
reputed to have very loose morals]" (*Sanhedrin* 38b).

Among Oshaya's other teachers were Ammi (*Pesachim* 63b)
and Rava (*Chullin* 52b). Oshaya's disciples included Ze'eira, Abba
(both mentioned in *Ketubbot* 79a), and Yosef (*Shabbat* 127a).

Oshaya lived in Nehardea. From time to time he would visit the academies of Palestine, where he would transmit the teachings of the Babylonian scholars (*Shabbat* 145b and *Niddah* 21b). In *Yoma* 41a he is referred to as Hoshaya.

Oshaya bar Zavda (fourth century)

Babylonian amora. In *Ta'anit* 26b he states that a Priest is not forbidden to drink wine before pronouncing the Priestly Benedictions.

Oshaya ben Chiyya (third century)

Palestinian tanna. In *Yevamot* 46b he is listed as a colleague of Chiyya bar Yehudah.

Oshaya ben Judah

See Oshaya ben Yehudah.

Oshaya ben Yehudah (first/second century)

Palestinian tanna. Son of a spice maker, Oshaya ben Yehudah is recorded in *Chullin* 55b testifying before Akiva ben Yosef and quoting Tarfon that an animal stripped of its hide may not be used as food.

Oshaya Berabbi (third century)

Palestinian tanna. Oshaya is noted in *Yevamot* 46b as a colleague of Safra.

Oshaya of Nehardea

See Oshaya.

Oshaya of Usha (third century)

Palestinian amora. In *Bekhorot* 38b he is listed as a colleague of Rabbah bar Bar Chana.

Oshaya Rabbah (third century)

Also known as Hoshaya Rabbah.

Palestinian amora. Known in English as Oshaya the Great, there is some confusion in the Talmud about the identity of his father. In *Mo'ed Katan* 24a his father is recorded as a scholar named Nachmani. It is noted in *Ketubbot* 62b, however, and is the consensus among historians, that Oshaya Rabbah's father was Chama bar Bisa, a man who, like Akiva ben Yosef, spent twelve years away from home studying. Oshaya became an outstanding scholar, even greater than his father, Chama bar Bisa, who is said to have stood in his son's presence as a sign of respect (*Bava Batra* 59a).

Oshaya Rabbah opened a school in Caesarea that, in time, rivaled the prestigious academy in Tiberias. Many important scholars are numbered among Oshaya's disciples, which led Yehudah ha-Nasi to say of Oshaya that "he was as great a man in his generation as Me'ir had been in his."

Among Oshaya Rabbah's teachers were Chiyya (*Shabbat* 38b) and Assi (*Shabbat* 18a). Among Oshaya's disciples were Acha (*Berakhot* 3b), Elazar (*Pesachim* 103b and *Gittin* 78a), Eli'ezer (*Kiddushin* 6a), Yitzchak bar Nachman (*Shabbat* 37a), Yochanan bar Nappacha (*Eruvin* 53a), Ya'akov ben Idi (*Berakhot* 29b), Shimon ben Lakish (*Niddah* 18b and 25a), and Chama ben Yosef (*Niddah* 19a and *Avodah Zarah* 44b).

Pesachim 113b reveals that Oshaya and his colleague Chanina earned their livelihoods as cobblers. Both were said to have lived on a street inhabited by harlots and to have made shoes for these women. Rava notes that while the harlots would look at the Rabbis, the Rabbis would not look at them.

Oshaya is sometimes referred to as Hoshaya (*Eruvin* 43a) and occasionally as Hoshaya Rabbah to distinguish him from the Babylonian amora Oshaya.

Oshaya Ze'eira of Chaverya (third/fourth century)

Babylonian amora. He is referred to in *Chullin* 12b and 31a, and in *Niddah* 26a.

P

Panda (first/second century)

Palestinian tanna. In *Berakhot* 55b he is mentioned as an associate (and possibly a teacher) of Akiva ben Yosef and a disciple of Nachum. This is the only reference to Panda in the Talmud.

Pappa (fourth century)

Also known as Pappa bar Chanan of Bei Khelochit.

Babylonian amora. Almost always referred to as Pappa, without patronymic, he was a close friend and colleague of Huna bar Yehoshu'a (*Bava Metzi'a* 67b), though the two often disagreed on penalties to be imposed for violations of law.

Pappa studied under Rava (*Eruvin* 51a) and Abbayei (*Berakhot* 20a). His other prestigious teachers included Rav (*Shabbat* 93b) and Shemu'el (*Sotah* 35b). Upon Rava's death, Pappa established his own academy in the town of Naresh; he drew many students (*Ketubbot* 106a), and Huna bar Yehoshu'a (*Yoma* 49a and *Berakhot* 22b) became his deputy. In *Ketubbot* 40b, where he is referred to as Pappa bar Chanan of Bei Khelochit, Pappa is mentioned as a colleague of Shimi bar Ashi.

The Talmud offers two accounts of how Pappa became rich. In *Pesachim* 49a Pappa is quoted as saying: "Had I not married a Priest's daughter, I would not have become wealthy." In *Pesachim* 113a Pappa remarks: "Were I not a beer manufacturer, I would not have become wealthy." Huna bar Yehoshu'a and Pappa were partners (*Gittin* 73a) in the beer business, which Pappa furthered by announcing, "Everyone can drink beer, but drinking wine violates [the precept] 'Thou shalt not waste'" (*Shabbat* 140b). So vast were Pappa's holdings that he had to lease additional land to grow fodder to feed his many animals (*Bava Metzi'a* 46a and 109a).

Pappa was married twice. His second wife was the daughter of Abba of Sura (*Ketubbot* 39b), with whom he apparently was unhappy. This may have led him to say: "Be quick to buy land but deliberate in choosing a wife" (*Yevamot* 63a).

Bava Metzi'a 84a describes Pappa as being extremely obese; fasting did not agree with him (*Ta'anit* 24b). Yet once, when he spoke unkindly about a fellow scholar, he imposed a fast upon himself as an act of repentance (*Sanhedrin* 100a).

Pappa was very heartened when he found students who were particularly wise and on one occasion offered Huna bar Nachman his daughter's hand in marriage (*Horayot* 12b). Whenever Pappa visited a town on business, he always paid his respects to the local scholars; this practice exemplified his deep regard for teachers and learned students (*Niddah* 33b).

Widely acclaimed for his erudition and compassionate manner in handling legal disputes, many colleagues turned to him for opinions and rulings. Among the cases he handled, the following were typical:

- May dough be kneaded with milk? (*Bava Metzi'a* 91a)
- May two animals of the opposite sex and of diverse kinds be housed in the same enclosure? (*Bava Metzi'a* 91a)
- If a man sells a field to two persons, the ground to one and the trees to the other, how can the owner of the trees have access to their fruit if the owner of the land refuses him permission to tread on his property? (*Bava Batra* 37a)

Though Pappa was a legal force in the Talmud, he also was influenced by superstition. In *Pesachim* 110a his belief in the power of demons is described. In *Berakhot* 19a he claims that a beam fell on and killed a man who was following the funeral cortege of Shemu'el because the man had made some disparaging remarks about the famous scholar. In *Pesachim* 112b Pappa cautions that one should not remove his shoes when entering a home in which a cat resides, lest the cat, having eaten a snake, leaves the snake's bones on the floor and a bone becomes embedded in a person's foot, endangering him. *Sanhedrin* 93a quotes Pappa as saying: "A white horse seen in a dream is a favorable omen [because it signifies appeasement]," which is in keeping with Pappa's favorite proverb: "He who takes vengeance destroys his own house" (*Sanhedrin* 102b).

Pappa headed the Naresh academy for nineteen years, until his death in approximately 376.

Pappa bar Acha bar Adda (fourth century)

Babylonian amora. In *Sanhedrin* 29b he is noted as a disciple of Rav and in *Eruvin* 21b as a disciple of Acha bar Ulla.

Pappa bar Chanan (third/fourth century)

Babylonian amora. In *Bava Batra* 153a he is said to have been the scribe of Rava, writing out documents for him.

Pappa bar Chanan of Bei Khelochit

See Pappa.

Pappa bar Channin (third century)

Babylonian amora. In *Menachot* 28b he is noted as a disciple of Yosef, who claimed that in order for a candlestick to be used in the Temple it had to be made of gold.

Pappa bar Joseph

See Pappa bar Yosef.

Pappa bar Nachman (third century)

Babylonian amora. In *Bava Metzi'a* 113a, he is mentioned as a disciple of Yosef.

Pappa bar Shemu'el (third century)

Babylonian amora. A disciple of Chisda (*Shabbat* 54b) and of Rava (*Rosh Hashanah* 27a and 34b), Pappa bar Shemu'el was recognized in *Sanhedrin* 17b as the most celebrated judge in Pumbedita. Pappa's wife's name was Yalta (*Shabbat* 54b).

Pappa bar Yosef (third century)

Babylonian amora. According to *Bava Metzi'a* 113a, he was a disciple of Yosef.

Pappa ben Abba (fourth century)

Palestinian amora. In *Yevamot* 46a he is said to have been a member of a wealthy family of moneylenders, who were reputed to force into slavery borrowers unable to repay their loans. Pappa ben Abba is portrayed in *Bava Kamma* 10b as a very corpulent man and in *Chullin* 54a as a fowler who used to kill birds by striking them on the kidney. In *Yoma* 66b he is noted as a colleague of Ravina I.

Pappa Sabba (third century)

Babylonian amora. Known in English as Pappa the Elder, he is listed in *Sanhedrin* 49b and *Menachot* 33b as a disciple of Rav.

Pappa the Elder

See Pappa Sabba.

Pappeyas (first century)

Palestinian tanna. In *Sanhedrin* 94a, one of Pappeyas's disciples quotes his master's view that it was a disgrace that Moses and the 600,000 Israelites who left Egypt had not offered thanks to God until Jethro came and did so. Pappeyas is listed as a colleague of Yehoshu'a ben Chananyah in *Rosh Hashanah* 6a and as a colleague of Yehudah ben Beteira in *Beitzah* 29b.

Pappi (fourth century)

Babylonian amora. A devoted disciple of Rava (*Yoma* 62a, *Ketubbot* 8a, and *Bava Batra* 126a), Pappi quotes Rava in *Megillah* 26b as saying that one may convert a synagogue into a school but may not convert a school into a synagogue. Rava believed that nothing was more important than the study of Torah.

In an interesting case that came before Pappi for adjudication, he ruled, in opposition to his contemporary Beivai bar Abbayei, that a person may demand payment for improvements he makes in a field that he had leased.

Among Pappi's colleagues were Kahana (*Sotah* 45a), Pappa (*Ketubbot* 7a) and Ashi (*Chullin* 77a and *Rosh Hashanah* 29b).

Pappus ben Judah

See Pappus ben Yehudah.

Pappus ben Yehudah (second century)

Palestinian tanna. Pappus ben Yehudah tried to discourage Akiva ben Yosef from publicly teaching Torah to large assemblies of students after the Romans had decreed death to anyone who did so. When asked by Pappus whether he did not fear the Romans, Akiva responded with the following parable of the fox and the fish (*Berakhot* 61b):

A fox walking alongside a river saw a fish scurrying from one place to another. "From what are you fleeing?" he asked. "From the nets cast for us by men," the fish replied.

The fox said: "Would you like to come ashore so that you and I can live together in the way that my ancestors lived with your ancestors?" "Are you the one they call the cleverest of animals?" asked the fish. "You are not clever but foolish. If we are afraid in the element in which we live now, how much more would we have to fear in a strange environment!"

"If such is our condition when we sit and study the Torah," said Akiva to Pappus, "what would happen to us if we neglect the Torah?"

Parnakh (third century)

Palestinian amora. He is listed in *Shabbat* 14a as a disciple of Yochanan bar Nappacha. In *Megillah* 32a Parnakh condemns anyone who takes hold of a Torah scroll without its covering, thus handling the parchment itself.

Pas

See Efes.

Pedat (third century)

Palestinian amora. In *Ketubbot* 64a he is listed as a disciple of Yochanan bar Nappacha. According to *Berakhot* 55b, Pedat was a teacher of Huna ben Ammi and according to *Pesachim* 101a, a teacher of Abbayei.

Pelimo (second century)

Palestinian tanna. In *Menachot* 37a he asks Yehudah ha-Nasi: "If a man has two heads, on which head should he wear *tefillin?*" Yehudah dismissed him angrily for asking such a ridiculous question. Just then a man came in and said: "A child with two heads has been born to me. How much must I give the *Kohen* for his redemption [of the firstborn]?"

In *Sanhedrin* 10b Pelimo comments that "If the New Moon appears at its due time [on the thirtieth of the month], it does not have to be sanctified [blessed]; if it does not appear at its due time, sanctification is to be proclaimed."

Perida (third/fourth century)

Palestinian amora. In *Menachot* 52b he is noted as a disciple of Ammi bar Natan. *Sanhedrin* 82a describes a skull that Perida's grandfather found lying near the gates of Jerusalem on which these words were inscribed: "This and yet another." When Perida's grandfather tried to bury the skull, it refused to remain underground and would resurface. Perida's grandfather said, "This must be the skull of King Jehoiakim, about whom Jeremiah wrote (22:19): 'He shall be buried with the burial of an ass' but who, as king, although he was evil, deserved a decent interment."

Perida lived to a ripe old age and when asked the secret of his longevity replied: "I was always the first to appear in the house of study and never refused to pay a Priest his Priestly dues" (*Megillah* 27b–28a).

Phinehas

See Pinchas.

Pinchas

See Pinchas bar Chama.

Pinchas Achuha de-Mar Shemu'el (second/third century)

Babylonian amora. Known in English as Pinchas, Brother of Mar Shemu'el, he is mentioned in *Mo'ed Katan* 18a.

Pinchas bar Ammi (fifth century)

Babylonian amora. He is listed in *Pesachim* 100a as a colleague of Mereimar, in *Zevachim* 7b as a colleague of Ashi, and in *Ketubbot* 85a as a colleague of Pappa and Huna bar Yehoshu'a.

Pinchas bar Chama (fourth century)

Palestinian amora. Often referred to as Pinchas, without patronymic, or as Pinchas ha-Kohen, he probably was born in Sikhnin, in the Galilee. His teacher was Yirmeyahu, and Pinchas had a brother named Shemu'el. For a while Pinchas lived in Babylonia, where he displayed great interest in *aggadah*. One of his more popular maxims was: "The name that a man gains for himself is worth more than the one given him by his father and mother."

In *Ketubbot* 105a Pinchas is mentioned as a disciple of Oshaya and in *Yevamot* 29b as a disciple of Rava.

Pinchas bar Chisda (third/fourth century)

Babylonian amora. *Kiddushin* 32b recounts how Pinchas bar Chisda offended Rava by not rising as a sign of respect when Rava served him a drink at his son's wedding. Pinchas is the brother of Mari bar Chisda, as noted in *Ketubbot* 61a.

Pinchas bar Mari (fourth/fifth century)

Babylonian amora. In *Zevachim* 4a he is mentioned as a contemporary of Ashi.

Pinchas ben Aruva (first century)

Palestinian tanna. *Gittin* 56b mentions his visit with the notables of Rome.

Pinchas ben Ya'ir (second century)

Palestinian tanna. Born in Lydda, Pinchas ben Ya'ir is noted in *Shabbat* 33b as the son-in-law of Shimon bar Yochai, with whom he studied. The Zohar (3:240), however, refers to Pinchas as the father-in-law of Shimon bar Yochai, who was the leader of a group of mystics of whom Pinchas was a part. Pinchas ben Ya'ir was widely praised as a legal scholar, although few of his decisions are recorded.

In Mishnah *Sotah* 9:15 Pinchas offers a ladder of saintliness: "Caution [against evil] leads to cleanliness, and cleanliness leads to purity, and purity leads to abstinence [asceticism], and abstinence leads to holiness, and holiness leads to humility, and humility leads to fear of God, and fear of God leads to saintliness, and saintliness leads to [the gift of] the Holy Spirit, and the Holy Spirit leads to the resurrection of the dead, and the resurrection of the dead shall come through Elijah of blessed memory. Amen."

Widely known for his piety and for acts of charity, Pinchas is associated with many unusual and often miraculous happenings. *Chullin* 7a describes a journey he took to raise funds to redeem captives. As he approached a river, he saw that its bridge was out and that he could not cross it. Addressing the river, Pinchas cried: "Make way that I may cross!" The river answered, "You are about to do the will of the Creator, and I always do His will. You are not certain whether your journey will be successful, but my path [to the sea] has been laid out by God. I therefore need not change my course . . ." "If you will not make way for me, I will decree that your sources be dried up," replied Pinchas. Upon hearing this, the river was frightened and immediately made a path for him.

Pinchas ben Ya'ir's piety extended even to his animals. *Chullin* 7a recounts that once, when traveling with his donkey, Pinchas stopped at an inn to feed his animal. Barley was placed before it, but the donkey would not eat. The barley was sifted to cleanse it, but still the donkey would not eat. "Perhaps," said Pinchas, "the barley has not been tithed." Thereupon, it was tithed and the animal ate his fill.

In *Sotah* 49a Pinchas is quoted as saying: "Since the destruction of the [Second] Temple, scholars and noblemen were ashamed and covered their heads," implying that it was customary for the masses to go bareheaded. Elsewhere the Talmud indicates that when people would pass learned scholars, they would cover their heads as a sign of respect.

Pinchas, Brother of Mar Samuel
See Pinchas Achuha de-Mar Shemu'el.

Pinchas ha-Kohen
See Pinchas bar Chama.

R

Rab

See Rav.

Raba

See Rava.

Rabbah

See Rabbah bar Nachmani.

Rabbah bar Abbuha

See Rabbah bar Avuha.

Rabbah bar Abina

See Rabbah bar Avina.

Rabbah bar Adda (fourth century)

Babylonian amora. In *Ketubbot* 7b he is mentioned as a disciple of Yehudah bar Yechezkel and a brother of Ravin bar Adda.

Rabbah bar Aivu (third/fourth century)

Babylonian amora. In *Gittin* 32a and *Keritot* 24a he is noted as a disciple of Sheshet.

Rabbah bar Avina (third century)

Also spelled Rabbah bar Abina.

Babylonian amora. A colleague of Yosef, Rabbah bar Avina (misspelled as Ahina) comments in *Menachot* 37b on the subject of *tzitzit* required for garments.

Rabbah bar Avuha (third century)

Also spelled Rabbah bar Abbuha.

Babylonian amora. A relative of the exilarchs, Rabbah bar Avuha is believed by some authorities to have been an exilarch himself. Until the year 259, when it was destroyed by the Palmyrenes, Nehardea was the home of Rabbah bar Avuha. Afterward, he went to live in Machoza with his disciple and son-in-law, Nachman bar Ya'akov (*Bava Metzi'a* 91b and *Yevamot*

80b). Rabbah bar Avuha's daughter and Nachman's wife, Yalta, was well-known and is mentioned several times in the Talmud.

Rabbah bar Avuha apparently was less than an outstanding scholar, an admission he makes in *Bava Metzi'a* 114b; often he relies on the views of Rava (*Sanhedrin* 63a and *Gittin* 62b). An interesting comment of Rabbah bar Avuha is noted in *Ketubbot* 37b. In referring to *Leviticus* 19:18 he says: "The commandment to love one's neighbor must be observed even when a criminal is being executed. He should be granted as easy a death as possible."

Rabbah bar Aza (third/fourth century)

Babylonian amora. He is listed in *Temurah* 21a as a contemporary of Abbayei.

Rabbah bar Bar Chana (third century)

Babylonian amora. Born in Babylonia, he studied in Palestine under Yochanan bar Nappacha for many years. When Rabbah bar Bar Chana returned to Babylonia, disappointed over the lack of respect accorded him in Palestine (*Yoma* 9b), he transmitted the teachings of Yochanan to the scholars of Pumbedita and Sura.

In Pumbedita, Rabbah became very friendly with Yehudah bar Yechezkel and consulted with him on many matters (*Mo'ed Katan* 17a). In Sura, where Chisda was principal of the academy, Rabbah tried to introduce the recitation of the Ten Commandments into the daily liturgy of Babylonia, as it had been done in the Temple. Chisda convinced him that the idea was unwise (*Berakhot* 12a). One of Rabbah's mentors was Shemu'el bar Marta.

Rabbah became famous when news of his fantastic adventures spread. As noted in *Bava Batra* 73a–74a, he traveled a great deal on sea and land and related greatly exaggerated accounts of his experiences, products of his active imagination. One such story goes like this: "Once, while on a ship, we came upon a gigantic fish at rest, which we thought was an island. The fish had sand on its back and grass was growing in the sand. We landed, made a fire, and cooked our meal. But when the fish felt the heat of the cooking, he rolled over. Had our ship not been so close by, we all would have drowned" (*Bava Batra* 73b).

Because of his fantastic tales, one colleague remarked, "All Rabbahs are asses and all bar Bar Chanas are fools."

Rabbah was a serious student, a devoted teacher, and a virtuous individual. One of his most memorable aphorisms is, "The soul of one pious man is worth the entire world." Because of his travels, he felt safe in asserting that the Land of Israel truly was a land flowing with milk and honey, as noted in *Numbers* 13:27.

Berakhot 47a records that Rabbah bar Bar Chana made a marriage feast for his son in the home of Shemu'el bar Kettina.

Rabbah bar Beruna (third/fourth century)

Babylonian amora. In *Shabbat* 110a he comments on two species of palm trees in Palestine.

Rabbah bar Chana (third century)

Also known as Abba bar Chana.

Babylonian amora. Born in Kafri, Babylonia, Rabbah bar Chana was the nephew of Chiyya and a cousin of Rav (*Sanhedrin* 5a). Little else is known about Rabbah's personal life except that he was married and was a wine merchant (*Bava Metzi'a* 83a).

Rabbah migrated to Palestine, where he studied under Yochanan bar Nappacha (*Zevachim* 62a and *Beitzah* 40a) and Yehudah ha-Nasi, who authorized him to decide legal questions when he returned to Babylonia.

In *Ta'anit* 7a Rabbah bar Chana asks, "Why are the words of the Torah likened to fire?" He answers: "To teach you that just as fire does not ignite itself, so, too, the words of the Torah do not endure with he who studies alone."

Rabbah bar Chanina (fourth century)

Babylonian amora. In *Bava Batra* 113b and *Sanhedrin* 34b he is a listed as a student of Nachman bar Ya'akov.

Rabbah bar Channin (third/fourth century)

Babylonian amora. In *Eruvin* 38b and 45a he is noted as a disciple of Abbayei.

Rabbah bar Chiyya of Ketisfon (second/third century)

Babylonian amora. According to *Yevamot* 104a, he was censured by Shemu'el for performing the *chalitzah* ceremony in a manner rejected by the majority of rabbis, using a felt sock instead of a shoe, conducting the ceremony at night, and allowing no men to be present.

Rabbah bar Huna (third/fourth century)

Also known as Abba bar Huna *and* Rava bar Huna.

Babylonian amora. Son of Huna, principal of the academy at Sura, Rabbah studied under his father, who also encouraged him to attend classes conducted by the great scholar Chisda, who would succeed Huna as principal of the academy at Sura.

At first Rabbah was not drawn to Chisda, but later in life a closer association developed between the two men, and Chisda even appointed Rabbah to be a judge (*Shabbat* 10a). After the death of Chisda, Rabbah was appointed principal of the academy at Sura.

Shemu'el (*Eruvin* 49a) and Rav (*Bava Batra* 136b) also were Rabbah bar Huna's teachers.

Although he was quite wealthy (*Bava Metzi'a* 107b reports that "he owned a forest near the river bank"), Rabbah bar Huna was modest and unassuming. His illustrious colleague Rava once expressed the hope that he might emulate him (*Mo'ed Katan* 29a).

Among the statements of Rabbah that reflect his fine character are:

- An insolent person is considered a sinner. (*Ta'anit* 7b)
- When a man loses his temper it proves that even God is unimportant in his eyes. (*Nedarim* 22b)
- He who possesses learning but is without fear of God is like the steward to whom has been given the keys of the inner storehouse but not the outer storehouse. He, therefore, cannot gain access to the treasures. (*Shabbat* 31a–b)

It is reported in *Mo'ed Katan* 25b that while Rabbah died in Babylonia in 322, his body was transported to the Land of Israel for burial, where many eulogies were delivered to honor his memory.

Rabbah bar Huna Zuti (fourth century)

Also known as Rava bar Huna Zuti.

Babylonian amora. In *Bava Batra* 66b he is noted as a teacher of Nechemyah bar Yosef. Rabbah taught at the academy in

Nehardea, where he was referred to as Rava bar Huna Zuti (*Beitzah* 29b).

Rabbah bar Isaac
See Rabbah bar Yitzchak.

Rabbah bar Isi (third century)
Babylonian amora. In *Sotah* 30a, where he is referred to as Rabbah ben Isi, he is noted as a disciple of Rav.

Rabbah bar Lima (second/third century)
Babylonian amora. In *Rosh Hashanah* 4a and *Megillah* 13b he is said to have been a disciple of Rav.

Rabbah bar Livai (fourth century)
Babylonian amora. A contemporary of Rava, Rabbah bar Livai is listed in *Niddah* 46b as a colleague of Yehudah, who was a disciple of Shemu'el. In *Pesachim* 40b Rabbah bar Livai disputes a ruling by Rava permitting grain, upon which a cask of wine used by idolators had fallen, to be sold to Gentiles.

Rabbah bar Mari (third/fourth century)
Babylonian amora. A colleague and close friend of Rava (*Berakhot* 42b), Rabbah bar Mari resided for a short time in Palestine and then returned home to Babylonia (*Yoma* 78a). He is remembered for the following aphorism: "Just as the lentil has no mouth [or "cleft," like other types of beans] so does a mourner have no mouth [the ability or desire to converse]" (*Bava Batra* 16b). In *Sukkah* 32b he is mistakenly listed as a disciple of Yochanan ben Zakkai, who lived three centuries earlier. Rabbah bar Mari was a frequent visitor at the home of Rava (*Berakhot* 42b) and answered many of Rava's questions (*Bava Kamma* 92a).

Rabbah bar Mattnah (fourth century)
Babylonian amora. In *Horayot* 14a Rabbah is noted as a fellow student of Abbayei, Rava, and Ze'eira. Rava considered Abbayei to be the most learned of the three, and Abbayei eventually was selected to head the academy in Pumbedita following the deaths of Rabbah bar Nachmani and Yosef.

Rabbah bar Mechasya (third century)
Babylonian amora. In *Ta'anit* 12b he is noted as a disciple of Chama bar Gurya.

Rabbah bar Memel

See Abba bar Memel.

Rabbah bar Nachmani (third/fourth century)

Babylonian amora. Scion of a Priestly family whose roots could be traced back to Eli, the *Kohen Gadol* (*Rosh Hashanah* 18a), Rabbah bar Nachmani raised his orphaned nephew Abbayei. In *Berakhot* 48a Rabbah predicted that both Rava and Abbayei would become great rabbis. Rabbah bar Nachmani is sometimes referred to simply as Rabbah, without the patronymic.

Although he was born in Memel, a city in Galilee, according to *Eruvin* 17a, Rabbah left Palestine to study in Babylonia under Huna in Sura and also under Yehudah bar Yechezkel in Pumbedita. Rabbah's teachers respected his scholarship greatly, and Huna, it is said (*Gittin* 27a, *Bava Metzi'a* 18b, and elsewhere), would not issue a ruling without first consulting Rabbah.

Ketubbot 111a speaks of how Rabbah's brothers, who lived in Palestine, tried to convince him to return to Palestine so that he might study under the great scholar Yochanan bar Nappacha, but apparently Rabbah was not convinced of the wisdom of that course. Instead, he spent most of his life in Babylonia in the company of his close friend and colleague Yosef, who had an encyclopedic memory and who was referred to as "Sinai." Rabbah himself was highly skilled in analysis and dialectics, and was referred to in *Berakhot* 64a as "Uprooter of Mountains."

When Yehudah bar Yechezkel, master of the academy in Pumbedita, died in 299, Yosef was offered the position there but declined because astrologers had told him that he would hold the post for only two years (*Berakhot* 64a). Rabbah was elected to the position and served as principal of the academy in Pumbedita for twenty-two years. When Rabbah died, Yosef succeeded him and served for two and a half years before he died.

Under Rabbah's leadership, the academy in Pumbedita attracted four hundred students (*Ketubbot* 106a), the greatest number in its history. During the *kallah* months (Adar and Elul), when thousands of students would gather at the Babylonian academies to attend lectures by the greatest scholars of the day, as many as twelve thousand Jews flocked to hear Rabbah, who always introduced his remarks with a humorous anecdote (*Shabbat* 30b).

Bava Metzi'a 86a records that Rabbah died a tragic death. Local tax collectors, frustrated over their inability to collect money from students who were away during the *kallah* months, blamed Rabbah and set out to arrest him. He fled, running from town to town, and finally back to Pumbedita where, according to one view, on the outskirts of town, in the woods, he was found dead, entrapped in a thicket.

It was said that at the moment of his death, a heavenly voice was heard to proclaim: "Happy art thou, O Rabbah bar Nachmani, whose body is pure, and whose soul has departed unblemished." According to *Rosh Hashanah* 18a and *Mo'ed Katan* 28a, he was only forty years old when he died, although this figure is disputed, and many scholars believe he was sixty years old.

Mo'ed Katan 25b notes that when Rabbah bar Nachmani died, followed two and a half years later by Yosef, it seemed as though the cliffs on both sides of the Euphrates kissed each other, meaning that mourners were so numerous they could have forced the water to be pushed aside.

Rabbah bar Natan (third century)

Babylonian amora. A student of Huna (*Bava Kamma* 32a), Rabbah bar Natan was in touch with the Palestinian scholar Yochanan bar Nappacha. The two men consulted on the question of property that can be recovered by a lender if the debtor's signature on a note has been legally certified by a court as bona fide (*Bava Batra* 176a).

Rabbah bar Nathan

See Rabbah bar Natan.

Rabbah bar Rav (second/third century)

Babylonian amora. In *Bava Metzi'a* 67a he is in agreement with Rava on what constitutes indirect usury; for example, a merchant overcharging a customer.

Rabbah bar Rav Chanan (third/fourth century)

Babylonian amora. *Eruvin* 92a states that Rabbah bar Rav Chanan, Abbayei, Rabbah, and Ze'eira studied together.

Berakhot 45a relates an interesting bit of advice that one of Rabbah bar Rav Chanan's teachers offered when Rava asked, in a moot case, "What is the law?" The response he received was: "Go out and see how the people are accustomed to act."

Bava Batra 26a describes a disagreement between Rabbah bar Rav Chanan and Yosef. Rava had some date trees adjoining Yosef's vineyard. Birds would roost on the date trees and swoop down, damaging Yosef's grapevines. Yosef asked Rava to remove the date trees, but Rava refused, basing his decision on the opinion of Rav, who said that one may not cut down fruit-bearing trees.

Rabbah bar Rav Nachman (third/fourth century)

Babylonian amora. Son of the noted amora Nachman bar Ya'akov, Rabbah bar Rav Nachman was considered by his colleague Rabbah bar Huna as a master of learning (*Yevamot* 25a). *Bava Metzi'a* 108a describes a clash that occurred between them, which ended in Rabbah bar Huna cursing Rabbah bar Rav Nachman and his children. The conflict arose when Rabbah bar Rav Nachman ordered that some of Rabbah bar Huna's trees be cut down because they interfered with the flow of traffic on a nearby river.

Rabbah bar Samuel

See Rabbah bar Shemu'el.

Rabbah bar Shemu'el (third century)

Also known as Abba bar Shemu'el.

Babylonian amora. Thought to have been the son of the renowned amora Shemu'el, Rabbah bar Shemu'el was a disciple of Chiyya (*Berakhot* 40a) and a colleague of Pappa and Huna bar Yehoshu'a (*Berakhot* 22b). In *Zevachim* 105a, where Rabbah bar Shemu'el addresses a question to Chiyya, he is referred to as Abba bar Shemu'el. Among Rabbah bar Shemu'el's very learned disciples were Rav (*Yoma* 36b) and Chisda (*Chullin* 102a). In *Eruvin* 11b and 39b Rabbah is noted as a teacher of Sheshet. In *Yoma* 82a Rabbah cautions against forcing children to fast on Yom Kippur at too early an age. He suggests that they be trained gradually, one year or two before they reach maturity.

Rabbah bar Shila (fourth century)

Babylonian amora. Rabbah bar Shila is thought to have lived near Machoza; his name appears in association with Rava, who also lived in Machoza, where he was principal of an academy. According to *Shabbat* 81a–b, *Chullin* 102a, and *Bava Metzi'a* 70a, Rabbah bar Shila was a disciple of Chisda, whose teaching he cites with regard to the handling of funds belonging to orphans. Rabbah bar Shila also studied with Mattnah II (*Chagigah* 23a and *Chullin* 42b) and Nachum bar Ya'akov (*Bava Batra* 155b).

After being appointed judge, Rabbah bar Shila insisted upon a strict interpretation of the law and warned other judges that it was wrong to borrow anything from litigants who appeared before them, lest they compromise their impartiality (*Ketubbot* 104b and 105b).

In *Chagigah* 15b Rabbah bar Shila is portrayed as a mystic who fantasized that he met the prophet Elijah and asked him why the teachings of Me'ir were not being transmitted. Elijah responded by saying, "Because his learning came from his teacher Acher [Elisha ben Avuyah] who became an apostate." To which Rabbah replied, "But why? Me'ir merely found a [beautiful] pomegranate. He ate its [juicy] fruit and discarded the peel."

In *Ta'anit* 2a Rabbah bar Shila comments on the texts that suggest that rain can be described as a reflection of God's power. In *Berakhot* 8a Rabbah comments on *Psalms* 32:6: "Let everyone who is godly pray unto Thee in the time of finding." He ascribes to the phrase "a time of finding" the following meaning: "A man should pray for peace even until the last clod of earth is placed on his grave."

Rabbah bar Shimi (third/fourth century)

Babylonian amora. He studied with several notable teachers, including Ravina I (*Pesachim* 6b) and Yosef (*Chullin* 29b). In *Yoma* 63a, Rabbah bar Shimi is listed as a teacher of Dimi.

Rabbah bar Tachlifa (fourth century)

Babylonian amora. He was a disciple of Ravina I (*Eruvin* 40a), Rav (*Shabbat* 120b), and Yirmeyahu ben Abba, a disciple of Rav (*Chullin* 45b and 49a).

Rabbah bar Ulla (fourth century)

Palestinian amora. In *Eruvin* 8a he is noted as a colleague of Beivai bar Abbayei. In *Bava Kamma* 39b Rabbah bar Ulla is noted as a colleague of Ya'akov and in *Bava Metzi'a* 93a as a contemporary of Acha bar Huna.

Rabbah bar Yitzchak (third century)

Also known as Rava bar Yitzchak.

Babylonian amora. In *Chullin* 45b, *Sanhedrin* 99b, and *Yevamot* 71b he is noted as a disciple of Rav, and in *Avodah Zarah* 55a as a colleague of Yehudah bar Yechezkel. Rabbah bar Yitzchak sometimes is referred to as Rava bar Yitzchak (*Kiddushin* 27a).

Rabbah bar Yonatan (second/third century)

Babylonian amora. According to *Yoma* 47a and *Nedarim* 41b, Rabbah bar Yonatan was a disciple of Yechi'el.

Rabbah bar Yosef bar Chama

See Rava.

Rabbah ben Maryon (third century)

Palestinian amora. He is listed in *Eruvin* 19a as a disciple of Yehoshu'a ben Levi. Rabbah's father, Maryon, also was an amora.

Rabbah ben Ofran (third century)

Palestinian amora. According to *Megillah* 15b, he was a disciple of Elazar ben Pedat.

Rabbah ben She'ilta (fourth century)

Palestinian amora. In *Gittin* 81b he is noted as a teacher of Ze'eira.

Rabbah ben Toviyyah (third century)

Palestinian amora. In *Eruvin* 28a he is listed as a disciple of Yitzchak.

Rabbah ben Zavda (third century)

Babylonian amora. In *Shabbat* 19b reference is made to his dispute with Huna, which is detailed in *Shabbat* 120a. The issue under discussion relates to moving articles from one domain to another on the Sabbath. In this instance, a fire broke out in a house and the question was how many meals the owner could remove to feed humans and animals.

Rabbah of Kubi (fifth century)

Babylonian amora. *Kiddushin* 8a reports that Mar bar Ashi bought from the mother of Rabbah of Kubi a scarf worth ten *sela* for thirteen *sela*. The point being made is that one cannot assume that both parties evaluated the scarf in the same way. Thus, for example, if one pays a Priest the five *sela* fee for the redemption of his firstborn son with a garment less than five *sela* in value, the transaction is valid if the Priest accepts the garment as full payment.

Rabbah the Younger

See Rabbah Zuti.

Rabbah Tosfa'ah (fifth century)

Babylonian amora. A pupil of Ravina I and a contemporary of Ravina II (*Mo'ed Katan* 4a), Rabbah Tosfa'ah served as head of the academy in Sura and was succeeded after his death by Ravina II.

In *Berakhot* 50a Rabbah Tosfa'ah comments on what constitutes a quorum for the public recitation of Grace After Meals; in *Yevamot* 80b he indicates that a woman's pregnancy may extend from nine to twelve months.

One of the last of the amora'im, Rabbah Tosfa'ah was of great assistance to Ashi in completing the compilation of the Babylonian Talmud. Some believe that he was called Tosfa'ah, which means "additions," because of his ability to explain and expand upon Talmudic discussions. It is more likely that he was named for his birthplace, Thospia.

Rabbah Zuta

See Rabbah Zuti.

Rabbah Zuti (fourth/fifth century)

Also known as Rabbah Zuta.

Babylonian amora. Known in English by the name Rabbah the Younger—*zuti* and *zuta* mean "small" or "junior"—Rabbah Zuti is mentioned in *Bekhorot* 36a as a disciple of Ravina I, and in *Menachot* 31b and 52a as a colleague of Ashi. *Beitzah* 32b and *Bava Batra* 120a, in which he is referred to as Rabbah Zuta, also note that he was a colleague of Ashi.

Rabbanai Achu de-Rabbi Chiyya bar Abba
(third century)
Also spelled Rabbenai Achu de-Rabbi Chiyya bar Abba.

Babylonian amora. Known in English as Rabbanai, Brother of Chiyya bar Abba, he is listed in *Chullin* 76b and *Yoma* 21a as a disciple of Shemu'el, whom he consulted frequently, and in *Ketubbot* 21b as the brother of Chiyya bar Abba. In *Avodah Zarah* 39a Rabbanai is noted as a contemporary of Huna and Yosef.

Rabbanai, Brother of Chiyya bar Abba
See Rabbanai Achu de-Rabbi Chiyya bar Abba.

Rabbenai Achu de-Rabbi Chiyya bar Abba
See Rabbanai Achu de-Rabbi Chiyya bar Abba.

Rabin bar Adda
See Ravin bar Adda.

Rabina
See entries under Ravina.

Rafram (fourth/fifth century)
Babylonian amora. A pupil of Ashi, to whom he often addressed questions (*Ketubbot* 95b), and a colleague of Ravina II (*Yoma* 78a and *Gittin* 11a), Rafram succeeded Geviha of Bei Katil as principal of the academy in Pumbedita and served from 433 until his death in 443. The name Rafram is likely a contraction of the title "Rav" and the name Efrayim.

Rafram bar Pappa (fourth century)
Babylonian amora. Sometimes referred to simply as Rafram, Rafram bar Pappa studied in his youth under Chisda (*Eruvin* 83a and *Bava Batra* 25b) and later under Rava, who once reprimanded him for not reciting the Torah blessings properly. "You black pot!" said Rava. "Why do you want to create controversy?" (*Berakhot* 50a). Rafram also was a student of Shemu'el, whom he quotes in *Mo'ed Katan* 24a.

Among Rafram's colleagues were Ashi (*Gittin* 42a), Rava and Huna (*Ta'anit* 20b), and Natan (*Yoma* 78a). Many scholars, along with the exilarch, attended lectures given by Rafram in Natan's house. Rafram was so well regarded that he succeeded Dimi as principal of the academy in Pumbedita. According to some scholars, Rafram died in 387; others date the year of his death as 395.

Rafram of Pumbedita (second century)

Babylonian amora. *Bekhorot* 36b reports what happened when a firstling given to a *Kohen* by Rafram was blemished by the Priest and disqualified for sacrifice.

Rafram of Sikhra (fourth/fifth century)

Babylonian amora. In *Bava Metzi'a* 42a Rafram of Sikhra is noted as a contemporary of Ashi. Sikhra was a town on the Tigris near Machoza.

Rakhish bar Pappa (fourth century)

Babylonian amora. According to *Chullin* 42b, he was a disciple of Rav.

Rama bar Chama

See Rami bar Chama.

Rami

See Ammi bar Natan.

Rami bar Abba (third/fourth century)

Babylonian amora. In both *Chullin* 111a and *Beitzah* 29b he is noted as the father-in-law of Ashi. According to *Eruvin* 10a and 61a, Rami bar Abba was a disciple of Huna; *Berakhot* 59b lists Rami as a disciple of Yitzchak. *Megillah* 26b describes Rami bar Abba's dilemma in erecting a synagogue.

Rami bar Berabbi

Babylonian amora. He is mentioned in *Sanhedrin* 17b. In Rashi's commentary on *Beitzah* 8b he is referred to as Beribbi.

Rami bar Chama (fourth century)

Also known as Rama bar Chama.

Babylonian amora. According to *Bava Batra* 29b, Rami bar Chama and his brother Ukba bar Chama jointly bought a maidservant. A subsequent dispute over the maidservant had to be adjudicated by Rava. *Bava Batra* 151a notes another dispute between the two brothers, this one over their mother's estate.

Berakhot 44a and *Bava Batra* 12b discuss the marriage of Chisda's daughter, first to Rami bar Chama and later, after Rami's death, to Rava; Ukba bar Chama married another of Chisda's daughters. In *Beitzah* 29b Ashi testifies to the fine character of Rami, his father-in-law, when he says: "My wife is the daughter of Rami bar Chama, a man of pious deeds . . ."

Rami was a disciple of Rav (*Ta'anit* 9a), Yirmeyahu of Difti (*Megillah* 18b), and Yitzchak (*Avodah Zarah* 31b), whom he quotes as expressing the view that beer prepared by heathens is forbidden because it might lead to socializing with them, which might lead to intermarriage.

In *Yoma* 19a he is referred to as Rama bar Chama.

Rami bar Dikoli (third/fourth century)
Also known as Rami bar Dikoli of Pumbedita.

Babylonian amora. In *Yevamot* 80a he quotes his teacher Shemu'el. Some scholars believe that Rami bar Dikoli was the son-in-law of Rami bar Tamrei.

Rami bar Dikoli of Pumbedita
See Rami bar Dikoli.

Rami bar Ezekiel
See Rami bar Yechezkel.

Rami bar Judah
See Rami bar Yehudah.

Rami bar Pappa (third century)
Babylonian amora. According to *Yoma* 77b, Rami bar Pappa was a colleague of Yehudah bar Ila'i and Shemu'el bar Yehudah. In *Bava Batra* 100b it is reported that Rami bar Pappa's sister was married to Aviya.

Rami bar Rav (second/third century)
Babylonian amora. In *Makkot* 23b Rami bar Rav comments on the tithe to be brought to the Temple.

Rami bar Samuel
See Rami bar Shemu'el.

Rami bar Shemu'el (fourth century)
Babylonian amora. In *Ketubbot* 97a he is mentioned as a colleague of Nachman bar Ya'akov. In *Niddah* 17b Rami bar Shemu'el and Yitzchak bar Yehudah are listed as students of Huna.

Rami bar Tamrei (third/fourth century)
Babylonian amora. A native of Pumbedita, Rami bar Tamrei went to Sura one Yom Kippur eve and ate some cow's udder for his pre-fast meal. The natives criticized him roundly for violating custom: the people of Sura did not eat udder at all, although the residents of Pumbedita did (*Chullin* 110a). Rami was then hauled before the great scholar Chisda, with whom he had a sharp debate. In the end, Chisda recognized that Rami was a profound scholar.
In *Menachot* 29b of some manuscripts, Rami bar Tamrei is referred to as the father-in-law of Rami bar Dikoli.

Rami bar Yechezkel (third/fourth century)
Babylonian amora. Son of the amora Yechezkel, Rami was born in Babylonia but moved to Palestine, where he settled in Bene Berak. According to *Eruvin* 102a, he was a disciple of Amram. *Ketubbot* 111b reports that Rami bar Yechezkel visited his older brother, Yehudah bar Yechezkel, in Babylonia; Yehudah was founder and principal of the academy in Pumbedita.

Rami bar Yehudah (second/third century)
Babylonian amora. In *Zevachim* 55b he is listed as a disciple of Rav.

Rami bar Yeiva (third/fourth century)
Babylonian amora. A brother of Chanin bar Yeiva and Safra bar Yeiva, Rami bar Yeiva is mentioned in *Arakhin* 11b as a contemporary of Abbayei. Rami is also quoted in *Beitzah* 8b and *Shabbat* 83a.

Rami ben Avin (fourth century)
Palestinian amora. In *Shabbat* 20b he offers his view on a by-product of pitch that is unacceptable for use as a Sabbath candle.

Rami ben Yud (second century)
Palestinian tanna. In *Ta'anit* 22b he comments on the circumstances under which an alarm may be sounded on the Sabbath.

Rav (second/third century)
Also known as Abba Arikha *and* Abba bar Aivu.
Babylonian amora. Rav, whose real name was Abba bar Aivu, also was known as Abba Arikha—"Tall Abba"—because of his

exceptional height. *Niddah* 24b says that "Rav was the tallest man of his generation, and Yehudah bar Yechezkel reached only up to his shoulder." Rav also was a very handsome man, as noted in *Bava Metzi'a* 84a.

Born in Kafri, in southern Babylonia, Rav was a descendant of a distinguished Babylonian family that traced its ancestry back to Shimei, a brother of King David (*Ketubbot* 62b). Rav's father, Aivu, was a brother of Chiyya, who lived in Palestine, where he was a highly esteemed scholar in the circle of the patriarch, Yehudah ha-Nasi.

In his youth, Rav moved from Babylonia to Palestine, where he studied under his uncle Chiyya, who introduced him to Yehudah ha-Nasi. The patriarch was so impressed with Rav's keen mind that he entered into many legal discussions with him (*Chullin* 137b). It was most unusual for a tanna to engage an amora in such disputes. Thus, Rav occupies a unique position as the link between tanna'im and amora'im. In fact, he is said to be the last of tanna'im and the first of the amora'im.

While Yehudah ha-Nasi was still living, Rav, having been ordained as a rabbi—though not without certain limitation (he could not ordain others)—was appointed to Yehudah's court and remained in Palestine for some time before returning to Babylonia.

At first he settled in Nehardea, where he served as an assistant to Shila, principal of the academy. After Shila's death, Rav left Nehardea to found his own academy in Sura, which soon became the intellectual center of Babylonian Jewry. Its reputation was so remarkable that it attracted as many as twelve hundred students at one time (*Ketubbot* 106a).

Rav's closest friend and his adversary in halakhic discussions was Shemu'el, a longtime resident of Nehardea (*Shabbat* 108a). Their controversies are recorded throughout the Talmud. In matters of ritual law the *halakhah* follows Rav, and in civil matters it follows Shemu'el.

In one striking statement governing ritual matters Rav said: "The *mitzvot* were given only to refine people, for what difference does it make to God whether one slaughters an animal from the front or the back of the neck" (*Genesis Rabbah* 44:1).

A member of the affluent family of the *reish galuta,* Rav was appointed commissioner of markets. In this capacity, he supervised and controlled the price of commodities throughout the Jewish communities of Babylonia, for which he was well paid. He also was associated with the beer manufacturing business and owned real estate. But despite his financial security, his domestic life was not pleasant. For some unspecified reason his wife made his life miserable and tormented him. *Yevamot* 63a reports that when he asked her to prepare lentils for him, she would prepare beans, and when he asked for beans, she would serve him lentils.

One of Rav's two sons, Chiyya (the other was Aivu), came to his rescue and would tell his mother that his father wanted the opposite of what he really desired. One day Rav said to Chiyya, "Your mother has grown to like me." He once advised Chiyya, "Do not take drugs," apparently aware of the fact that they are habit-forming (*Pesachim* 113a). Chiyya was later recognized as a master of the Talmud.

The Talmud contains a plethora of Rav's sage expressions. Among the most meaningful are:

- Do not accept pupils who are less than six years old. From that age on you can accept them and stuff them with learning the way you would stuff an ox. (*Bava Batra* 21a)
- When you wish to punish a pupil, hit him with nothing harder than a shoelace. (*Bava Batra* 21a)
- Man will be called to account in the hereafter for each pleasure he denied himself without sufficient cause. (Palestinian Talmud, *Kiddushin* 4:12)
- Whoever can pray for his fellowman and does not do so must be called a sinner. (*Berakhot* 17a)
- A man must always accustom himself to think that whatever the Almighty does is for the best. (*Berakhot* 60b)
- One must not eat before feeding his animals. (*Berakhot* 40a)
- The future world is not like this world. In the world to come there will be no eating or drinking, no propagating or business activity, no envy or hatred or contention. The

righteous will be sitting on thrones with crowns on their heads, enjoying the brilliance of God's splendor. (*Berakhot* 17a)

- The number of pupils that should be assigned to each teacher is twenty-five . . . If there are forty, appoint an assistant. (*Berakhot* 17a)
- A meal without salt is no meal. (*Berakhot* 44a)
- The study of Torah is more important than the rebuilding of the Temple. (*Megillah* 16b)
- If all the seas were ink and all the reeds in the swamps were pens, they would not suffice to describe all the evil torment a ruler can invent for his subject. (*Shabbat* 11a)

Rav died in approximately 248 at an advanced age and was mourned for an entire year not only by his family and his many disciples, but by Babylonian Jewry as a whole. When Shemu'el was told that Rav had died, he tore twelve of his garments (as a sign of mourning) and said: "Gone is the man before whom I stood in awe" (*Mo'ed Katan* 24a). After Rav's death, it is noted in *Sanhedrin* 47b, it became customary to take some earth from Rav's grave and apply it as a remedy on the first day of an attack of fever.

Rav bar Shabba (fourth century)
Babylonian amora. In *Shabbat* 14a he is listed as a disciple of Ravina I, for whom he would prepare meals, and in *Bava Metzi'a* 66b as a colleague of Kahana.

Rava (third/fourth century)
Also known as Abba bar Yosef bar Chama, Rabbah bar Yosef bar Chama, Rava bar Yosef bar Chama, *and* Rava brei de-Rav Yosef bar Chama.

Babylonian amora. Son of Yosef bar Chama (*Bava Kamma* 97a), Rava's full name is given as Abba bar Yosef bar Chama in *Eruvin* 54a. In *Bava Kamma* 70a he is referred to as Rabbah bar Yosef bar Chama. Rava is short for Rav Abba.

Bava Batra 12b states that Rava married the daughter of Chisda (Chisda was principal of the academy in Sura and Rava's teacher), widow of his colleague Rami bar Chama. Rava's advice to single men was that they should always marry into a better family and should inquire well into the character of the prospective bride's brothers (*Bava Batra* 110a). One of Rava's sons, Acha, would become a disciple of Ashi (*Megillah* 28b).

Rava's name generally is linked with Abbayei. After Abbayei's death, Rava was appointed principal of the prestigious academy in Pumbedita at the beginning of the fourth century. Yosef bar Chiyya succeeded Rabbah as principal, and though Rava was a contender to succeed Yosef, the post was offered to Abbayei. This prompted Rava to return to Machoza, the town of his birth and in which he had studied as a youth under Nachman bar Ya'akov, and establish an academy there (*Shabbat* 4a). After Abbayei died, in 338, many of his students moved to Machoza to study under Rava. Over the next fourteen years, until Rava's death, his academy in Machoza was one of the most distinguished centers of learning in Babylonia, attracting large numbers of students (*Bava Batra* 22a).

In addition to Chisda, Rava's most outstanding teachers were Yosef, head of the academy in Pumbedita (*Chullin* 133a), and Nachman bar Ya'akov (*Shabbat* 4a). *Eruvin* 54a relates that Yosef had a grievance against Rava, son of Yosef bar Chama, and when the eve of Yom Kippur was approaching, Rava decided to placate his teacher, Yosef, by offering him a cup of wine that he had mixed in his expert manner. In *Ta'anit* 9a, among Rava's students and disciples are listed Huna bar Mano'ach, Shemu'el bar Idi, and Chiyya of Vastanya.

Among the many issues Rava discussed in his lectures and debated with Abbayei was the question of whether it is permissible to cook food for Shabbat on a festival immediately preceding the Sabbath (*Beitzah* 15a). In *Yoma* 10b Rava discusses whether a *sukkah* should have a *mezuzah* affixed to its doorpost.

In *Mo'ed Katan* 28a Rava characterized himself as having been blessed with the wisdom of Huna and the wealth of Chisda, but not the modesty of Rabbah bar Huna. That Rava was not overly modest is evident from a description of his demeanor in *Nedarim* 40a: Once, when Rava became ill, he requested that his condition not be made public. Apparently, he felt that if people discussed his condition it might tempt fate. But after the first day, he said to his servants: "Go out into the marketplace and announce my sickness so that anyone who is an enemy may rejoice, and anyone who is a friend may pray for me."

According to *Bava Metzi'a* 73a, Rava was a wealthy man who owned vineyards and was involved in the wine trade (*Berakhot* 56a). We also know from the Talmud that he owned a number of slaves. *Kiddushin* 33a reports that while the great scholar Yochanan bar Nappacha would rise to show respect when an older person passed by—even if he were a heathen—Rava would not rise. He would, however, send a servant to assist an aged person, if necessary. In *Makkot* 22b Rava rejects uncultured people who stand up to show deference to the Torah scroll but do not stand to show respect for a great or learned person.

Rava did not subscribe to the notion that the study of Torah is an end in itself. In *Berakhot* 17a, he stated succinctly: "The goal of wisdom is repentance and good deeds, so that a man should not study Torah and Mishnah and then despise his father and mother, his teacher, and his superior in wisdom and rank." Yet it is reported in *Shabbat* 10a that "When Rava saw Hamnuna prolonging his prayers, he said, 'There are people who give up [study, which is] eternal life, and occupy themselves with [praying for] transient needs.'"

Rava revealed his ideal of a truly religious person in a statement recorded in *Shabbat* 31a: "When a man is led in for judgment [in the world to come] he is asked: 'Did you deal faithfully [honestly] in your business dealings, did you set aside definite times for study, did you engage in procreation, did you hope for salvation, did you engage in the dialectics of wisdom, and did you differentiate one thing from another?'"

Sanhedrin 65b reveals that Rava was a mystic. In commenting on *Isaiah* 59:2, "But your iniquities have made a separation between you and God, and your sins have hidden His face from you . . . ," Rava said: "If the righteous people so desired, they could create the world. It is only man's sins that separate him from God." The Talmud then relates that Rava, after having studied the *Sefer Yetzirah* (*Book of Creation*) and learned the proper combination to form the divine name, once created a person. When Rava sent his creation to Ze'eira, Ze'eira talked to it, but it was unable to answer for it lacked the faculty of speech. Ze'eira then said to the creature, "You were created by one of the Torah scholars who mastered the secrets of creation. Return to your dust."

In *Pesachim* 25b Rava reveals how precious he regards the life of each individual. A man came to him and said: "The ruler of my city ordered me to slay so-and-so or he will kill me. What shall I do?" Rava responded: "Let yourself be slain, rather than you slay another. What makes you think your blood is more red than his? Perhaps his is redder."

Just before Rava died, he managed to say to Se'oram, his brother (*Moed Katan* 28a), "Tell the angel of death not to torment me."

Se'oram asked, "Are you [—a Torah teacher—] not an intimate friend of the angel of death?"

Rava replied: "Since my *mazzal* [lucky star] is already in his hands, the angel of death cares little about me."

When Rava died, Se'oram forced people in the street to come in and help carry Rava's litter. Later, Rava appeared to Se'oram in a dream, and Se'oram asked him: "Master, did you suffer pain when your life exited your body?"

"Not more," said Rava, "than one feels from the prick of the cupping needle [as blood is being drawn]."

According to tradition, when Rava died, Ashi was born.

Rava bar Abba (third century)
Babylonian amora. In *Pesachim* 30b he is noted as a disciple of Chiyya bar Ashi, who was a disciple of Shemu'el.

Rava bar Acha bar Huna (third/fourth century)
Babylonian amora. In *Niddah* 31b he is listed as a disciple of Sheshet.

Rava bar Achilai (third century)
Babylonian amora. He was a contemporary of Rav (*Bava Kamma* 64b).

Rava bar Avin (third/fourth century)
Babylonian amora. He is quoted in *Pesachim* 40a and *Ketubbot* 23a.

Rava bar Chaklai (third century)
Babylonian amora. In *Eruvin* 67b he is noted as a colleague of Huna.

Rava bar Chinena (third/fourth century)

Babylonian amora. He is listed in *Chullin* 18a as a teacher of Zutra and Ashi. *Bava Batra* 13b recounts the case that Rava bar Chinena and his brother, Dimi bar Chinena, brought before Rava regarding two servants left to them by their father. The issue was whether one brother could claim the more valuable of the servants and pay his brother compensation. Rava ruled against this, prohibiting one from saying to the other, "You name a price or let me name a price."

Rava bar Chinena Sabba (third century)

Also known as Rava bar Chinena the Elder.

Babylonian amora. In *Berakhot* 12a he is listed as a disciple of Rav.

Rava bar Chinena the Elder

See Rava bar Chinena Sabba.

Rava bar Huna

See Rabbah bar Huna.

Rava bar Huna Zuti

See Rabbah bar Huna Zuti.

Rava bar Iti (fourth century)

Babylonian amora. According to *Keritot* 24a, he was a disciple of Shimon ben Lakish; in *Bava Metzi'a* 14a he is noted as a colleague of Idi bar Avin.

Rava bar Jeremiah

See Rava bar Yirmeyahu.

Rava bar Joseph

See Rava bar Yosef.

Rava bar Kisna (second/third century)

Babylonian amora. He is quoted in *Bava Batra* 12a.

Rava bar Mechasya (third/fourth century)

Palestinian amora. In *Shabbat* 10b he is noted as a disciple of Chama bar Gurya, who was a disciple of Rav.

Rava bar Mesharshya (third/fourth century)

Babylonian amora. According to *Nazir* 40b, he was a colleague of Rava.

Rava bar Pappa (third/fourth century)
Babylonian amora. He is quoted in *Shabbat* 66b.

Rava bar Rabbah (third century)
Babylonian amora. In *Eruvin* 93b he is noted as a contemporary of Rabbah bar Ulla. In *Shabbat* 123a and *Ketubbot* 98a he is mentioned as a disciple of Yosef.

Rava bar Rabbah bar Huna (fourth century)
Babylonian amora. In *Eruvin* 55b he is listed as a contemporary of Rabbah bar Huna. In *Chullin* 76a Rava bar Rabbah bar Huna is noted as a disciple of Assi.

Rava bar Sharshum (third/fourth century)
Babylonian amora. In *Bava Batra* 33a he is noted as a junior contemporary of Abbayei.

Rava bar Ulla (fourth century)
Babylonian amora. He is listed in both *Menachot* 34a and *Chullin* 91a as a teacher of Shemu'el bar Acha.

Rava bar Yirmeyahu (third/fourth century)
Also known as Abba bar Yirmeyahu.
Babylonian amora. In *Pesachim* 36a and *Mo'ed Katan* 4a he is mentioned as a disciple of Shemu'el, and in *Avodah Zarah* 16b as a disciple of Rav. Rava bar Yirmeyahu is noted in *Gittin* 74a and *Ketubbot* 109a as a teacher of Ze'eira.

Rava bar Yishma'el (third/fourth century)
Babylonian amora. Rava bar Yishma'el is mentioned in *Ketubbot* 10b and *Mo'ed Katan* 6b.

Rava bar Yitzchak
See Rabbah bar Yitzchak.

Rava bar Yosef (third/fourth century)
Also known as Rabbah bar Yosei.
Babylonian amora. He is noted in *Bava Metzi'a* 67b as a disciple of Rava and, in *Arakhin* 5b, where he is referred to as Rabbah bar Yosef, he is noted as a disciple of Rav.

Rava bar Yosef bar Chama
See Rava.

Rava bar Zimmuna (third century)
Babylonian amora. According to *Shabbat* 112b, he was a teacher of Ze'eira.

Rava bar Zutra (third century)
Babylonian amora. In *Avodah Zarah* 28b he is mentioned as a disciple of Chanina.

Rava ben Ila'i (third century)
Palestinian amora. In *Shabbat* 62b he is mentioned as a disciple of Ammi and a colleague of Yitzchak.

Rava of Barneish (fourth/fifth century)
Babylonian amora. He is noted in *Rosh Hashanah* 26b and *Bava Metzi'a* 73b as a colleague of Ashi. Barneish was a canal near the town of Mechasya, adjacent to Sura.

Rava of Parzikya (fourth/fifth century)
Babylonian amora. According to *Pesachim* 76b, he was a contemporary of Kahana bar Chinena Sabba. In several Talmudic tractates, Rava of Parzikya is mentioned as a colleague of Ashi (*Pesachim* 76b, *Sotah* 26b, *Bava Kamma* 36a, *Bava Batra* 4b, and *Temurah* 30a); Rava's son, Huna Mar bar Rava of Parzikya, was Ashi's colleague as well (*Ketubbot* 10a).

Ravin bar Adda (fourth century)
Also spelled Rabin bar Adda. *Also known as* Avin bar Adda
Babylonian amora. Both he and has brother, Rabbah bar Adda, were disciples of Rav (*Yoma* 53b) and Yehudah bar Yechezkel, principal of the academy in Pumbedita (*Beitzah* 33b and *Ketubbot* 7b). Ravin bar Adda also was a disciple of Yitzchak (*Pesachim* 8b) and a colleague of Rava (*Yoma* 50a and *Zevachim* 93b). In *Berakhot* 6a Ravin bar Adda quotes Yitzchak on the importance of having a *minyan* for public prayer.

Ravin bar Chama (third/fourth century)
Also spelled Rabin bar Chama.
Babylonian amora. In *Ketubbot* 53a he is listed as a disciple of Chisda.

Ravin bar Chinana (fourth century)
Also spelled Rabin bar Chinena.
Babylonian amora. A disciple of Ulla (*Menachot* 30b), Ravin

bar Chinena is noted in *Pesachim* 109b as a colleague of Ashi and in *Chullin* 122a as a colleague of Ze'eira.

Ravin bar Nachman bar Jacob
See Ravin bar Nachman bar Ya'akov.

Ravin bar Nachman bar Ya'akov (third/fourth century)
Also spelled Rabin bar Nachman bar Ya'akov.

Babylonian amora. He is noted as a colleague of Yehudah bar Yechezkel in *Bava Metzi'a* 107a.

Ravin bar Samuel
See Ravin bar Shemu'el.

Ravin bar Shava (third/fourth century)
Also spelled Rabin bar Shava.

Babylonian amora. In *Chullin* 48a he is mentioned as a teacher of Rava.

Ravin bar Shemu'el (third century)
Also spelled Rabin bar Shemu'el.

Babylonian amora. According to *Bava Batra* 43a and 44b, he was a disciple of Shemu'el.

Ravin of Naresh (fourth/fifth century)
Also spelled Rabin of Naresh.

Babylonian amora. In *Gittin* 69b he prescribed a remedy of pepper grains and wine for the daughter of Ashi, who was suffering from stomach pains. According to the Talmud, she was cured.

Ravin Sabba
See Avin.

Ravin the Elder
See Avin.

Ravina I (fourth/fifth century)
Babylonian amora. Ravina, whose name is an abbreviation of Rav Avina, was the maternal uncle of Ravina II, final editor of the Talmud. After Ravina II's father died, Ravina I became his guardian.

Bava Metzi'a 104b notes that Ravina had a daughter in whose *ketubbah* Ravina wrote an amount of dowry larger than he intended to give her, and *Shabbat* 61a refers to Ravina's son,

Rabbana, as being a God-fearing person who always put his right sandal on first, but without tying it. Then he would put on his left sandal, tie it, and then tie the right one. When he removed his sandals at the end of the day, he would reverse the order. Many Rabbis believed that because the right half of the body was stronger, more honor must be shown it. By removing the left sandal first, greater respect was shown the right one, for it remained on the foot longer.

From an incident that is described in *Kiddushin* 33a, it seems that it was customary for scholars to wear head coverings and for laymen who entered their presence to cover their heads as a sign of respect. When Ravina was sitting outdoors with Yirmeyahu of Difti, a man passed by who did not cover his head. "How impudent is that man!" Ravina exclaimed. To which Yirmeyahu responded: "Perhaps he is from the town of Mechasya [where scholars are so commonplace and people are lax in carrying out the custom]." (*Kiddushin* 29b contains a discussion about covering one's head.)

Among Ravina I's principal teachers were Rava (*Berakhot* 20b, 33b, and 38a), and Chisda (*Pesachim* 59a). His colleagues included Acha bar Abbayei (*Shabbat* 4a and *Bava Kamma* 39b) and Yehudah of Difti (*Berakhot* 25a). Ravina I had little respect for his disciple, Rav bar Shabba (*Berakhot* 14a).

Ravina I was a fellow student of Ashi at the Sura academy. Later, when Ashi became principal of the academy and transfered it to Mata Mechasya, Ravina returned and became his intimate colleague (*Eruvin* 63a). When Ashi took on the project of editing the Babylonian Talmud, he depended greatly on Ravina, who had a phenomenal memory.

Ravina died in 422 at an advanced age. Many eulogies by prominent scholars were delivered at his funeral (*Mo'ed Katan* 25a).

Ravina II (fifth century)
Also known as Ravina bar Huna.

Babylonian amora. Like his uncle, Ravina I, who became his guardian after his father's death, Ravina II assisted Ashi in the monumental task of editing and finalizing the text of the

Babylonian Talmud. Ravina II's mother, who apparently was quite learned, communicated to him opinions held by her husband, who had died when Ravina II was very young (*Berakhot* 39b and *Menachot* 68b).

Shortly after Ashi's death, Ravina II served as a judge in Sura. Among the cases on which he worked, he helped Ashi's daughter collect her inheritance from her brother (*Ketubbot* 69a). Whenever possible, Ravina II tried to make the commandments easier to observe. He believed that the dignity of man was more important than the dignity of the commandments.

A charitable man, Ravina II raised money from the rich to care for the poor. Wealthy women would remove their jewelry and give it to him to aid the needy.

Ravina II's son married the daughter of Chanina of Sepphoris.

Following the death of Rabbah Tosfa'ah, principal of the academy in Sura, Ravina II headed the school for a year. Ravina died in 499, his death marking the close of the amoraic period as well as the task of editing the Talmud.

Ravina bar Huna
See Ravina II.

Ravina bar Shila (third century)
Babylonian amora. In *Sukkah* 13a and *Mo'ed Katan* 17b and 19b he is noted as a teacher of Chisda.

Ravina ben Ulla (third/fourth century)
Palestinian amora. According to *Beitzah* 3b, he was a contemporary of Yehudah bar Yechezkel.

Rechavah of Pumbedita (third/fourth century)
Babylonian amora. Rechavah, who studied in Pumbedita under Yehudah bar Yechezkel (*Pesachim* 52b), also was a disciple of Rava (*Eruvin* 22b) and a colleague of Huna bar Chanina (*Eruvin* 26b). Rechavah was married to Choma, daughter of Isi. After Rechavah's death, Choma would go on to marry Yitzchak bar Rabbah bar Chana and, following Yitzchak's death, Abbayei.

Rechumi I (fourth century)
Also known as Nechumi.

Babylonian amora. Listed as a colleague of Yosef bar Chama in *Eruvin* 11a, Rechumi I questioned Abbayei as to the kind of herb that is meant by the word *maror*, as noted in *Pesachim* 39a. According to *Ketubbot* 62b, Rechumi attended the school of Rava in Machoza. Rechumi is referred to as Nechumi in *Bava Batra* 131a. He died when a roof he was sitting on collapsed.

Rechumi II (fifth century)

Babylonian amora. In *Zevachim* 77a he is noted as a pupil of Ravina I. Rechumi II succeeded Rafram as head of the academy in Pumbedita and served from 443 to 456.

Reish Lakish

See Shimon ben Lakish.

Reuben ben Itztrobili

See Re'uven ben Itztrobili.

Re'uven ben Itztrobili (second century)

Palestinian tanna. In *Mo'ed Katan* 18b he is noted as a teacher of Rav. Rav quotes him as saying: "A person does not arouse suspicion unless he has done something that makes him a suspect."

Romanos (fourth century)

Palestinian amora. According to *Shabbat* 47a, he was a disciple of Ze'eira.

S

Safra (fourth century)

Babylonian amora. A businessman (*Bava Batra* 144a) who was praised for his honesty, Safra is lauded in *Pesachim* 113a as a bachelor who lived in a large city, yet who never succumbed to the temptation of prostitutes.

Safra's principal teachers were Abbayei (*Chullin* 51a), Abba (*Berakhot* 62b), and Ammi bar Natan (*Shabbat* 5b). When visiting his brother, Dimi Achuha de-Rav Safra, who lived in Palestine, Safra studied in various academies and carried the teachings of these Palestinian scholars back to the teachers in Babylonia. Apparently Safra himself was not esteemed as an all-around scholar, for Abbahu commented, "He is a scholar of the Talmud, not of the Bible" (*Avodah Zarah* 4a). Safra's decisions are not quoted in the Palestinian Talmud.

In fact, when Safra died in Pumbedita, the Rabbis did not rend their clothes for him, as was commonly done to mark the death of a scholar, because, they claimed, they did not learn anything directly from him. *Mo'ed Katan* 25a reports that Abbayei was one of the few who defended Safra.

It was said of Safra (*Berakhot* 16b–17a) that after concluding the prescribed prayers, he would add: "May it be Thy will, O Lord our God, to establish peace among the celestial family, and among the earthly family, and among the disciples who occupy themselves with Thy Torah, whether for its own sake or for other motives; and may it please Thee that all who do so for other motives may some day study it for its own sake!" (*Berakhot* 16b–17a).

Safra bar Yeiva (third/fourth century)

Babylonian amora. A brother of Channin bar Yeiva and Rami bar Yeiva, Safra bar Yeiva is referred to in *Bava Batra* 5a as a colleague of Ravina I.

Salla (fourth century)

Palestinian amora. In *Beitzah* 31a he is listed as a disciple of Yirmeyahu, and in *Ta'anit* 7b and *Kiddushin* 70a as a disciple of Hamnuna.

Salla Chasida (third century)

Babylonian amora. Known in English as Salla the Pious, he is mentioned in *Chullin* 74b as the father of Yosef and a colleague of Pappa. *Berakhot* 5b refers to Salla's brother, Yehudah Achuha de-Rav Salla Chasida.

Salla the Pious

See Salla Chasida.

Samma bar Ashi (fourth/fifth century)

Babylonian amora. Samma bar Ashi is believed to have been a colleague of Ravina II (*Bava Kamma* 18a and *Zevachim* 19b), but there is some confusion about his true identity. In *Ketubbot* 33b he is referred to as Samma bar Assi, a colleague of Ashi.

Samma bar Assi

See Samma bar Ashi.

Samma bar Chilkiyah (third/fourth century)

Babylonian amora. According to *Chullin* 38a, Samma was a colleague of Ravina I.

Samma bar Mari (fourth century)

Babylonian amora. In *Berakhot* 62b he is noted as a teacher of Chana bar Adda.

Samma bar Mesharshya (third/fourth century)

Babylonian amora. He is listed in *Chullin* 17b as a colleague of Ashi and a colleague of Ravina I.

Samma bar Rakta (fifth century)

Babylonian amora. According to *Kiddushin* 9a, he was a contemporary of Ravina II.

Samma bar Rava (fifth century)

Babylonian amora. He is quoted in *Chullin* 47b and *Bava Metzi'a* 42b, and for twenty years he served as head of the academy in Pumbedita.

Samma ben Jeremiah

See Samma ben Yirmeyahu.

Samma ben Yirmeyahu (fourth century)
Palestinian amora. He is quoted in *Ketubbot* 33a.

Samuel
See Shemu'el.

Samuel, Father of
See Abba bar Abba.

Saul ben Botnit
See Abba Sha'ul ben Botnit.

Sechorah (third century)
Babylonian amora. A disciple of Huna (*Shabbat* 24a) and a teacher of Rava (*Berakhot* 5a, *Eruvin* 54b, and *Menachot* 40b), Sechorah was highly praised in *Nedarim* 22b by Rava, who declared him to be "a great man."

Se'oram (second/third century)
Also known as Se'orim.
Babylonian amora. Rava's brother (*Mo'ed Katan* 28a and *Bava Metzi'a* 73b), Se'oram was at Rava's bedside during his dying moments.

Se'orim
See Se'oram.

Shabbetai (fourth century)
Palestinian amora. In *Gittin* 26b and *Bava Batra* 163a he is noted as a disciple of Chizkiyyah and in *Niddah* 27b as a teacher of Yitzchak of Magdala. *Ketubbot* 96a makes reference to Shabbetai's widowed daughter-in-law, who seized a bag full of money from her deceased husband's estate; the Sages had no power to make her return the money.

Shabbetai bar Marinus (fourth century)
Babylonian amora. In a *ketubbah* that Shabbetai bar Marinus wrote for his daughter-in-law, he promised to give her a fine cloak should she be widowed or divorced. The *ketubbah* was lost, and Shabbetai denied ever making such a promise. He is accused by Chiyya in *Bava Metzi'a* 17a of lying.

Shalman (third century)
Babylonian amora. In *Bava Batra* 13b he is mentioned as a contemporary of Shemu'el.

Shalmon of Bei Keluchit (third/fourth century)

Babylonian amora. In *Beitzah* 5b he is noted as a colleague of Adda bar Ahava.

Shaman bar Abba

See Shimon bar Abba.

Shaman of Sikara

See Shemen of Subara.

Shammai (first century B.C.E./first century C.E.)

A contemporary of Hillel, Shammai, together with Hillel, formed the last of the *zugot*. Born in Palestine, Shammai served as *av beit din* of the Sanhedrin, while Hillel served as *nasi*. Some scholars identify Shammai as the leader of the Pharisees during the reign of Herod; others dispute the identification.

Shammai took an extremely rigid stance in the interpretation and application of Jewish law, while Hillel was more lenient. Shammai founded a school known as Beit Shammai. In their interpretation of the law, Shammai's many disciples rarely deviated from Shammai's example.

A case in point is the treatment of the *agunah*, whose husband is not known with certainty to be alive or dead. Hillel (and most of his colleagues) ruled that she could remarry, even on the basis of indirect evidence of her husband's death. Beit Shammai, on the other hand, insisted that witnesses come forth with direct testimony.

Shammai's irascible nature was particularly evident by the manner in which he treated ignorant people. This led the Rabbis to remark: "One should always be as gentle as Hillel, and not as impatient as Shammai" (*Shabbat* 30b). Yet Shammai, later in life, would say: "Make the study of Torah your chief occupation. Speak little and do much, and receive every person in a friendly manner" (*Avot* 1:15).

Shammai displayed his gentler side when his daughter-in-law gave birth on Sukkot: He broke open the plastered ceiling of the room in which the baby's crib had been placed and covered it with branches so that the child would have the merit of having "lived" in a sukkah as prescribed in the Torah (Mishnah *Sukkah* 2:8).

Sanhedrin 88b notes that because the students of Shammai and Hillel grew so numerous, many had not studied sufficiently and issued conflicting rulings, making it appear as though two Torahs were given to Israel on Mount Sinai. Still, as *Yevamot* 14b points out, the adherents of these two opposing schools accepted each other socially, including marriage between their families.

Sha'ul ben Botnit
See Abba Sha'ul ben Botnit.

Shava (third/fourth century)
Also spelled Shabba.
Babylonian amora. In *Horayot* 5b Shava is mentioned as a colleague of Kahana.

Shayya (fourth/fifth century)
Babylonian amora. In *Zevachim* 34b he is listed as a contemporary of Ashi.

Shefatyah (third century)
Palestinian amora. A disciple of Yochanan bar Nappacha, in *Megillah* 32a Shefatyah quotes his master, who derides a student for reciting a passage from the Torah or Mishnah without chanting the appropriate melody, for the melody serves as an aid to one's memory.

Sheisha bar Idi (fourth century)
Also known as Shinena bar Idi.
Babylonian amora. A disciple of Pappa, to whom he refers as his master in *Chagigah* 9b, and of Yochanan bar Nappacha (*Shabbat* 146b), Sheisha bar Idi also was a colleague of Yosef (*Shabbat* 114b). In *Gittin* 89b Sheisha's name appears as Shinena bar Idi. It is recorded in *Sukkah* 46b that Sheisha accepted the ruling of Abbayei with regard to the observance of an extra day of Sukkot in the Diaspora.

Some scholars are of the opinion that Sheisha bar Idi and Sheshet bar Idi are one and the same person.

Shemayah
Two scholars were known by this name:
1. The first-century B.C.E. *nasi* of the Sanhedrin during the

reign of King Herod, who, together with Avtalyon, formed the fourth of the five *zugot*. While some scholars posit that Shammai was the leader of the Pharisees, others speculate that it was Shemayah. Like Avtalyon, Shemayah was a native of Alexandria; according to *Gittin* 57b both men were converts or the sons of converts. Their most famous pupil was Hillel. All that is known of Shemayah during his student days is that he was a pupil of Yehudah ben Tabbai. One of Shemayah's favorite maxims was: "Love labor, shun power, and do not become intimate with the ruling authorities" (*Avot* 1:10).

2. A third/fourth-century Babylonian amora who, in *Pesachim* 27b, is noted as a colleague of Rami bar Chama and, in *Niddah* 73a, as a colleague of Rava.

Shemayah bar Ze'eira (third/fourth century)
Babylonian amora. In *Ketubbot* 81a and *Eruvin* 93a he is mentioned as a disciple of Abbayei.

Shemayah of Kalenbo (third/fourth century)
Palestinian amora. He is noted as a contemporary of Abbayei in *Yoma* 21a and *Zevachim* 96a.

Shemen bar Abba
See Shimon bar Abba.

Shemen of Subara (fourth century)
Also known as Shaman of Sikara.
Babylonian amora. In *Chullin* 16b he is listed as a colleague of Ashi and Ravina I.

Shemu'el (second/third century)
Also known as Mar Shemu'el.
Babylonian amora. One of the most renowned scholars of his age, Shemu'el also was a physician and an astronomer. Because of his expertise in astronomy and his skill in fixing the calendar, the name Yarchina'a (*Bava Metzi'a* 85b), which is derived from the Hebrew word *yerach*, meaning "month" or "moon," was conferred upon him.

Shemu'el also was occasionally referred to as Mar Shemu'el (*Eruvin* 6b) and by the Persian name Aryokh, a variant form of *ari*, meaning "lion," because he pursued his studies with the strength of a lion. He was also sometimes called Shakud, "the diligent one," because of the diligence he applied to his studies, and as Shabur or Shavur Malkah, the Aramaic form of the name King Shapur, the Persian monarch with whom Shemu'el was extremely friendly (*Berakhot* 54a and *Nedarim* 49b). *Sukkah* 53a states that Shemu'el used to juggle eight cups of wine in the presence of the king.

A native of Babylonia and son of Abba bar Abba (*Berakhot* 18b), a dealer in silks who was entrusted with money belonging to orphans, Shemu'el studied under such scholars as Levi ben Sisi (*Nedarim* 82a), a close friend of his father (*Megillah* 29a), and Chiyya (*Shabbat* 138a). Shemu'el then spent many years in Palestine studying in the town of Tiberias under Yehudah ha-Nasi and Chama ben Chanina (*Gittin* 67a).

When Shemu'el was asked how he had time to study Torah and engage in astronomy, he replied, "I engage in astronomy only when I am free from studying Torah." "And when is that?" he was asked. "When I go to the privy," he reportedly responded. *Berakhot* 58b quotes Shemu'el as saying, "Except for the comet, whose nature I do not understand, I know the lanes of heaven as well as I know the streets of Nehardea."

In *Arakhin* 10b–11a Shemu'el recounts that "In the Sanctuary there was a [musical instrument called a] *magreifah* that had ten holes, each of which produced ten different sounds. Thus, it produced a total of one hundred different kinds of sounds." Nachman ben Yitzchak believed this statement of Shemu'el to be pure hyperbole.

The story of how Shemu'el cured Yehudah ha-Nasi's eye affliction also seems an exaggeration. Shemu'el said to Yehudah ha-Nasi, "I will put medicine in your eye."

Yehudah responded, "I cannot bear such a thing."

"Then let me apply it as a poultice."

"That, too, I cannot bear."

So Shemu'el placed a vial containing the medicine under Yehudah ha-Nasi's pillow, and he was cured.

Bava Metzi'a 85b–86a reveals that Yehudah ha-Nasi was most anxious to ordain Shemu'el and confer upon him the title "Rabbi" but somehow never got around to doing it. Although Shemu'el may have been disappointed, he said to his mentor, "Let it not upset you, for I have seen it written in the stars: 'Yarchina'ah [Shemu'el] will be called Sage, but not Rabbi, and Rabbi's [Yehudah ha-Nasi's] healing shall come through him.'"

Shemu'el cared for Yehudah ha-Nasi during his illness. In a pensive mood Shemu'el said to Yehudah: "Great scholar! Hurry and eat; hurry and drink [and enjoy life]. This world that we all must leave lasts no longer than a wedding feast" (*Eruvin* 54a). After Yehudah ha-Nasi's death, Shemu'el returned to Babylonia where, upon the death of Shila, he was elevated to the post of principal of the academy in Nehardea. At this time Rav, a colleague of Shemu'el at the academy in Nehardea, left the city to found his own academy in Sura. Throughout their lives, the two scholars were intellectual opponents, and the views of both are cited prominently throughout the Talmud. Shemu'el was considered superior to Rav in civil law but inferior to him in ritual matters. After Rav's death, Shemu'el would be recognized as the leading authority in Babylonia.

Shemu'el would often ask Rav for his opinion on ritual matters, such as: "Should one respond 'Amen' after a young child recites a blessing?" Rav replied: "No, because he is merely at the learning stage [and is not obligated to recite a blessing]" (*Berakhot* 53b).

Shemu'el, a stickler for the administration of absolute justice, often was quite liberal in interpreting the law. For example, regarding the question of rending a garment upon the simultaneous death of one's father, mother, brother, and sister, Shemu'el ruled that one tear—*keri'ah*—suffices for all (*Mo'ed Katan* 26b). In *Eruvin* 79b he maintained that it was permissible to kindle a fire on the Sabbath for a woman in childbirth or for one who was sick and in need of warmth to survive.

Shemu'el refused to countenance even the appearance of impropriety by litigants or judges. A strict constructionist, Shemu'el once ruled that a man who had stolen a wooden beam and used it in building a castle had to raze the entire structure and return the beam to its owner (*Ta'anit* 16a).

In another instance Shemu'el was on a ferryboat crossing a river. When the boat landed, a man offered to help him off with his luggage. Shemu'el asked him: "What business do you have here?" "I have a lawsuit being tried here," the man replied. Knowing that he would be the judge trying the case, Shemu'el recused himself: "I am disqualified from ruling on your lawsuit as judge [since it might be construed as showing partiality should he rule in favor of the man who had been kind to him]" (*Ketubbot* 105b).

Rosh Hashanah 24b recounts that a synagogue that housed the statue of a king was moved to Nehardea and that Shemu'el's father used to pray there. Like his father, Abba bar Abba, a prominent scholar in the city of Nehardea, Shemu'el was unafraid of being criticized for violating the second of the Ten Commandments. And, like his father, he was friendly to all men, and declared: "It is forbidden to deceive anyone, be he Jew or pagan (*Chullin* 94a). He also said, "Before the throne of the Creator there is no difference between Jews and pagans, since there are many noble and virtuous among the latter" (Palestinian Talmud, *Rosh Hashanah* 57a).

Among Shemu'el's many outstanding students, Nachman bar Ya'akov was one of the most prominent (*Eruvin* 47a, *Beitzah* 25b, and *Ketubbot* 108b); he inherited Shemu'el's position as head of the academy in Nehardea. A second outstanding student was Yehudah bar Yechezk'el, who founded the academy in Pumbedita (*Berakhot* 19a and 25a).

Because of Shemu'el's friendship with the Persian king, many privileges were granted the Jews. He therefore urged Jews to be involved in communal affairs, commenting: "Do not separate yourself from the community" (*Berakhot* 50a).

Although he surely had no intention of degrading women, his innocent comment in *Berakhot* 24a, "A woman's voice stimulates sexual desire," became the basis later on to separate men and women in the synagogue by establishing a women's gallery or using a partition (*mechitzah*). When his two daughters were taken captive in Nehardea by Roman soldiers, he saw to it that his coreligionists provided ransom money for their release (*Ketubbot* 23a).

After Shemu'el's death in Nehardea in 257 C.E., his life was greatly glorified.

Shemu'el bar Abba (third/fourth century)

Palestinian amora. Not to be confused with the illustrious Shemu'el, whose father's name also was Abba, *Megillah* 23b records that Shemu'el bar Abba was a student of Yochanan bar Nappacha and often translated and interpreted his lectures, although apparently he never was ordained by Yochanan bar Nappacha. Shemu'el bar Abba's other teachers were Assi and Ze'eira (*Kiddushin* 59b). In *Eruvin* 7b Shemu'el bar Abba is noted as a colleague of Sheshet and in *Beitzah* 19b as a contemporary of Adda bar Yitzchak.

Shemu'el bar Abba of Hagronia (third century)

Babylonian amora. According to *Bava Kamma* 88a–b, the second marriage of Shemu'el's mother was to a man named Abba, also the name of Shemu'el's father. Shemu'el's mother willed her entire estate to her son. After she died, her husband disputed the matter, making claim to a portion of it. A long debate ensued among the Rabbis, and Rava announced that the surviving husband had no legitimate claim.

Shemu'el bar Abbahu (fourth century)

Babylonian amora. Shemu'el bar Abbahu was a contemporary of Achai, and *Chullin* 59b records a disagreement between the two men about whether a goat from the Caucasus (on the Black Sea), which has horns and sharp, pointed hooves, qualifies as a kosher animal. In *Chullin* 49a Shemu'el bar Abbahu remarks that his father, as a student, attended Rafram's lectures during the *kallah* months.

Shemu'el bar Acha (fourth century)

Babylonian amora. In *Menachot* 34a he is noted as a disciple of Rava bar Ulla. According to *Bava Metzi'a* 46a, Shemu'el bar Acha was a close friend of Pappa.

Shemu'el bar Achitai (third century)

Also known as Shemu'el bar Chattai.

Babylonian amora. In *Gittin* 39b he is noted as a disciple of Hamnuna Sabba. In *Sukkah* 42a, where he is referred to as Shemu'el bar Chattai, he deals with a problem raised by Hamnuna Sabba relating to the culpability of a man who brought, on the Sabbath, an animal for the daily offering that had not been properly examined.

Shemu'el bar Ammi (fourth century)

Palestinian amora. Son-in-law of Shemu'el Sabba, Shemu'el bar Ammi is mentioned in *Yevamot* 105a and *Rosh Hashanah* 18a as a disciple of Yonatan ben Elazar. *Pesachim* 16b records a disagreement between Shemu'el bar Ammi and Chiyya bar Avin, a disciple of Yochanan bar Nappacha, on the question of defilement caused by the blood of sacrifices.

Shemu'el bar Bar Chama (third century)

Babylonian amora. In *Shabbat* 29a, 59b, and 146b he is listed as a colleague of Yosef, who was a disciple of Rav.

Shemu'el bar Bidri (second/third century)

Babylonian amora. In *Menachot* 35b he is mentioned as a disciple of Rav.

Shemu'el bar Bisna (third/fourth century)

Babylonian amora. A disciple of Nachman bar Ya'akov (*Ketubbot* 100a) and Yosef, it is noted in *Kiddushin* 26b that Yosef was displeased with Shemu'el bar Bisna's unimpressive scholarly achievements. In *Niddah* 42a Shemu'el consults Abbayei on a question involving a woman's ritual purity.

Shemu'el bar Chattai

See Shemu'el bar Achitai.

Shemu'el bar Idi (fifth century)

Babylonian amora. He is noted in *Pesachim* 104a as the brother of Chananyah bar Idi and a colleague of Menachem bar Simai. *Ta'anit* 9a records that Shemu'el bar Idi attended lectures by Rava with his colleagues Huna bar Mano'ach and Chiyya of Vastanya.

Shemu'el bar Ika (third/fourth century)

Babylonian amora. In *Avodah Zarah* 69a he contends that if a forbidden food falls into a vat of beer, the beer may be consumed if the food occupies less than one-sixtieth of the volume. This rule continues to apply today.

Shemu'el bar Inya (second/third century)

Babylonian amora. In *Eruvin* 63b he quotes Rav as saying: "The study of Torah is more important than the offering of the daily sacrifices." Commenting on the words in *Jeremiah* 13:17,

"My soul will weep in secret," Shemu'el bar Inya said, "The Holy One, blessed be He, has a place [residence] and its name is "Secret" (*Chagigah* 5b).

Shemu'el bar Judah

See Shemu'el bar Yehudah.

Shemu'el bar Kettina (third century)

Babylonian amora. *Berakhot* 47a reports that Rabbah bar Bar Chana made a marriage feast for his son in the home of Shemu'el bar Kettina.

Shemu'el bar Marta (third century)

Babylonian amora. Noted in *Bava Kamma* 51b as a mentor of Rabbah bar Bar Chana, Shemu'el bar Marta is quoted in *Megillah* 16b as saying: "The study of Torah is more important than the [re]building of the Temple." Some Sages say this statement was made by Rav.

Shemu'el bar Nachman

See Shemu'el bar Nachmani.

Shemu'el bar Nachmani (third century)

Also known as Shemu'el bar Nachman.

Palestinian amora. A disciple of Yonatan ben Elazar, Shemu'el bar Nachmani quotes his mentor frequently throughout the Talmud. Shemu'el's mother was well acquainted with Yonatan, and in *Bava Metzi'a* 85a Shemu'el quotes Yonatan as saying, "He who teaches his neighbor's son Torah will merit a place in the heavenly academy." In *Nedarim* 20b Shemu'el quotes Yonatan as saying, "If one's wife requests him to perform his marital duty [and he obliges], he will father children such as did not exist since the generation of Moses," and in *Nedarim* 22a, "He who loses his temper will be exposed to the torments of Gehenna."

Shemu'el bar Nachmani was a colleague of Yochanan and Ya'akov ben Idi, according to *Berakhot* 9b and 62b, respectively.

When Palestine suffered a period of pestilence and famine, Shemu'el recommended that a prayer be recited to bring it to an end (*Ta'anit* 8b).

In *Pesachim* 39a Shemu'el comments on why the Egyptians have been compared to *maror*. "To teach us," he says, "that just as *maror* is soft when it begins to grow and hard at the end, so were the Egyptians soft at the beginning but tough at the end."

Shemu'el bar Nadav (third century)

Babylonian amora. In *Arakhin* 16b he is listed as the son-in-law, as well as a disciple, of Chanina bar Chama.

Shemu'el bar Natan (fourth century)

Palestinian amora. In *Shabbat* 38a and *Sukkah* 43b he is noted as a disciple of Chanina bar Chama and in *Bava Batra* 78b as a disciple of Yochanan bar Nappacha.

Shemu'el bar Nathan

See Shemu'el bar Natan.

Shemu'el bar Pappa (fourth century)

Babylonian amora. He is listed in *Yoma* 37a as a disciple of Adda.

Shemu'el bar Sasartai (third century)

Babylonian amora. He is mentioned in *Ta'anit* 14a as a disciple of Rav.

Shemu'el bar Shilat (second/third century)

Babylonian amora. In *Ketubbot* 50a and *Bava Batra* 21a Rav advises Shemu'el bar Shilat, who was devoted to teaching children, not to accept a student under the age of six; above that age, Rav notes, you can "stuff him like an ox." Rav, who was Shemu'el's mentor, also warned him to "Be fervent in delivering my funeral eulogy. For I will be standing there" (*Shabbat* 153a). *Yoma* 76b lists Yehudah bar Yechezkel as Shemu'el bar Shilat's disciple. Shemu'el's son, Yehudah bar Shemu'el bar Shilat, was a disciple of Rav (*Ta'anit* 14a).

Shemu'el bar Shimi (fourth century)

Babylonian amora. In *Keritot* 27b he is mentioned as a student of Pappa.

Shemu'el bar Yehudah (fourth century)

Babylonian amora. A proselyte, he was a disciple of Yehudah bar Yechezkel. Shemu'el bar Yehudah later taught in the academy in Tiberias, until the Roman persecutions in Palestine began in 337 C.E., at which time he returned to Babylonia, bringing with him the teachings of Yochanan bar Nappacha and Elazar ben Pedat. Shemu'el bar Yehudah was one of Abbayei's teachers.

Shemu'el bar Yitzchak (second/third century)

Babylonian amora. *Ketubbot* 17a describes how the affable, beloved Shemu'el bar Yitzchak would join in wedding festivities, dancing before the bride as he juggled three twigs, throwing each in the air and catching them.

According to *Bava* Metzi'a 41a and *Shabbat* 51a, Shemu'el bar Yitzchak was a disciple of Rav, whom he quotes as saying: "Whatever may be eaten in its raw [natural] state, may be eaten even if it was cooked by Gentiles." Shemu'el later became a disciple of Huna, and like many of Huna's students, he migrated to Palestine. It was probably in Palestine that Yehudah's only daughter married the amora Oshaya.

Shemu'el bar Yitzchak's closest friend was Ze'eira (*Pesachim* 72b). It is reported in *Mo'ed Katan* 25b that when Shemu'el died, the entire community was so upset that even the trees are said to have uprooted themselves.

Shemu'el bar Zerukinya (fourth/fifth century)

Babylonian amora. According to *Chullin* 111a, he was a contemporary of Ashi.

Shemu'el bar Zutra (third/fourth century)

Babylonian amora. In *Niddah* 46a he is noted as a disciple of Rava. Shemu'el bar Zutra is reputed to have been so honest (*Bava Metzi'a* 49a) that he would not violate a promise if given all the riches of the world.

Shemu'el ben Chiyya (third century)

Palestinian amora. In *Bava Metzi'a* 72b he is noted as a disciple of Elazar ben Pedat.

Shemu'el ben Nachum (third century)

Babylonian amora. In *Bava Kamma* 55a there is a dispute as to whether Shemu'el ben Nachum was the brother or father of Acha bar Chanina's mother, making him either the uncle or grandfather of Acha bar Chanina.

Shemu'el ben Nadav (third/fourth century)

Palestinian amora. He was the son-in-law of Chanina bar

Chama and a contemporary of Yehoshu'a ben Levi (*Arakhin* 16b).

Shemu'el ben Yeiva (third/fourth century)

Palestinian amora. In *Niddah* 15b he is mentioned as a colleague of Abba.

Shemu'el, Father of

See Abba bar Abba.

Shemu'el ha-Katan (first century)

Palestinian tanna. A famous pupil of Hillel, Shemu'el ha-Katan is known in English as Shemu'el the Small because of his great modesty. When Gamli'el II, the patriarch, convened seven scholars and eight appeared, Shemu'el ha-Katan, not wanting the extra man to feel embarrassed, stood and said, "I am the one who has come without an invitation." Gamli'el knew that it was not Shemu'el ha-Katan and praised him for his self-effacement. In *Avot* 4:19 Shemu'el quotes from *Proverbs* 24:17: "Rejoice not when your enemy falls, and when he stumbles do not allow your heart to be glad" (*Avot* 4:19).

A humble scholar and not yet expert in calendar intercalation, Shemu'el nevertheless was invited to join the deliberations of Gamali'el II and his inner circle, who worked on fixing the calendar (*Sanhedrin* 11a). According to *Berakhot* 28b, it was Shemu'el ha-Katan who composed *Birkat ha-Minim*, the prayer condemning apostates, which was added to the *Amidah*.

Based on a report in *Shabbat* 33a, Shemu'el suffered from edema and died childless while still a young man.

Shemu'el of Cappodocia (first century)

Palestinian tanna. Believed to have been a contemporary of Yochanan ben Zakkai, Shemu'el of Cappodocia is quoted in *Chullin* 27b, where he comments on the *kashrut* of certain animals. He says that fowl are related to fish, "for the skin of chicken's feet resembles the scale-covered skin of fish."

Shemu'el of Difti (fourth/fifth century)

Babylonian amora. A colleague of Acha bar Rava (*Shabbat* 22a), the two disagreed about the placement of the Chanukkah *menorah*. In Talmudic times, when houses did not open directly onto the street but into a courtyard, the *menorah* was placed outside, close to the door. Acha said it was to be placed on the right-hand side of the door; Shemue'l of Difti said to the left, as one enters the house. The law is in accordance with Shemu'el's view.

Shemu'el Sabba (third century)

Palestinian amora. Known in English as Shemu'el the Elder, Shemu'el Sabba is mentioned in *Berakhot* 62b as the son-in-law of Chanina and in *Sotah* 10b as the father-in-law of Shemu'el bar Ammi.

Shemu'el the Elder

See Shemu'el Sabba.

Shemu'el the Small

See Shemu'el ha-Katan.

Sherevya (third/fourth century)

Palestinian amora. According to *Yevamot* 112a, he was a disciple of Rava and, according to *Bava Metzi'a* 64a, a disciple of Abbayei. Pappa was a colleague of Sherevya (*Ketubbot* 102b and *Kiddushin* 9b), as was Ravina I (*Shabbat* 136b).

Sheshet (second/third century)

Babylonian amora. Sheshet lived in Nehardea, where he studied in the synagogue (*Megillah* 29a) before leaving to study at the academy in Machoza (*Nedarim* 78a and *Bava Batra* 121a). After Machoza, he moved to Shilche on the Tigris, where, according to some scholars, he founded an academy. Though Sheshet was blind (*Berakhot* 58a), his memory was so extraordinary (*Shevu'ot* 41b) that he knew by heart not only the entire Mishnah but all of the *baraitot*. *Pesachim* 68b notes that every thirty days Sheshet would review his studies.

Sheshet had a great deal of respect for Huna, who would succeed Rav as principal of the academy in Sura. According to *Yevamot* 62b and 64b, Sheshet attended Huna's lectures, but because they were so long and because Sheshet would not disturb Huna by leaving in the middle of a lecture to relieve himself, Sheshet became impotent.

Sheshet did not have the same regard for Rav, one of the most learned scholars of his generation, nor did he appreciate the casuistry employed by students in the academy in Pumbedita. Of the latter Sheshet said sarcastically to one student, "Are you from

Pumbedita where they draw an elephant through the eye of a needle?" (*Bava Metzi'a* 38b). Rav ruled that if a man is suspected of having intercourse with a married woman, "This must be confirmed by witnesses." Sheshet contemptuously exclaimed, "It seems that Rav made this statement while he was sleeping or was about to doze off" (*Yevamot* 24b). Sheshet himself remarked, "A woman's hair stimulates sexual desire" (*Rosh Hashanah* 24a).

Among Sheshet's many disciples were Adda bar Chama (*Bava Metzi'a* 30a), Chiyya bar Avin (*Ketubbot* 13a), Yosef bar Chama (*Shabbat* 63a and *Sotah* 21b), Huna bar Yehudah (*Bava Metzi'a* 53b), Huna bar Yehoshu'a (*Yoma* 70a), and Yirmeyahu ben Abba (*Eruvin* 12a). Sheshet often engaged in debate on difficult legal issues with Abbayei (*Megillah* 27a) and Chisda (*Berakhot* 30a and *Eruvin* 57a).

Eruvin 39b describes a dinner held in the home of the exilarch, Rabbah bar Avuha, to which Sheshet, Nachman bar Ya'akov, and Chisda were invited. A stag that had been caught by a non-Jew on the first day of a Jewish holiday and slaughtered on the second day was served; Nachman and Chisda ate it, but Sheshet refused because he regarded both days of the holiday to be of equal importance in the Diaspora.

Berakhot 12b states that when Sheshet recited the *Amidah*, "He bowed and would bend like a reed, and when he raised himself, he would rise like a serpent," slowly, with effort.

When Sheshet was near death, it is said that the Angel of Death met him on the street and tried to take away his soul. Sheshet said to him, "You want to kill me on the street like a steer? If you want to take my soul, come into my house" (*Mo'ed Katan* 28a).

Sheshet bar Idi (fourth century)

Babylonian amora. Some scholars believe that Sheshet bar Idi and Sheisha bar Idi are one and the same person. *Pesachim* 49a relates that Idi bar Avin married the daughter of a *Kohen* and that their sons, Sheshet bar Idi and Yehoshu'a bar Idi, were both ordained. In *Bava Metzi'a* 65a and 67b Sheshet is mentioned as a colleague of Pappa, with whom he disputed legal issues. In *Berakhot* 23b Sheshet comments on how one should store his *tefillin* when they are not in use by placing them on a stool and covering them with a cloth. In *Sukkah* 56a Sheshet rules that upon entering a *sukkah* the prayer ending with "to dwell in a *sukkah*" is recited followed by the *She-hecheyanu* blessing (presumably both following the *Kiddush*).

Sheshet of Katruya (fourth/fifth)

Babylonian amora. He once read the Purim Megillah in the presence of Ashi (*Megillah* 21b).

Shila

In addition to Shila of Kefar Tamarta (see below), who in the Palestinian Talmud is referred to simply as Shila, two scholars were known by this name:

1. A second/third-century Palestinian tanna who is named in *Avodah Zarah* 23a as a contemporary of Eli'ezer ben Hurkanos. In *Sukkah* 26a Shila rules that a bridegroom is not obligated to pray on his wedding day.

2. A third-century Babylonian amora whose mentor, according to *Berakhot* 49b, was Rav, for whom Shila served as a *meturgeman* ("translator") at one of his public lectures. Chisda was another of Shila's prominent teachers (*Berakhot* 15b). Shila served as principal of an academy in Nehardea, where he left a whole school of disciples known as De-Bei Rabbi Shila.

Berakhot 58a records that after Shila administered lashes to a man (rather than put him to death) who had had intercourse with a non-Jewish woman, he commented, "Since we have been exiled from the land, we have no authority to put anyone to death."

Shila bar Abimi

See Shila bar Avimi.

Shila bar Abina

See Shila bar Avina.

Shila bar Avimi (third century)

Also spelled Shila bar Abimi.

Babylonian amora. He is listed in *Avodah Zarah* 15a as a disciple of Rav.

Shila bar Avina (second/third century)

Also spelled Shila bar Abina.

Babylonian amora. Together with his colleague Assi, Shila bar Avina tended Rav on his deathbed. One of Shila's prominent disciples was Tachlifa (*Avodah Zarah* 22b).

Shila Mari (third century)

Babylonian amora. He is listed as a contemporary of Kahana II and of Shemu'el bar Yehudah in *Shabbat* 32b and 43b, respectively.

Shila of Kefar Tamarta (third century)

Palestinian amora. In the Babylonian Talmud Shila is identified by the name of his native city in Palestine, Tamarta. In the Palestinian Talmud he simply is called Shila. In *Sotah* 35a he is listed as a teacher of Chanina ben Pappa. In *Megillah* 16b Shila comments on the style scribes employ in writing a Torah scroll.

Shila of Shelanya (fourth/fifth century)

Babylonian amora. In *Mo'ed Katan* 12b he is listed as a colleague of Ashi.

Shimi (third/fourth century)

Babylonian amora. In *Chullin* 11b he is noted as a colleague of the Babylonian Kahana. In *Bava Metzi'a* 11b he is listed as a disciple of Pappa and in *Yoma* 62a as a disciple of Rava.

Shimi bar Abba (third/fourth century)

Babylonian amora. In *Berakhot* 31a he is noted as a colleague of Mordekhai.

Shimi bar Adda (fourth century)

Babylonian amora. In *Nazir* 50b he is mentioned as a colleague of Pappa.

Shimi bar Ashi (fourth/fifth century)

Babylonian amora. He was a teacher of the Babylonian Kahana (*Chullin* 53a). It is recorded in *Berakhot* 31a and *Sotah* 46b that Kahana escorted Shimi bar Ashi from Pum Nahara to Bei Zinyata, a section of Babylonia rich in palm trees. *Yoma* 27a and *Kiddushin* 48b relate how Shimi observed Abbayei teaching his son. When Shimi asked Abbayei to give him lessons, Abbayei responded, "I use my time for my own studies" (*Gittin* 60b).

One of Shimi's principal teachers was Pappa, whose discourses he attended often (*Nazir* 26b and *Ta'anit* 9b). In time Shimi became sufficiently learned and sharp-witted to challenge Chisda's ruling on the question of which birds may be used for sacrificial purposes.

It is possible that Shimi bar Ashi was a physician.

Shimi bar Chiyya (third century)

Babylonian amora. Grandson of Rav (*Chullin* 111b), Shimi was very close to his grandfather and was invited to join Rav when he dined with the great scholar Shemu'el (*Berakhot* 47a). Nevertheless, Shimi did disagree with Rav in a number of cases. In one instance the issue was the type of ritual conversion that should be conducted for a slave purchased by an Israelite (*Avodah Zarah* 57a). On a lighter note, in *Bekhorot* 44a Shimi and Rav disagree about the height of Moses.

Shimi apparently was knowledgeable about medical matters; when Rav was experiencing eye trouble, Shimi prepared an ointment to alleviate his pain (*Chullin* 111b).

Shimi bar Chizkiyyah (second/third century)

Babylonian amora. In *Ketubbot* 6a he is listed as a disciple of Rav.

Shimi bar Hezekiah

See Shimi bar Chizkiyyah.

Shimi bar Ukba (third century)

Babylonian amora. According to *Berakhot* 10a, Shimi bar Ukba was a constant companion of Shimon.

Shimi bar Ziri (fourth century)

Babylonian amora. In *Temurah* 24a he is noted as a student of Pappa.

Shimi ben Abbayei (fourth century)

Palestinian amora. A disciple of Yochanan bar Nappacha, Shimi ben Abbayei reports the observation of Yitzchak, also a disciple of Yochanan, that a child under fifty days of age will not nurse from any woman except his mother (*Ketubbot* 60a).

Shimi of Choza'ah (third century)

Babylonian amora. He is mentioned in *Pesachim* 42b as a contemporary of Chiyya.

Shimi of Fort Shichori (third century)
Palestinian amora. A disciple of Simlai and a contemporary of Adda, Shimi comments in *Sotah* 38b on a situation in which a congregation consists wholly of *Kohanim*. Some *Kohanim* ascend the platform to bless the people, he says, while the others respond "Amen."

Shimi of Machoza (second/third century)
Babylonian amora. From a reference in *Makkot* 16a, he appears to have been a contemporary of Rav.

Shimi of Nehardea (third century)
Babylonian amora. In *Bava Kamma* 32b he is noted as a colleague of Rava and in *Shevu'ot* 12b as a contemporary of Nachman bar Yitzchak.

Shimon
Also known as Simeon *and* Simon.
In addition to Shimon bar Yochai (see below), whose name often appears without patronymic, two other scholars share this name:
1. A first-century Palestinian tanna whose brother, Azaryah, was a wealthy merchant. Shimon is mentioned only once in the Mishnah, in *Zevachim* 1:2.
2. A first-century Palestinian tanna about whom little is known except that he was the son of Hillel (and is sometimes referred to as Shimon ben Hillel) and the father of Gamli'el I. He succeeded Hillel as *nasi* of the Sanhedrin (*Shabbat* 15a).

Shimon, Achi Azaryah (first century)
Palestinian tanna. Known in English as Shimon, Brother of Azaryah, he is quoted in *Sotah* 21a and *Tohorot* 8:7.

Shimon bar Abba (third/fourth century)
Also known as Shaman bar Abba *and* Shemen bar Abba.
Palestinian amora. Born in Babylonia, where he studied under the celebrated amora Shemu'el, whom Shimon bar Abba referred to as "our master" (*Ketubbot* 107b), Shimon later moved to Palestine. There he lived in poverty and, according to one tradition, eked out an existence as a grave digger (*Genesis Rabbah* 89:2).

In Palestine, he studied under Yochanan bar Nappachah (*Ketubbot* 67a and *Berakhot* 21b), becoming his prize pupil. Because of Shimon's poverty, Yochanan applied the words of *Ecclesiastes* 9:11 to him, "Bread is not to the wise."

While Shimon was on a trip abroad, Yochanan ordained several of his pupils. Yochanan never ordained Shimon, a missed opportunity that distressed Yochanan greatly (*Sanhedrin* 14a).

Chanina bar Chama was another of Shimon's outstanding teachers in Palestine (*Ketubbot* 23a). On the advice of Chanina, Shimon married, successively, the two daughters of Shemu'el, head of the academy in Nehardea. Earlier in their lives the women had been taken prisoner by the Romans. Both women died shortly after marrying Shimon (Palestinian Talmud, *Ketubbot* 2:6; Babylonian Talmud, *Ketubbot* 23a).

Shabbat 119b refers to Amram, the son of Shimon.

One of Shimon's *aggadic* sayings, based on *Ecclesiastes* 7:2, is especially poignant, considering the circumstances of his life: "There are two ways of showing love: that of participating in a wedding ceremony, and that of participating in a funeral. When the two happen at the same time, and you can attend only one and do not know where to go, follow the advice of Solomon, who said, 'It is better to go to the house of mourning than to go to the house of feasting.'"

Shimon bar Kappara (third century)

Palestinian amora. A disciple of Yehudah ha-Nasi, it is believed that Shimon bar Kappara was well versed in the law and, at the same time, possessed great poetic talent. He composed fables and satirical poetry, though very little of it has come down to us.

Shimon bar Pazzi (third/fourth century)

Palestinian amora. Known in Palestine by the Greek name Simon, a form of the Hebrew Shimon, in Babylonia he was called by his full name, Shimon bar Pazzi. According to the *tosafot* (*Bava Batra* 149a), Pazzi was his mother's name. Others contend that Pazzi is a masculine name, hence the name of his father.

The Pazzi family lived in Tiberias, where it was highly respected. Shimon moved to Lydda where he became a pupil of

Yehoshu'a ben Levi (*Berakhot* 34a) and a colleague of Abbahu and Yitzchak Nappacha, and Yitzchak bar Nachman. Shimon's son, Yehudah, was a tanna of the next generation.

Although some halakhic teachings are recorded in his name, most of Shimon's teachings were aggadic (*Pesachim* 56a, *Sotah* 41b, and *Avodah Zarah* 18a) and were drawn from lectures he delivered in Babylonia.

One of Shimon's homilies, recorded in the Midrash (*Genesis Rabbah* 8:5), is as follows:

> When God was about to create the first man, he consulted with His angels. Some were in favor of creating man; others opposed it. God then consulted Mercy, and Mercy said, "Man *should* be created, for he will perform good works." Then He consulted with Truth, and Truth said, "He should *not* be created for he will be full of deceit." He consulted with Benevolence, and Benevolence said, "He *should* be created, for he will do good works." Finally, Peace was consulted, and Peace said, "He should *not* be created, for he will be filled with strife." God then took Truth and cast her to the ground.

In commenting on why the Hebrew word *va-yyitzer* ("and He created," *Genesis* 2:7) is written with two *yuds*, Shimon states that one *yud* refers to *Yotzri* ("my Creator") and the other to *yitzri* ("my evil inclination"), and "Woe is me if I follow my evil inclination rather than the will of my Creator" (*Berakhot* 61a and *Eruvin* 18a).

Shimon bar Yochai (second century)

Palestinian tanna. Often referred to as Shimon, without patronymic, an indication of how well known and respected he was, Shimon bar Yochai was born in the Galilee in approximately 100 C.E.

Early in his career, Shimon studied for thirteen years under Akiva ben Yosef, who opened an academy in Bene Berak. *Shabbat* 11a comments that "study" was Shimon's profession. Akiva said of him: "It is sufficient that I and your Creator know your power." Along with Me'ir, Shimon was one of Akiva's prize pupils; the two were the only scholars Akiva ever ordained. Shimon remained devoted to Akiva throughout his life, and even when Akiva was imprisoned for teaching Torah in violation of Roman law, Shimon found a way to sneak into his cell so that he could continue his studies with his master (*Pesachim* 112a). After Akiva's death, Shimon was ordained once again by Yehudah ben Bava (*Sanhedrin* 14a). In his later years, Shimon established an academy in Tekoa, in the Upper Galilee.

Shimon is the author of the *Mechilta de-Rabbi Shimon bar Yochai*, a commentary on *Exodus*. The original work was lost but has been reconstructed from uncovered fragments, as well as from quotations and references found in other books of the period, particularly the *Midrash ha-Gadol* of thirteenth-century Yemenite origin.

Although Shimon's father believed in appeasing the Romans, Shimon was outspoken against them. Legend has it that after being reported to Hadrian by his pupil Yehudah ben Gerim, Shimon and his son, Elazar, fled from Rome, where Shimon had been sent as an emissary. Father and son lived in a cave for thirteen years, subsisting on dates and the fruit of a carob tree. Shimon's body was covered with sores by the time he left the cave. He then bathed in the warm springs of Tiberias and his sores disappeared; many versions of this story can be found in the Talmud.

Shimon gained a reputation as a miracle worker. Legends about him flourished, especially after his death, and to this day his tomb in Meron is a place of pilgrimage, particularly on Lag b'Omer, the date on which it is said that Shimon bar Yochai died. Kabbalists ascribed to him mystical powers and attributed the Zohar to him.

Although Shimon was one of the authorities of his generation on halakhic matters, his ethical pronouncements are equally thoughtful. Among them are the following:

- So great is the power of repentance that even a man who was completely wicked in his lifetime, if he repents before his death, is considered perfectly righteous. (*Kiddushin* 40b)

- If you are My witness, I am God. If you are not My witness, it is as if I am not God. (Midrash *Sifri* 346)
- One should throw himself into a burning furnace rather than shame his neighbor. (*Berakhot* 43b)
- To honor one's parents is more important than honoring God. (Palestinian Talmud, *Pe'ah* 1:1)
- A bird does not fall into a trap unless God willed it. (Palestinian Talmud, *Shevi'it* 9:10)
- Three who have eaten at one table and have not indulged in discussing matters of Torah are like people who have eaten of the sacrifices of the dead. . . . But if three who have eaten at one table spend time discussing Torah, it is as if they had eaten from the table of God. (*Avot* 3:3)
- There are three crowns—the crown of Torah, the crown of Priesthood, and the crown of kingship—but the crown of a good name supersedes them all. (*Avot* 4:13)
- All Israel are royal children. (*Shabbat* 128a)

A classic example of Shimon bar Yochai's approach to *halakhah* is evident in his logical analysis of the verse, "You shall not take a woman's garment as a pledge" (*Deuteronomy* 24:17). While the Rabbis in the Mishnah (*Bava Metzi'a* 115a) say this applies to all widows, whether rich or poor, Shimon said it must only apply to poor widows.

If a garment was taken from a poor widow as a pledge, the creditor would return it every evening as prescribed in *Exodus* 22:25–26, because it might be the widow's only garment (in which she would sleep at night). By going to her house every morning to take the pledged garment and then returning it every evening, the creditor might compromise the widow's reputation. Shimon therefore ruled that the prohibition applied only to a poor widow. In the case of a rich widow, there would be no need to return the garment every evening.

Among Shimon bar Yochai's disciples were Shimon ben Yehudah ha-Nasi (*Rosh Hashanah* 15a), Shimon ben Elazar (*Shabbat* 69a), and Yochanan bar Nappacha (*Yoma* 5b). Among Shimon bar Yochai's most prominent students was the outstanding Yehudah ha-Nasi, editor of the Mishnah. Shimon's son, Elazar, also was a famous Sage.

Shimon ben Akashya (second century)

Palestinian tanna. Mentioned only once in the Mishnah, he is quoted in Mishnah *Kinnim* 3:6 as saying that an uneducated person loses intelligence as he grows older, while a learned person gains intelligence with the passage of time.

Shimon ben Avishalom (second century)

Palestinian tanna. He is quoted in *Berakhot* 7b and *Megillah* 14a.

Shimon ben Avtolemos (second century)

Palestinian tanna. He is quoted in *Bava Batra* 68a.

Shimon ben Azzai (second century)

Also known as Ben Azzai. Azzai is a contraction of the name Azaryah.

Palestinian tanna. When the Talmud speaks of a matter as having been brought "before the Sages," it often refers to Shimon ben Azzai, a highly regarded scholar, as we learn from *Sanhedrin* 17b. Shimon's interests ranged beyond Torah study, into philosophy and mysticism as well.

In *Yevamot* 63b Shimon ben Azzai's colleagues criticized him for not marrying: "You preach well but do not act well." He responded: "What shall I do if my soul is in love with the Torah? The world can be carried on by others."

According to some sources, Shimon ben Azzai married the daughter of Akiva ben Yosef; according to others, they may have been betrothed but never married. Like Akiva's wife, Shimon's wife encouraged him to leave home and study. As it is written in *Ketubbot* 63a: "Ewe follows ewe; a daughter's actions are like those of her mother."

In contrast to Eli'ezer ben Hurkanos, who said, "Anyone who teaches Torah to his daughter, it is as though he taught her lewdness," Ben Azzai remarked, "A man is required to teach his daughter Torah" (*Sotah* 20a).

Several of Shimon ben Azzai's sayings are recorded in *Avot*, including "Run to perform even a minor commandment, and flee from sin; for one good deed leads to another, and one sin brings on another . . ." (*Avot* 4:2). He also said: "Do not despise any man, and do not regard anything as impossible; for there is no man who does not have his hour, and there is nothing that does not have its place" (*Avot* 4:3).

As a younger disciple of and then companion to Akiva ben Yosef, *Chagigah* 14b describes how the two men, along with Shimon ben Zoma and Elisha ben Avuyah, "entered the *pardes* [orchard]"—a metaphor for speculation into mystical, and generally forbidden, studies. The experience was devastating. As a result, Shimon ben Zoma became demented, Shimon ben Azzai died, and Elisha ben Avuyah rejected Judaism altogether. Only Akiva came out unscathed.

Shimon ben Bathyra
See Shimon ben Beteira.

Shimon ben Beteira (first/second century)
Palestinian tanna. He is quoted in *Chagigah* 23b and *Eduyyot* 8:1.

Shimon ben Chalafta (second century)
Palestinian tanna. A student of Yehudah ha-Nasi, Shimon ben Chalafta was one of the scholars of the transition period between tanna'im and amora'im. He lived in extreme poverty in Ein Tina, a town near Sepphoris, where Yehudah ha-Nasi lived. Yehudah often offered Shimon support and invited him to his home (*Shabbat* 152a). Once, when Shimon took leave of Yehudah ha-Nasi, Yehudah ordered his son to ask Shimon for a blessing. Shimon responded: "God grant that you will neither cause shame to others nor be shamed by others" (*Mo'ed Katan* 9b).

In *Sotah* 41b Shimon ben Chalafta observed: "Since the fist of hypocrisy has become all-powerful, justice has become perverted; good deeds of individuals are destroyed, and no one may claim, 'My merits are greater than yours.'"

Many stories are told about Shimon's interest in zoology and the experiments he conducted. This earned him the title *askan,* "the busy one." It is reported that Shimon once saved the life of a hen by attaching a reed, for added support, to her dislocated hipbone. He made feathers grow on another hen (*Chullin* 57b). Still other experiments, which he conducted in his orchard, are reported in Midrash *Leviticus Rabbah* 22:4.

In the Mishnah (*Uktzin* 3:12) a famous saying of Shimon ben Chalafta's is recorded: "God has found no better vessel than peace to hold the blessing to be given to Israel. As it is written, 'The Lord gives strength to His people; the Lord will bless His people with peace'" (*Psalms* 29:11). These became the final words in the Babylonian Talmud.

Shimon ben Chanina (second century)

Also known as Shimon ben ha-Segan.

Palestinian tanna. Most often referred to in the Talmud as Shimon ben ha-Segan (*segan* means "assistant" or "deputy"), he served as Deputy High Priest, as noted in *Avot* 3:2, *Yoma* 7:1, and *Pesachim* 14a. In *Sanhedrin* 101a he is mentioned as a mentor of Shimon ben Elazar and in *Pesachim* 47a as an authority whose views were respected by Shimon ben Gamli'el II.

Shimon ben Chiyya (third century)

Babylonian amora. In *Shabbat* 111a he is mentioned as a disciple of Rav.

Shimon ben Elazar (second century)

Palestinian tanna. He lived near Tiberias, but little is known about his life. Like his teachers, Me'ir (*Shabbat* 134a) and Shimon bar Yochai (*Shabbat* 69a), Shimon ben Elazar engaged in polemics with the Samaritans, who did not believe that the bodies of the dead would be resurrected before the Day of Judgment. Shimon also is quoted frequently in halakhic discussions as an adversary of Yehudah ha-Nasi, with whom he was friends, but few of Shimon's views are included in the Mishnah.

In *Pesachim* 92a and *Shabbat* 135a Shimon discusses the views of the schools of Shammai and Hillel regarding the application of the circumcision rite to converts. In *Mo'ed Katan* 25a Shimon rules that "One who is in the presence of a dying person who has breathed his last breath must tear his garment."

Many of Shimon's maxims have been preserved. One very meaningful one states: "There are two kinds of friends: one who reproves you, and the other who praises you. Love him who reproves you, and hate him who praises you. The former leads you into the future world, while the latter simply removes you from this world" (*Avot de-Rabbi Natan* 29).

Shimon also said: "Do not try to pacify your friend in his hour of anger; do not try to comfort him while his dead lies before him . . ." (*Avot* 4:18).

Shimon ben Eliakim

See Shimon ben Elyakim.

Shimon ben Elyakim (third/fourth century)

Also known as Shimon ben Yakim.

Palestinian amora. He was a disciple of the scholar Elazar ben Pedat (*Ketubbot* 50b and *Bava Batra* 81a), whom he criticized for making rulings that were merciful but that went beyond the demands of justice. In the Palestinian Talmud Shimon ben Elyakim is known as Shimon ben Yakim. He was a contemporary of Ulla (*Nedarim* 42b) and Shimon ben Lakish (*Avodah Zarah* 34b).

According to *Sanhedrin* 30b, Shimon ben Elyakim was anxious to ordain Yosei bar Chanina but was unable to procure the attendance of two other rabbis for the ordination to take place.

Shimon ben Gamli'el I (first century)

Palestinian tanna. Son of Gamli'el I, Shimon served as *nasi* of the Sanhedrin in the last two decades before the destruction of the Temple in 70 C.E. His rule of life is recorded in *Avot* 1:17: "All my days I have grown up among Sages, but I have found no better prescription for life than silence; deeds are more important than intellectual speculation; too much talk leads to sin."

It is reported in *Sukkah* 53a that at the Simchat Beit ha-Sho'eivah ceremony—the "Festival of Water Drawing"—on Sukkot, Shimon ben Gamli'el I would juggle eight flaming torches and do pushups using only his thumbs.

Shimon ben Gamli'el I, executed by the Romans, was one of the Ten Martyrs. Upon his death, he was succeeded as *nasi* by Yochanan ben Zakkai.

Shimon ben Gamli'el II (second century)

Palestinian tanna. Son of Gamli'el II and father of the celebrated Yehudah ha-Nasi, Shimon ben Gamli'el II went into hiding when the Bar Kokhba Revolt broke out, eventually emerging to become *nasi* of the Sanhedrin when it was reconvened in Usha.

Shimon opposed prohibiting an act which was not, in itself, a violation of Jewish law but was instituted simply because it might lead to a violation of *halakhah*. He declared: "Fear should not be admitted as a factor in decision making" (*Shabbat* 13a, *Yoma* 77b, and *Bava Metzi'a* 69b).

In addition to Torah study, Shimon was educated in other disciplines. He seems to have been learned in Greek philosophy, and some of his children were given Greek instruction.

Because of the severe persecution inflicted on the Jews by the Romans during his years of incumbency, Shimon devoted himself to achieving peace. While lamenting the oppressive conditions under which Jews lived, he managed to organize the community so efficiently that he garnered the admiration and respect of the Romans (*Shabbat* 13b). He once remarked, "Great is peace, for Aaron the Priest became famous only because he sought peace."

In *Avot* 1:18 Shimon ben Gamli'el II taught: "The world rests on three things: on truth, on judgment, and on peace," basing his message on *Zechariah* 8:16. He also declared that justice must be accorded non-Jews and Jews alike.

Upon his death, Shimon was succeeded as *nasi* by his illustrious son, Yehudah ha-Nasi.

Shimon ben Gudda (first/second century)
Palestinian tanna. In *Avodah Zarah* 32a he is mentioned as a contemporary of Chanina ben Gamli'el.

Shimon ben ha-Pekoli (second century)
Palestinian tanna. Known in English as Shimon, Son of the Cotton Dealer, he was a contemporary of Gamli'el II at Yavneh, where he formulated the sequence of the *Shemoneh Esrei* ("Eighteen") prayer, the *Amidah* (*Megillah* 17b). According to Rashi, Shimon's father probably was a cotton dealer.

Shimon ben ha-Segan
See Shimon ben Chanina.

Shimon ben Hillel
See Shimon.

Shimon ben Isi ben Lakonya (second/third century)
Also known as Shimon ben Yosei ben Lakonya.
Palestinian tanna. A *Kohen* (*Bekhorot* 38b) and the brother-in-law of Elazar ben Shimon, he is mentioned in *Bava Metzi'a* 85a. According to *Pesachim* 51a, Shimon was a colleague of Yochanan ben Elazar, and in *Shabbat* 49b he is mentioned as a mentor of Yonatan ben Elazar.

In *Shevuot* 18b Shimon ben Isi ben Lakonya is asked an impertinent question by Yonatan ben Yosei ben Lakonya: "Where in the Torah is there a prohibition against having intercourse with a menstruating woman?" He answered that the prohibition can be found in *Leviticus* 18.

Shimon ben Jacob of Tyre
See Shimon ben Ya'akov of Tyre.

Shimon ben Jehozadak
See Shimon ben Yehotzadak.

Shimon ben Judah
See Shimon ben Yehudah ha-Nasi.

Shimon ben Kisma (third century)
Palestinian amora. In *Shabbat* 75b he is noted as a disciple of Shimon ben Lakish.

Shimon ben Lakish (third century)
Also known as Reish Lakish.
Palestinian amora. According to some authorities, he was born in Bostra, east of Jordan, around the year 200 but spent his early years in Sepphoris and his later years in Tiberias as an assistant to his friend and brother-in-law Yochanan bar Nappacha, with whom he debated many halakhic issues.

Shimon ben Lakish was widely celebrated for his scholarship as well as his brute strength. Legends abound describing his physical prowess (*Gittin* 47a) and how he was forced to give up Torah study because of acute financial straits and fight wild beasts in the arena as part of a circus. When Yochanan bar Nappacha saw Shimon bathing in the Jordan one day, he was so impressed by Shimon's beautiful physique that he plunged into the water to say to him: "Your strength would be more appropriate if dedicated to the study of Torah."

Shimon ben Lakish responded: "And your beauty [would be appreciated by and suited] for women" (*Bava Metzi'a* 84a).

The two men then made a deal: Yochanan bar Nappacha promised that if Shimon ben Lakish would resume his Torah studies, he would give him his beautiful sister as a wife. Shimon ben Lakish agreed (*Bava Metzi'a* 84a) and became such a diligent student that it was said he would review a section of Mishnah forty times before listening to the analysis of his teacher Yochanan (*Ta'anit* 8a). Ulla said of Shimon ben Lakish (*Sanhedrin* 24a), "When he discussed halakhic questions, he was so incisive that it appeared as though he were uprooting mountains and rubbing them together." When Yochanan bar Nappacha was appointed head of the prestigious academy in Tiberias, he invited Shimon to be his assistant (*Bava Kamma* 117a).

Later in life, Shimon ben Lakish became an ascetic and would no longer laugh or speak to anyone he deemed untruthful (*Berakhot* 31a). It was reported that Shimon was so respected that if anyone with whom he associated applied for a loan, the loan would be granted without a cosigner.

A number of Shimon ben Lakish's comments and observations are worthy of mention:

- A man does not commit a sin unless a mad spirit enters into him. (*Sotah* 3a)
- Decorate [improve] thyself first; afterward decorate [improve] others. (*Bava Metzi'a* 107b)
- Greater is he that lends than he that gives alms; but he that helps by taking part in a business venture is greater than either. (*Shabbat* 63a)
- He who commits the sin of adultery, if only with his eyes, is an adulterer. (*Leviticus Rabbah* 23:12)
- He who has a synagogue in his town and does not go there to pray is an evil neighbor. (*Berakhot* 8a)
- A man should never speak in such a way as to give Satan an opening [to cause harm]. (*Berakhot* 19a)
- The world exists only by virtue of the breath coming from the mouths of schoolchildren [engaged in their studies]. (*Shabbat* 119b)

- The Holy One does not smite Israel unless he has created the healing remedy beforehand. (*Megillah* 13b)

In *Berakhot* 5a Shimon's disciple, Levi bar Chama, quotes his master as saying: "A man should always encourage the good impulse [in his soul] to fight against the evil impulse. If he subdues it, good and well. Otherwise let him study Torah." Shimon added: "If one studies the Torah, suffering is kept at bay."

Shimon ben Lakish made the following observations regarding the selection of a mate:

An unusually tall man should not marry an unusually tall woman, lest their children turn out to be as tall as a mast of a ship; a dwarf should not marry a dwarf, lest their children turn out to be the size of a finger; a man whose complexion is unusually white should not marry a woman whose complexion is unusually white, lest their children turn out to be albino; a man whose complexion is abnormally black should not marry a woman whose complexion is abnormally black, lest their children turn out to be pitch-black. (*Berakhot* 45b)

Hundreds of debates are reported in the Talmud between Shimon ben Lakish and Yochanan bar Nappacha. Except in three cases, the law follows the interpretation of Yochanan bar Nappacha (*Yevamot* 36a). Nevertheless, Yochanan appreciated the wisdom and learning of his brother-in-law, so much so that when Shimon ben Lakish died, in approximately 275, and Yochanan no longer had anyone worthy of debating, Yochanan said that he felt like a person with one hand trying to applaud.

Yochanan was devastated by the death of Shimon and was inconsolable. It is said that he kept calling: "Where is bar Lekisha? Where is bar Lekisha?" Soon after, Yochanan followed Shimon ben Lakish to the grave (*Bava Metzi'a* 84a).

Shimon ben Menasya (second/third century)

Palestinian tanna. A contemporary of Yehudah ha-Nasi, with whom he engaged in legal debate, Shimon ben Menasya and his colleague Yosei ben Meshulam were part of a group called the Edah Kedoshah—Holy Congregation—whose members devoted one-third of each day to prayer, one-third to study, and one-third to work.

One of Shimon ben Menasya's interpretations of a biblical verse has become very popular. Commenting on *Exodus* 31:13, "You shall keep the Sabbath, for it is holy unto you," Shimon says, "'Unto you' implies that the Sabbath is given to you, and you are not given to the Sabbath." In other words, the Sabbath is a God-given gift.

Shimon is quoted in *Bava Metzi'a* 106b, *Shabbat* 95a, and *Yoma* 85b.

Shimon ben Mitzpah
See Shimon of Mitzpah.

Shimon ben Nannas (second century)
Also known as Ben Nannas.

Palestinian tanna. A contemporary of Akiva ben Yosef (*Gittin* 81b) and Yishma'el ben Elisha (*Gitin* 81b*)*, Shimon ben Nannas often is referred to simply as Ben Nannas (*Menachot* 45b). The Mishnah *Bava Batra* 10:8 indicates that Shimon was an expert in civil jurisprudence and suggests that those who wish to become proficient in civil law should model themselves after him.

Shimon ben Nathaniel
See Shimon ben Netanel.

Shimon ben Netanel (first century)
Palestinian tanna. Son-in-law of Gamli'el I and descendant of a noble Priestly family, Shimon ben Netanel was praised by his teacher, Yochanan ben Zakkai, for his piety (*Avot* 2:8).

Shimon ben Nezira
See Shimon Nezira.

Shimon ben Rabbi
See Shimon ben Yehudah ha-Nasi.

Shimon ben Shetach (first century B.C.E.)
During the reign of Alexander Yannai and Salome Alexandra, who was Shimon's sister, the Sanhedrin was composed mainly of Sadducees. Alexander Yannai persecuted the Pharisees, killing many and exiling others. It was Shimon ben Shetach who per-

suaded Alexander Yannai to let the exiled Pharisees return, including Yehudah ben Tabbai; together Shimon ben Shetach and Yehudah ben Tabbai constituted one of the *zugot*, although sources differ about which one served as *nasi* and which as *av beit din*.

Shimon instituted a written *ketubbah*—marriage contract—as well as elementary education for the young. In order to eradicate witchcraft, it is reported that Shimon ben Shetach once had eighty women hanged as witches (*Sanhedrin* 45b). In revenge, their relatives swore that Shimon's own son was a murderer, and Shimon had no choice but to put his son to death.

Shimon's attitude toward non-Jews is demonstrated by the following story:

Shimon was very poor and supported himself and his family by conducting a small linen business. Once, his pupils presented him with an ass that they had purchased from an Ishmaelite [Arab]. On the neck of the animal they found a costly jewel. The students hoped that it would be so valuable that their master would be able to sell it, give up his business, and devote himself to his studies and his teaching. Shimon, however, cut their joy short, saying, "The jewel must be returned. I bought only the ass, not the jewel." Shimon returned the jewel to the Ishmaelite, who exclaimed: "Praised be the God of Shimon ben Shetach!" (*Deuteronomy Rabbah* 3:3).

In *Shabbat* 14b Shimon proposed new legislation for the purpose of making divorce more difficult. In *Berakhot* 19a and *Ta'anit* 19a Shimon says of Choni ha-Me'aggel that he deserved to be excommunicated for acting too "familiar" with Heaven by praying for rain.

Shimon ben Tachlifa (second century)
Palestinian tanna. Often confused with Shimon ben Chalafta, Shimon ben Tachlifa is quoted in *Ketubbot* 111b.

Shimon ben Tarfon (first/second century)
Palestinian tanna. He is quoted in *Shevu'ot* 39b.

Shimon ben Ya'akov of Tyre (third century)
Palestinian amora. He is listed as a disciple of Yochanan bar Nappacha in *Berakhot* 33a.

Shimon ben Yakim
See Shimon ben Elyakim.

Shimon ben Yannai (third century)
Palestinian amora. He transmitted the views of his famous father, although, according to the Palestinian Talmud, many of the views he transmitted came to him via his sister.

Shimon ben Yehotzadak (second/third century)
Palestinian tanna. A Priest who is widely quoted in the Babylonian Talmud, he is mentioned in *Sukkah* 27a as a teacher of Yochanan bar Nappacha and in *Ta'anit* 22b as a teacher of Ulla. According to *Sanhedrin* 26a, Shimon ben Yehotzadak was a colleague of Chiyya ben Zarnuki and Shimon ben Lakish.

Shimon ben Yehudah ha-Nasi (second/third century)
Also known as Shimon ben Rabbi *and* Shimon Berabbi.
Palestinian tanna. The youngest son of Yehudah ha-Nasi, Shimon ben Yehudah ha-Nasi was much more learned than his older brother Gamli'el III (*Ketubbot* 103b), who succeeded his father as *nasi*. Yehudah recognized Shimon's brilliance and therefore called him "the light of Israel" (*Arakhin* 10a and *Menachot* 88b). Shimon was Yehudah's closest disciple, and the two engaged in many legal discussions. Shimon succeeded his father as head of the academy in Sepphoris. One of Shimon ben Yehudah's other principal teachers was Shimon bar Yochai (*Sotah* 45a and *Shabbat* 79b).

In *Bava Batra* 8a Shimon is presented as a kindhearted person and in *Bava Batra* 164b as truthful and forthright. *Bava Batra* 16b relates his disappointment when his wife gave birth to a girl. Mishnah *Makkot* 3:15 records one of Shimon's memorable teachings: "If man is rewarded for abstaining from drinking blood, for which he does not have a natural craving, how much more should he be rewarded for abstaining from robbery and fornication, to which he has an inborn inclination."

Shimon ben Yehudah of Kefar Akko
See Shimon of Kefar Akko.

Shimon ben Yosei (second century)
Palestinian tanna. It is noted in *Shabbat* 61a that Shimon ben Yosei studied under his father, whom he quotes. In *Horayot* 11a Shimon ben Yosei is listed as a disciple of Shimon bar Yochai.

Shimon ben Yosei ben Lakonya
See Shimon ben Isi ben Lakonya.

Shimon ben Ze'eira (second/third century)
Palestinian amora. He is quoted in *Kiddushin* 76b.

Shimon ben Zeirud (third century)
Palestinian amora. His ordination by Yochanan bar Nappacha is discussed in *Sanhedrin* 14a.

Shimon ben Zevid (third/fourth century)
Palestinian tanna. In *Nedarim* 8b Shimon ben Zevid quotes his teacher, Yitzchak bar Chakla, who also was known as Yitzchak bar Tavla. *Berakhot* 38a mentions Shimon's father, Zevid, and his brother, Ze'eira, who was a great man, well versed in benedictions.

Shimon ben Zoma (second century)
Also known as Ben Zoma.

Palestinian tanna. A disciple of Yehoshu'a ben Chananyah and a colleague of Shimon ben Azzai, with whom he shared theosophic speculations, much of Shimon ben Zoma's scholarly activity was devoted to the story of Creation, which was his undoing (*Chagigah* 14b). As a result of his intense concentration on the subject, he became demented.

Shimon ben Zoma generally is referred to as Ben Zoma, just as Shimon ben Azzai is referred to as Ben Azzai. *Zoma* is a Greek word meaning "broth" or "soup."

Ben Zoma, who died at a very young age, is the author of the popular saying: "Who is wise? He who learns from every man . . . Who is strong? He who controls his evil inclination . . . Who is rich? He who is satisfied with his lot . . . Who is respected? He who respects his fellowman" (*Avot* 4:1).

Shimon Berrabi

See Shimon ben Yehudah ha-Nasi.

Shimon, Brother of Azariah

See Shimon, Achi Azaryah.

Shimon ha-Chasid

See Shimon ha-Tzadik.

Shimon ha-Imsoni

Tanna. Of unknown date and origin, he is known in English as Shimon of Amasia. In *Bava Kamma* 41b and *Pesachim* 22b he comments on the significance of the Hebrew word *et*, an untranslatable particle that occurs often in the Torah before a noun.

Shimon ha-Nasi (second/third century)

Palestinian tanna. Known in English as Shimon the Prince, he expresses the view in *Gittin* 14b that if an agent of the deceased cannot deliver money he holds to a person named by the deceased, the funds must be returned to the heirs of the deceased.

Shimon ha-Timni (first/second century)

Also known as Shimon of Teman.

Palestinian tanna. Known in English as Shimon the Temanite, according to *Sanhedrin* 17b he was a colleague of Akiva ben Yosef, Eliezer ben Hurkanos, and Yehoshu'a ben Chananyah; in *Beitzah* 21a he is noted as a colleague of Yehudah ben Bava. Shimon's name derives from the town of Teman.

Shimon ha-Tzadik (fourth century B.C.E.)

Also known as Shimon ha-Chasid.

Teacher of the pre-Tannaitic period. Known in English as Shimon the Just or Shimon the Pious, he is not mentioned in the Mishnah, and the years of his scholarly activity are unknown. He served as *Kohen Gadol* during the rule of Alexander the Great of Macedonia and was a direct descendant of the Priest who had served as *Kohen Gadol* following the return of the Jews from Babylonian captivity in about 510 B.C.E.

Yoma 69a records a dramatic legend about Shimon ha-Tzadik and the conquest of Jerusalem by Alexander the Great:

Alexander the Great, who was conducting a war against Persia, wanted the Jews of Palestine to help him. The Jews informed him that they could not, because they had sworn loyalty to King Darius of Persia. Alexander, announcing that he would take revenge, marched into Jerusalem with a great army. The Jews were overcome with fear.

Shimon ha-Tzadik dressed himself in the elaborate Priestly vestments that, as *Kohen Gadol,* he wore only when entering the Holy of Holies on the Day of Atonement. As soon as Alexander saw him, Alexander descended from his chariot and bowed down to Shimon.

The commanders of Alexander's armies asked the king why the conqueror of so many lands, the man who had crushed so many enemies, would bow before a Jew whom he previously had threatened to destroy. Alexander answered that every night preceding a victory he saw an old man in his dream who resembled the Jewish High Priest. He therefore refused to harm Shimon, believing that, by being kind to him, he would have luck in future wars.

Shimon ha-Tzadik then led Alexander into the Temple. Alexander was fascinated by what he saw and asked that a stone image of himself be placed under the altar. Shimon replied that this was impossible because the Jewish faith does not permit images in the Temple, but he promised to memorialize Alexander's kindness in another way. Shimon ordered that all boys born that year be named Alexander. The king was highly pleased.

During Shimon's forty years of leadership, many rituals were introduced that are still practiced. Among them are the recitation of the *Kiddush* and *Havdalah.* The rule that even the poorest person must drink no less than four glasses of wine at the *Seder* on Passover eve also was introduced. Blessings over food were established, and the reading of the *haftarah* was initiated for Sabbath mornings and festivals.

A famous maxim attributed to Shimon is this: "The world is founded upon three principles: Torah, worship, and kindness" (*Avot* 1:2).

Shimon ha-Tzadik was one of the last survivors of the Great Assembly. His date of death is generally given as 300 B.C.E. He was survived by two sons: Shimi and Chonyo (known as Onias in English).

Shimon Nezira (third century)

Also known as Shimon ben Nezira.

Palestinian amora. Known in English as Shimon the Nazarite, he is quoted in *Yevamot* 97a. In *Shabbat* 33b he is referred to as Shimon ben Nezira.

Shimon of Amasia

See Shimon ha-Imsoni.

Shimon of Kefar Akko (third century)

Also known as Shimon ben Yehudah of Kefar Akko.

Palestinian amora. In *Sanhedrin* 110b he is noted as a disciple of Shimon bar Yochai.

Shimon of Machoza (second century)

Palestinian amora. In *Sukkah* 45b he is noted as a teacher of Shimon bar Yochai and Yochanan bar Nappacha.

Shimon of Mitzpah (first century)

Also known as Shimon ben Mitzpah.

Palestinian tanna. A colleague of Gamli'el I, Shimon of Mitzpah is noted for his collection of laws pertaining to the service in the Temple on Yom Kippur (*Yoma* 14b). In *Yoma* 15a he is referred to as Shimon ben Mitzpah.

Shimon of Shezor (first/second century)

Also known as Shimon Shezori.

Palestinian tanna. According to *Rosh Hashanah* 13b, he was a disciple of Yosei ben Kippar. In *Gittin* 13b and 65b Shimon's view—that if a man on his deathbed orders a *get* to be delivered to his wife on his behalf, it must be carried out—is dominant. In *Shabbat* 26a he says: "One may kindle Sabbath lights without oil that comes from gourds and with naphtha." In *Shabbat* 26a, Shimon of Shezor is referred to as Shimon Shezori. Shezor, sometimes called Shegor, was a town in the Galilee.

Shimon of Shikmonah (second century)

Palestinian tanna. A native of Shikmonah, a town near Mount

Carmel, Shimon is referred to in *Bava Batra* 119a as a disciple of Akiva ben Yosef and a colleague of Chidka.

Shimon of Shiloh

Of unknown date and origin, his lecture on what happened to the four princes who were cast into the fiery furnace by Nebuchadnezzar is quoted in *Pesachim* 118a.

Shimon of Teman

See Shimon ha-Timni.

Shimon Shezori

See Shimon of Shezor.

Shimon, Son of the Cotton Dealer

See Shimon ben ha-Pekoli.

Shimon the Just

See Shimon ha-Tzadik.

Shimon the Nazarite

See Shimon Nezira.

Shimon the Pious

See Shimon ha-Tzadik.

Shimon the Prince

See Shimon ha-Nasi.

Shimon the Temanite

See Shimon ha-Timni.

Shimon Yasinya (third century)

Palestinian tanna. He is mentioned in *Bekhorot* 47b as a disciple of Shimon ben Lakish.

Shizvi (third/fourth century)

Babylonian amora. Shizvi studied under many outstanding amora'im, including Chisda (*Shabbat* 136b and *Eruvin* 8b), Rava (*Bava Metzi'a* 114b), Rabbah bar Nachmani (*Bava Kamma* 51b), and Nachman bar Ya'akov (*Eruvin* 77a).

It is recounted in *Shabbat* 23b that Chisda frequently passed the house of Shizvi's father and observed it habitually illuminated with lamps. Chisda commented: "A great man will issue from this house."

Sima bar Idi (fourth/fifth century)

Babylonian amora. According to *Menachot* 25a, he was a colleague of Ashi. In an alternative textual reading, it was Sima bar Ashi who was a colleague of Ashi.

Simai (third century)

Palestinian tanna. One of the last tanna'im and a young contemporary of Yehudah ha-Nasi, Simai was a teacher of Yonatan ben Elazar (*Bava Metzi'a* 90b). Simai taught at the Babylonian academy in Nehardea and was greatly admired by his students, one of whom was Chiyya bar Abba (*Sotah* 11a).

Chullin 56b reports that Simai and his colleague Tzadok went to Lydda to intercalate the year and spent the Sabbath in Ono, a town three miles north of Lydda. *Rosh Hashanah* 19b records Simai's view concerning the month of Adar Sheini, which is inserted into the Jewish calendar after the month of Adar during leap years.

Simai bar Chilkai (third century)

Babylonian amora. In *Zevachim* 103a Simai questions Ravina I regarding the status of a proselyte.

Simi bar Abba (third/fourth century)

Babylonian amora. In *Nedarim* 36a he disagrees with a teaching of Yehudah bar Yechezkel.

Simeon

See Shimon.

Simlai (third century)

Palestinian amora. Simlai, whose father's name was Abba, earned his livelihood as an assessor under the patriarch Yehudah Nesi'ah, an occupation that required constant travel between the Galilee in Palestine and Babylonia. Simlai was born in Nehardea, Babylonia, and when a new school opened in Nehardea, Simlai left Palestine and moved back to his native town to study there.

At first, Simlai was not an outstanding legal scholar. His forte was *aggadah*, as is demonstrated in his lecture on the formation of an embryo. In *Niddah* 30b he comments:

What does an embryo resemble when in the bowels of its mother? Folded writing tablets. Its hands rest on its two temples, respectively; its two elbows on its two legs; and its two heels against its buttocks. Its head lies between its knees, its mouth is closed and its navel is open, and it eats what its mother eats and drinks what its mother drinks. It produces no excrement because this might kill its mother. As soon, however, as it sees the light of day the closed organ [its mouth] opens and the open one [its navel] closes; otherwise the embryo could not live even one single hour.

Simlai was one of the first scholars to note that 613 commandments were revealed to Moses on Mount Sinai, of which 365 are prohibitions and 248 are positive mandates (*Makkot* 23b). The 365 negative commandments, he said, correspond to the number of days in the year and the 248 positive commandments to the number of bones in the human body.

Avodah Zarah 37a records that on one occasion Yehudah Nesi'ah said to Simlai: "You were not present in the academy yesterday when we declared the oil of heathens permitted." To which Simlai countered: "Would that in our days you permitted their bread also!"

Because Simlai favored closer contact with the non-Jewish community, he was especially qualified to enter into discussion with the Church Fathers and dispute arguments that they drew from the Torah in support of the dogmas of Christianity.

In *Berakhot* 32a and *Avodah Zarah* 7b Simlai suggests how one should prepare for serious prayer: One "should always recount the praises of the Omnipresent and then offer his supplications."

In keeping with Simlai's particular interest in *aggadah*, he once asked his teacher Yochanan bar Nappacha to teach him the Book of Genealogies, a commentary on the book of *Chronicles* (*Pesachim* 62b).

One of Simlai's teachers was Elazar ben Shimon, whom Simlai quotes as saying: "The Messiah, son of David, will not come until all [corrupt] judges and officers are gone from Israel" (*Sanhedrin* 98a).

Simon

   See Shimon.

Simya (third century)

   Palestinian tanna. In *Yevamot* 74a he is noted as a teacher of Shimon ben Lakish.

Sumkhos

   See Summakhos.

Summakhos (second century)

   Also spelled Sumkhos. *Also known as* Summakhos ben Yosef.

   Palestinian tanna. Known in English as Symmachus, he was a distiniguished disciple of Me'ir (*Yoma* 18a and *Yevamot* 90a). In *Bava Metzi'a* 29b Summakhos rules on the proper conduct to be followed by one in whose safekeeping a Torah scroll has been left. In *Shabbat* 26a he comments on the type of oil that may be used to kindle the Sabbath lights and in *Berakhot* 13b on the laws governing the recitation of the *Shema*. "Whoever prolongs the word *echad* ["one," meaning God],"when reciting the *Shema*, says Sumkhos, "will have his days and years prolonged" (*Berakhot* 13b).

   Abbahu, quoting Yochanan bar Nappacha, said that Summakhos had such an incisive mind that he was able to argue forcefully both sides of an issue and that "for every law regarding ritual uncleanness he was able to produce forty-eight reasons in favor of the ruling, and for every law governing ritual cleanness he was able to muster forty-eight reasons to support its cleanness" (*Eruvin* 13b).

   It appears that Summakhos lived to a ripe old age, for even the prominent amora Rav was taught by him.

Summakhos ben Yosef

   See Summakhos.

Symmachus

   See Summakhos.

T

Tabi
See Tavi.

Tabi bar Kisna
See Tavi bar Kisna.

Tabi bar Mattnah
See Tavi bar Mattnah.

Tachlifa (third century)
Babylonian amora. In *Mo'ed Katan* 25a he is noted as a contemporary of Huna, and in *Avodah Zarah* 15a and 22b as a disciple of Shila bar Avina, who was a disciple of Rav.

Tachlifa Achuha de-Rabbannai Choza'ah
(third/fourth century)
Palestinian amora. Known in English as Tachlifa, Brother of Rabbannai of Choza'ah, he states in *Beitzah* 15b that a person's finances for the year are set between Rosh Hashanah and Yom Kippur.

Tachlifa Avuha de-Rav Huna bar Tachlifa
(third/fourth century)
Babylonian amora. Known in English as Tachlifa, Father of Rav Huna bar Tachlifa, he is noted in *Yoma* 6b and *Keritot* 25b as a disciple of Rava.

Tachlifa bar Abina
See Tachlifa bar Avina.

Tachlifa bar Avdimi (third century)
Babylonian amora. In *Avodah Zarah* 6a and *Bava Batra* 8b he is noted as a disciple of Shemu'el.

Tachlifa bar Avina (third/fourth century)
Also spelled Tachlifa bar Abina.

Babylonian amora. In *Chullin* 60b he is noted as a disciple of Chisda.

Tachlifa bar Chisda (third/fourth century)

Babylonian amora. He is mentioned in *Gittin* 31b as a disciple of Chisda.

Tachlifa bar Gizza (fourth century)

Babylonian amora. In *Avodah Zarah* 69a he is listed as a colleague of Ravina I.

Tachlifa bar Ma'arava (third/fourth century)

Palestinian amora. Known in English as Tachlifa, Son of the West, he was so-called because he visited Babylonia, which is to the west of Palestine (*Ketubbot* 8a). According to *Berakhot* 55a, he was a colleague of Abbahu; *Nedarim* 56b lists him as a colleague of Ravin. Abbahu was one of Tachlifa bar Ma'arava's students (*Gittin* 52b).

Tachlifa bar Samuel

See Tachlifa bar Shemu'el.

Tachlifa bar Shemu'el (third century)

Babylonian amora. He is quoted in *Megillah* 23b on the issue of when the translator may interject his comments during a Torah reading.

Tachlifa ben Avimi (third century)

Babylonian amora. In *Ketubbot* 64a and *Chullin* 107b he is listed as a disciple of Shemu'el.

Tachlifa ben Sha'ul

See Chalafta ben Sha'ul.

Tachlifa, Brother of Rabbannai of Choza'ah

See Tachlifa Achuha de-Rabbannai Choza'ah.

Tachlifa, Father of Rav Huna bar Tachlifa

See Tachlifa Avuha de-Rav Huna bar Tachlifa.

Tachlifa, Son of the West

See Tachlifa bar Ma'arava.

Taddai (fourth century)

Babylonian amora. In *Shabbat* 38b he is noted as a teacher of Abba, who was a pupil of Zerika.

Tanchum (third/fourth century)

Palestinian amora. *Sanhedrin* 39a indicates that Tanchum was on friendly terms with the Roman emperor. Tanchum's teachers included Yochanan bar Nappacha (*Shabbat* 9b), Yehoshu'a ben Levi (*Sotah* 39b and *Megillah* 22a), Assi (*Berakhot* 29a), and Tavla (*Sanhedrin* 28b). In *Shabbat* 21b and *Bava Kamma* 62b Tanchum is noted as a teacher of Natan bar Minyomi.

Tanchum bar Chanilai (third/fourth century)

Also known as Tanchum bar Ila'i.

Palestinian amora. Sometimes referred to as Tanchum bar Ila'i, he is noted in *Bava Kamma* 55a as a very close friend of Yehoshu'a ben Levi.

Commenting on *Exodus* 34:28, which says that Moses, who had ascended on high to receive the Torah, ate no bread and drank no water for forty days and forty nights, and on *Genesis* 18:8, in which the ministering angels descended to visit Abraham and, like other mortals, did eat bread, Tanchum draws the lesson, "A person should never deviate from local custom," or, as we would say, "When in Rome, do as the Romans do."

In *Ta'anit* 7b Tanchum bar Chanilai states: "No rain falls unless the sins of Israel have been forgiven."

Tanchum bar Ila'i

See Tanchum bar Chanilai.

Tanchum ben Ammi (third/fourth century)

Palestinian amora. He is mentioned in *Sanhedrin* 5b as a teacher of Mani of Tyre.

Tanchum ben Chakhinai (second century)

Palestinian tanna. In *Shevu'ot* 36a he explains Me'ir's view as to how the guilt of a *sotah*, a woman suspected of adultery, is to be ascertained.

Tanchum ben Chiyya of Kefar Akko (third century)

Palestinian amora. A wealthy man whose mother was very philanthropic (*Leviticus Rabbah* 34:1), Tanchum ben Chiyya of Kefar Akko was a disciple of Shimon bar Pazzi and the Babylonian amora Ya'akov bar Acha (*Mo'ed Katan* 16b). In *Ta'anit* 7b Tanchum is quoted as saying: "The rains are not withheld unless the enemies of Israel have been condemned to destruction [for their sins]"; by "enemies of Israel" Tanchum meant the sinners within Israel itself. *Mo'ed Katan* 25b reports that Tanchum's death was deeply felt by the Jewish community. It was said in Babylonia that when Tanchum died all the statues in Tiberias (Palestine) moved from their places.

Tanchum of Noy

Amora. Of unknown date and origin, Tanchum of Noy is referred to in *Shabbat* 30a.

Tanchum of Parud (second/third century)

Palestinian amora. Tanchum of Parud is mentioned in *Avodah Zarah* 31a; Bar Kappara had once resided in Parud as had Yochanan bar Nappacha. Parud is believed to have been located southwest of Safed.

Tanchuma bar Abba (fourth century)

Palestinian amora. A master of *aggadah*, Tanchuma bar Abba was fond of using symbolism in his teachings, as the following quotation exemplifies: "Just as the spice box contains all kinds of fragrant spices, so must a youngster be filled with all kinds of biblical, Mishnaic, halakhic, and aggadic knowledge" (*Song of Songs Rabbah* 5:13). Tanchuma's many sayings form the basis of the group of aggadic *midrashim* called *Tanchuma-Yelammedenu*.

His frequent association with Gentiles led him to say: "When a non-Jew greets you with a blessing, answer him, 'Amen.'"

The Talmud relates the following interesting incident in the life of Tanchuma:

> The emperor said to him, "Let us all become one people." To this Tanchuma replied, "But we who are circumcised cannot become like you. However, you can circumcise yourselves and become like us."
>
> The emperor said, "You have answered me correctly. But he who outwits the king must be thrown to the wild beasts." This was done, but the animals did not harm Tanchuma. A disbeliever who watched the proceedings remarked, "Perhaps the animals were not hungry!" Whereupon, the disbeliever was thrown into the arena and was torn to pieces. (*Sanhedrin* 39a)

Tarfon (first / second century)

Palestinian tanna. Born into a Priestly family, Tarfon served in the Second Temple during its last years. It is reported that during a period of famine, he married three hundred women so that they could share with him his Priestly allotment of food. So considerate of women was he that legend has it that whenever his mother would get in or out of bed, Tarfon would bend down and let her step on his back to make it easier for her (*Kiddushin* 31b). Once, when she had to cross the courtyard and was not wearing sandals, Tarfon placed his hands under her feet to alleviate her pain. On festivals and holidays, Tarfon would delight his family with the finest fruits and delicacies.

One of Tarfon's most famous sayings is recorded in *Avot* 2:15–16: "The day is short, and the work is great . . . the laborers are lazy, the wages are high, and the employer is demanding . . . It is not incumbent upon you to finish the work, but neither are you free to desist from it."

While Tarfon subscribed to the philosophy of Shammai, who followed a stricter interpretation of the civil law than did Hillel, Tarfon shared the view of Akiva ben Yosef, a disciple of Hillel. Tarfon and Akiva agreed that if they were members of the Sanhedrin, capital punishment would be totally abolished (*Makkot* 7a).

In addition to Akiva, Tarfon's colleagues included Yishma'el ben Elisha and Elazar of Modi'in. *Sukkah* 31a indicates that Yehudah bar Ila'i was Tarfon's disciple. In *Megillah* 20a Yehudah bar Ila'i recalls how he once read the book of *Esther* before Tarfon and the Elders in Lydda.

After the destruction of the Temple, Tarfon became one of the leading authorities in Yavneh. While he is said to have lived in Yavneh, it is evident that he also lived in Lydda (Mishnah *Bava Metzi'a* 4:3).

Tavi

Also spelled Tabi.

Two scholars were known by this name:

1. A third/fourth-century Palestinian amora who, in *Rosh Hashanah* 22a, quotes his teacher Mari Tavi. In *Berakhot* 15b, *Yoma* 65b, *Megillah* 29b, and *Sanhedrin* 92a Tavi is noted as a disciple of Yoshiyyahu.

2. A fourth-century Babylonian amora who is listed as a disciple of Nachman bar Ya'akov in *Temurah* 34a.

Tavi bar Kisna (third century)

Also spelled Tabi bar Kisna. Also *known as* Tavyomi bar Kisna. Babylonian amora. In *Ketubbot* 64a and *Nedarim* 12b he is noted as a disciple of Shemu'el. In *Menachot* 70a he is referred to as Tavyomi bar Kisna.

Tavi bar Mattnah (third/fourth century)

Also spelled Tabi bar Mattnah.

Babylonian amora. He was a disciple of Yoshiyyahu (*Temurah* 29a) and Yosef (*Chullin* 39b), and a contemporary of Abbayei (*Bava Batra* 58a) and Rava (*Mo'ed Katan* 68a). *Bava Batra* 151a notes that Tavi and Achadvoi bar Mattnah were colleagues.

Tavla (third/fourth century)

Babylonian amora. In *Sanhedrin* 28b he is noted as a teacher of Tanchum, and in *Bava Metzi'a* 94a and *Shabbat* 101a as a disciple of Rav. In *Eruvin* 75a Tavla is mentioned as a colleague of Yosef and in *Chullin* 132b as a colleague of Nachman bar Ya'akov. According to *Menachot* 78a, Nachman bar Rav Chisda was Tavla's disciple.

Tavut (third/fourth century)

Babylonian amora. In *Chullin* 44a he is mentioned as a colleague of Rava. According to *Sanhedrin* 97a, Tavut was so honest he said that even if offered all the treasures in the world he would not go back on his word.

Tavyomi (third/fourth century)

Babylonian amora. In *Bava Kamma* 41b he is listed as a disciple of Rava and in *Bava Batra* 163b as a disciple of Rav. In *Nedarim* 16b Tavyomi quotes Giddal, a disciple of Shemu'el; in *Bava Metzi'a* 54b Tavyomi quotes Abbayei's interpretation of *Levitcus* 27:15.

Tavyomi bar Kisna

See Tavi bar Kisna.

Totai (third/fourth century)

Babylonian amora. In *Kiddushin* 16b he is noted as a contemporary of Sheshet and Yosef.

Tzadok (first / second century)

Palestinian tanna. Of Priestly descent, Tzadok was a pupil of the school of Shammai, although often he ruled in accordance with the legal interpretations of Hillel. As an extremely influential member of Gamli'el II's Sanhedrin, Tzadok always sat to Gamli'el's right (*Kiddushin* 32b). Together with Eli'ezer ben Hurkanos and Yehoshu'a ben Chananyah, Tzadok was present at the marriage of the son of Gamli'el II in Yavneh (*Kiddushin* 32b).

According to *Gittin* 56a–b, Tzadok had foreseen the eventual fall of Jerusalem and had taken to fasting in the hope that disaster could be averted. A short time before the Temple was destroyed, Yochanan ben Zakkai appeared with his disciple Tzadok before Vespasian in the Roman camp. When Vespasian noticed that Yochanan displayed greater reverence to Tzadok than to him, he asked, "What distinction has this man?"

Yochanan replied, "I can assure you that had there been another one like him, you could not have triumphed over our people, even if you had employed twice as many soldiers as you did."

"Wherein lies his strength?" Vespasian asked.

"For forty years he neither ate nor drank anything more than the juice of one fig, which he consumed every night," Yochanan answered. "Tzadok also taught a host of disciples all day. Had there been another like him, God would have had to spare our city for the sake of two such holy men."

When Jerusalem finally fell, Tzadok, who was in poor health, was taken captive by the Romans. Titus, now in charge of the Roman legions, released him upon the intercession of Yochanan ben Zakkai.

One of Tzadok's most famous maxims was: "Do not make of the Torah a crown to glorify yourself, nor a spade with which to dig" (*Avot* 4:5).

Tzadok ben Chalokah (third century)

Palestinian amora. In *Yoma* 78a Tzadok ben Chalokah is listed as a junior colleague of Yosei ben Zimra.

U

Ukba (third century)

Also spelled Ukva. *Also known as* Mar Ukba.

Palestinian amora. A kindly, modest scholar, who acted tenderly toward his wife, Ukba was known for giving charity to the poor, making sure to keep his identity a secret (*Bava Batra* 10b). The following story is told about his generosity: Each day Ukba would leave four silver coins on a particular man's doorstep. The recipient wished to find out the identity of his benefactor. On one occasion he opened the door suddenly as Ukba put down the coins. In order not be recognized, Ukba fled and hid in a furnace. According to *Ketubbot* 67b, there was no fire in the furnace, but it was still very hot, and Ukba burned his feet.

Ukba was a disciple of Shemu'el (*Eruvin* 81a and *Shabbat* 108b) and Chanina bar Chama (*Ketubbot* 60b). In *Ketubbot* 72b Ukba is mentioned as a contemporary of Rabbah bar Bar Chana, and in *Sanhedrin* 70a, *Berakhot* 10b, and *Sotah* 39a, he is listed as a teacher and friend of Chisda. *Chullin* 43b speaks of an ox belonging to Ukba's family that was improperly slaughtered and ruled *tereifah*.

Ukba bar Chama (third century)

Also known as Mar Ukba.

Babylonian amora. In *Zevachim* 55b he is noted as a disciple of Yosei bar Chanina. Like his brother, Rami bar Chama, Ukba bar Chama married a daughter of Chisda (*Berakhot* 44a).

Ukva

See Ukba.

Ulla (second/third century)

Also known as Ulla ben Yishma'el.

Palestinian tanna. In his youth Ulla's primary teacher was

Elazar, the third-century Babylonian-born amora who moved to Palestine. Later, Ulla would transmit some of Elazar's rulings (a number are found in *Bava Kamma* 11a and 11b) to Babylonian scholars, whom he visited often. In *Sanhedrin* 92a Ulla is referred to as Ulla ben Yishma'el; in the Palestinian Talmud his name often appears as Ulla ben Yishma'el.

During his travels to Babylonia the *reish galuta* would invite Ulla to deliver lectures. A strict constructionist, Ulla once heard Huna offer an interpretation with which he did not agree and applied to him the verse from *Proverbs* 10:26, "Like vinegar to the teeth, like smoke to the eyes, so is the lazy man to those who sent him on a mission" (*Kiddushin* 45b).

Because of Ulla's frequent trips to Babylonia to teach Torah, Yalta, wife of Nachman bar Ya'akov, described him as a "peddler" (*Berakhot* 51b).

One of Ulla's most important teachers in Palestine was Yochanan bar Nappacha, whose many teachings he conveyed to Babylonian scholars (*Berakhot* 38b).

Ulla believed that honoring one's parents was of paramount importance. To demonstrate his point, he recalls in *Kiddushin* 31a the extent to which a heathen, Dama, son of Netinah of Ashkelon, went to honor his father (it should be noted that this same story is attributed to Eli'ezer ben Hurkanos in *Avodah Zarah* 23b):

Sages wanted to buy some precious stones from Netinah, for which he would earn a profit of six hundred thousand gold denarii. However, the key to the cupboard in which the stones were stored lay under Netinah's pillow, and Dama refused to disturb his father. [The Palestinian Talmud says that Dama's father's feet were resting on the chest containing the merchandise.]

The following year God rewarded Dama: A red heifer was born to his herd. When the Sages went to buy the precious cow, Dama said to them: "I know, if I asked, you would pay me all the money in the world for the heifer. I ask you only for what I lost because I honored my father."

Ulla died in Babylonia prior to the death of his teacher Elazar and was taken to Palestine for burial. He believed that only in the Land of Israel would the dead be resurrected (*Ketubbot* 111a). The learned Ulla Rabbah is believed to have been Ulla's son.

Ulla bar Abba (third century)

Palestinian amora. Praised by his colleagues as a humble, devoted student of the Torah, destined for the world to come (*Sanhedrin* 88b), he is noted in *Ketubbot* 74a as the teacher of the third/fourth-century Palestinian amora Kahana.

Ulla bar Chanina (third century)

Babylonian amora. In *Nazir* 65a he is mentioned as a contemporary of Yehudah bar Yechezkel.

Ulla bar Chinena (fourth century)

Palestinian amora. A contemporary of Yirmeyahu. In *Sukkah* 33a Ulla bar Chinena and Yirmeyahu disagree over whether a myrtle branch whose tip is defective may be used on Sukkot.

Ulla bar Ila'i (third/fourth century)

Babylonian amora. A contemporary of Hamnuna (*Shabbat* 129a), Ulla bar Ila'i is quoted in *Beitzah* 22a as saying: "All the needs of a sick man may be performed for him by a heathen on the Sabbath." *Shavuot* 30a recounts that Ulla participated in a legal case that was tried before Nachman.

Ulla bar Menashya (third century)

Babylonian amora. *Gittin* 79a records that he was a disciple of Avimi.

Ulla bar Rav (third/fourth century)

Babylonian amora. *Pesachim* 117b records that Ulla bar Rav visited Rava and was not criticized by him for reciting *Kiddush* in accordance with the customs of the elders of Pumbedita. In *Megillah* 24b Ulla is listed as a disciple of Abbayei, of whom he once asked whether "a boy [presumably thirteen years old or above] in rags [improperly clad] may be the Torah reader." The answer was given in the negative, *mi-shum kevod tzibbur*, that is, to preserve the dignity of the congregation.

Ulla ben Idi (first/second century)
Palestinian tanna. In *Bava Kamma* 42a he is noted as a contemporary of Akiva ben Yosef and Yosei ha-Gelili.

Ulla ben Ishma'el
See Ulla.

Ulla ben Yishma'el
See Ulla.

Ulla of Bira'a (third/fourth century)
Palestinian amora. According to *Ta'anit* 31a, he was a disciple of Elazar ben Pedat. Ulla quotes his master as saying: "In the days to come, God will hold a celebration for the righteous, and He will sit in their midst in the Garden of Eden." *Mo'ed Katan* 26a lists Chelbo as one of Ulla's disciples.

Ulla Rabbah (third century)
Palestinian tanna. Known in English as Ulla the Elder or Ulla the Great, *Kiddushin* 31a reports that Ulla Rabbah used to lecture at the entrance of the *nasi*'s house, a location where popular discourses were usually given. Scholars believe that Ulla Rabbah was the son of Ulla.

Ulla the Elder
See Ulla Rabbah.

Ulla the Great
See Ulla Rabbah.

Uzzi'el
An amora of unknown date and origin, Uzzi'el was a grandson of Uzzi'el Rabbah and is quoted in *Mo'ed Katan* 5a on the subject of impurity.

Uzzi'el Rabbah
See Uzzi'el.

ϒ

Ya'akov

In addition to Ya'akov bar Korshai (see below), often referred to simply as Ya'akov, two other scholars shared this name:

1. A third-century Palestinian amora who, in *Shabbat* 81a and *Sanhedrin* 22a, is noted as a disciple of Yochanan bar Nappacha.

2. A fourth-century Babylonian amora who, in *Bava Batra* 60b and *Sanhedrin* 81b, is noted as a teacher of Yirmeyahu bar Tachlifa. According to *Bava Batra* 147a, Ya'akov came from Nehardea.

Ya'akov bar Abba

Two scholars were known by this name:

1. A third-century Babylonian amora who, in *Zevachim* 70b, is listed as a younger colleague of Rav.

2. A fourth-century Babylonian amora who, in *Menachot* 17a and *Bava Metzi'a* 23b, is noted as a disciple of Abbayei. Ya'akov's father's name sometimes appears as Avina, Avuha, Abbuha, Avun, Aibu, or Aivu.

Ya'akov bar Abbuha

See Ya'akov bar Abba.

Ya'akov bar Acha

Three scholars were known by this name:

1. A third-century Babylonian amora noted in *Ta'anit* 27b as a disciple of Assi.

2. A third-century Babylonian amora who, in *Mo'ed Katan* 27a, quotes Yehoshu'a ben Levi.

3. A fourth-century Palestinian amora who, according to *Pesachim* 103a, visited Rava's home and observed his conduct as he recited repeated blessings over wine. In *Shabbat* 31b, Ya'akov bar Acha is said to have been highly respected by his younger

colleague Elazar ben Pedat, and in *Berakhot* 23a Ya'akov is noted as a disciple of Ze'eira.

Ya'akov bar Acha bar Ya'akov (third/fourth century)
Babylonian amora. Though sent by his father to study under Abbayei, Ya'akov bar Acha bar Ya'akov turned out to be a poor student (*Kiddushin* 29b).

Ya'akov bar Adda (second/third century)
Babylonian amora. In *Sanhedrin* 66b he is listed as a disciple of Rav.

Ya'akov bar Aibu
See Ya'akov bar Abba.

Ya'akov bar Aivu
See Ya'akov bar Abba.

Ya'akov bar Avina
See Ya'akov bar Abba.

Ya'akov bar Avuha
See Ya'akov bar Abba.

Ya'akov bar Avun
See Ya'akov bar Abba.

Ya'akov bar beratei Acha bar Ya'akov
(third/fourth century)
Babylonian amora. Known in English as Ya'akov, Grandson of Acha bar Ya'akov, and though he was reared by his grandfather, he contends in *Sotah* 49a that one does not have the same obligation to honor one's grandparents as one has to honor one's parents.

Ya'akov bar Chanina (third century)
Babylonian amora. In *Shabbat* 79b and *Menachot* 32b he is mentioned as a teacher of Achai.

Ya'akov bar Idi (third century)
Palestinian amora. In *Berakhot* 29b he is noted as a disciple of Oshaya, in *Shabbat* 150a as a disciple of Yochanan, and in *Berakhot* 62b as a colleague of Shemu'el bar Nachmani.

Ya'akov bar Korshai (second century)
Palestinian tanna. Often referred to simply by the name Ya'akov,

he was a contemporary of Me'ir and Shimon ben Gamli'el II (*Horayot* 13b and *Ketubbot* 34a). Ya'akov bar Korshai is remembered for his saying, "This world is like a vestibule leading to the world to come. Prepare yourself in the vestibule so that you may enter the banquet hall" (*Avot* 4:16).

Ya'akov bar Nachmani (second/third century)

Babylonian amora. In *Chullin* 52b he is noted as a disciple of Shemu'el.

Ya'akov bar Zavda

See Ya'akov bar Zavdai.

Ya'akov bar Zavdai (fourth century)

Also known as Ya'akov bar Zavda.

Palestinian amora. In *Kiddushin* 33b he is noted as a contemporary of Ila'i and Shimon bar Abba.

Ya'akov ben Dostai (third century)

Palestinian amora. In *Ketubbot* 111b he is noted as a contemporary of Shimon ben Lakish.

Ya'akov berei de-vat Shemu'el (fourth century)

Babylonian amora. Known in English as Ya'akov, Son of the Daughter of Shemu'el, he is mentioned in *Berakhot* 25b as a teacher of Bali.

Ya'akov berei de-vat Ya'akov (third/fourth century)

Babylonian amora. He was known in English as Ya'akov, Son of the Daughter of Ya'akov, and Rashi notes in *Eruvin* 80a that since Ya'akov's father was an unworthy person, his name is not used. Ya'akov's colleague Ze'eira advised him to visit Ya'akov ben Idi when he made a trip to Palestine (*Eruvin* 80a).

Ya'akov Gavlaya (third century)

Also known as Ya'akov Gevula'a *and* Ya'akov Gevulaya.

Palestinian amora. In the Palestinian Talmud (*Yevamot* 9b) he is mentioned as a disciple of Yochanan bar Nappacha and Chanina bar Chama.

Ya'akov Gevula'a

See Ya'akov Gavlaya.

Ya'akov Gevulaya

See Ya'akov Gavlaya.

Ya'akov, Grandson of Acha bar Ya'akov
See Ya'akov bar beratei Acha bar Ya'akov.

Ya'akov Karchah (third/fourth century)
Babylonian amora. In *Chullin* 22b he comments on pigeons that are permissible to be used for sacrifice.

Ya'akov of Adiabene
See Ya'akov of Hadyaiva.

Ya'akov of Hadyaiva (third century)
Babylonian amora. Known in English as Ya'akov of Adiabene, he is listed in *Bava Batra* 26b as a disciple of Chisda.

Ya'akov of Karchina (second century)
Palestinian tanna. In *Eruvin* 86a he is noted as a contemporary of Yehudah bar Ila'i.

Ya'akov of Kefar Chittayya (second century)
Palestinian tanna. In *Chagigah* 5b he is described as a student who shows respect for his teacher by visiting him every day.

Ya'akov of Nehar Pekod (fourth/fifth century)
Babylonian amora. In *Chullin* 107a and *Ketubbot* 33b he is mentioned as a contemporary of Ashi, and in *Ketubbot* 93a and 98b as a disciple of Ravina I.

Ya'akov, Son of the Daughter of Shemu'el
See Ya'akov berei de-vat Shemu'el.

Ya'akov, Son of the Daughter of Ya'akov
See Ya'akov berei de-vat Ya'akov.

Yaddu'a ha-Bavli (second century)
Palestinian tanna. Known in English as Yaddu'a the Babylonian, he was a disciple of Me'ir.

Yaddu'a the Babylonian
See Yaddu'a ha-Bavli.

Yakim (first/second century)
Palestinian tanna. He is listed in Mishnah *Eduyyot* 7:5 as a colleague of Yehoshu'a ben Chananyah.

Yannai (second/third century)
Also known as Yannai Rabbah *or* Yannai Sabba.

Palestinian amora. Often referred to as Yannai Rabbah ("Yannai the Great") or Yannai Sabba ("Yannai the Elder"), he was a very wealthy descendant of a Priestly family. Upon the death of his teacher, Yehudah ha-Nasi, Yannai ruled that even Priests may attend the funerals of great teachers (Palestinian Talmud, *Berakhot* 4:6).

Bava Batra 14a refers to four hundred vineyards that Yannai cultivated. Growing up in wealth, his daughters demanded expensive gifts before they would agree to marry (*Kiddushin* 11a). One of Yannai's daughters married Yehudah, the son of his friend and colleague Chiyya.

Yannai was not only a very spiritual man, but a very practical one as well. He established an important academy at Akbara, in the Galilee, where the students studied and, at the same time, worked on Yannai's estate, thus earning their keep.

Yannai is the author of the following prayer:

Lord of the world, I have sinned before You! May it be Thy will to grant me a good heart, good desires, a good name, a good eye, a modest soul, and a humble spirit. May Thy name not be profaned through us, and preserve us from being the subject of gossip among people. Bring us not to destruction, nor our hopes to frustration, and spare us from depending on the favors of men whose gifts are small but whose shame is great. Grant that our share be in Your Torah and among those who do Your will. Build Your house, and Your palace, and Your city, and Your Temple, soon in our days.

Yannai was exemplary in his relationships with his fellow-man. He wisely admonished people to correct their own defects before castigating others (*Bava Batra* 60b); encouraged people to give charity in private rather than in public, which could cause embarrassment to the recipient (*Chagigah* 5a); and said that "If a patient says, 'I need food,' but the doctor says, 'He does not need food,' we listen to the patient" (*Yoma* 83a; Yannai quotes *Proverbs* 14:10 as proof).

In *Berakhot* 30b Yannai is listed as a teacher of Chanina Kera. Later, in *Berakhot* 44b, Yannai quotes Yehudah ha-Nasi as saying that "an egg is superior [in food value] to any other kind of food."

To remind us that first things must come first, Yannai says, "Woe is the man who builds the door before he builds the house" or "Woe to him who has no courtyard yet erects a gate" (*Shabbat* 31b).

Yannai influenced a generation of prominent scholars, among whom were Yochanan bar Nappacha (*Rosh Hashanah* 15a), Shimon ben Lakish (*Eruvin* 11b), Aivu (*Ketubbot* 54b and *Kiddushin* 19a), Chanina (*Ketubbot* 56a), and Dimi (*Eruvin* 75a).

As Yannai's death approached, he instructed his children not to bury him in a white shroud, lest he be destined for Gehenna, where he would appear like a groom among mourners, nor in a black shroud, lest he be destined for Paradise, where he would appear as a mourner among grooms (*Shabbat* 114a).

Yannai's students compared their teacher to a phoenix, a bird that lives for a thousand years, is consumed by flames, and then is reborn from a single egg that remains intact in its nest (*Genesis Rabbah* 19:5).

Yannai bar Nachmani (third century)

Babylonian amora. According to *Tamid* 29a, he was a disciple of Shemu'el.

Yannai ben Ammi (fourth century)

Palestinian amora. In *Chullin* 111a he is noted as a colleague of Abbayei.

Yannai ben Ishmael

See Yannai ben Yishma'el.

Yannai ben Yishma'el (third century)

Palestinian amora. A contemporary of Ze'eira and Abba ben Kahana, according to *Avodah Zarah* 30a, when Yannai was sick, his colleague Yishma'el ben Zerud and other scholars came to visit him. Yannai is thought to have been the brother of Yudan ben Yishma'el.

Yannai, Brother of Rabbi Chiyya bar Abba

See Yannai Achuha de-Rabbi Chiyya bar Abba.

Yannai Achuha de-Rabbi Chiyya bar Abba
(third/fourth century)

Palestinian amora. Known in English as Yannai, Brother of Rabbi Chiyya bar Abba, he is quoted in *Sanhedrin* 74b.

Yannai Rabbah
See Yannai.

Yannai Sabba
See Yannai.

Yannai the Elder
See Yannai.

Yannai the Great
See Yannai.

Yannai the Lesser
See Yannai Ze'eira.

Yannai Ze'eira (fourth/fifth century)

Palestinian amora. Grandson of Yannai, he was known in English as Yannai the Lesser to distinguish him from his grandfather.

Yanuka bar Chisda (fourth/fifth century)
Also known as Mar Yanuka bar Chisda.

Babylonian amora. He was the brother of Kashisha bar Chisda, as noted in *Bava Metzi'a* 66b and *Pesachim* 107a.

Yechezkel (third century)

Babylonian amora. In *Berakhot* 11a he gives equal validity to the teachings of Hillel and Shammai. In *Kiddushin* 32a Yechezkel is mentioned as the father of Rami bar Yechezkel and Yehudah bar Yechezkel.

Yechi'el (third century)

Babylonian amora. In *Mo'ed Katan* 10a he is mentioned as a contemporary of Yehudah bar Yechezkel. In *Nedarim* 41b and *Yoma* 47a, Rabbah bar Yonatan is noted as Yechi'el's disciple.

Yehoshu'a
See Yehoshu'a ben Chananyah.

Yehoshu'a bar Abba (third century)

Babylonian amora. In *Mo'ed Katan* 5b he is mentioned as a

disciple of Ulla. In *Menachot* 30a, Yehoshu'a bar Abba cites a ruling by Giddal, a pupil of Rav, about the superior value of writing one's own Torah scroll as opposed to buying one in the marketplace.

Yehoshu'a bar Avin (fourth century)
Palestinian amora. He is noted in *Exodus Rabbah* 21:5 as an expert in *aggadah.*

Yehoshu'a bar Idi (fourth century)
Babylonian amora. Son of Idi bar Avin and brother of Sheshet bar Idi, Yehoshu'a bar Idi was a colleague of Kahana (*Pesachim* 3b) and a teacher of Ashi, as well as a guest in Ashi's home (*Shabbat* 11a). In *Eruvin* 82a–b, Yehoshu'a bar Idi comments on a view expressed by Assi that a six-year-old child may walk beyond the Sabbath limits within an *eruv* established by his mother. Yehoshu'a was married to a Priest's daughter (*Pesachim* 49a), and his own mother was also the daughter of a Priest.

Yehoshu'a ben Akiba
See Yehoshu'a ben Akiva.

Yehoshu'a ben Akiva (second century)
Palestinian tanna. In *Pesachim* 112a Akiva ben Yosef offers his son Yehoshu'a advice on how to conduct his life.

Yehoshu'a ben Bathyra
See Yehoshu'a ben Beteira.

Yehoshu'a ben Beteira (first/second century)
Palestinian tanna. In *Shabbat* 104b he comments on how much writing constitutes a violation of Sabbath law; in *Parah* 1:5 he comments on how many black hairs on the red heifer (*parah adummah*), whose ashes were used to purify one who had come into contact with a human corpse, would invalidate it as a sacrifice.

Yehoshu'a ben Chananiah
See Yehoshu'a ben Chananyah.

Yehoshu'a ben Chananyah (first/second century)
Palestinian tanna. Quoted widely throughout the Babylonian Talmud, he is known as Yehoshu'a, without patronymic, except in *Chagigah* 5b, *Kiddushin* 30a, and *Sukkah* 53a, where he is referred to as Yehoshu'a ben Chananyah.

In *Eruvin* 11b it is noted that Yehoshu'a studied Torah at the academy of Yochanan ben Nuri and later established his own school in Beki'in, a small town between Yavneh and Lydda. According to *Nedarim* 50a, Yehoshu'a and Eli'ezer ben Hurkanos tutored the unschooled Akiva ben Yosef for twelve years; in the end, Akiva became their equal in learning. Yehoshu'a also taught Shimon ben Zoma.

As a *Levi*, Yehoshu'a sang in the Temple choir in his youth; to support his family, he later became a needleworker, continuing in this humble occupation even when he became principal of his own academy. At the same time he was an activist, helping his teacher, Yochanan ben Zakkai, escape from Jerusalem during the Roman siege of the city in 70 C.E.

While Gamli'el II was *nasi* and head of the *beit din*, Yehoshu'a ben Chananyah became one of its prominent members, though he and Gamli'el often argued with each other. One time (*Rosh Hashanah* 25a) they disagreed about calendar calculations, specifically the date of Yom Kippur; on another occasion (*Berakhot* 27b) they disagreed about those circumstances under which one may recite an abbreviated *Amidah.* On several occasions, their disagreements were violent, and, in the year 90, Gamli'el II was temporarily removed from his post for publicly embarrassing Yehoshu'a. Gamli'el was replaced by Elazar ben Azaryah but after a while was reinstated.

Yehoshu'a was an independent thinker, and on many occasions he carried out religious rituals that deviated from the norm. *Rosh Hashanah* 11a records a dispute with his colleagues over when the world was created; in *Rosh Hashanah* 11b, Yehoshu'a identifies the seventeenth day of the Hebrew month of Iyyar as being the day on which the Flood (*Genesis* 7:11) engulfed the world. In *Sukkah* 37b it says that Yehoshu'a waved the *lulav* only when the words *hosha na* ("Save us, please") were recited (*Psalms* 118:25).

In *Mo'ed Katan* 21a Yehoshu'a says, "A mourner is forbidden to put on *tefillin* during the first two days of mourning. In *Mo'ed Katan* 27a he pronounced that mourning begins from the moment "the rolling stone closes the tomb."

Despite Yehoshu'a's disagreements with Gamli'el II, in 95 C.E.

he joined Gamli'el II, Akiva ben Yosef, and Elazar ben Azaryah (*Sukkah* 41b) on a visit to Rome to raise funds for their schools. This brought Yehoshu'a into contact with the non-Jewish world. He also visited Athens, where he debated with philosophers and Christians, and came to the attention of Hadrian, the Roman emperor (*Chagigah* 5b).

Yehoshu'a had several confrontations with Hadrian and later with the Elders of Athens. They tried to entrap him with trick questions (*Chullin* 59b–60a and *Ecclesiastes Rabbah* 9:4). His responses are classic. Once they asked him, "Where is the middle of the world?" Yehoshu'a pointed to the spot where he stood. When they asked him how he knew this was the middle of the world, he told them to take a line and measure the distance to convince themselves.

Again, attempting to confuse him, the Elders said, "We have a well in the desert and we want you to bring it into the city." Yehoshu'a replied, "For that I need a rope of bran, for only such a rope can be used for moving wells."

Again they said to him, "We have a broken mill and we want you to patch it." He answered, "For this a thread of sand is needed."

Another time he was asked, "When a bird dies, how does its soul leave its body?" Yehoshu'a replied, "The soul leaves through the same place that it enters at birth."

In Yehoshu'a's debates with Hadrian, the Roman emperor once inquired, "You say that God creates new angels every day to praise Him, and after they finish their praise they go away. I would like to know where they go." Yehoshu'a replied, "They go to the place where they were created. They go to the River of Fire, which flows day and night even as the Jordan flows day and night. And this River of Fire comes from the perspiration of the sacred animals that carry the Throne of Glory."

Then Hadrian said, "I have noticed that God's name is mentioned in the first five of the Ten Commandments but that it does not occur in the other five. How can you explain that?" Yehoshu'a retorted, "Why is it that wherever a person looks, he sees your statue, but in those places where a person goes to relieve himself he does not find your likeness?" The emperor answered, "It is not fitting to place my image in unclean places."

"Neither is it fitting to mention God's name together with murderers, adulterers, thieves, false witnesses, and other sinners who are the refuse of humanity," Yehoshu'a responded.

On another occasion Hadrian asked Yehoshu'a, "Why do the Sabbath dishes have such a fragrant aroma?" Yehoshu'a answered, "We have a particular seasoning called 'Sabbath' that we put into a dish and that gives it its fragrant aroma . . ." (*Shabbat* 119a).

Yehoshu'a was said to have been very ugly. When the king's daughter asked how so much wisdom got into so frightful a person, he replied, "Wine is not kept in casks of gold."

In *Avot* 2:16 Yehoshu'a warned, "The evil eye, the evil impulse, and hatred of fellow human beings destroy a person's life."

A poignant example of Yehoshu'a's critical attitude toward Jews who were overzealous in their observance of Jewish ritual is detailed in *Bava Batra* 60b. Yehoshu'a noticed that a group of ascetics could not stop grieving over the destruction of the Second Temple. To express their grief they avoided all pleasure, even denying themselves the luxury of eating meat and drinking wine.

When Yehoshu'a questioned them about this practice, they replied, "Do you expect us to eat flesh, which used to be brought as an offering on the altar, now that the altar is no longer in existence? Shall we drink wine that was once poured on the altar as a libation, but which act no longer can be carried out?"

"If that is so," Yehoshu'a responded, "we should not eat bread either, because meal offerings can no longer be brought on the altar."

"We can manage with fruit," the ascetics said.

"You should not eat fruit either," Yehoshu'a said to them, "because fruit offerings that were once brought to the Temple can no longer be brought." "And," he added, "you should no longer drink water because once there was a water-drawing ceremony on the second night of Sukkot, to induce God to bring on the rainy season—and that can no longer be carried out."

To this the ascetics had no answer. "Listen my sons, listen to me," Yehoshu'a concluded. "Not to mourn at all is impossible because the loss of the Temple has been so grievous. But to

MASTERS OF THE TALMUD

mourn too much is impossible, because we must never impose upon the community a hardship that the majority cannot endure."

Yehoshu'a ben Elisha (first century)

Palestinian tanna. In *Nazir* 44a Yitzchak ha-Kohen consults Yehoshu'a ben Elisha about the laws regarding the reburial of his father, who had died three years earlier, without Yitzchak ha-Kohen's knowledge.

Yehoshu'a ben Gamla (first century)

During the reign of Herod Agrippa II (28–92 C.E.), the High Priesthood often was for sale. Yehoshu'a ben Gamla had married a widow of great wealth, Miryam (Martha), a daughter of the High Priest Boethus. It is said that she induced Agrippa II, by the offer of a large bribe, to confer the High Priesthood upon her husband.

Yehoshu'a did not occupy the office for very long, but during his tenure he spent much money to beautify the Temple. It is said that he had a golden vessel made that was used for the casting of lots to determine which of the two he-goats was to be sacrificed on Yom Kippur, and which, as the symbolic bearer of the sins of Israel, was to be thrown off a cliff.

Despite the fact that Yehoshu'a ben Gamla is reputed to have paid a bribe to be appointed High Priest, the Talmud mentions his name respectfully. He is praised for having insisted that there must be teachers in every city in Judea to instruct the children so that the Torah would not be forgotten (*Bava Batra* 21a).

Yehoshu'a ben Hurkanos (first/second century)

Palestinian tanna. In *Sotah* 31a he speculates on whether the word *lo* in *Job* 13:15 should be spelled with an *alef* or a *vav*.

Yehoshu'a ben Hyrcanus

See Yehoshu'a ben Hurkanos.

Yehoshu'a ben Karchah (second century)

Palestinian tanna. Quoted several times in the Talmud, he explains to Yehudah ha-Nasi in *Megillah* 28a why he (Yehoshu'a) has attained a ripe old age: "Never in my life have I gazed at the countenance of a wicked man." In *Megillah* 2b Yehoshu'a rules on when the book of *Esther* is to be read in walled cities and, in

13a, offers a description of Queen Esther's appeal. In *Nedarim* 31b Yehoshu'a ben Karcha comments on the importance of fulfilling the commandment of circumcision and in *Nazir* 23b remarks: "A man should always be prepared to perform a *mitzvah*." In *Ketubbot* 68a and *Bava Batra* 10a he says: "Whoever turns his eyes away from [one who appeals for] charity is like one who worships idols." In *Sanhedrin* 6b Yehoshu'a is quoted as saying: "Settling conflicts by arbitration is a meritorious course."

In *Yoma* 39b and *Megillah* 14a Yehoshu'a is noted as a teacher of Chiyya bar Avin.

Yehoshu'a ben Kepusai (second century)

Palestinian tanna. In *Shabbat* 147a he is mentioned as a son-in-law of Akiva ben Yosef. In *Avodah Zarah* 32a he is noted as a teacher of Shimon ben Gamli'el.

Yehoshu'a ben Levi (third century)

Palestinian amora. Born in Lydda, where he established an academy, he instructed many students who were destined to become great scholars. Among his disciples were Ya'akov ben Idi (*Gittin* 39a), Shimon bar Pazzi (*Shabbat* 40a), Ulla (*Bava Metzi'a* 9b), and Zerika (*Berakhot* 3b).

Yehoshu'a respected the scribes who wrote religious articles, as noted in *Pesachim* 50b where he remarks that the Men of the Great Assembly observed twenty-four fasts [to implore Heaven] that those who write Torah scrolls, *tefillin*, and *mezuzot* not get rich, for if they did get rich, they would no longer be willing to continue the tedious task [of writing religious articles]. It was Yehoshu'a ben Levi who instructed worshippers to take three steps back at the conclusion of the *Amidah* (*Yoma* 53b) and then recite the sentence, "May He who makes peace in His high places . . ."

On one occasion, the patriarch Yehudah Nesi'ah sent Yehoshu'a ben Levi on a mission to Rome to collect funds from wealthy Jews for support of the patriarchate. Yehoshu'a ben Levi's son, Yosef, would later marry Yehudah Nesi'ah's daughter.

Yehoshu'a trained his children to cherish education and live piously. In *Berakhot* 8a he admonishes them: "Come to the synagogue early and leave late, that you may live long." And in

Berakhot 47b he says: "A man should always come early to synagogue so that "he may merit being among the first ten [for a *minyan*]." In *Berakhot* 59a his disciple Aleksandri quotes him as saying: "Thunder was created to straighten out the crookedness of the heart." And in *Kiddushin* 30a Yehoshu'a ben Levi is credited with the words: "He who teaches his grandson Torah [is regarded] as though he had received the Torah [directly] from [God on] Mount Sinai."

In *Ta'anit* 3b Yehoshu'a ben Levi says that the verse in *Zechariah* 2:10, "I have spread you abroad [in exile] as the four winds of heaven," implies that "As the world cannot endure without winds, so the world cannot endure without Israel."

He died in approximately 275.

Yehoshu'a ben Levi ben Lachma (third century)

Palestinian amora. In *Bava Batra* 15a he claims that Job was a contemporary of Moses.

Yehoshu'a ben Matya (second century)

Palestinian tanna. He is mentioned in the Mishnah *Eduyyot* 2:5.

Yehoshu'a ben Memel (first/second century)

Palestinian tanna. In *Nazir* 56b he is listed as a disciple of Eli'ezer ben Hurkanos and a colleague of Yehoshu'a ben Chananyah.

Yehoshu'a ben Perachyah (first/second century B.C.E.)

Pre-tannaitic Palestinian teacher. He was a member of one of the *zugot*—Nittai of Arbela was his partner—and served as president of the Sanhedrin. At the time of the persecution of the Pharisees by King Alexander Yannai, Yehoshu'a fled with Jesus to Alexandria, Egypt (*Sotah* 47a). According to early manuscripts of the Talmud, Jesus was a disciple whom Yehoshu'a ben Perachyah "thrust away with both hands."

One of Yehoshua's maxims was this: "Provide yourself with a teacher, find yourself a companion, and judge everyone favorably" (*Avot* 1:6).

Yehoshu'a ben Uza'a (second century)

Palestinian tanna. In *Yoma* 47b he is quoted by Yochanan bar Nappacha.

Yehoshu'a ben Ziruz (second century)
Palestinian tanna. According to *Shabbat* 147a and *Chullin* 6b, he was the brother-in-law of Me'ir—Me'ir's wife was the sister of Yehoshu'a ben Ziruz.

Yehoshu'a Deromah (third century)
Palestinian amora. Known in English as Yehoshu'a of the South, he is quoted in *Avodah Zarah* 30b by his disciple Safra as remarking, "The older the snake, the less potent its venom."

Yehoshu'a ha-Garsi (first/second century)
Palestinian tanna. Known in English as Yehoshu'a the Grits Maker, he was the brother of Nimos ha-Gardi, ("Nimos the Weaver"; *Bekhorot* 10b). According to *Eruvin* 21b, Yehoshu'a ha-Garsi tended to the needs of Akiva when Akiva was imprisoned by the Romans, bringing him water every day.

Yehoshu'a of Sikhnin (third century)
Palestinian amora. Sikhnin was a town in the Galilee fortified by Josephus when he was in command of the area during the uprising against Rome in 66 C.E. Yehoshu'a of Sikhnin is mentioned only once in the Talmud (*Bava Batra* 75b), as a teacher of Pappi.

Yehoshu'a of the South
See Yehoshu'a Deromah.

Yehoshu'a the Grits Maker
See Yehoshu'a ha-Garsi.

Yehudah
See Yehudah bar Ila'i, Yehudah bar Yechezkel, *and* Yehudah ben Bava.

Yehudah I
See Yehudah ha-Nasi.

Yehudah II
See Yehudah Nesi'ah.

Yehudah III (third century)
Palestinian amora. He succeeded his father, Gamli'el IV, as patriarch and head of the Sanhedrin. Like his grandfather, Yehudah Nesi'ah (with whom he is often confused), he devoted himself to the furtherance of elementary education in Palestine.

During Yehudah III's tenure, he was charged with having been paid off to appoint to office certain judges who were unworthy administrators of justice. Gradually the scholars became disenchanted with the patriarchate and leadership eventually passed out of its control. Yehudah III was succeeded by his son, Hillel II.

Yehudah IV (fourth century)

Palestinian amora. In 380, Yehudah IV succeeded his father, Gamli'el V, as patriarch of Palestine. Upon his death, Yehudah IV was succeeded by his son, Gamli'el VI.

Yehudah Achuha de-Rav Salla Chasida (third century)

Babylonian amora. Known in English as Yehudah, Brother of Salla Chasida, he and other scholars went to visit Huna, where they learned that four hundred jars of his wine had turned sour. It was suggested that this was punishment for Huna's bad actions (*Berakhot* 5b).

Yehudah bar Abba (fourth/fifth century)

Babylonian amora. In *Menachot* 31b he is listed as a contemporary of Ashi and Rabbah bar Nachmani.

Yehudah bar Abbayei (second/third century)

Babylonian amora. In *Pesachim* 92b he is noted as a disciple of Rav.

Yehudah bar Achotai (third century)

Babylonian amora. In *Keritot* 13b he agrees with Elazar ben Pedat that (in *Leviticus* 10:9) the words *strong drink*, which Priests should avoid, refer to something intoxicating.

Yehudah bar Ammi (fourth century)

Palestinian amora. In *Eruvin* 30b, *Ketubbot* 28b, and *Niddah* 57a he is noted as a disciple of Yehudah bar Yechezkel, who was a disciple of Shemu'el, and in *Mo'ed Katan* 5b as a disciple of Ulla.

Yehudah bar Chanina (third century)

Palestinian amora. In *Eruvin* 11a he is mentioned as a teacher of Shimon ben Lakish. Yehudah bar Chanina often is confused with Yehudah bar Chinena.

Yehudah bar Chaviva (third century)

Palestinian amora. He is listed in *Ketubbot* 60a as a disciple of Shemu'el. Some scholars believe that he is one and the same as Yehudah bar Chanina. *Berakhot* 42a, however, notes that Yehudah bar Chanina gave a wedding feast for his son in the house of Yehudah bar Chaviva.

Yehudah bar Chinena (fourth century)

Babylonian amora. In *Bava Kamma* 14b he is noted as a colleague of Huna bar Yehoshu'a.

Yehudah bar Ezekiel

See Yehudah bar Yechezkel.

Yehudah bar Gamda

See Yehudah ben Agra of Kefar Akko.

Yehudah bar Idi (second/third century)

Palestinian amora. In *Rosh Hashanah* 31a he is noted as a disciple of Yochanan bar Nappacha.

Yehudah bar Ila'i (second century)

Palestinian tanna. Often referred to simply as Yehudah, he was born in Usha in the Galilee. He was one of the last five disciples of Akiva ben Yosef, all of whom fled to Babylonia upon Akiva's death at the hands of the Romans. After the persecutions, Yehuda bar Ila'i returned to his school in Usha. He has been characterized as "modest, wise, diplomatic, and eloquent," and was one of Yehudah ha-Nasi's most important students.

In *Shabbat* 33b Yehudah bar Ila'i is mentioned as a colleague of Elazar ben Yosei, who was a member of the Sanhedrin in Yavneh, which had been established by Yochanan ben Zakkai after the destruction of the Temple in 70 C.E.

Nedarim 49b notes how poor Yehudah bar Ila'i was. His wife bought some wool of mixed colors out of which she knitted a shawl. Yehudah shared it with her and used it as a cloak when he went to pray in the synagogue. Yet, he prepared for the Sabbath like no other scholar. *Shabbat* 25b notes that it was his practice on the eve of the Sabbath to have a tub filled with warm water in which he would wash his face, his hands, and his feet. He would then wrap himself in fringed robes which gave him the appearance of an angel of the Lord.

Ketubbot 17a reports that Yehudah bar Ila'i was so devoted to studying Torah that he would interrupt his studies only to perform the *mitzvah* of joining a funeral procession or leading a bride to the *chuppah*, the wedding canopy. At weddings, he would take a twig of myrtle, hold it aloft, and dance before the bride, singing: "O bride! How beautiful and graceful!"

In *Sukkah* 51b Yehudah is quoted as saying that "one who has not seen the double colonnade [of the great synagogue] in Alexandria, Egypt, has never seen the glory of Israel." The synagogue was so large that when the time came for the congregation to say "Amen," an attendant would wave a scarf to notify the congregation, many of whom were beyond earshot. Goldsmiths, silversmiths, blacksmiths, metalworkers, and weavers sat in separate sections, so that when a poor man entered the synagogue he could easily sit with his fellow craftsmen and seek employment.

In *Avot* 4:13, the following maxim is quoted in Yehudah bar Ila'i's name: "Be cautious in study, for an error in study amounts to an intentional sin." Yehudah considered study to be of the utmost importance but also emphasized the value of labor. Among the duties of a father toward his son, Yehudah asserted, is to teach him a trade: "One who does not teach his son a trade may cause him to become a thief" (*Kiddushin* 29a).

Yehudah bar Ila'i used to say: "Ten strong things have been created in the world. A mountain is strong, but iron cleaves it. Iron is strong, but fire melts it. Fire is strong, but water quenches it. Water is heavy, but clouds carry it away. Clouds are heavy, but a wind scatters them. The wind is strong, but the body withstands it. The body is strong, but fear crushes it. Fear is strong, but wine dissipates it. Wine is strong, but sleep overcomes it. Stronger than all these, however, is death" (*Bava Batra* 10a).

Yehudah bar Isaac
See Yehudah bar Yitzchak.

Yehudah bar Ishmael
See Yehudah bar Yishma'el.

Yehudah bar Joshua
See Yehudah bar Yehoshu'a.

Yehudah bar Kaza (fourth century)

Babylonian amora. In *Ketubbot* 104a he is listed as a contemporary of Nachman bar Yitzchak.

Yehudah bar Ma'arava (fourth century)

Palestinian amora. Known in English as Yehudah the Palestinian, he is said in *Sotah* 41b to have been an older contemporary of Shimon bar Pazzi.

Yehudah bar Mereimar

See Yehudah Mar bar Mereimar.

Yehudah bar Natan (fourth century)

Babylonian amora. According to *Berakhot* 60a, he was a disciple of Hamnuna.

Yehudah bar Nathan

See Yehudah bar Natan.

Yehudah bar Oshaya (fourth century)

Babylonian amora. In *Chullin* 93a he is noted as a colleague of Levi bar Huna bar Chiyya.

Yehudah bar Pazzi

See Yehudah bar Shimon.

Yehudah bar Safra (third/fourth century)

Palestinian amora. In *Pesachim* 70b, Ila'i is listed as Yehudah bar Safra's disciple.

Yehudah bar Samuel

See Yehudah bar Shemu'el.

Yehudah bar Samuel bar Shilat

See Yehudah bar Shemu'el bar Shilat.

Yehudah bar Shalom (fourth/fifth century)

Palestinian amora. *Bava Batra* 10a records his preachings on man's fate: "Just as a man's livelihood is determined for him on Rosh Hashanah, so is his lack of success."

Yehudah bar Shemu'el (fourth century)

Babylonian amora. In *Avodah Zarah* 20b he is mentioned as a colleague of Pappa and in *Shabbat* 38a as a disciple of Abba, who was a disciple of Kahana.

Yehudah bar Shemu'el bar Shilat (third century)

Babylonian amora. In *Berakhot* 47a, *Eruvin* 97a, *Ta'anit* 14a, and *Mo'ed Katan* 16a Yehudah bar Shemu'el bar Shilat, son of amora Shemu'el bar Shilat, is noted as a disciple of Rav. *Shabbat* 118b contains some of Yehudah's unique observations about the Sabbath. On one occasion he was asked, "How does one prove that he delights in the Sabbath?" Yehudah responded, "By preparing a dish of beets, a large fish, and cloves of garlic." On another occasion Yehudah commented on the fact that while in the desert many Israelites disregarded the warning that manna would not appear on the Sabbath day and went out to search for it (*Exodus* 17:27). Yehudah said, "Had Israel kept the first Sabbath, no nation would ever have had dominion over them."

Yehudah bar Shila (third/fourth century)

Also known as Yehudah bar Shilat.

Palestinian amora. According to *Yevamot* 21b, Yehudah bar Shila visited Babylonia, where he advised scholars about the Palestinian ruling concerning marriage to one's mother-in-law or father-in-law after the death of his or her spouse. In *Zevachim* 22a and *Shabbat* 126b he is listed as a disciple of Assi, who was a disciple of Yochanan bar Nappacha.

Yehudah bar Shilat

See Yehudah bar Shila.

Yehudah bar Shimon

Two scholars were known by this name:

1. A second/third-century Palestinian tanna who is quoted in *Sanhedrin* 100a as saying, "He who undergoes privation in this world in order to study Torah will be rewarded by God in the world to come."

According to *Chullin* 48a, Yehudah bar Shimon was a mentor to Yochanan bar Nappacha.

2. A fourth-century Palestinian amora who was also known as Yehudah bar Pazzi *and* Yehudah bar Shimon bar Pazzi. In *Berakhot* 9b Yehudah bar Shimon says that David composed 103 (of the 150) chapters of *Psalms* and notes that the first and last verses of these chapters contain the word "happy." In

Menachot 4b Yehudah is mentioned as a colleague of Yirme-yahu. *Chullin* 111a recounts how Zerika and Yannai ben Ammi visited Yehudah bar Shimon and were served a meal.

In the following parable Yehudah bar Shimon expounds on God's love for Israel:

A king once had an orchard in which he grew figs, vines, pomegranates, and apples. The king turned the orchard over to a caretaker and left. Sometime later he returned to see how his orchard was thriving and found it full of thorns and weeds. In great anger he commanded that the trees be cut down. However, when he looked closely between the thorns he noticed a beautiful rose. He bent over, inhaled its fragrance, and said, "Because of this rose I will save the whole orchard." Twenty-six generations after the creation of the world God saw its wickedness and decided to anni-hilate it. But among the thorns He saw a rose, the Jews, who accepted the Ten Commandments, and, for their sake, He spared the whole world. (*Leviticus Rabbah* 23:3)

Yehudah bar Shimon bar Pazzi
See Yehudah bar Shimon.

Yehudah bar Simon
See Yehudah bar Shimon.

Yehudah bar Yechezkel (third century)
Babylonian amora. Son of the amora Yechezkel and brother of Rami bar Yechezkel, Yehudah bar Yechezkel was born around the time that Yehudah ha-Nasi completed the task of editing the Mishnah. Yehudah bar Yechezkel was so widely known that in the hundreds of references to him in the Talmud he generally is referred to as Yehudah or Rav Yehudah, without patronymic.

Yehudah studied under several teachers, including Tarfon (*Chagigah* 10a), Kahana (*Yoma* 11a), and Zerika (*Beitzah* 75b). His most influential teachers, however, were Rav, whom he quotes in *Berakhot* 17b and 19b and numerous other tractates, and Shemu'el, whom he quotes in *Berakhot* 19a and 21a, as well as in other tractates.

Shemu'el admired Yehudah's keen mind and referred to him as *shinena,* "the sharp one" (*Shabbat* 152a and *Rosh Hashanah* 24b); likewise, Chisda recognized Yehudah's sharpness (*Chullin* 110a–b). It is said that Shemu'el respected Yehudah so much that when Yehudah entered a room, Shemu'el would rise for him (*Kiddushin* 33b). Yehudah commanded great respect both at home and abroad. Surprisingly, as noted in *Rosh Hashanah* 35a, Yehudah prayed only once every thirty days—because he was so committed to his studies. Equally surprisingly, Yehudah made no effort to find a wife for his learned son Yitzchak (*Kiddushin* 71b and *Yevamot* 63b), explaining that he did not know where to find one.

If Yehudah bar Yechezkel was inclined to favor the legal rulings of Shemu'el over those of Rav, Yehudah quotes Rav considerably more often on philosophical subjects and matters of personal relationships:

- Giving a kindly reception to a stranger is even more meritorious than receiving God's presence. (*Shabbat* 127a)
- The Holy One, blessed be He, did not create even one thing in this world without a purpose. He created the snail as a cure for the scab; he created the fly as an antidote to the [sting of the] hornet; the mosquito for the serpent's bite, etc. (*Shabbat* 77b)
- Wherever the Sages have forbidden an action because of how it might be perceived by the public, it also is forbidden when performed in the utmost privacy. (*Beitzah* 9a)

Yehudah believed that everything was foreordained and that nothing happened by mere chance. In *Sotah* 2a he quotes Rav as saying: "Forty days before the creation of a child, a heavenly voice [*bat kol*] announces: 'The daughter of A is for B, the house of C is for D, the field of E is for F.'" And in *Yoma* 21a, where it is suggested that ten miracles were wrought in the Temple of Jerusalem, Yehudah quotes Rav on one of them: "When the Israelites came up to observe the festivals, [the crowd was so great that the people] stood pressed together, but when they had to prostrate themselves . . . there was ample open space."

Yehudah bar Yechezkel's philosophy is summed up in *Rosh Hashanah* 17b: "Great is the power of repentance, for it can rescind any pronouncement as to the fate of man."

Yehudah founded an academy in Pumbedita in 259, which became, after the destruction of Nehardea by the Palmyrenes, the center of Jewish scholarship in northern Babylonia, just as Sura, under Rav and his successors Huna and Ashi, had become the center of Jewish scholarship in southern Babylonia. Under the inspired leadership of Yehudah and his successors, who included Abbayei and Rava, Pumbedita would outstrip the academy in Sura (though later it would go into decline and be moved from Pumbedita to Machoza). When Huna died in 297, Yehudah was chosen by the Sura academy as its principal; thus, during Yehudah bar Yechezkel's lifetime, the academies of Sura and Pumbedita were under a single leadership. Yehudah died two years later, in 299, but the academies of Pumbedita and Sura continued for hundreds of years, well into the geonic period that culminated in the eleventh century.

Yehudah bar Yehoshu'a (third/fourth century)
Babylonian amora. In *Avodah Zarah* 43b he is noted as a contemporary of Abbayei.

Yehudah bar Yishma'el (fifth century)
Babylonian amora. In *Chullin* 118b he is listed as a colleague of Chaviva.

Yehudah bar Yitzchak (third/fourth century)
Babylonian amora. In *Ta'anit* 6b he is mentioned as a contemporary of Pappa and Abbayei.

Yehudah bar Zavdi
See Yehudah bar Zevida.

Yehudah bar Zevida (third century)
Also known as Yehudah bar Zavdi *and* Yehudah bar Zevina.
Palestinian amora. According to *Yevamot* 83b, he was the brother of Abba. In *Kiddushin* 73b, where he is referred to as Yehudah bar Zavdi, he is listed as a disciple of Rav, while *Berakhot* 12b records that he taught Abbahu bar Zutrati. In *Bava Batra* 120a he comments on the youthfulness and beauty of the mother of Moses. In *Sotah* 12a he is referred to as Yehudah bar Zevina.

Yehudah bar Zevina

See Yehudah bar Zevida.

Yehudah ben Achoto shel Rabbi Yosei ben Chanina

(third century)

Palestinian amora. In *Ketubbot* 49b and *Bava Batra* 139a Yehudah ruled that if a man died and left a widow and a daughter, his widow was to receive maintenance out of his estate. If the daughter married and died, and her husband inherited her possessions, her widowed mother still has the right to receive everything she is entitled to under her *ketubbah*.

Yehudah ben Agra of Kefar Akko (second century)

Also known as Yehudah bar Gamda.

Palestinian tanna. In *Niddah* 53a Yehudah ha-Nasi agrees with Yehudah ben Agra's ruling on when a woman's "clean days" have begun after a menstrual discharge. In *Chullin* 134a Yehudah ben Agra is mentioned as a disciple of Me'ir, and in *Sotah* 43b, where he is referred to as Yehudah bar Gamda, he is said to have been a colleague of Shimon ben Gamli'el II.

Yehudah ben Bathyra I

See Yehudah ben Beteira I.

Yehudah ben Bathyra II

See Yehudah ben Beteira II.

Yehudah ben Bava (second century)

Palestinian tanna. Yehudah ben Bava is sometimes referred to simply as Yehudah, without patronymic. In *Berakhot* 27a he is mentioned as the source of five teachings, among them that a woman may remarry even if only one witness testifies that her husband has died. Rav heaps high praise upon Yehudah ben Bava in *Sanhedrin* 13b.

To ensure the continuation of rabbinic tradition during the Hadrianic persecutions, Yehudah ordained five leading pupils of the martyred Akiva ben Yosef—Me'ir, Yehudah bar Ila'i, Shimon bar Yochai, Yosei ben Chalafta, and Elazar ben Shammu'a. When the six men were caught by the Romans, Yehudah ben Bava told the others to flee and was himself murdered (*Sanhedrin* 14a and *Avodah Zarah* 8b) at the age of seventy.

Yehudah ben Beteira I (first century)

Babylonian tanna. Known in English as Yehudah ben Bathyra I, he was a prolific scholar. Though he was born in Palestine, he left before the destruction of the Temple and became principal of an academy in Nisibis, Babylonia (*Sanhedrin* 32b). Members of his family were reputed to have been leaders of the Sanhedrin during Herod's reign over Judea.

Yehudah ben Beteira is quoted frequently in the Talmud, and his decisions generally prevailed. Among his most famous and learned colleagues were Akiva ben Yosef (*Shabbat* 17a), Yehoshu'a (*Kiddushin* 75a), and Yehudah ben Bava (*Chullin* 41a). In *Ta'anit* 2b Yehudah ben Beteira engages in a dispute over the proper time to cease reciting the prayer for rain. In *Mo'ed Katan* 26b he expresses the opinion that upon the death of any close relative, one makes a single tear in one's garment as a sign of mourning, but for a parent the tear is extended. Yehudah ben Beteira is quoted in *Berakhot* 22a as saying: "Just as fire is not susceptible to uncleanness, so words of Torah are not susceptible to it."

Yehudah ben Beteira II (second century)

Palestinian tanna. Known in English as Yehudah ben Bathyra II, he probably was born in Rome, though he studied in Palestine, where he was an associate of Akiva ben Yosef (*Shabbat* 96b). Yehudah disputed Akiva's view that the man in the Torah who violated the Sabbath by gathering sticks and was stoned to death (*Numbers* 15:32–36) was Zelophehad. Zelophehad was the father of five famous daughters (*Numbers* 27), who, after vigorous protest, were finally granted the right to inherit their father's estate.

At some point Yehudah left Palestine and, like Yehudah ben Bathyra I (both men were probably from the same family), settled in Nisibis, Babylonia. He established a yeshiva there, which, according to *Sanhedrin* 32b, was noted for its high academic standing. *Yevamot* 108b indicates that Yehudah was of equal status with Akiva in deciding matters of law.

Yehudah ben Bizna (second century)

Palestinian tanna. He is quoted in *Nedarim* 32a, where he

discusses the laxity of Moses in performing the circumcision of his sons, leaving it to his wife, Zipporah (*Exodus* 4:25).

Yehudah ben Chiyya (third century)

Palestinian amora. Yehudah, his twin brother Chizkiyyah, and their father, Chiyya, were all disciples of Yehudah ha-Nasi. A native of Babylonia, Yehudah ben Chiyya moved to Palestine with his family. The circumstances of Yehudah's birth are detailed in *Yevamot* 65b.

Ketubbot 62b describes the marriage of Yehudah to the daughter of Yannai. Yannai so respected his son-in-law for his scholarship and piety that it is said Yannai would seat himself atop a hill each Friday afternoon to observe his son-in-law's return from the academy. As soon as Yehudah would draw near, Yannai would rise out of respect. When Yannai's students questioned his actions, he explained that his son-in-law "equaled Mount Sinai in sanctity, and no one was allowed to sit down in front of Mount Sinai."

Yehudah ben Chiyya died in the Galilee (while Yannai was still alive) and was honored as a saintly person.

Yehudah ben Dama (first/second century)

Palestinian tanna. One of the Ten Martyrs put to a merciless death by the Romans, Yehudah ben Dama was reportedly slain on the eve of Shavuot, immediately after the execution of Yehudah ben Bava.

Yehudah ben Dostai (first century)

Palestinian tanna. In *Makkot* 7a he is noted as one who transmitted the teachings of Shimon ben Shetach.

Yehudah ben Durtai (first century)

Palestinian tanna. It is said that he moved far away from Jerusalem to avoid having to bring a paschal offering for Pesach. He is quoted in *Pesachim* 70b.

Yehudah ben Gadish (first/second century)

Also known as Yehudah ben Gadush *and* Yehudah ben Garush.

Palestinian tanna. His father's name is spelled in a variety of ways. In *Eruvin* 27a–b, Yehudah ben Gadish is noted as a colleague of Eli'ezer ben Hurkanos.

Yehudah ben Gamaliel
>   *See* Yehudah ben Gamli'el.

Yehudah ben Gamli'el (third century)
>   *Also known as* Yehudah ha-Nasi III.
>   Palestinian amora. Grandson of Yehudah ha-Nasi, as noted in *Gittin* 76b, Yehudah ben Gamli'el generally is referred to as Yehudah ha-Nasi III. In *Ta'anit* 24a he prayed for rain, but it did not come. After he felt humiliated, however, rain did fall.

Yehudah ben Gadush
>   *See* Yehudah ben Gadish.

Yehudah ben Garush
>   *See* Yehudah ben Gadish.

Yehudah ben Gerogrot (third century)
>   Palestinian amora. In *Yoma* 78a he is mentioned as a contemporary of Yehoshu'a ben Levi.

Yehudah ben Gurya (first/second century)
>   Palestinian tanna. In *Eruvin* 63a he is noted as a disciple of Eli'ezer ben Hurkanos. It is reported that Yehudah ben Gurya died because he had the audacity to render a legal decision in the presence of his teacher.

Yehudah ben Ishtata
>   *See* Yehudah ben Ishtita.

Yehudah ben Ishtita (third century)
>   *Also spelled* Yehudah ben Ishtata.
>   Palestinian amora. *Eruvin* 52a reports that one Sabbath eve Yehudah ben Ishtita brought a basket of fruit to Natan ben Oshaya and was invited to spend the night at his home. The understanding was that Yehudah would be allowed to return to his home the next day, which was within the Sabbath parameters.

Yehudah ben Lakish (second century)
>   Palestinian tanna. In *Chagigah* 9b he is noted as a colleague of Shimon bar Yochai.

Yehudah ben Leiva'i
>   *See* Yehudah ben Levi.

Yehudah ben Levi (second/third century)
Also known as Yehudah ben Leiva'i.
Palestinian amora. In *Shabbat* 113a and *Niddah* 60a he is noted as a teacher of Yochanan bar Nappacha.

Yehudah ben Menashya (third century)
Palestinian amora. In *Berakhot* 10a he is mentioned as a colleague of Shimon bar Pazzi.

Yehudah ben Nachman
See Yehudah ben Nachmani.

Yehudah ben Nachmani (third century)
Also known as Yehudah ben Nachman.
Palestinian amora. In *Sotah* 37b, *Gittin* 60b, and *Temurah* 14b he is referred to as the *meturgeman*—"interpreter"—of Shimon ben Lakish, expounding on Shimon ben Lakish's lectures in the academy in Tiberias.

Yehudah ben Nakosah (second century)
Palestinian tanna. In *Bava Kamma* 81b he is said to have been a disciple of Chiyya and in *Chullin* 118b a disciple of Ya'akov bar Korshai. In *Bava Batra* 71a Yehudah ben Nakosah is noted as a colleague of Yehudah ha-Nasi and in *Niddah* 56a as a colleague of Yirmeyahu.

Yehudah ben Nechemyah (first/second century)
Palestinian tanna. In *Menachot* 68b he is listed as a younger contemporary of Yehudah bar Ila'i.

Yehudah ben Nehemiah
See Yehudah ben Nechemyah.

Yehudah ben Ro'etz (second century)
Palestinian tanna. He is quoted in *Sanhedrin* 4a in connection with the pronunciation of the Hebrew word *shevu'ayim* ("two weeks"), which appears in *Leviticus* 12:5.

Yehudah ben Shammu'a (second century)
Palestinian tanna. According to *Rosh Hashanah* 19a, he was a disciple of Me'ir.

Yehudah ben Tabbai (first century B.C.E.)
As *nasi* of the Sanhedrin during the first century B.C.E., he and the *av beit din*, Shimon ben Shetach (some believe their

positions were reversed and Shimon ben Shetach was *nasi* while Yehudah ben Tabbai was *av beit din)*, constituted one of the five pairs, or *zugot.* Yehudah fled to Alexandria when Alexander Yannai persecuted the Pharisees.

Makkot 5b records a disagreement between Yehudah and Shimon over the degree of punishment for witnesses who testify falsely in murder cases. In *Chagigah* 16a Yehudah comments on the practice of the laying on of hands on the head of an animal to be sacrificed; he says that on a holiday this ritual may not be performed.

One of Yehudah ben Tabbai's maxims was this: "Do not [when serving as a judge] assume the role of counselor. When both parties in a lawsuit are standing before you, regard them both as guilty. But when they depart, having submitted to your judgment, regard them both as innocent [since they have accepted the sentence that will be placed upon them]" (*Avot* 1:8).

Yehudah ben Teima (second century)

Palestinian tanna. In *Chagigah* 14a he is referred to as "Master of the Mishnah." *Mo'ed Katan* 21a records his comments on the donning of *tefillin* during mourning. Disagreeing with the Rabbis who forbade the wearing of *tefillin* during the first three days of mourning, Yehudah permitted a mourner to wear *tefillin* from the second day onward but felt the mourner should remove the *tefillin* when receiving visitors and don them again when the visitors departed.

In *Sanhedrin* 4b Yehudah is noted as the mentor of Yochanan ben Dahabai, while in *Sanhedrin* 59b, Yehudah reveals himself as a mystic, fantasizing about Adam reclining in the Garden of Eden while ministering angels roasted flesh and strained wine for him, all of which made the serpent envious.

The following popular maxims of Yehudah ben Teima are quoted in *Avot*:

- Be bold as a leopard, light as an eagle, swift as a gazelle, and strong as a lion to do the will of your Father in heaven. (*Avot* 5:23 and *Pesachim* 112a)
- Five years is the age for the study of Torah; ten, for the

study of Mishnah; thirteen, for the fulfillment of commandments; fifteen, for the study of Talmud; eighteen, for marriage; twenty, for seeking a livelihood; thirty, for full strength; forty, for full understanding; fifty, for giving counsel; sixty, to be an elder; seventy, for gray hair; eighty, for special strength; ninety, for a bowed back; and at one hundred, it is as if one were [already] dead and had passed out of the world. (*Avot* 5:21)

Yehudah ben Ya'ir (second century)
Palestinian tanna. In *Yevamot* 80b he is noted as a teacher of Shimon ben Gamli'el II.

Yehudah ben Yochanan ben Zakkai (first/second century)
Palestinian tanna. Son of the renowned Yochanan ben Zakkai, Yehudah is quoted in *Niddah* 15a, where he ruled that a man may enter the Temple and burn incense even during the time when his wife is "unclean."

Yehudah Berabbi (second century)
Palestinian tanna. In *Menachot* 34b he is said to have been a colleague of Yosei bar Chalafta, with whom he discusses how to handle a situation in which one has no *tefillah* for the hand but two *tefillin* for the head. Yehudah agrees with Yosei that in such a case, the worshipper may cover up one *tefillah* and place it on his arm.

Yehudah, Brother of Salla Chasida
See Yehudah Achuha de-Rav Salla Chasida.

Yehudah, Brother of Salla the Pious
See Yehudah Achuha de-Rav Salla Chasida.

Yehudah Chayyata (second/third century)
Palestinian tanna. He is referred to in *Bava Batra* 164b as having written a deed to whose legitimacy Yehudah ha-Nasi attested.

Yehudah ha-Gelostera (first/second century)
Palestinian tanna. Known in English as Yehudah the Locksmith, he is mentioned in *Berakhot* 22a as a colleague of Akiva ben Yosef.

Yehudah ha-Kohen (second century)
Palestinian tanna. Known in English as Yehudah the Priest,

he is listed in Mishnah *Eduyyot* 8:2 as a colleague of Yehudah
ben Bava.

Yehudah ha-Nachtom (first/second century)
Palestinian tanna. Known in English as Yehudah the Baker,
he was a contemporary of Eli'ezer ben Hurkanos. *Bava Batra*
132a recounts a discussion between the two men about a husband who had given his wife, in writing, the right to use and
enjoy all the advantages and profits of his property and whether,
as a widow, she could collect all she was entitled to under her
ketubbah.

Yehudah ha-Nasi (second/third century)
Palestinian tanna. Known in English as Judah the Prince, he
was the son and successor of Shimon ben Gamli'el II, ascending
to the post of patriarch (*nasi*) of Palestine and presiding over
the Sanhedrin. So highly regarded was Yehudah ha-Nasi for his
piety and scholarship that the title *Rabbenu ha-Kadosh*, "Our
Holy Teacher," was bestowed upon him. Throughout the pages
of the Talmud he is constantly referred to simply as "Rabbi."
His disciples were sometimes given the honorific "Berabbi [or
Beribbi]," a contraction of the words *Bei* or *Beit*, meaning
"house," and "Rabbi."

Yehudah grew up in Usha, where he studied under many of
the most prominent teachers of the time, including Shimon bar
Yochai, Yehudah bar Ila'i, and Elazar ben Shammu'a. Although
he was born into a wealthy family, Yehudah achieved even greater
wealth through his own efforts. *Bava Metzi'a* 85a notes that even
Yehudah's steward was wealthier than King Shapur of Persia.
Bava Batra 8a reports that Yehudah had a storehouse filled with
food. One year, when provisions were scarce, he offered food
free of charge to any learned person but denied it to anyone
ignorant of the teachings of the Bible and Mishnah.

Yehudah ha-Nasi's *beit din* met first in Tiberias, then in Beit
She'arim, and finally, for the last seventeen years of his life, in
Sepphoris, where the high altitude offered Yehudah ha-Nasi re-
lief from his physical ailments.

According to *Bava Metzi'a* 85a, Yehuda ha-Nasi bravely endured years of pain, which he believed was punishment for his

failure to show compassion to a calf that was about to be slaughtered. The calf tried to hide under Yehudah ha-Nasi's cape.

"Go back!" Yehudah ha-Nasi told it. "It is for this very purpose that you were created! You were created to serve man as food."

Having witnessed the incident, the heavenly court decreed: "Since Yehuda ha-Nasi showed no compassion to the calf, let suffering be his lot."

One day, many years later, as Yehudah's maid was sweeping his house, she came across some small animals on the floor (some say they were baby weasels) and swept them up. Yehudah ha-Nasi said to her, "Let them go, for it is written 'And His [God's] mercies are over all his works.'" The heavenly court, having again witnessed Yehudah's actions, said, "Since Rabbi Yehudah shows compassion, we will show compassion to him." Thereupon, Yehudah ha-Nasi's suffering came to an end. Because of this, Yehudah ha-Nasi said, "Suffering is precious."

Beyond question, the most important contribution of Yehuda ha-Nasi was his redaction of the Mishnah, the first part of the Talmud, which consists of the teachings of the tanna'im, scholars who lived prior to 220 C.E., the year in which Yehudah died. Yehudah and his associates sifted through, evaluated, and edited a vast number of legal opinions that had been expressed over the centuries in the academies of learning, primarily in Palestine.

The completed effort was divided into six sections, known as *sedarim* ("orders"), arranged as follows:

1. *Zera'im*, dealing with laws pertaining to agriculture
2. *Mo'ed*, dealing with laws pertaining to the Sabbath and holidays
3. *Nashim*, dealing with marriage and divorce
4. *Nezikin*, dealing with civil and criminal matters
5. *Kodashim*, dealing with laws regulating ritual slaughter and sacrifices
6. *Tohorot*, dealing with laws of ritual purity

Each order is subdivided into tractates, of which there are a total of sixty-three.

Scholars of the next several generations, in both the Palestinian and Babylonian academies, studied and analyzed the teachings of the Mishnah and offered their commentary on the conclusions of the tanna'im. These interpreters of the law were known as amora'im, and their commentary, called Gemara, is the second part of the Talmud.

According to *Gittin* 59a, Acha bar Rava said that between the death of Yehudah ha-Nasi in 220 and the birth of Ashi, the redactor of the Babylonian Talmud, "No one was as erudite in Torah studies and worldly affairs as Yehudah ha-Nasi."

In his capacity as patriarch of Palestine Jewry, it was necessary for Yehudah to maintain cordial relations with the Romans, who controlled Palestine. *Shabbat* 33b reports how pleased Antoninus Pius, emperor of Rome from 138 to 161, was with Yehudah's attitude. He heard, with great pleasure, that in a debate with Shimon bar Yochai and other scholars, Yehudah praised the Romans, saying, "How noble is the work of this [Roman] nation! They laid out streets, they built bridges, and they have erected bathhouses." But the price of acceptance was not cheap. *Avodah Zarah* 16a reports that on each Roman festive day, Yehudah ha-Nasi had to present the emperor with "a fattened ox plus 120,000 coins."

Among the popular maxims attributed to Yehudah ha-Nasi and recorded in *Avot* are:

- What is the proper course a man should choose for himself? One that brings honor to himself and to his fellowman. (*Avot* 2:1)
- Be careful to adhere to the light commandments as well as to the more weighty ones, for a person does not know how to weigh the importance of a commandment. (*Avot* 2:1)
- Bear in mind three things and you will not be tempted to sin: "Know what is above you: a seeing eye; an ear that hears and remembers; and above everything, that all your deeds are recorded in the Book of Life." (*Avot* 2:1)

In *Shabbat* 77b Yehudah quotes the following statement in the name of Rav: "Of all the things that God created in His world, not one was created that is useless." And in *Kiddushin* 49a Yehudah ha-Nasi notes that "He who translates a verse [of the Torah] literally is a liar; he who adds [his own words] is a blasphemer."

Yehudah ha-Nasi died in 220, adored and respected by his people. It is reported in *Kiddushin* 72b that on the day Akiva ben Yosef died, Yehudah ha-Nasi was born. *Ketubbot* 103b notes that, "On the day Rabbi [Yehudah] died a voice from heaven [a *bat kol*] announced, 'Whoever was present at the death of Rabbi is destined to enjoy life in the world to come.'" Yehudah ha-Nasi was succeeded by his eldest son, Gamli'el III.

Yehudah ha-Nasi II
See Yehudah Nesi'ah.

Yehudah ha-Nasi III
See Yehudah ben Gamli'el.

Yehudah ha-Nedu'a (fifth century)
Babylonian amora. Known in English as Yehudah the Indian, he is described in *Kiddushin* 22b as a proselyte who had no heirs. When he fell sick, he was visited by Mar Zutra.

Yehudah ha-Sabbar (second/third century)
Babylonian amora. Known in English as Yehudah the Interpreter, he was, according to *Eruvin* 72b, an interpreter of the law whose rulings were approved of by Rav.

Yehudah Mar bar Mereimar (fourth/fifth century)
Also known as Yehudah bar Mereimar.

Babylonian amora. In *Ketubbot* 80a he is noted as a colleague of Pappa. According to *Berakhot* 45b, Yehudah Mar bar Mereimar, Mar bar Rav Ashi, and Acha of Difti dined together. In *Bava Metzi'a* 111a Yehudah Mar bar Mereimar is said to have been friends with Mar Zutra.

Yehudah, Nephew of Yosei ben Chanina
See Yehudah ben Achoto shel Rabbi Yosei ben Chanina.

Yehudah Nesi'ah (third century)
Also known as Yehudah II *and* Yudan Berabbi.

Palestinian amora. Grandson of Yehudah ha-Nasi and son of Gamli'el III, he is referred to in *Kiddushin* 21b as Yudan Berabbi. Although he was tutored and supported by Yochanan bar Nappacha, who was head of the *beit din*, Yehudah Nesi'ah was not reputed to be a great scholar. However, in *Mo'ed Katan* 20a and *Avodah Zarah* 6b he is mentioned as a teacher of Shimon ben Lakish. When economic conditions in Palestine were at their worst, Yehudah Nesi'ah imposed a tax upon scholars, which Shimon ben Lakish deplored (*Bava Batra* 7b). According to some scholars, the tax was imposed by Yehudah III.

In *Megillah* 7b Yehuda Nesi'ah is mentioned as a friend and colleague of Osha'ya Rabbah, to whom he sent a choice calf and a barrel of wine. Among Yehudah Nesi'ah's other close colleagues were Yannai (*Bava Batra* 111a) and Ammi bar Natan (*Rosh Hashanah* 20a and *Avodah Zarah* 33b).

Much of Yehudah Nesi'ah's time and effort was devoted to advancing the system of elementary education, including organizing schools in the smaller towns and villages of Palestine (*Shabbat* 119b).

Yehudah Nesi'ah died in 250 and was succeeded by his son, Gamli'el IV.

Yehudah of Difti (third/fourth century)

Babylonian amora. In *Berakhot* 25a he is said to have been a colleague of Ravina I.

Yehudah of Diskarta (third/fourth century)

Babylonian amora. In *Nazir* 35a and *Niddah* 35a he is noted as a pupil of Rava. In *Sotah* 6b and *Gittin* 28b Yehudah of Diskarta is listed as a colleague of Mesharshya, and in *Niddah* 39a a colleague of Pappa.

Yehudah of Hagronia (third century)

Babylonian amora. In *Avodah Zarah* 39a he is said to have been a colleague of Huna bar Minyomi. Hagronia was a town along the Euphrates.

Yehudah of Kefar Gibbor Chayil (fourth century)

Also known as Yehudah of Kefar Nibburayya.

Babylonian amora. In *Megillah* 18a he is listed as a contemporary of Dimi. In *Ketubbot* 65a Yehudah is referred to as Yehudah of Kefar Nibburayya.

Yehudah of Kefar Nibburayya

See Yehudah of Kefar Gibbor Chayil.

Yehudah of Sura (third/fourth century)
Babylonian amora. In *Tamid* 27a he is noted as a contemporary of Abbayei.

Yehudah the Baker
See Yehudah ha-Nachtom.

Yehudah the Indian
See Yehudah ha-Nedu'a.

Yehudah the Interpreter
See Yehudah ha-Sabbar.

Yehudah the Locksmith
See Yehudah ha-Gelostera.

Yehudah the Palestinian
See Yehudah bar Ma'arava.

Yehudah the Priest
See Yehudah ha-Kohen.

Yehudah the Prince
See Yehudah ha-Nasi.

Yeimar (fifth century)
Babylonian amora. In *Bava Kamma* 62a and *Bava Metzi'a* 61b Yeimar is noted as a disciple of Ashi.

Yeimar bar Chashu (fourth century)
Babylonian amora. He is listed in *Ketubbot* 84b as a colleague of Pappa and Huna.

Yeimar bar Hillel (fourth century)
Babylonian amora. *Zevachim* 9a records a disagreement between Yeimar bar Hillel and Mar Zutra ben Nachman over a ruling concerning the remainder of a Pesach offering.

Yeimar bar Shelemya (third/fourth century)
Babylonian amora. A disciple of many prominent teachers, his masters included Rav (*Shabbat* 156a), Abbayei (*Shabbat* 66b and *Chullin* 107b), Rava (*Bava Batra* 9a), and Pappa (*Menachot* 31a).

Yeimar bar Shizvi (fifth century)
Babylonian amora. He is mentioned in *Berakhot* 53b as a colleague of Mar Zutra.

Yeimar of Difti (third century)

Babylonian amora. In *Shabbat* 146b he comments on the practice of shaping a myrtle leaf on the Sabbath to serve as a funnel.

Yeimar Sabba (third/fourth century)

Babylonian amora. Known in English as Yeimar the Elder, in *Bava Kamma* 49b and *Ketubbot* 53a he is noted as a disciple of Nachman bar Ya'akov. *Chullin* 86b recounts that Yeimar Sabba served a meal to Rav's disciples Berona and Chananel.

Yeimar the Elder

See Yeimar Sabba.

Yeiva (third century)

Palestinian amora. He was the father of several sons, including Rami (*Shabbat* 83a and *Avodah Zarah* 15a), Channin (*Bava Batra* 174a), and Safra (*Bava Batra* 5a).

Yeiva Sabba (third century)

Palestinian amora. Known in English as Yeiva the Elder, he is listed in *Bava Kamma* 49b as a disciple of Nachman bar Ya'akov and is sometimes confused with Yeimar Sabba.

Yeiva the Elder

See Yeiva Sabba.

Yeshevav (first century)

Palestinian tanna. In *Chullin* 32a he is mentioned as a disciple of Yehoshu'a ben Chananyah, and in *Kiddushin* 64a and *Nazir* 65a as a colleague of Akiva ben Yosef.

Yeshevav ha-Sofer (second century)

Palestinian tanna. Known in English as Yeshevav the Scribe, he served as the clerk of the Sanhedrin in Yavneh and made copies of the Torah. He was one of the Ten Martyrs put to death by the Romans for defying the rule prohibiting the teaching of Torah.

Yeshevav the Scribe

See Yeshevav ha-Sofer.

Yirmeyahu

In addition to the fourth-century Yirmeyahu bar Abba (see below), who usually is referred to simply as Yirmeyahu, two other scholars share this name:

1. A second-century Palestinian tanna who, according to *Bava Metzi'a* 114a, was a disciple of Ilfa. In *Menachot* 32b Yirmeyahu quotes Yehudah ha-Nasi as saying that *tefillin* and *mezuzot* may be written from memory, without reference to a printed text for accuracy, and that they need not be written on ruled lines. The final ruling of the Sages, however, is that *mezuzot* must be written on ruled lines while *tefillin* need not be.

2. A second/third-century Palestinian tanna who was a colleague of Ya'akov bar Korshai (*Me'ilah* 14a) and a mentor of Yosei ha-Gelili (*Horayot* 8b).

Yirmeyahu bar Abba

Two scholars were known by this name:

1. A third-century Babylonian amora who is referred to as Yirmeyahu ben Ammi in *Mo'ed Katan* 9a. In *Chullin* 45b and *Megillah* 18b Yirmeyahu is noted as a disciple of Rav and, in a variety of tractates, including *Berakhot* 56a, *Chullin* 49a, and *Ta'anit* 12b, as a teacher of Rava, Rabba bar Tachlifa, and Chisda.

In *Ta'anit* 11b, where he is mentioned as a disciple of Shimon ben Lakish, Yirmeyahu bar Abba notes that in Babylonia none of the fasts were observed more fastidiously than that of Tishah b'Av. One of his classic statements appears in *Sotah* 42a: "Four types of people will not be admitted to the presence of the Shekhinah: scoffers, flatterers, liars, and slanderers."

2. A fourth-century Babylonian amora generally cited in the Talmud without patronymic. He was born in Babylonia but migrated to Palestine where he studied under Abbahu and Ze'eira in Tiberias. Although a bright student, Yirmeyahu was expelled from the academy for asking questions in a disrespectful manner; he subsequently was reinstated. He had great contempt for the Babylonians, as is evident from his comment in *Yoma* 57a, where he refers to Rava and other Babylonian scholars as foolish people. Yet, according to *Yoma* 63a, he does appear to have been in contact with scholars such as Dimi.

In *Shabbat* 10a he is noted as a student of Ze'eira, and in *Sukkah* 12a the two disagree about the type of covering one may use on a *sukkah*. In *Sukkah* 37b Yirmeyahu ben Abba inquires of Zerika why a blessing is made only over a *lulav* when both the *etrog* and *lulav* are held together.

Yirmeyahu bar Acha (third century)

Babylonian amora. In *Chullin* 51b he is mentioned as a disciple of Rav.

Yirmeyahu bar Samuel

See Yirmeyahu bar Shemu'el.

Yirmeyahu bar Shemu'el (third century)

Babylonian amora. He is quoted in *Pesachim* 76a.

Yirmeyahu bar Tachlifa (second century)

Palestinian tanna. According to *Yoma* 78a and *Mo'ed Katan* 18a, he was a teacher of Ya'akov bar Korshai.

Yirmeyahu ben Ammi

See Yirmeyahu bar Abba.

Yirmeyahu ben Elazar (third century)

Palestinian amora. An authority on *aggadah*, he theorizes in *Sanhedrin* 109a that there was a difference of opinion among the inhabitants of Babel as to why a tower should be built to reach to heaven. In *Berakhot* 61a and *Eruvin* 18a he is quoted as saying: "God created Adam with two faces, and from one he fashioned Eve."

One of Yirmeyahu's favorite maxims was this: "Only praise should be recited in a person's presence, and all in his absence" (*Eruvin* 18b). He also said: "Any house in which the words of Torah are heard at night will never be destroyed" (*Eruvin* 18b).

Yirmeyahu ben Eleazar

See Yirmeyahu ben Elazar.

Yirmeyahu Bira'ah (third century)

Babylonian amora. In *Eruvin* 25a and *Bava Batra* 53b he is mentioned as a disciple of Yehudah bar Yechezkel. As noted in *Gittin* 34a, Yehudah once forced Yirmeyahu's son-in-law to give his wife a *get* and then cancelled it.

Yirmeyahu of Difti (fourth century)

Babylonian amora. In *Megillah* 18b he is said to have been a teacher of Rami bar Chama; in *Shabbat* 18b and 74a he is mentioned as a colleague of Ashi and in *Bava Batra* 171b as a colleague of Kahana.

Yirmeyahu Rabbah (third century)
Babylonian amora. Known in English as Yirmeyahu the Great, he is mentioned in *Shabbat* 29b as a contemporary of Yehudah.

Yirmeyahu the Great
See Yirmeyhau Rabbah.

Yishma'el
See Yishma'el ben Elisha.

Yishma'el bar Shimon (fourth/fifth century)
Babylonian amora. In *Avodah Zarah* 11b he is listed as a contemporary of Ashi.

Yishma'el bar Simeon
See Yishma'el bar Shimon.

Yishma'el ben Abba (second century)
Palestinian tanna. Even though Yishma'el ben Abba lived before Shimon ben Lakish, *Chullin* 122a records Yishma'el's comments on a question raised by Shimon: "Until what age is a camel considered young? As long as he had not yet borne a burden."

Yishma'el ben Beroka (second/third century)
Palestinian tanna. In *Shabbat* 26a he claims that a Sabbath lamp may be lighted only with oil tapped from a fruit tree.

Yishma'el ben Elazar (third century)
Babylonian amora. In *Shabbat* 32a he is listed as a contemporary of Acha.

Yishma'el ben Eleazar
See Yishma'el ben Elazar.

Yishma'el ben Elisha (first/second century)
Palestinian tanna. A descendant of a wealthy Priestly family, Yishma'el ben Elisha was a contemporary of Akiva ben Yosef, with whom he often differed in interpretation of the law. Yishma'el's full name was Yishma'el ben Elisha, but in the Babylonian Talmud he generally is referred to without patronymic. Among the few tractates in which he is called by his full name are *Berakhot* (7a), *Shabbat* (12b), and *Ketubbot* (105b).
Yishma'el, reputed to be very handsome (*Gittin* 58a), was the son and grandson of a High Priest. Yishma'el's grandfather,

Yishma'el ben Eliyyahu, was executed by the Romans around 69 C.E., after they conquered Jerusalem. Like his grandfather, Yishma'el ben Elisha defied the Romans, who forbade the teaching of Torah, and paid for it with his life. An account of Yishma'el's death is described in the Yom Kippur liturgy in the story of the Ten Martyrs.

Among the points of law on which Yishma'el and Akiva disagreed were the retention of uncircumcised slaves (*Yevamot* 48b); the requirements for a valid *etrog* and *lulav* (*Sukkah* 34b); the offering of the Passover sacrifice while leaven is still in one's home (*Pesachim* 5a); whether it is permitted to transact business with idolators (*Avodah Zarah* 6a–7b); whether the tearing of a garment applies to a High Priest in mourning (*Horayot* 12b); and how many *aliyyot* are to be awarded on the Sabbath, festivals, and Yom Kippur (*Megillah* 23a).

But despite their disputes, Yishma'el and Akiva were congenial and often took trips together to raise funds for their respective academies, as reported in *Chagigah* 12a.

Akiva's academy was in Lydda. Yishma'el established his academy in Usha (*Bava Batra* 28b), an ancient site in the vicinity of Haifa; his school was known as Bei Rabbi Yishma'el. Later Me'ir and Yosei ha-Gelili I established academies there. It was in Usha that Yishma'el introduced his thirteen rules of hermeneutics, the principles by which Scripture can be interpreted. Among Yishma'el's disciples were Zekharyah (*Nedarim* 32b) and Yochanan bar Nappacha (*Chagigah* 9a).

Four times a year judgment is pronounced on the world, it was taught at Yishma'el's academy (*Rosh Hashanah* 16a): "On Pesach with respect to produce, on Shavu'ot with respect to fruit, on Sukkot with regard to rain. Man himself is judged on Rosh Hashanah and his fate sealed on Yom Kippur."

Yishma'el believed that one should greet all people cheerfully (*Avot* 3:13), and he joined Akiva and Shimon ben Gamli'el in asserting that all Israel are royalty (*Shabbat* 128a) and may anoint their wounds with oil on the Sabbath, just as they do on weekdays.

Yishma'el ben Isaac

See Yishma'el ben Yitzchak.

Yishma'el ben Johanan ben Beroka

See Yishma'el ben Yochanan ben Beroka.

Yishma'el ben Sitri'el (second/third century)

Palestinian tanna. Mentioned as a contemporary of Yehudah ha-Nasi in *Bekhorot* 57b, he lived at the northwestern foot of Mount Lebanon.

Yishma'el ben Yitzchak (second century)

Palestinian tanna. In *Kiddushin* 54a he is noted as a colleague of Me'ir.

Yishma'el ben Yochanan ben Beroka (second century)

Palestinian tanna. Son of the tanna Yochanan ben Beroka, Yishma'el was a contemporary of Shimon ben Gamli'el II and a member of the synod of Usha, an assembly of rabbis that gathered at this city near Haifa in approximately 140 C.E., after the Bar Kokhba defeat. In *Eruvin* 38b Yishma'el ben Yochanan ben Beroka is listed as one of the four Elders of his time, along with Shimon ben Gamli'el II, Elazar ben Shimon, and Yosei ben Yehudah.

In *Avodah Zarah* 25b Yishma'el ben Yochanan ben Beroka advises that if a person sees an idolator carrying a sword, he should walk on the idolator's right side; in *Rosh Hashanah* 34a he comments on the procedure for blowing the *shofar*. In *Yevamot* 42b he repeats the view of the Sages of Yavneh that after the death of a husband, or a divorce, a woman should wait three months before remarrying. The same rule applies today, to make sure the woman is not pregnant.

In *Avot* 4:6 Yishma'el ben Yochanan ben Beroka is quoted as follows: "He who studies so that he may teach is given the opportunity to learn and teach. He who learns with a view to doing is given the opportunity to learn and teach, to observe and to do."

Yishma'el ben Yosei (second century)

Palestinian tanna. Son of the great scholar Yosei ben Chalafta, who was a leather worker and an authority on animals (*Shabbat* 49b and 51b), Yishma'el ben Yosei is noted in *Pesachim* 112b as an advisor to Yehudah ha-Nasi and in *Yevamot* 104a as a colleague of Yishma'el ben Elisha. As reported in the Palestinian Talmud (*Megillah* 1:1), Yishma'el ben Yosei had a phenomenal memory and was able to transcribe the entire text of Scripture from memory. Rashi (*Shabbat* 51a) considered him as great as his learned father.

In *Bava Metzi'a* 84a he is described as extremely portly; there it also says that Yishma'el ben Yosei and his colleague Elezar ben Shimon had waists that were so large that when they stood facing each other there was room for a team of oxen to pass underneath. On one occasion, *Pesachim* 86b reports, when he visited the home of his colleague Shimon ben Yosei ben Lakonya, Yishma'el ben Yosei gulped down a drink.

In *Eruvin* 80a Yishma'el ben Yosei quotes his father as advising him: "Whenever you have an opportunity to relax the laws of *eruv*, seize it." Contrary to the view of the Sages, Yishma'el, following Mattya ben Cheresh, permitted one who had a pain in his mouth to be given medicine on the Sabbath (*Yoma* 84a).

Yishma'el was a judge who assisted the Roman government in the arrest of Jewish criminals. It is recorded in *Bava Metzi'a* 84a that Yishma'el ben Yosei and Elazar ben Shimon were condemned by their coreligionists for informing on fellow Jews who opposed Roman authority. Yishma'el's response was this: "What can I do? It is a royal decree." Although he was a man of integrity, his fellow Jews hated him, which led him to say: "Judge not alone, for no one may judge alone except One [God]."

Yishma'el ben Zerud (third century)

Palestinian amora. In *Avodah Zarah* 30a he is noted as a colleague of Yannai ben Yishma'el, upon whom he paid a call when Yannai was ill.

Yishma'el of Kefar Yama (third century)

Palestinian amora. He is quoted in *Nedarim* 57b. Kefar Yama was a town located near Tiberias.

Yitzchak (second/third century)

Palestinian amora. In *Berakhot* 36a he is noted as a disciple of Yochanan bar Nappacha and in *Eruvin* 20b as a disciple of Yehudah bar Ila'i. An able teacher, Yitzchak numbered among his students Chisda (*Sukkah* 44b and *Berakhot* 43a), Ravin bar

Adda (*Pesachim* 8b), Mari ben Avuha (*Pesachim* 83a), Yosef (*Beitzah* 3b), Huna (*Eruvin* 17a), and Amram and Nachman bar Ya'akov (*Chullin* 41a).

Yitzchak was the author of many interesting observations and rulings. In *Kiddushin* 30b he states: "Man's evil desire renews itself daily"; in *Sotah* 34b he comments on the names of the spies listed in *Numbers* 13. In *Yoma* 9b Yitzchak suggests that women attract men sexually through the use of myrrh and balsam; in *Chullin* 63b he comments on which birds are kosher. In *Berakhot* 23b, Yitzchak says, "One who wishes to partake of a regular meal should first take off his *tefillin*," which would indicate that the wearing of *tefillin* all day long was a common practice in Talmudic times. And in *Sanhedrin* 102a he says, "No punishment comes upon the [Jews of the] world that is not, in some small measure, retribution for the sin of the golden calf."

In *Bava Metzi'a* 42a Yitzchak offers some very practical advice. He says, "A man should allocate his possesions into three parts: one-third should be invested in land, one-third in merchandise, and one-third in readily transportable assets." (In *Bava Metzi'a* 42a this statement is attributed to Yitchak Nappacha.) In *Berakhot* 55a Yitzchak expresses the true essence of democracy when he says: "We must not appoint a community leader without first consulting the community."

Yitzchak bar Abba (second/third century)
Babylonian amora. In *Mo'ed Katan* 12a, Yitzchak bar Abba seems to agree with the view of Yosei that a person may do work on a festival when the probability for financial loss exists, if he makes a slight modification in his work pattern. In *Zevachim* 5a Yitzchak bar Abba is noted as a colleague of both Ze'eira and Abbayei, and in *Menachot* 17a and 93b he is portrayed as a scholar highly respected by the tanna'im of Palestine.

Yitzchak bar Adda (third century)
Also known as Yitzchak bar Idi.
Babylonian amora. In *Chullin* 15b he is noted as a disciple of Rav; in *Berakhot* 4a he is referred to as Yitzchak bar Idi.

Yitzchak bar Ammi (fourth century)
Babylonian amora. In *Berakhot* 60a and *Niddah* 25b he is

quoted as saying: "If the woman is first to emit the semen, she bears a male child. If the male is first to do so, she bears a female child." This probably reflects the most advanced understanding of human reproduction at the time.

Yitzchak bar Ashi (second century)
Babylonian amora. In *Pesachim* 45b he is listed as a disciple of Rav.

Yitzchak bar Ashyan (third century)
Babylonian amora. In *Berakhot* 30b he is noted as a disciple of Rav, and in *Berakhot* 14a and *Chullin* 33a as a teacher of Idi bar Avin.

Yitzchak bar Avdimi (third century)
Also spelled Yitzchak bar Avdumi.
Palestinian tanna. In *Chullin* 110a and *Yevamot* 45a he is referred to as Yitzchak bar Avdumi. In *Shabbat* 40b he is mentioned as a disciple of Yehudah ha-Nasi and in *Bava Batra* 87a as a student of Rav. Apparently Yitzchak bar Avdimi spent much time studying in Babylonia as well as in Palestine. *Zevachim* 43b quotes Rava as stating, "Any biblical verse not elucidated by Yitzchak bar Avdimi remains unexplained." Yitzchak's interpretations were transmitted by scholars of later generations, including those in the academy of Sura, where Chisda had taught, and Pumbedita, where Rabbah bar Nachmani had conducted classes.

Yitzchak bar Avdumi
See Yitzchak bar Avdimi.

Yitzchak bar Avin (second century)
Palestinian tanna. In *Zevachim* 42a he is mentioned as a contemporary of Me'ir.

Yitzchak bar Bar Chana (fourth century)
Babylonian amora. In *Yoma* 77b he is said to have been a contemporary of Ze'iri and his disciple Ashi.

Yitzchak bar Bizna (third century)
Babylonian amora. In *Shabbat* 110a he is noted as a younger contemporary of Rav and in *Zevachim* 20a as a younger contemporary of Ilfa. In *Gittin* 54b Yitzchak is mentioned as a colleague of Ammi bar Natan, Assi, and Yochanan bar Nappacha.

When Rav died, as an expression of mourning Yitzchak decreed that "Myrtles and palm branches, accompanied by the sound of the *tabla* [small bells that form an instrument], should not be brought to a wedding" (*Shabbat* 110a).

Yitzchak bar Chakla (third/fourth century)
Also known as Yitzchak bar Ila'a *and* Yitzchak bar Tavla.
Palestinian amora. A contemporary of Yehoshu'a ben Levi, he was a member of the school of Elazar ben Pedat. *Pesachim* 113b says: "Yitzchak bar Tavla is identical to Yitzchak bar Chakla and to Yitzchak bar Ila'a," and *Nedarim* 8b identifies Yitzchak bar Tavla as a teacher of Shimon ben Zevid.

Yitzchak bar Chananiah
See Yitzchak bar Chananyah.

Yitzchak bar Chananyah (third century)
Babylonian amora. In *Nedarim* 38b he is noted as a disciple of Huna.

Yitzchak bar Chanina (third century)
Babylonian amora. In *Ketubbot* 4b he is mentioned as a colleague of Huna and in *Ketubbot* 61a as a contemporary of Chisda.

Yitzchak bar Idi
See Yitzchak bar Adda.

Yitzchak bar Ila'a
See Yitzchak bar Chakla.

Yitzchak bar Joseph
See Yitzchak bar Yosef.

Yitzchak bar Judah
See Yitzchak bar Yehudah.

Yitzchak bar Maryon (third century)
Palestinian amora. He was a contemporary of Elazar ben Pedat.

Yitzchak bar Mesharshya (fourth/fifth century)
Babylonian amora. An esteemed scholar, as noted in *Avodah Zarah* 14a, he comments on Rav's interpretation of what constitutes an *eruv* in *Eruvin* 32b. According to *Chullin* 97b and 104b, Yitzchak bar Mesharshya once paid a visit to the home of Ashi, where he was served cheese, which he ate, and then meat, which he also ate, without washing his hands between courses.

He explained his conduct by saying that the rule of washing hands between courses of cheese and meat applies only at night, "but by day, I can see that my hands are clean."

Yitzchak bar Nachman (third century)

Also known as Yitzchak bar Nachmani.

Palestinian amora. Yitzchak bar Nachman studied under many prominent scholars, including Shemu'el (*Sukkah* 30a and *Chullin* 90b), Shimon ben Lakish (*Bekhorot* 13a), and Elazar ben Pedat (*Niddah* 48a). In *Yoma* 78b Yitzchak bar Nachman is noted as a colleague of Yehoshu'a ben Levi and in *Sanhedrin* 10b as a colleague of Shimon bar Pazzi.

Yitzchak bar Nachmani

See Yitzchak bar Nachman.

Yitzchak bar Naphtali (sixth century)

Babylonian amora. A colleague of Ravina II, Yitzchak bar Naphtali is mentioned in *Ketubbot* 96a.

Yitzchak bar Rabbah bar Chana (third/fourth century)

Babylonian amora. In *Sukkah* 43b he is noted as a junior colleague of Rava. According to *Yevamot* 64b, Yitzchak married Choma, widow of Rechavah of Pumbedita and daughter of Isi, who was the son of Yitzchak bar Yehudah. After Yitzchak bar Rabbah bar Chana's death, Choma would marry Abbayei.

Yitzchak bar Redifa (fourth century)

Palestinian amora. He translated the aggadic sayings of Ammi bar Natan, who was his teacher, as noted in *Ketubbot* 106a. In *Shabbat* 23b Yitzchak bar Redifa is noted as a disciple of Huna.

Yitzchak bar Samuel

See Yitzchak bar Shemu'el.

Yitzchak bar Shemu'el (third century)

Babylonian amora. In *Berakhot* 3a he is noted as a disciple of Rav and in *Menachot* 30b as a teacher of Rabbah bar Bar Chana.

Yitzchak bar Shemu'el bar Marta (third/fourth century)

Babylonian amora. In *Berakhot* 25b Achai attempted to arrange a marriage for his son with a member of Yitzchak's family but was not successful.

In *Chullin* 35a Yitzchak bar Shemu'el bar Marta is listed as a disciple of Nachman and in 74a as a disciple of Rav. It is in *Chullin* 74a that Yitzchak rules that one may eat an animal that had a limb hanging loose when it was slaughtered.

In *Megillah* 16b Yitzchak's disciple, Rabbah bar Nachmani quotes his master as saying: "The study of Torah is more important than honoring [one's] parents."

Yitzchak bar Shula (fourth century)
Babylonian amora. In *Kiddushin* 32a he is noted as a disciple of Matna, who was a student of Chisda.

Yitzchak bar Tavla
See Yitzchak bar Chakla.

Yitzchak bar Ya'akov bar Giyyora
See Yitzchak bar Ya'akov bar Giyyorei.

Yitzchak bar Ya'akov bar Giyyorei (third/fourth century)
Also known as Yitzchak bar Ya'akov bar Giyyora.
Palestinian tanna. In *Ta'anit* 29b, *Chullin* 101b, and *Eruvin* 62a he is mentioned as a disciple of Yochanan bar Nappacha. In *Mo'ed Katan* 18a he is referred to as Yitzchak bar Giyyora.

Yitzchak bar Yehudah (third century)
Babylonian amora. Son of Yehudah bar Yechezkel, founder of the academy in Pumbedita, Yitzchak bar Yehudah was a contemporary of the Palestinian amora Ulla, who, on occasion, visited Pumbedita (*Pesachim* 104b and *Kiddushin* 71b). Yitzchak bar Yehudah's father quotes his son on matters of law in *Eruvin* 80b and *Shabbat* 151a. Yitzchak's son, Isi bar Yitzchak bar Yehudah, also was an amora.

It is reported in *Kiddushin* 32b that Yitzchak bar Yehudah attended the wedding of Abba Mar ben Pappa.

Yitzchak bar Yosef (third/fourth century)
Palestinian amora. In *Pesachim* 72a and *Chullin* 101a he is noted as a disciple of Abbahu, and in *Shabbat* 45b and 58a as a disciple of Yochanan bar Nappacha. Yitzchak bar Yosef was one of the most prominent intermediaries between the Rabbis of Palestine and those of Babylonia, transmitting, among other teachings, the rulings of Abbahu and Yochanan with regard to the appropriate time at which to recite the *Hashkivenu* prayer, and the views of Acha ben Chanina and Yehoshu'a ben Levi on

the recitation of the *Shema* (*Berakhot* 9a). In *Berakhot* 11b Yitzchak bar Yosef comments on other prayers.

In *Nazir* 11b, Yitzchak bar Yosef cites Yochanan bar Nappacha's view that if a man instructs his representative to arrange a marriage for him, without specifying which woman, it is presumed that the messenger carried out the man's wishes and he therefore is forbidden to marry any other woman. According to *Berakhot* 42b, Yitzchak visited his master, Abbayei, on a festival and noted that each time Abbayei took a drink of wine during the meal he recited a blessing over it, contrary to the ruling of Yehoshu'a ben Levi.

Yitzchak bar Yosef was banished from Judea by Constantine, the first Christian emperor of Rome, and settled in Babylonia.

Yitzchak ben Acha
See Yitzchak ben Pinchas.

Yitzchak ben Chalov (third century)
Babylonian amora. In *Chullin* 99b he is said to have been a colleague and teacher of Ammi bar Natan.

Yitzchak ben Chiyya (fourth century)
Also known as Yitzchak ha-Sofer.

Palestinian amora. In *Ta'anit* 23b Mani complains to Yitzchak ben Chiyya that members of the household of the patriarch are annoying him. Yitzchak ben Chiyya was sometimes referred to as Yitzchak ha-Sofer, in English, Yitzchak the Scribe.

Yitzchak ben Elazar
Two Palestinian scholars were known by this name:

1. A second-century tanna who was related to Yochanan bar Nappacha and who was a colleague of Chiyyah bar Abba.

2. A fourth-century amora, who was a native of Caesarea, where he taught and was beloved by his students. One of Yitzchak's favorite teachings was this: "The Prophets know that their God is true, hence they do not flatter Him" (Palestinian Talmud, *Berakhot* 7:4).

In *Shabbat* 29b, Yitzchak ben Elazar is noted as a colleague of Avin of Sepphoris. In *Sukkah* 35b Yitzchak comments on the *kashrut* of an *etrog* and its *pittam*.

The Midrash tells the following story about Yitzchak: Near

Caesarea was a cliff that extended into the sea. One day, as Yitzchak was walking along this cliff, he saw a large bone lying in the road. He covered it with earth so that no one would hurt himself. But as soon as he had covered it, the earth disappeared and the bone was visible again. Yitzchak repeated his actions several times, but the bone refused to stay buried; Yitzchak concluded that this was an omen from God. A while later, an imperial messenger passed by, stumbled over the bone, and died as a result of the fall. It turned out that this messenger had been carrying with him an edict that would have resulted in the persecution of the Jews of Caesarea.

Yitzchak ben Elazar of Caesarea
See Yitzchak ben Elazar.

Yitzchak ben Eleazar
See Yitzchak ben Elazar.

Yitzchak ben Eliashib
See Yitzchak ben Elyashiv.

Yitzchak ben Elyashiv (fourth century)
Palestinian amora. He is quoted in *Sukkah* 19a on what constitutes a valid *sukkah*. In *Ta'anit* 23b he is noted as a teacher of Mani and other scholars who attended his lectures.

Yitzchak ben Phinehas
See Yitzchak ben Pinchas.

Yitzchak ben Pinchas (third century)
Also known as Yitzchak ben Acha.
Palestinian amora. In *Chullin* 27b he argues logically that, according to the Torah, birds do not require ritual slaughtering. In *Pesachim* 113b he is identified as Yitzchak ben Acha.

Yitzchak ben Savarin (fourth century)
Palestinian amora. In *Zevachim* 9a he is listed as a contemporary of Yosei ben Avin.

Yitzchak ben Ze'eira (fourth century)
Also known as Yitzchak ben Zita.
Palestinian amora. *Shabbat* 20b records a discussion in which he prohibits a wick made of *gushkera*, a cottonlike plant, from being used for the Sabbath lights.

Yitzchak ben Zita
See Yitzchak ben Ze'eira.

Yitzchak de-Bei Rabbi Ammi (third/fourth century)
Babylonian amora. Known in English as Yitzchak of the School of Ammi (presumably Ammi bar Natan), his comments are found in *Sotah* 9b and *Bava Batra* 116a concerning the stipulation that daughters of the tribe of Benjamin are not to be heirs to their fathers' estates along with their brothers because the tribe was so small and many women married men of other tribes.

Yitzchak de-Bei Rabbi Yannai (second century)
Palestinian amora. Known in English as Yitzchak of the School of Yannai, he is quoted in *Yoma* 86a as saying: "If one is ashamed of a colleague's reputation, that constitutes a profanation of God's name."

Yitzchak ha-Kohen (first century)
Palestinian tanna. Known in English as Yitzchak the Priest, he is noted in *Nazir* 44a as a contemporary of Yehoshu'a ben Elisha. When Yitzchak ha-Kohen's father died in Persia, Yitzchak was not notified until three years later. He inquired of Yehoshu'a ben Elisha whether he might personally arrange to have his father's remains removed to the family sepulcher. The reply was negative, since his father's body would have disintegrated by then.

Yitzchak ha-Sofer
See Yitzchak ben Chiyya.

Yitzchak Kaskesa'ah (fourth century)
Palestinian amora. In *Berakhot* 51a he is noted as a disciple of Yosei ben Avin and Yochanan bar Nappacha.

Yitzchak Nappacha (third/fourth century)
Palestinian amora. A smith by trade (*nappacha* is Aramaic for "smith"), Yitzchak was a pupil of Yochanan bar Nappacha and developed into both a halakhic and an aggadic authority. When Ammi bar Natan became head of the academy in Tiberias, an occasion arose on which Ammi and Assi forbade Yitzchak Nappacha to lecture: one insisted that he lecture on halakhic matters; the other demanded that he discourse on aggadic matters. Yitzchak responded by relating the following parable:

A man had two wives, one young, the other old. The young one pulled out all of the man's gray hairs because she wanted her husband to look young, while the older wife pulled out his black hairs so that he would appear old. Between the two of them, the man became bald.

Yitzchak Nappacha favored *aggadah*, hoping to bring words of comfort and inspiration, rather than legal discussion, to the Jews of Palestine during what was a period of rampant poverty. This, however, did not mean that legal rulings were outside his province. In *Gittin* 29b he is mentioned as a member of a *beit din* along with his distinguished colleagues Abbahu and Chanina ben Pappa. It is noted in *Shabbat* 126b that Yitzchak Nappacha would deliver lectures at the entrance of the home of the *reish galuta*, the titular head of Babylonian and Persian Jewry.

Yitzchak of Carthage (second/third century)

Palestinian tanna. While many scholars believe that Yitzchak of Carthage lived or spent time in that city, others believe that the Hebrew, Kartigna, may refer to a city in Spain. In *Berakhot* 29a Yitzchak comments on the liturgy of Rosh Hashanah, remarking that the nine blessings that are part of the *Musaf Amidah* correspond to the nine times Hannah mentions God's name in her prayer (*1 Samuel* 2:1–10), which is contained in the *haftarah* for the first day of Rosh Hashanah.

Yitzchak of Kartigna

See Yitzchak of Carthage.

Yitzchak of Magdala (fourth century)

Palestinian amora. In *Niddah* 27b he is mentioned as a contemporary of Shabbetai. In *Yoma* 81b he is referred to as a colleague of Kahana.

Yitzchak of the School of Ammi

See Yitzchak de-Bei Rabbi Ammi.

Yitzchak of the School of Yannai

See Yitzchak de-Bei Rabbi Yannai.

Yitzchak Sumka (third/fourth century)

Babylonian amora. Known in English as Yitzchak the Red, he is listed in *Yevamot* 64b as a contemporary of Rava.

Yitzchak the Priest
> *See* Yitzchak ha-Kohen.

Yitzchak the Red
> *See* Yitzchak Sumka.

Yitzchak the Scribe
> *See* Yitzchak ben Chiyya.

Yochana bar Chana bar Adda (third century)
> *Also known as* Mar Yochana bar Chana bar Adda.
> Babylonian amora. In *Chullin* 133a he is noted as a colleague of Rava and Safra.

Yochana bar Chana bar Bizna (third/fourth century)
> Babylonian amora. Sometimes confused with Yochana bar Chana bar Adda, Yochana bar Chana bar Bizna is mentioned in *Chullin* 133a.

Yochanan
> *See* Yochanan bar Nappacha.

Yochanan Achuha de-Mar bar Rabbana
(third/fourth century)
> Babylonian amora. Known in English as Yochanan, Brother of Mar bar Rabbana, he is named as a colleague of Nachman bar Yitzchak in *Shabbat* 49b.

Yochanan bar Chanina (third/fourth century)
> Babylonian amora. In *Sanhedrin* 38b he says that during Creation, the day consisted of twelve hours, and in the first hour God began fashioning Adam out of the dust of the earth.

Yochanan bar Marya (fifth century)
> Palestinian amora. He was a contemporary of Ashi.

Yochanan bar Nappacha (third century)
> *Also known as* Yochanan ben ha-Napach.
> Palestinian amora. Generally known as Yochanan, without patronymic, he was born in Sepphoris during the patriarchate of Yehudah ha-Nasi. According to *Kiddushin* 31b, Yochanan bar Nappacha's father died soon after Yochanan was conceived, and his mother died soon after giving birth to him; Yochanan was raised by his grandfather. In the Palestinian Talmud, where he is widely quoted, he is called Yochanan ben ha-Napach.

His cognomen, Nappacha, means "smith." It is thought that his father was a smith (*Sanhedrin* 96a), and for a while Yochanan probably earned a livelihood following in his father's footsteps. But apparently his father had also been engaged in farming and had become wealthy from investments in land and vineyards. Yochanan inherited all of these holdings upon his father's death but sold the entire estate when he was of age, using the funds to further his education. He once offered this advice to people pursuing wealth: "Whoever wishes to become rich should [avoid other difficult occupations and] get involved in the breeding of small catttle" (*Chullin* 84b).

In pursuing his education, Yochanan first studied under Yehudah ha-Nasi. Although Yochanan was unable to follow the intricate discussion, Yehudah ha-Nasi predicted that he would develop into a fine teacher (*Chullin* 137b and *Pesachim* 3b). Later, Yochanan studied in Caesarea under Oshaya Rabbah, Yannai, and Chanina bar Chama.

Yochanan apparently was a very handsome young man and bragged about his appearance. In *Bava Metzi'a* 84a he is quoted as saying that if women looked at his beautiful face, they would have beautiful children.

Yochanan's brother-in-law and very close friend was Shimon ben Lakish, a renowned, pious scholar who also was Yochanan's disciple (*Shabbat* 15b). When Shimon ben Lakish died, Yochanan could not be consoled. He seemed to feel responsible for his brother-in-law's death and suffered periods of depression. It is said that Yochanan had ten sons, all of whom died during his lifetime (*Berakhot* 5b). Despite these terrible tragedies, Yochanan was an extremely sympathetic individual and one of the most productive amora'im of his generation. In *Shabbat* 114a he speaks of the disciples of the wise as the builders of the world; in *Sanhedrin* 22a he acknowledges how difficult it is to arrange a union between a man and a woman and expresses deep sympathy for a man who has lost his wife.

When Yehudah Nesi'ah became principal of the academy in Sepphoris, Yochanan became his assistant. Later, Yochanan became principal of an academy in Tiberias, where he attracted many students from Babylonia and influenced numerous scholars. Over one hundred amora'im were said to have accepted Yochanan's rulings and promoted his decisions. Among the more prominent of these scholars were Rabbah bar Chana (*Berakhot* 13b and 25a), Chiyya bar Abba (*Shabbat* 110b), Abbahu (*Berakhot* 14a), Huna (*Berakhot* 24b), Ammi bar Natan (*Shabbat* 5b), Assi (*Shabbat* 20a), and Rabbah bar Bar Chana (*Shabbat* 21b).

At the height of Yochanan's career, Rav and Shemu'el were masters of the academies in Babylonia. Yochanan respected Rav, whom he addressed as "Our Master in Babylonia," but considered Shemu'el inferior in learning and after Rav's death refused to recognize Shemu'el as a legal authority. Yochanan later recanted and gave his approval to Shemu'el's rulings. In *Bava Metzi'a* 30b Yochanan reaches the conclusion that catastrophe befalls the Jewish people when judges base decisions on the letter of the law rather than its spirit. One of Yochanan's greatest contributions was that he assembled all of the material that would later become the foundation of the Palestinian Talmud.

In *Ta'anit* 5b Yochanan cautions: "One should not talk during a meal, lest the windpipe precede the gullet [and the food go down the wrong pipe]." One of Yochanan's most widely quoted maxims, on the importance of attending synagogue, is this: "Whenever the Holy One, blessed be He, enters a synagogue and does not find ten persons there, He becomes very angry [because important prayers cannot be recited without a *minyan*" (*Berakhot* 6b).

Yochanan is quoted in *Shabbat* 149b as saying, "as long as that wicked man [Nebuchadnezzar, king of Babylonia, who destroyed the First Temple and sent the Jews into exile] lived, the sound of joy never left the mouth of any living creature." With regard to a slanderer, Yochanan said, "He who slanders another person denies the existence of God" (*Arakhin* 15a). In *Sanhedrin* 74a, Yochanan reports on a meeting held by the Sages in Lydda, where they ruled that if a man is told to transgress all the commandments of the Torah or he will be killed, he may do so in order to save himself. The only exceptions to this rule are idol worship, committing incest, or committing murder. He must submit to death rather than transgress these three prohibitions.

One of the more interesting comments made by Yochanan

appears in *Eruvin* 100b, where he says, "Had the Torah not been given to Israel, we might have learned modesty from the cat, honesty from the ant, chastity from the dove, and good manners from the cock who first coaxes and then mates."

When Yochanan died in Tiberias around the year 279, Yitzchak ben Elazar eulogized him as follows: "This day is as depressing for the Jews as if the sun had suddenly set at noon."

Yochanan ben Bag Bag
See Ben Bag Bag.

Yochanan ben Bathyra
See Yochanan ben Beteira.

Yochanan ben Beroka (second century)
Palestinian tanna. A disciple of Yehoshu'a ben Chananyah, he and Elazar ben Chisma traveled to pay their respects to Yehoshu'a in his old age. In *Avot* 4:5 Yochanan is quoted as saying: "Whoever profanes God's name in secret will receive his punishment publicly." Yochanan's son, Yishma'el ben Yochanan ben Beroka, also was a tanna.

Yochanan ben Beteira (first century B.C.E.)
Palestinian tanna. A contemporary of Hillel and Shammai, Yochanan ben Beteira is quoted in *Zevachim* 63a and *Menachot* 41b.

Yochanan ben Dahabai (second century)
Palestinian tanna. In *Menachot* 42b he disputes with Chanina ben Gamli'el the amount of dye required for the blue thread of the *tallit*. In *Sanhedrin* 4b Yochanan ben Dahabai is noted as a colleague of Yehudah ben Teima.

Yochanan ben Elazar (third century)
Palestinian amora. In *Pesachim* 51a and *Bekhorot* 38b he is noted as a colleague of Rabbah bar Bar Chana.

Yochanan ben Eleazar
See Yochanan ben Elazar.

Yochanan ben Gudgada (second/third century)
Palestinian tanna. According to *Chullin* 55b, he was a colleague of Eli'ezer ben Yosei ha-Gelili and, according to *Chagigah* 3a, a contemporary of Yehudah ha-Nasi.

Yochanan ben ha-Napach
See Yochanan bar Nappacha.

Yochanan ben he-Choranit (first century)
Palestinian tanna. In *Berakhot* 11a he is mentioned as a disciple of Hillel. According to two accounts—in *Eruvin* 13b and *Sukkah* 28a—the elders of Beit Hillel and Beit Shammai visited Yochanan ben he-Choranit on Sukkot and found him at mealtime sitting with the greater part of his body within the *sukkah*, while the table itself was in the house. *Yevamot* 15b recounts that Yochanan and Elazar ben Tzadok studied Torah together. *He-Choranit* probably means "the honorable one."

Yochanan ben Ila'i (first/second century)
Palestinian tanna. He lived in Upper Galilee and was a close friend of Eli'ezer ben Hurkanos (*Sukkah* 27b).

Yochanan ben Joseph
See Yochanan ben Yosef.

Yochanan ben Joshua
See Yochanan ben Yehoshu'a.

Yochanan ben Matya (second century)
Palestinian tanna. According to *Bava Metzi'a* 49a and 83b, Yochanan ben Matya sent his son to hire laborers, and his son, without consulting Yochanan, promised to provide them with food, something not normally done for day workers. His son was reprimanded for not advising them that they had no claim for not being fed.

Yochanan ben Meshulam (first/second century)
Palestinian tanna. Brother of Yosei ben Meshulam, Yochanan was a disciple of Elazar ben Chisma (*Gittin* 62a).

Yochanan ben Nizuf (second century)
Palestinian tanna. In *Shabbat* 115a Yosei bar Chalafta relates that his father once visited Shimon ben Gamli'el II at his home in Tiberias and found him studying the Targum of the book of *Job* with Yochanan ben Nizuf.

Yochanan ben Nuri (first/second century)
Palestinian tanna. He was a devoted disciple of Gamli'el II. After Gamli'el's death, one of Yochanan ben Nuri's students,

Yehoshu'a ben Chananyah, wanted to abolish various ordinances that had been enforced by Gamli'el. Yochanan opposed him and was supported by most of the tanna'im (*Eruvin* 41a). Yochanan was reputed to be familiar with general science and particularly adept at geometry. Yehudah ha-Nasi characterized Yochanan as being "a basket full of *halakhot*," and in *Gittin* 67a Isi ben Yehudah characterized Yochanan as "a basket full of fancy goods."

Akiva ben Yosef was one of Yochanan's closest colleagues, and the two engaged in many debates (*Pesachim* 32a, *Nazir* 52b, and *Sanhedrin* 84a).

Yochanan ben Saul

See Yochanan ben Sha'ul.

Yochanan ben Sha'ul (second century)

Palestinian tanna. In *Eruvin* 81a he comments on the preparation of an *eruv*.

Yochanan ben Torta (first/second century)

Palestinian tanna. A contemporary of Akiva ben Yosef, Yochanan ben Torta speculates in *Yoma* 9a about why Shiloh, the seat of the Tabernacle, was destroyed. He ascribes it to the people's immorality and their lack of respect for sanctified objects.

Yochanan ben Yehoshu'a (second century)

Palestinian tanna. He is referred to in Mishnah *Yadayim* 3:5 as the son of the father-in-law of Akiva ben Yosef, Akiva's brother-in-law.

Yochanan ben Yosef

Palestinian tanna. Of uncertain date, he is quoted in *Chullin* 139a.

Yochanan ben Zakkai (first century)

Palestinian tanna. A pupil of Hillel and Shammai (*Pesachim* 3b and *Avot* 2:9), Yochanan ben Zakkai emerged as a leading Pharisee who battled the views of the Sadducees. A towering figure in Jewish history, he earned his livelihood as a tradesman while being engaged in study. Hillel was quick to recognize Yochanan's potential and encouraged him.

Once, when Hillel was ill, a group of disciples came to visit him. Yochanan remained outside the sick room. When Hillel didn't see him, he asked, "Where is the small Yochanan?" He then predicted that this young man would grow to be "a father in wisdom for future generations."

The most famous legend concerning Yochanan tells how he was able to escape from Jerusalem during the Roman siege immediately preceding the destruction of the Second Temple. Yochanan pretended to be dead, and, since Jewish law did not permit a body to remain in the city of Jerusalem unburied overnight, Roman officials agreed to allow Yochanan's coffin to be carried out of the city for burial. When Yochanan emerged from the coffin, he faced the Roman general Vespasian, predicting that Vespasian would soon become emperor. Flattered by the prediction, Vespasian granted Yochanan his wish, namely that Yochanan's students be permitted to leave Jerusalem and reestablish their academy in Yavneh, a town south of present-day Tel Aviv. Yavneh emerged as the spiritual center of Judaism and the seat of the Sanhedrin, of which Yochanan became head, succeeding Shimon ben Gamli'el, the patriarch who was a leader in the failed revolt against Rome in 66 C.E. and who died during the seige of Jerusalem in the year 70, one of the Ten Martyrs.

Yochanan's foresight and courageous action, which had allowed for the continuation of Jewish scholarship in Yavneh, was a prime factor in the rejuvenation of Jewish life following the destruction of the Temple.

True to Hillel's prognostication, Yochanan ben Zakkai's disciples would become Talmudic giants. His most distinguished pupils were Akiva ben Yosef, Yehoshu'a ben Chananyah, Chanina ben Dosa, Eli'ezer ben Hurkanos, Yosei ha-Kohen, Elazar ben Arakh, and Shimon ben Netanel. They, along with other scholars, admired Yochanan greatly and dubbed him Rabban— "teacher extraordinaire."

Yochanan was a role model for all of his students. It was said that, despite his prominence, he was friendly to everyone with whom he came in contact. It is noted in *Berakhot* 17a that "He was first to greet every person he passed on the street, even a heathen." *Sukkah* 28a notes that throughout his life "He never uttered profane talk, nor walked four cubits [six feet] without studying Torah or wearing *tefillin.*"

Yochanan also was renowned as a teacher to the masses. In the days of the Temple, *Pesachim* 26a reports, Yochanan would sit in the shade of its high walls and lecture all day long on the laws of upcoming festivals because the crowds were so great that they could not be accommodated in the confines of his own academy. Of those who were very learned, he said, "Take no special credit for it, for this is the purpose of your existence" (*Avot* 2:9).

After finishing the book of *Job*, Yochanan would say, "The end of a man is to die, and the end of a beast is to be slaughtered; all are doomed to die. Happy is he who was brought up in Torah, whose labor was in the Torah, who has given pleasure to his Creator, and who was raised with a good name and departed the world with a good name" (*Berakhot* 17a). (Some manuscripts say Yochanan was quoting a statement of Me'ir.) In the final analysis, Yochanan believed, "A good heart is the most important thing in life."

When Yochanan retired, Gamali'el II, a direct descendant of Hillel, became *nasi.* Hillel and his descendants served as heads of the Sanhedrin for over 400 years; Yochanan ben Zakkai was the only outsider in this long line.

As Yochanan grew old, he feared his approaching death. When his disciples came to visit him, he wept in their presence, unsure of whether he was destined for Paradise or Gehenna. They asked him, "Rabbi, why do you weep?" He replied, "When a man has to appear for trial before a king whose rule is only temporary, whose kindness is passing, and whose anger does not last, he is seized by terror; how much more understandable is the terror that seizes one who has to be tried by the King of Kings, whose rule is eternal, whose anger is everlasting, and whose kindness endures forever" (*Berakhot* 28b).

It is written in *Sotah* 49b that "When Yochanan ben Zakkai died, the luster of wisdom vanished."

Yochanan, Brother of Mar bar Rabbana

See Yochanan Achuha de-Mar bar Rabbana.

Yochanan ha-Makoti (third century)

Palestinian amora. His disciples included Yochanan bar Nappacha and Yirmeyahu ben Abba (*Sukkah* 45b).

Yochanan ha-Sandelar (second century)

Palestinian tanna. Known in English as Yochanan the Sandal Maker, he was a native of Alexandria and a sandal maker by profession. In *Berakhot* 22a he is noted as a disciple of Akiva ben Yosef. Yochanan once remarked to Me'ir, also a disciple of Akiva, "I have served Akiva standing longer than you have served him sitting." After the death of Akiva, Yochanan planned to escape to Nisbis with Elazar ben Shammu'a, but both turned back, unable to forsake Palestine, the land of their people. Thus Yochanan was in a position to transmit Akiva's teachings to future generations.

According to *Yevamot* 104a, Yochanan was a colleague of Shimon bar Yochai.

In *Avot* 4:11, Yochanan is quoted as saying, "Every assembly that is for the sake of Heaven will endure, but every assembly whose purpose is not for the sake of Heaven will not endure."

Yochanan of Alexandria (second century)

Palestinian tanna. He was one of the seven disciples of Akiva ben Yosef who fled to Babylonia upon the death of Akiva at the hands of the Romans.

Yo'ezer of the Birah (first/second century)

Palestinian tanna. He is mentioned in Mishnah *Orlah* 2:12.

Yochanan the Sandal Maker

See Yochanan ha-Sandelar.

Yonah (fourth century)

Palestinian amora. Yonah was a highly regarded scholar who lectured at the academy earlier established by Yehudah ha-Nasi in Sepphoris (*Shabbat* 155b). In *Niddah* 11b Yonah is listed as a colleague of Rava and in *Shabbat* 10a as a colleague of Ze'eira and Yirmeyahu, with whom he differed on the point at which a lawsuit is considered to have begun.

Possessed of a mystical bent, Yonah is described as one of the great men in Israel who, when the community was in dire need of rain, would implore God on its behalf. He would don sack-

cloth, stand on a low spot, and pray. It is said that his prayers
for rain were answered. In *Berakhot* 14a he quotes his teacher
Ze'eira who said, "Whoever goes seven days without a dream is
called evil."

Ta'anit 23b notes that Yonah had a son named Mani who
was associated with the academy at Sepphoris.

Yonah bar Tachlifa (fourth century)

Babylonian amora. According to *Chullin* 30b, he was a colleague of Rava.

Yonatan

Three scholars were known by this name:

1. A second-century Palestinian tanna who was the brother-
in-law of Dosa ben Harkinas and a contemporary of Yochanan
ben Zakkai. In *Chullin* 35a Yonatan is noted as a disciple of
Yehudah ha-Nasi and in *Sanhedrin* 93a as a disciple of Shimon
bar Yochai.

In *Yoma* 58a, *Nedarim* 72b, and *Chagigah* 18a, Yonatan is
described as a close friend and colleague of Yoshiyyahu, with
whom he studied in the academy of Yishma'el ben Elisha and
with whom he engaged in discussions on a variety of subjects.
In later years, Yonatan leaned toward the interpretation of Jewish law as propounded by Akiva ben Yosef and became one of
Akiva's disciples.

One unusual experience of Yonatan is described in *Avodah
Zarah* 17a. He and his friend Chanina decided to test their re-
sistance to temptation by entering a house of prostitution. When
they approached the house, the harlots withdrew, noting that
the visitors were rabbis.

2. A third-century Babylonian amora who, in *Megillah* 10b,
is noted as a contemporary of Levi and in *Bava Metzi'a* 96a as a
colleague of Rava. In *Bava Kamma* 67a he is listed as a teacher
of Chisda.

3. A third-century Palestinian amora who is mentioned in
Yoma 53a as a teacher of Elazar ben Pedat and in *Yevamot* 86a as
a colleague of the minor scholar Savya. According to *Yoma* 3b,
the Babylonian scholar Yoshiyyahu was said to have been in
contact with Yonatan. In *Yoma* 86a, Shemu'el quotes Yonatan

as saying: "Great is repentance, for it prolongs a man's life"; in *Avodah Zarah* 5a, Shemu'el again quotes Yonatan: "Every good deed that a man does in this world walks before him into the world to come."

Yonatan bar Chanina (third century)

Babylonian amora. According to *Gittin* 66a, he taught his father that "Demons have a shadow but not a shadow of a shadow." He was commenting on the remote possibility that a demon, trapped in a pit, overheard Yonatan order that a divorce decree be transmitted to his wife.

Yonatan bar Saul

See Yonatan bar Sha'ul.

Yonatan bar Sha'ul (third/fourth century)

Babylonian amora. In *Sanhedrin* 74a he is noted as a contemporary of Abbayei.

Yonatan ben Akhmai (third century)

Also known as Yonatan ben Asmai.

Palestinian amora. Because the Hebrew letters *mem* and *samekh* are very much alike, the name Akhmai is sometimes confused with Asmai, and *Mo'ed Katan* 9a renders Yonatan's name as Yonatan ben Asmai. *Shabbat* 49a describes Yonatan ben Akhmai, along with Yonatan ben Elazar and Chanina ben Chama, discussing the handling of fresh hides on the Sabbath. *Sanhedrin* 14a mentions Yonatan ben Akhmai as a colleague of Shimon ben Zirud.

Yonatan ben Amram (third century)

Palestinian amora. In *Chagigah* 20a he is noted as a colleague of Yonatan ben Elazar. When Dimi came from Palestine to Babylonia, he quoted Yonatan ben Amram as saying: "Whosoever departs from the words of the Torah falls into Gehenna" (*Bava Batra* 79a).

Yonatan ben Asmai

See Yonatan ben Akhmai.

Yonatan ben Avtolemos (second/third century)

Palestinian tanna. In *Niddah* 19a he is mentioned as a contemporary of Elazar ben Shimon.

Yonatan ben Elazar (third century)

Palestinian tanna. In *Chagigah* 20a Yonatan ben Elazar is listed as a colleague of Yonatan ben Amram and in *Ketubbot* 49b as a colleague of Yonatan ben Akhmai. Chanina bar Chama was a colleague of Yonatan as well. Yonatan ben Elazar's closest colleague probably was Chiyya bar Abba, to whom he transferred debts due him through the courts, in keeping with the *perozbol* established by Hillel (*Gittin* 37a).

Of all Yonatan's disciples, Shemu'el bar Nachmani was most notable. In *Ketubbot* 9a–b Shemu'el bar Nachmani quotes his master as saying: "Everyone who goes to war . . . should write a *get* for his wife [to be executed should he not return]."

Of Yonatan's many teachings transmitted through Shemu'el the following are representative:

- He who loses his temper will be exposed to all the torments of Gehenna. (*Nedarim* 22a)
- When one fulfills a *mitzvah* in this world, it precedes him in the world to come. When one commits a transgression, it clings to him and precedes him to the day of judgment. (*Sotah* 3b)
- He who teaches his neighbor's son Torah will be privileged to sit in the heavenly academy. (*Bava Metzi'a* 85a)
- He who teaches his neighbor's son Torah is considered as though he had begotten him. (*Sanhedrin* 19b)

Yonatan ben Eleazar

See Yonatan ben Elazar.

Yonatan ben Harkinas (first century)

Palestinian tanna. He was a disciple of Shammai and a contemporary of Elazar ben Azaryah.

Yonatan ben Joseph

See Yonatan ben Yosef.

Yonatan ben Yosef (second century)

Palestinian tanna. In *Avot* 4:9 he says: "Whoever fulfills the Torah though he lives in a state of poverty, will, in the end, fulfill it from a position of wealth." In *Yoma* 85b Yonatan ben Yosef is quoted as saying: "The Sabbath is committed to your hands, not you to its hands."

Yonatan ben Yosei ben Lakonya (second century)

Palestinian tanna. In *Shevu'ot* 18b he impudently inquires of Shimon ben Yosei ben Lakonya: "Where is the prohibition in the Torah against having intercourse with a menstruating woman?"

Yonatan ben Uzziel

See Yonatan ben Uzzi'el.

Yonatan ben Uzzi'el (first century)

Palestinian tanna. A student of Hillel (*Bava Batra* 134a and *Sukkah* 28a), Yonatan ben Uzzi'el is reported to have had a disagreement with Shammai relating to a man who was dissatisfied with the conduct of his sons and who proceeded to assign his estate to Yonatan ben Uzzi'el (*Bava Batra* 133b). In *Megillah* 3a it is said that the Targum—the Aramaic translation—of the Prophets was composed by Yonatan ben Uzzi'el "from the mouths of [the prophets] Haggai, Zechariah, and Malachi."

Yonatan ha-Kitoni (first/second century)

Palestinian tanna. Known in English as Yonatan the Kitonite, he was a contemporary of Akiva ben Yosef. In *Eruvin* 96a Yonatan ha-Kitoni rules that "*Tefillin* may not be worn at night," contrary to the view of Akiva.

Yonatan of Beit Guvrin (third century)

Also known as Natan of Beit Guvrin.

Palestinian amora. He was a senior colleague of Shimon ben Pazzi and a junior colleague of Yehoshu'a ben Levi.

Yonatan the Kitonite

See Yonatan ha-Kitoni.

Yosef (third/fourth century)

Babylonian amora. He owned a small date farm on which he made wine (*Bava Batra* 26a) and was a friend and colleague of Rabbah bar Nachmani. Both were great scholars: Yosef's knowledge of Jewish tradition and practice was encyclopedic, and he was nicknamed "Sinai"; Rabbah was proficient in the logical analysis of texts and became known as "Uprooter of Mountains." Once when Yosef took sick, he forgot his learning, and Abbayei restored it to him (*Nedarim* 41a) by reminding him often of his teachings. Yosef, thankful, always showed Abbayei great deference (*Kiddushin* 33a).

Upon the death of Huna bar Chiyya it became necessary to appoint a new principal for the academy in Pumbedita. Yosef was offered the post but refused it because astrologers told him he would head the academy for only two years. It was then offered to Rabbah bar Nachmani, who remained principal for twenty-two years. Yosef succeeded him, but served for only two and a half years before he died in 333 (*Berakhot* 64a).

Another example of Yosef's belief in the supernatural can be found in *Pesachim* 109b, where he comments on a rabbinic enactment that states, "Men must not eat in pairs, nor drink in pairs, nor cleanse themselves twice." "The demon named Yosef," said Rabbi Yosef, "told me that Ashmedai, king of the demons, is appointed over all pairs," meaning that those who drink in pairs are at his mercy (*Pesachim* 110a).

Yosef was very witty, and a number of his sayings are worth noting. On his sixtieth birthday, he invited several colleagues to a party, at which time he remarked, "No matter how much I misbehave now, I will never die young." He also said, "A craftsman who makes a spoon will still burn his tongue if he eats hot soup from it" and "Even if you curse a dog's tail, it will continue to wag."

Yosef bar Abba (third/fourth century)
Babylonian amora. In *Bava Batra* 144b he is listed as a disciple of Ukba, in *Berakhot* 59b as a disciple of Yochanan, and in *Ketubbot* 74a as a disciple of Menachem.

Yosef bar Abbahu (third/fourth century)
Babylonian amora. In *Bava Kamma* 112b he is said to have been a colleague of Abbahu.

Yosef bar Avdimi (fourth century)
Babylonian amora. In *Eruvin* 8a he is noted as a contemporary of Nachman bar Ya'akov.

Yosef bar Chama (fourth century)
Also known as Yosei bar Chama.
Babylonian amora. According to *Bava Kamma* 97a, he was the father of Rava. In both *Shabbat* 63a and *Sotah* 21b Yosef bar

Chama is noted as a disciple of Sheshet, in *Bava Kamma* 112b as a disciple of Oshaya, and in *Gittin* 39b as a disciple of Yochanan bar Nappacha. In *Beitzah* 8b, where he is referred to as Yosei bar Chama, he is listed as a colleague of Ze'eira.

Yosef bar Chibo (third/fourth century)
Palestinian amora. According to *Yoma* 87a, he was a disciple of Abbahu.

Yosef bar Chiyya (third/fourth century)
Babylonian amora. In *Chullin* 18b he is mentioned as a colleague of Rav and Shemu'el.

Yosef bar Ila'i (third century)
Babylonian amora. He is quoted in *Sukkah* 26a.

Yosef bar Manasseh of Devil
See Yosef bar Menasheh of Devil.

Yosef bar Menasheh of Devil (third century)
Babylonian amora. A disciple of Rav (*Kiddushin* 79b) and Shemu'el, Yosef sent Shemu'el a query about whether it was permissible for a *Kohen* who had given his wife a *get* to continue to reside with her so that she could look after him (*Gittin* 81a); Shemu'el ruled that it was not permissible. In *Ketubbot* 65a Yosef bar Menasheh's widow appealed to Yosef for a monetary allowance from her husband's estate so that she could maintain her social standing in the community.

Yosef bar Minyomi (fourth century)
Also known as Yosei bar Manyumi.
Babylonian amora. In *Chullin* 13b and 46a, and elsewhere, he is noted as a disciple of Nachman bar Ya'akov. In *Bava Batra* 132b he is referred to as Yosei bar Manyumi.

Yosef bar Nechunya (third century)
Babylonian amora. In *Berakhot* 23b he asks Yehudah bar Yechezkel about the rule that applies to placing *tefillin* under one's pillow, apparently for safekeeping. Yehudah, quoting his teacher Shemu'el, permits it.

Yosef bar Rabba (fourth century)
Babylonian amora. *Ketubbot* 63a recounts how Yosef bar Rabba was sent by his father to study under Yosef. In *Chullin* 28b

Yosef bar Rabba's father insisted that his son was as knowledgeable about nonkosher animals as Yochanan bar Nappacha. According to *Ketubbot* 4a, Yosef bar Rabba was a colleague of Rava and, according to *Gittin* 40a, a disciple of Pappa. When Yosef bar Rabba died, Nechemyah bar Yosef was appointed executor of his estate and granted Yosef's wife "an allowance for board" (*Ketubbot* 65a).

Yosef bar Shemaya (fourth century)

Palestinian amora. In *Temurah* 14b and *Eruvin* 41b he is mentioned as a colleague of Pappa.

Yosef ben Ammi (second/third century)

Palestinian amora. He is quoted in both *Kiddushin* 6b and *Zevachim* 3b.

Yosef ben Channin (third/fourth century)

Palestinian amora. In *Shabbat* 116a he asks his teacher Abbahu about the permissibility of saving books from a fire on the Sabbath in Bei Avidan. The name Bei Avidan is presumed by scholars to refer to a Nazarene meeting place and the books to the Gospels. Abbahu's answer was "yes and no," without elaboration. The text appears to have been censored by Church authorities.

Yosef ben Chonai (second century)

Palestinian tanna. In *Pesachim* 73b he agrees with Yehoshu'a ben Chananyah about the eligibility of certain sacrifices slaughtered for the purpose of the Passover offering. Yosef ben Choni is noted in *Zevachim* 11a as a colleague of Eli'ezer ben Hurkanos.

Yosef ben Dosai (second century)

Palestinian tanna. In *Chullin* 49a he differs with the other Rabbis regarding the *kashrut* of an animal whose lung had been punctured by a worm. It was ruled that the animal is kosher if the worm punctured the lung after the animal had been slaughtered.

Yosef ben Eilim of Sepphoris (second/third century)

Also known as Yosef ben Elam of Sepphoris *and* Yosef ben Ulam of Sepphoris.

Palestinian tanna. According to Josephus in his work *Antiquities of the Jews,* Matthias, the *Kohen Gadol,* had a conversation with his wife in a dream, which disqualified him from serving as High Priest. Yosef ben Eilim of Sepphoris, who is mentioned in *Horayot* 12b, was appointed in his place. In *Yoma* 12b, Yosef's father's name appears as Elam or Ulam instead of Eilim.

Yosef ben Elam of Sepphoris
See Yosef ben Eilim of Sepphoris.

Yosef ben Joshua ben Levi
See Yosef ben Yehoshu'a ben Levi.

Yosef ben Petros (third century)
Palestinian amora. In the Palestinian Talmud, *Mo'ed Katan* 3:5, he is noted as the father of Yehoshu'a ben Levi's first wife, and a contemporary of Zavdai ben Levi and Bar Kappara.

Yosef ben Samuel
See Yosef ben Shemu'el.

Yosef ben Shemu'el (fourth century)
Palestinian amora. In *Zevachim* 6b he is said to have been a colleague of Pappa.

Yosef ben Simai (first century)
Palestinian tanna. In *Shabbat* 121a he is described as a steward of King Herod Agrippa II. Yosef ben Simai lived in Sikhnin, near Sepphoris.

Yosef ben Ulam of Sepphoris
See Yosef ben Eilim of Sepphoris.

Yosef ben Yehoshu'a ben Levi (third century)
Palestinian amora. *Pesachim* 50a and *Bava Batra* 10b report that Yosef became ill and fell into a trance. When he recovered, his father asked him what he had seen. Yosef replied: "I saw a topsy-turvy world in which the lower class was on top and the upper class was below." "My son, you saw the world clearly," replied his father.

Yehudah ha-Nasi was Yosef's father-in-law, and Yosef's own father would always rise when Yosef approached out of respect for the house of the patriarch (*Kiddushin* 33b).

Yosef ben Yo'ezer
See Yosei ben Yo'ezer.

Yosef ben Zimra
See Yosei ben Zimra.

Yosef brei de-Rav Salla Chasida (fourth century)
Palestinian amora. Known in English as Yosef bar Salla the Pious, he is mentioned in *Pesachim* 73b and *Arakhin* 33b as a student of Pappa.

Yosef brei de-Rav Salla the Pious
See Yosef Brei de-Rav Salla Chasida.

Yosef of Sidon (fourth century)
Babylonian amora. According to *Ketubbot* 46a, both he and Nachman bar Yitzchak were students at the school established by Shimon bar Yochai.

Yosei
Several tanna'im and amora'im with this name are quoted in the Talmud without patronymic. It often is difficult to distinguish between them. In addition to Yosei I, II, and III, Yosei bar Chanina and Yosei ben Chalafta often appear without patronymic.

Yosei I (second century)
Palestinian tanna. Quoted frequently in the Talmud, he is noted as one of four scholars who studied together at the academy in Yavneh; the three other scholars were Yehudah ben Ila'i, Nechemyah, and Eli'ezer ben Yosei ha-Gelili (*Berakhot* 63b and Midrash Rabbah on *Song of Songs* 2:5).

Yosei II (second/third century)
Palestinian tanna. In *Bava Metzi'a* 43b he is mentioned as a disciple of Yochanan ben Nuri.

Yosei III (third/fourth century)
Palestinian amora. In *Berakhot* 11b he is listed as a colleague of Abba.

Yosei bar Chama
See Yosef bar Chama.

Yosei bar Chanina
Two scholars were known by this name:
1. A first-century Palestinian tanna who is mentioned in *Eruvin* 27a as a colleague of Eli'ezer ben Hurkanos and in *Pesachim* 68b as a colleague of Elazar.

2. A third-century Palestinian amora about whom little is known except that he had several sons. *Ta'anit* 13a reports that when several sons died, one after the other, Yosei bar Chanina bathed in cold water during the seven-day mourning period, which was contrary to accepted practice of not bathing at all.

Yosei was a disciple of Eli'ezer ben Ya'akov I (*Berakhot* 10b) and Shimon ben Lakish (*Nazir* 28b–29a). Yosei's disciples included Chama bar Ukba (*Pesachim* 52b), Abbahu (*Pesachim* 100a), and Chiyya bar Gamda (*Sotah* 7b). Among Yosei's colleagues were Yochanan bar Nappacha and Yehoshu'a ben Levi (*Berakhot* 22b).

According to *Berakhot* 50b, Yosei agreed with the accepted view that the wine used to recite the Grace After Meals must be diluted with water (as was common practice in Talmudic times), but his disciple Abbahu disagreed.

On the question of when the traditional prayer services were instituted, Yosei bar Chanina contends that they were introduced by the patriarchs, while his colleague, Yehoshu'a ben Levi, argues that they were instituted by the Men of the Great Assembly to replace the daily sacrifices (*Berakhot* 26b).

Yosei bar Huna (second/third century)

Babylonian amora. In *Sanhedrin* 105b he speculates that the biblical Ruth was the daughter of Eglon, grandson of Balak, king of Moab.

Yosei bar Manyumi

See Yosef bar Minyomi.

Yosei bar Nathan

See Isi bar Natan.

Yosei ben Avin (fourth century)

Also known as Yosei ben Bun.

Palestinian amora. A disciple of Assi, he was well acquainted with the discussions and decisions of Babylonian scholars. In *Berakhot* 22a and 33b, and *Shabbat* 21b and 96a, he is mentioned as a colleague and friend of Yosei ben Zevida, and in *Berakhot* 51a as a disciple of Yochanan bar Nappacha. In *Shabbat* 35b he declares that the Sabbath is over when three medium-sized stars appear in the sky.

Yosei ben Bun

See Yosei ben Avin.

Yosei ben Chalafta (second century)

Also known as Yosei of Sepphoris.

Palestinian tanna. Generally referred to as Yosei, without patronymic, he was born in Sepphoris to a Babylonian family (*Yoma* 66b). In *Mo'ed Katan* 21a he is referred to simply as Yosei of Sepphoris. One of the great scholars of his generation, he earned a living as a leather worker. A student of Akiva ben Yosef, he was one of seven of Akiva's disciples who fled to Babylonia (*Yevamot* 63b) when Akiva was martyred at the hands of the Romans. One of Yosei ben Chalafta's pupils was the illustrious Yehudah ha-Nasi, compiler of the Mishnah.

Yosei's father, Chalafta, was an outstanding scholar, and Yosei often makes reference to him. In *Bava Kamma* 70b and *Bava Batra* 56b he speaks of his father going to study under Yochanan ben Nuri.

In *Shabbat* 115a Yosei recounts his father visiting Gamali'el II in Tiberias where he found him sitting "at the table" of Yochanan ben Nizuf studying the Targum of the book of *Job*. In *Sukkah* 26a Yosei permits Shimon ben Gamli'el II, who was suffering from eye trouble, to sleep indoors instead of in the *sukkah*.

Yosei is noted as the author of the following maxim, which appears in *Avot* 4:6: "Whoever honors the Torah will himself be honored by his fellowman; he who dishonors the Torah will himself be dishonored." In *Avot* 4:9 Yosei says, in response to a query by his teacher Yochanan ben Zakkai, that the best course for a person to follow is to be a "good neighbor."

In *Sanhedrin* 21b Yosei is quoted as saying: "Had Moses not preceded him, Ezra would have been worthy of receiving the Torah of Israel"; a similar quote appears in the Palestinian Talmud, in *Megillah* 1:9. *Niddah* 49a ascribes to Yosei authorship of *Seder Olam* ("Order of the World"), a book that chronicles events from Creation to the Bar Kokhba Revolt. Yosei was quite astute in analyzing and interpreting the Bible. He believed, as did many later scholars, that some parts of the Torah were to be understood as allegory and not taken literally. This is how he viewed the story of the Revelation on Mount Sinai. He is quoted in *Sukkah* 5a, regarding the meeting between Moses and God on Mount Sinai (*Exodus* 25:22), as saying: "Neither did the Shekhinah [God] ever descend to earth, nor did Moses or Elijah ever ascend to heaven." To further support his position, he quotes *Psalms* 115:16: "The heavens are the heavens of the Lord, but the earth He has given to the children of men."

Yosei often disputed with non-Jews, among them a matron who asked innumerable questions. Once she inquired of Yosei how God spent all His time; Yosei replied that God was busy making ladders on which He raised some people and lowered others, giving money to some and taking it away from some to give to others. The matron was dissatisfied with this answer. Yosei then said that God also was busy arranging marriages.

Hearing this, the matron exclaimed, "Is this all that God does? I can do the same. I have many male and female slaves, and in one hour I can marry them all to each other." Yosei replied, "That which seems easy in your eyes is as difficult for God as the dividing of the sea."

The matron then chose from her slaves one thousand men and one thousand women, arranged them in two lines, and proclaimed, "This man will marry this woman, and this woman will marry that man." In this manner she mated them all in a short time.

The following day they all came to her with various complaints. One slave had a black eye, another a broken leg. When the matron asked them what had happened, they protested that she had chosen the wrong mates for them. The matron then realized that a marriage between two human beings was not as simple as she had thought it to be.

In *Megillah* 24b Yosei comments on a biblical verse that had perplexed him all his life: "And you shall grope at noonday as a blind man gropes in darkness" (*Deuteronomy* 28:29). He asked, "What difference does it make to a blind man whether it is dark or light?"

Yosei found the answer when he was out walking one night and saw a blind man walking on the road with a torch in his hand. He said to the blind man, "My son, for what reason do you carry the torch?"

The man replied, "So long as I have this torch in my hand, people can see me and save me from stumbling into potholes and thorns."

Yosei's last years were spent in Sepphoris, the city of his birth, where he had established a flourishing school and attracted many pupils. After his death, around the year 180, Yehudah ha-Nasi said of him, "The difference between Yosei's generation and ours is like the difference between the Holy of Holies and the most profane."

According to the Palestinian Talmud (*Yevamot* 1b), Yosei married his deceased brother's childless wife and she bore him five sons, Yishma'el, Elazar, Menachem, Chalafta (who died in Yosei's lifetime), and Avdimos, all of whom were great scholars. As Yosei proudly stated, he "planted five cedar trees among the Jews."

Yosei ben Channin
See Abba Yosef ben Channin.

Yosei ben Choni (first/second century)
Palestinian tanna. Known in English as Yosei ben Onias, he is mentioned in Mishnah *Zevachim* 1:2. In *Sanhedrin* 105b he is quoted as saying: "A man is envious of everyone except his son and his disciple." *Zevachim* 2a notes him as a contemporary of Eli'ezer ben Hurkanos.

Yosei ben Dostai
See Abba Yosei ben Dostai.

Yosei ben Durmaskit (first/second century)
Palestinian tanna. Known in English as Yosei, Son of the Damascene, he is noted in Mishnah *Yadayim* 4:3 as a colleague of Eli'ezer ben Hurkanos in Lydda.

Yosei ben Eliakim
See Yosei ben Elyakim.

Yosei ben Elisha (fourth century)
Palestinian tanna. In *Shabbat* 139a he says: "If you see a generation overwhelmed by trouble, go examine the judges."

Yosei ben Elyakim (fourth century)
Palestinian tanna. In *Berakhot* 9b he comments on the sequence of the morning prayers.

Yosei ben ha-Meshulam
See Yosei ben Meshulam.

Yosei ben he-Choteif Efrati (second century)
Palestinian amora. In Mishnah *Kilayim* 3:7 he is listed as a disciple of Yishma'el. "He-Choteif" means "the grabber," one who takes by force.

Yosei ben Johanan
See Yosei ben Yochanan.

Yosei ben Joezer
See Yosei ben Yo'ezer.

Yosei ben Joshua
See Yosei ben Yehoshu'a.

Yosei ben Judah
See Yosei ben Yehudah.

Yosei ben Judah of Kefar ha-Bavli
See Yosei ben Yehudah of Kefar ha-Bavli.

Yosei ben Kippar (second century)
Also spelled Yosei ben Kifar.
Palestinian tanna. In *Niddah* 48a he is noted as a disciple of Eli'ezer ben Hurkanos, and in *Rosh Hashanah* 13b and *Menachot* 30b as a disciple of Shimon of Shezor. According to *Berakhot* 63a, Yosei was one of the scholars sent by the *beit din* in Palestine to the Diaspora, to see how they were intercalating the calendar.

Yosei ben Kisma (first/second century)
Palestinian tanna. According to *Sanhedrin* 103b, he was a teacher of Yochanan bar Nappacha. In *Yevamot* 96b Yosei ben Kisma reports that he was present in a synagogue in Tiberias when two scholars argued so vehemently over the simple matter of whether a door bolt had a knob at its end that they ripped apart a Torah scroll. When Yosei saw what was happening, he declared: "I would not be surprised if this synagogue [which permits scholars to argue so angrily] will one day be turned into a house of idolatry."

Yosei's devotion to the transmission of Torah was paramount in his life. He once related this story:

I was traveling on the road when a man greeted me. I returned his greeting. He said to me, "Rabbi, from what city do you come?" I answered, "I come from a great city of scholars and sages." He said to me, "Rabbi, if you are willing to live with us in our city, I will give you a million golden dinars, precious stones, and pearls." I answered him, "Even if you gave me all the silver, gold, precious stones, and pearls in the world, I would not live in any other place except one in which Torah is studied. As David said in the book of *Psalms* [119:72]: 'The Law of Thy mouth is better unto me than thousands of pieces of gold and silver.'" (*Avot* 6:9)

In *Shabbat* 152a Yosei posed the following riddle: "Two are better than three [meaning, the use of two legs in one's youth and the use of two legs plus a cane in old age], and woe for the thing that goes and does not return. What is it?"

Chisda replied: "One's youth."

Yosei ben Menachem
See Isi ben Menachem.

Yosei ben Meshulam (first/second century)
Also known as Yosei ben ha-Meshulam.
Palestinian tanna. He is listed in *Chullin* 57b as a colleague of Shimon bar Yochai. In *Bekhorot* 24b and 25a Yosei is referred to as Yosei ben ha-Meshulam.

Yosei ben Nehorai (third century)
Palestinian amora. A disciple of Yehoshu'a ben Levi (*Chullin* 57b), Yosei ben Nehorai's rulings were transmitted by his disciple Yochanan (*Bava Metzi'a* 40a).

Yosei ben Onias
See Yosei ben Choni.

Yosei ben Parta
See Yosei ben Perida.

Yosei ben Perida (second/third century)
Also known as Yosei ben Parta.
Palestinian tanna. In *Nedarim* 41a and *Eruvin* 11b he is mentioned as a disciple of Eli'ezer Ben Hurkanos.

Yosei ben Saul

See Yosei ben Sha'ul.

Yosei ben Sha'ul (third century)

Palestinian amora. In *Avodah Zarah* 52b and *Mo'ed Katan* 22a he is noted as a disciple of Yehudah ha-Nasi. According to *Beitzah* 14b and 27a, and *Tamid* 27b, Yosei ben Sha'ul was a disciple of Rav and a teacher of Yehoshu'a ben Levi. In *Rosh Hashanah* 24a and *Ketubbot* 104a, Yosei is listed as a teacher of Chiyya bar Gamda.

Yosei ben Ulam (second century)

Palestinian tanna. A native of Sepphoris, according to *Megillah* 9b Yosei ben Ulam was a colleague of Yosei bar Chalafta.

Yosei ben Yasyan (second/third century)

Palestinian tanna. He is mentioned in *Menachot* 6b and *Yevamot* 98a. In *Eruvin* 53b he is described as having a vitriolic nature.

Yosei ben Yehoshu'a (second/third century)

Palestinian amora. In *Niddah* 24a and *Chullin* 56b he is noted as a teacher of Yochanan bar Nappacha.

Yosei ben Yehudah (second century)

Palestinian tanna. Son of Yehudah bar Ila'i, Yosei is known, principally, for his halakhic discussions with Yehudah ha-Nasi. One of Yosei's popular comments was, "Let thy yea be yea, and let thy nay be nay."

Yosei told the following tale of the Sabbath:

> Two angels—a good one and a bad one—accompany a man home on Sabbath eve from the synagogue. When the man finds the lamp lit, the table set, and the bed made in his home, the good angel prays, "May it be Thy will, O Lord, that it be the same next Sabbath," to which the evil angel, against his will, responds, "Amen." If, however, the man finds his house in disorder, the wicked angel says, "May it be the same next Sabbath," to which the good angel is forced to say, "Amen."

Yosei ben Yehudah of Kefar ha-Bavli (second century)

Palestinian tanna. A disciple of Elazar ben Shammu'a and a contemporary of Yehudah ha-Nasi, Yosei is quoted as saying: "He who learns from the young, to whom may he be compared? To one who eats unripe grapes and drinks [unfermented] wine from his vat. He who learns from the old, to whom may he be compared? To one who eats ripe grapes and drinks aged wine" (*Avot* 4:20).

Yosei ben Yochanan (second century B.C.E.)

Member of the Great Assembly. He and his colleague Yosei ben Yo'ezer (*Shabbat* 14b) constituted the first of the five *zugot*, "pairs"; Yosei ben Yo'ezer was the *nasi*, Yosei ben Yochanan the *av beit din*. One of Yosei ben Yochanan's popular maxims was: "Let your house be wide open, and let the poor be members of your household. Do not talk too much with women . . ." (*Avot* 1:5).

Yosei ben Yo'ezer (second century B.C.E.)

Also known as Yosef ben Yo'ezer.

Member of the Great Assembly. He and Yosei ben Yochanan constituted the first of the *zugot*, "pairs," with Yosei ben Yo'ezer as the *nasi* and Yosei ben Yochanan as the *av beit din* (*Temurah* 15b).

Among the laws enacted by Yosei ben Yo'ezer and Yosei ben Yochanan was one that declared all heathen countries to be impure (*Shabbat* 15a). The first halakhic controversy recorded in the Talmud was between these two scholars. It arose over whether the laying of hands on the heads of sacrificial animals is permitted on holidays (Mishnah *Chagigah* 2:2). Yosei ben Yo'ezer said it may not be performed; Yosei (called here Yosef) permitted it.

Bava Batra 133b notes that Yosei had a son who married the daughter of King Alexander Jannai's wreath maker.

Yosei ben Yo'ezer is characterized in *Chagigah* 20a as "the most pious in the Priesthood." He served the Jewish community during the High Priesthood of Alcimus, who, according to legend, murdered many Hasideans, including Yosei ben Yo'ezer. One of Yosei ben Yo'ezer's maxims was this: "Let thy house be a meeting place for the wise" (*Avot* 1:4).

Yosei ben Zevida (fourth century)

Palestinian amora. In *Berakhot* 22a and 33b, and *Shabbat* 21b and 96a he is listed as a colleague of Yosei ben Avin. In *Menachot* 70b Yosei ben Zevida is noted as a colleague of Yonah.

Yosei ben Zimra (third century)

Also known as Yosef ben Zimra.

Palestinian amora. Among his disciples were Yochanan (*Berakhot* 10b and *Shabbat* 105a) and Elazar ben Pedat (*Berakhot* 31b). In *Yoma* 78a Tzadok ben Chalokah testifies to the greatness of Yosei, going so far as to say that Yosei was greater than Yehudah ha-Nasi.

In *Arakhin* 15b Yosei ben Zimra is referred to as Yosef ben Zimra.

Yosei Gelila'ah (third century)

Palestinian amora. *Shabbat* 46a mentions that he visited the town of Yosei bar Chanina.

Yosei ha-Gelili (first/second century)

Palestinian tanna. Known in English as Yosei the Galilean, he was one of the most highly respected scholars in Yochanan ben Zakkai's academy in Yavneh. A colleague of Akiva ben Yosef, Yosei engaged him in many debates (*Berakhot* 50a, *Yoma* 4a and 58b). In *Avot de-Rabbi Natan*, chapter 18, Yehudah ha-Nasi characterized Yosei ha-Gelili as "a discriminating gatherer [of traditions]," who was praiseworthy for his humility and willingness to acknowledge the erudition of his colleagues.

Yosei's married life was unhappy, and he divorced his wife. When she remarried, he was magnanimous enough to support her and her blind husband (*Genesis Rabbah* 17:3 and *Leviticus Rabbah* 34:14). It was said that Yosei's heart was "full of love for humanity." But he did have one encounter with a woman that proved embarrassing. *Eruvin* 53b relates that Yosei once met Beruryah, wife of Me'ir, at a crossroads and asked her, "What road should we take to go to Lydda?"

"Foolish Galilean!" she replied. "Didn't the Sages say, 'Do not engage in much talk with women'? You should have asked, 'By which [road] to Lydda?'"

Yosei's reputation for piety endured for many centuries. A

third-century amora said, "When because of their sins there is a drought in Israel and Yosei ha-Gelili prays for rain, the rains come immediately." A popular invocation that was still recited in the tenth century went: "O Yosei ha-Gelili, heal me!"

Yosei's son, Eli'ezer ben Yosei ha-Gelili, was one of Akiva ben Yosef's great disciples and, like his father, also taught in the academy of Yochanan ben Zakkai in Yavneh.

Yosei ha-Kohen (first/second century)
Also known as Yosei he-Chasid.
Palestinian tanna. Known in English as Yosei the Priest (Yosei ha-Kohen) and sometimes as Yosei the Pious (Yosei he-Chasid), he is praised in *Chagigah* 18b as one of the most pious of all the *Kohanim*. In *Avot* 2:8 he is listed as one of Yochanan ben Zakkai's most prominent disciples.

According to *Rosh Hashanah* 17b, Yosei ha-Kohen was a colleague of Gamli'el I; according to *Ketubbot* 27a, he was a colleague of Zekharyah ben ha-Katzav. One of Yosei ha-Kohen's favorite maxims was this: "Let the property of your friend be as precious to you as your own" (*Avot* 2:12).

Yosei he-Chasid
See Yosei ha-Kohen.

Yosei he-Chorem (second century)
Palestinian tanna. A contemporary of Natan, Yosei he-Chorem discusses the positioning of the *tefillin* for the hand in *Menachot* 37a and concludes that they should be placed on the left hand, which is the weaker one. The established practice is for right-handed people to wear them on their left hand and left-handed people to wear them on their right hand.

Yosei Ketanta
See Isi ben Yehudah.

Yosei Mada'ah (third century)
Palestinian amora. Known in English as Yosei the Mede, because he came from Media, he was associated with Yehudah ha-Nasi and Huna of Sepphoris (*Chullin* 51a).

Yosei of Nehar Bil
See Assi of Nehar Bil.

Yosei of Sepphoris
See Yosei ben Chalafta.

Yosei of Yokeret (fourth century)
Palestinian amora. *Ta'anit* 23b records that Yosei ben Avin attended the lectures of Yosei of Yokeret then left him and went to study under Ashi. Scholars have identified Yokeret as Derukeret, a town near where Huna lived (*Ta'anit* 21b).

Yosei, Son of the Damascene
See Yosei ben Durmaskit.

Yosei the Galilean
See Yosei ha-Gelili.

Yosei the Mede
See Yosei Mada'ah.

Yosei the Pious
See Yosei ha-Kohen.

Yoshiyyah Rabbah (second century)
Babylonian amora. Known in English as Yoshiyyah the Great, he is mentioned in *Sanhedrin* 19a as a teacher of Menashya bar Avat. Yoshiyyah instructed Menashya on the protocol for offering condolences to mourners in the cemetery. *See* Menashya bar Avat.

Yoshiyyah the Great
See Yoshiyyah Rabbah.

Yoshiyyahu
Two scholars were known by this name.

1. A second-century Palestinian tanna who was born in Babylonia and later moved to Palestine, where he studied with Yishma'el ben Elisha. According to *Nedarim* 72b, *Nazir* 6b and 39b, and many other sources, Yoshiyyahu was a colleague of Yonatan, with whom he engaged in debate. Yoshiyyahu is not mentioned in the Mishnah, possibly because he lived in southern Palestine (*Sanhedrin* 88b) and, according to some scholars, the compiler of the Mishnah, Yehudah ha-Nasi, lived in the north (Tiberias), so Yoshiyyahu's teachings were most likely unknown to Yehudah.

In *Bava Batra* 117a Yoshiyyahu says that the land of Canaan was divided in accordance with the number of people who left Egypt and not in accordance with the number who entered the new land. This means that if one person who left Egypt had four sons, and another person had only one son, upon entering Canaan each of the five sons received only a fifth of his father's estate, while the one son received his father's full share.

Yoshiyyahu was the father of Achai ben Yoshiyyahu.

2. A third-century Babylonian amora, who was a prominent scholar. In *Kiddushin* 36b and *Sotah* 19a, Yoshiyyahu is described as a contemporary of Elazar ben Pedat and in *Sotah* 25a as a disciple of Ze'eira. In *Sukkah* 2b Yoshiyyahu is listed as a disciple of Rav and in *Sukkah* 7b he is quoted by Abbayei. One of Yoshiyyahu's disciples, Tavi, is mentioned in *Berakhot* 15b, *Yoma* 65b, *Megillah* 29b, and *Sanhedrin* 92a.

Yoshiyyahu of Hutzal (third/fourth century)
Babylonian amora. In *Gittin* 61a he is noted as a contemporary of Kahana. Hutzal is located between Sura and Nehardea.

Yoshiyyahu of Usha (third century)
Palestinian amora. In *Menachot* 39a he is noted as a colleague of Rabbah bar Bar Chana, with whom he discussed the threads used in fashioning the *tzitzit*.

Yosna (third/fourth century)
Palestinian amora. In *Avodah Zarah* 33b he is noted as a disciple of Ammi bar Natan.

Yudah
See Yehudah.

Yudan (fourth century)
Palestinian amora. In the Palestinian Talmud *Ketubbot* 2:4 (26c) he carried on a discussion with Yosei, the head of the academy in Tiberias. Yudan is not mentioned in the Babylonian Talmud.

Yudan ben Channin (fourth century)
Palestinian amora. A disciple of Berekhyah, Yudan ben Channin quotes Berekhyah in the Palestinian Talmud, *Sanhedrin* 1:1, as saying that God spoke these words to Israel: "My children, when you see the merit of the fathers [patriarchs] and the

merit of the mothers [matriarchs] declining, go and beseech God's kindness directly."

Yudan ben Ishmael

See Yudan ben Yishma'el.

Yudan ben Shimon (third century)

Palestinian amora. A contemporary of Yochanan bar Nappacha, Yudan comments in *Genesis Rabbah* 19:5 on the life of the phoenix, referred to in *Job* 29:18.

Yudan ben Simeon

See Yudan ben Shimon.

Yudan ben Yishma'el (third century)

Palestinian amora. Thought to be the brother of Yannai ben Yishma'el, Yudan once was asked whether teachers of the Torah should be paid for their services. Certainly, Yudan replied, they should be remunerated for the time spent in teaching since they could have earned money doing some other kind of work.

Yudan Berabbi

See Yehudah Nesi'ah.

Yustai ben Maton (second/third century)

Palestinian amora. In *Zevachim* 99a he is noted as a disciple of Yochanan bar Nappacha.

Names that begin with the Hebrew letter tzadi *can be found under the letter* T.

Zadok

See Tzadok.

Zakkai

Two scholars were known by this name:

1. A second-century Palestinian tanna who was a contemporary of Yehudah ha-Nasi and a pupil of Shimon bar Yochai. Zakkai lived to a ripe old age. When asked by his pupils how he merited such longevity, he explained that he never called his neighbor by a nickname and never neglected to buy wine for the Sabbath *Kiddush* (*Megillah* 27b).

It is noted in *Sanhedrin* 62a that Zakkai lectured in the presence of Yochanan bar Nappacha.

2. A fifth-century Babylonian amora who, in *Ketubbot* 87a, is noted as a colleague of Zutra.

Zava

See Zuga of Adiabene.

Zavdai ben Levi (third century)

Palestinian amora. A member of the group of scholars headed by Oshaya Rabbah, Zavdai ben Levi is quoted in *Zevachim* 28b by Yochanan bar Nappacha.

Zavdi (third century)

Babylonian amora. In *Arakhin* 13b he is mentioned as a disciple of Huna.

Zechariah

See Zekharyah.

Ze'eira

Two scholars were known by this name:

1. A third-century Babylonian amora who was a disciple of Huna (*Ta'anit* 11a) and Yoshiyyahu (*Sotah* 25a), and a teacher of Yirmeyahu ben Abba (*Ta'anit* 12b). When Ze'eira's father died, his mother had to sell some land in order to pay taxes; Ashi and Kahana signed as witnesses to the deed of sale (*Gittin* 52b).

2. A third/fourth-century Palestinian amora who was born in Babylonia and who is known as Zera in the Babylonian Talmud; *Berakhot* 38a identifies him as the son of Zevid and brother of Shimon ben Zevid. After studying for many years in Babylonia under Yosef bar Chiyya, Ze'eira was offered the leadership of the academy in Pumbedita but declined. While well versed in the dialectical method of study used in Babylonia, he preferred the more direct method employed in Palestinian academies, so he immigrated to Palestine (*Bava Metzi'a* 85a) and undertook a hundred fasts so that he would forget the Babylonian method of study. The post of head of the academy in Pumbedita was filled in the year 333 by Ze'eira's colleague Rava, after Abbayei's death.

In addition to Yosef bar Chiyya, Ze'eira studied under Assi and Chisda (*Berakhot* 49a and *Beitzah* 33b) and under Nachman bar Shemu'el bar Marta (*Chullin* 30b) in Babylonia.

For a while Ze'eira studied at the school of Hamnuna (*Berakhot* 24b). There Ze'eira learned that if one sneezes when reciting his prayers it is a good omen; just as it gives him relief here on earth below, so does it offer relief to those in heaven above. The esteemed scholar Sheshet (*Eruvin* 66a) called Ze'eira *gavra rabbah,* "a great man."

Shabbat 27b reveals the playful nature of Ze'eira as a young student. He once found his teacher Yehudah bar Yechezkel in a cheerful mood and asked if Yehudah would reveal to him some of the secrets of the universe. Ze'eira then proceeded to ask Yehudah questions such as: Why do camels have short tails, and why do sheep have warm [wool] coats, while goats do not?

In Palestine Ze'eira studied under Abbahu (*Berakhot* 51a), who so admired him that he visited Ze'eira when Ze'eira fell ill

(*Berakhot* 46a). Ze'eira also studied at the school of Yannai (*Shabbat* 121b), where his colleague was Abba bar Chiyya bar Abba. One of Ze'eira's most illustrious teachers in Palestine was the esteemed Yochanan bar Nappacha (*Berakhot* 47b).

Although Ze'eira tried to avoid ordination because he had come from Babylonia, he and his colleagues Ammi and Assi were ordained, earning the title of "Rabbi" (*Sanhedrin* 14a). It was said of Ze'eira that, despite his slight stature, he was impressive and quite charming. He attracted many outstanding students to his lectures, among them Yonah (*Gittin* 59a), Ya'akov bar Acha (*Berakhot* 23a), and Yirmeyahu (*Bava Kamma* 19a). Ze'eira's colleague Shemu'el ben Yitzchak (*Gittin* 23b) considered him one of the most brilliant and outstanding authorities of his generation.

Aside from his brilliance, Ze'eira was known for his modesty and spirituality. Once, having had an argument with a man, Ze'eira was so upset over his lack of self-control that he searched out the person in order to apolgize to him and bring about a reconciliation (*Yoma* 87a).

With respect to ritual observance, Ze'eira once said: "To enhance the beauty of performing a *mitzvah*, one should spend up to one-third [in excess of the ordinary cost of a ritual item]" (*Bava Kamma* 9b).

Berakhot 16b records these words that were part of Ze'eira's prayer regimen: "May it be Thy will, O Lord our God, that we neither sin nor bring upon ourselves shame or disgrace more than our fathers."

With regard to child rearing, Ze'eira said: "A man should not say to a child, 'I will give you something' and not keep his promise, for it will teach the child to lie" (*Sukkah* 46b).

It is reported in *Berakhot* 28a that when Ze'eira was tired of studying he would sit at the door of the school of Natan bar Tavi so that he might rise when a scholar passed, thus earning a reward in the world to come for showing respect to learned people. *Eruvin* 28b identifies the academy as that of Yehudah bar Ammi.

When Ze'eira died, he was mourned with these words: "Babylonia gave birth to him; the Land of Glory [Palestine] had the pleasure of rearing him. 'Woe is me,' says Tiberias, for she has lost a precious jewel" (*Mo'ed Katan* 25b).

Ze'eira bar Chama (third/fourth century)

Palestinian amora. In *Yoma* 78a he states that on Yom Kippur he was "the host of Ammi [ben Natan], Assi, Yehoshu'a ben Levi, and all the Rabbis of Caesarea."

Ze'eira bar Memel (third/fourth century)

Babylonian amora. In *Kiddushin* 9a he disagrees with the view of Rava on what constitutes a legal document for a betrothal to be official.

Ze'iri (third/fourth century)

Babylonian amora. A disciple of Rav, Ze'iri moved to Palestine when Rav died and studied under Yochanan bar Nappacha. Yochanan was very fond of Ze'iri and wanted him to marry his daughter. Ze'iri, however, refused. One day, as Ze'iri and Yochanan were taking a walk, they reached a body of water. Ze'iri, who was young and strong, lifted Yochanan up and carried him across. Said Yochanan to Ze'iri, "My teachings seem to appeal to you, but my daughter does not" (*Kiddushin* 71b).

Chanina bar Chama was another teacher of Ze'iri (*Shabbat* 17a), and Ashi was one of Ze'iri's prominent disciples (*Yoma* 77b).

Sanhedrin 67b records an unhappy incident in the life of Ze'iri. While visiting Alexandria, Ze'iri bought from a vendor what he thought was an ass. Ze'iri had been deceived—the ass was a product of sorcery, fashioned from a kind of tree that dissolves when it comes into contact with water. When Ze'iri reached a body of water he stopped to let the ass have a drink, and the animal dissolved. All that was left was a wooden plank.

When he returned to the vendor to get his money back, the vendor replied, "Does anyone buy something here in Egypt, a land famous for sorcery, without first testing it with water?"

Ze'iri ben Chama (third/fourth century)

See Ze'eira bar Chama.

Zekharyah (third century)

Palestinian tanna. A disciple of Yishma'el ben Elisha, Zekharyah is quoted as saying that "God intended to bring forth the

Priesthood from Shem (Noah's oldest son) but gave preference to Abraham" (*Nedarim* 32b).

Zekharyah ben Avkolas (first century)
Palestinian scholar. A leader of the Zealots, a Second Temple sect fervidly opposed to Roman dominion of Palestine, Zekharyah ben Avkolas expressed his opinion in *Gittin* 56a on the use of a blemished animal as a sacrifice.

Zekharyah ben ha-Katzav (first century)
Palestinian tanna. Known in English as Zekharyah, Son of the Butcher, he was a colleague of Yochanan ben Zakkai. Like his father, Zekharyah was a butcher by profession and a Priest by lineage. Zekharyah's disciples include Yehoshu'a ben Chananyah (*Sotah* 27a), and Yosei ben Yehudah and Elazar ben Yosei (*Bava Batra* 111a).

Zekharyah ben Kevutal (first century)
Palestinian tanna. According to *Berakhot* 63a, he is reported to have read to the High Priest from the book of *Daniel.* They used to read to the High Priest on Yom Kippur to keep him awake.

Zekharyah, Son of the Butcher
See Zekharyah ben ha-Katzav.

Zerika (third/fourth century)
Palestinian amora. The disciple of many distinguished masters, Zerika's teachers include Yehoshu'a ben Levi (*Berakhot* 3b), Ammi bar Natan (*Bava Batra* 130b), Elazar ben Pedat (*Sotah* 4b), Abba (*Shabbat* 38b), and Yehudah (*Beitzah* 7b). In *Gittin* 44a and *Sukkah* 37b Zerika is noted as a teacher of Yirmeyahu ben Abba; *Pesachim* 73a notes that the son of Huna ben Chinena also was one of Zerika's students.

In *Sotah* 4b Zerika quotes these words of Elazar ben Pedat: "Whoever makes light of washing his hands [before and after a meal] will be uprooted from the world."

In Babylonia it was said that Zerika had called Safra's attention to the difference between the modesty of "pious Palestine" and the audacity of "bold Babylonia." Said Zerika, "The pious men of Babylonia pray for rain openly and brazenly in public, while the men of Palestine do so modestly in private (*Ta'anit* 23b).

Zevid (third/fourth century)

Babylonian amora. In *Berakhot* 38a Zevid is identified as the father of Ze'eira and Shimon ben Zevid. *Bava Batra* 151a reports that the mother of Zutra bar Toviyyah gave her property to her son because she intended to marry Zevid and did not want Zevid to acquire ownership of her property through their marriage. She married Zevid and then divorced him. The validity of her action was the subject of a debate between Beivai bar Abbayei and Huna bar Yehoshu'a.

Zevid was a contemporary of the Palestinian Abbayei, whose teachings he transmitted to scholars in Babylonia (*Avodah Zarah* 38b). Among Zevid's disciples were Rava (*Rosh Hashanah* 6b and *Sukkah* 44a) and Nachman bar Ya'akov (*Bava Metzi'a* 17a).

Avodah Zarah 38b notes that Zevid died from drinking poison that the exilarch's heathen servants had placed in "a draft of spiced vinegar."

Zevid of Nehardea (fourth century)

Babylonian amora. For eight years he served as principal of the academy in Nehardea. One of his most illustrious students, Kahana, delivered the eulogy at his funeral.

Zilai (third/fourth century)

Babylonian amora. In *Berakhot* 53b Zivai is mentioned as a colleague of Zivai and a contemporary of Nachman bar Yitzchak.

Zivai (third century)

Babylonian amora. In *Berakhot* 53b Zivai is named as a colleague of Zilai.

Zohamai (fourth century)

Babylonian amora. In *Berakhot* 53b he is noted as a contemporary of Nachman ben Yitzchak.

Zuga of Adiabene (third century)

Also known as Zava of Adiabene.

Babylonian amora. He is quoted in *Mo'ed Katan* 28a, where he comforts the students of Huna's academy who believed that their master was dying.

Zuti (third/fourth century)

Babylonian amora. In *Nedarim* 77a Zuti is mentioned as a member of the school of Pappi and in *Shabbat* 157a and *Yevamot* 25b as belonging to the school of Pappa.

Zutra

Also known as Mar Zutra.

Several scholars were known by this name. The two most prominent were:

1. A second-century Palestinian tanna of whom it is noted in *Yoma* 87a that when, at an advanced age, he was unable to walk, he was carried to the podium by his students to lecture on the laws of a forthcoming festival. He is referred to in *Nedarim* 76b as Mar Zutra.

2. A fourth/fifth-century Babylonian amora whose teacher, according to *Shabbat* 50a and *Beitzah* 8a, was Zutra Rabbah, of whom nothing more is known. A very close colleague of Ashi, Zutra and Ashi visited Persia together, notes *Ketubbot* 61a. *Berakhot* 50b describes how Zutra, Ashi, and several other colleagues shared a serving of dates and pomegranates. Mention is made in *Berakhot* 46b of the fact that when Ashi was in mourning Zutra paid a condolence call.

Among Zutra's more prominent teachers were Huna (*Eruvin* 41b), Pappa (*Kiddushin* 7a and *Bava Metzi'a* 67b), and Shemu'el (*Nazir* 57b). Among Zutra's colleagues and contemporaries were Mereimar (*Sanhedrin* 42a), Ravina II (*Bava Batra* 61a and 70b), and Pappi (*Sukkah* 46a).

According to *Sanhedrin* 94a, Zutra believed that Sennacherib exiled the ten tribes to Africa in the seventh century B.C.E.

"Even a poor man who subsists on charity should give charity," said Zutra (*Gittin* 7b). In *Megillah* 26b he states that worn-out Torah covers may be used to make shrouds for an unidentified dead person, whom the nearest community is responsible to bury at its own expense.

Zutra served as exilarch from the year 512 until his death in 520.

Zutra bar Huna bar Pappi (third/fourth century)

Babylonian amora. In *Chullin* 48a he is mentioned as a colleague of Ravina I.

Zutra bar Mari (fourth/fifth century)

Also known as Mar Zutra bar Mari.

Babylonian amora. According to *Kiddushin* 65b, he was the son of Adda bar Mari bar Isur and the brother of Adda Sabba. Zutra bar Mari and Adda Sabba consulted Ashi on the division of their father's estate.

In *Bava Kamma* 29a, *Chullin* 108a, *Menachot* 56a, and *Zevachim* 22a, Zutra bar Mari is listed as a colleague of Ravina II.

Zutra bar Nachman (fourth century)

Also known as Mar Zutra bar Nachman.

Babylonian amora. Son of Nachman bar Ya'akov (*Sotah* 9a) and a contemporary of Assi (*Niddah* 49a). *Mo'ed Katan* 12a describes Zutra bar Nachman as a very wealthy man who built a mansion for himself. He is referred to in *Bava Batra* 151b as Mar Zutra bar Nachman.

Zutra bar Tobiah

See Zutra bar Toviyyah.

Zutra bar Toviyyah (third century)

Also known as Mar Zutra bar Toviyyah.

Babylonian amora. In *Sanhedrin* 106a Zutra bar Toviyyah is noted as a disciple of Rav who, he reports, criticized the greediness of the soothsayer Balaam by likening him to a "camel [who] went to look for horns and as a consequence his ears were cut off." Balaam, who had been ordered by Balak, king of Moab, to curse the Israelites, failed to do so (*Numbers* 22–24); when Balaam went to Balak to collect his fee, not only did he not receive payment but he paid with his life.

In *Sanhedrin* 106a and *Bava Metzi'a* 59a Zutra bar Toviyyah is referred to as Mar Zutra bar Toviyyah. In *Yoma* 86a he is noted as a disciple of Yehudah bar Yechezkel.

In *Chagigah* 12a Zutra quotes his teacher Rav as saying that the world was created by "ten things [divine powers], namely, wisdom, understanding, reason, strength, rebuke, might, righteousness, judgment, lovingkindness, and compassion." Rav based his belief on verses from *Psalms* 25:6, 65:7, and 89:15, and *Proverbs* 3:19 and 3:20.

Zutra's mother was married to Zevid for a brief time.

Zutra bar Zeira (fourth century)

Babylonian amora. He is quoted in *Shabbat* 157a.

Zutra ben Ze'eira (second century)

Palestinian tanna. He is quoted in *Nedarim* 77a.

Zutra Chasida (third century)

Also known as Mar Zutra Chasida.

Babylonian amora. Known in English as Zutra the Pious, it is recorded in *Bava Kamma* 81b that he had a servant, so undoubtedly he was a well-to-do scholar. According to *Sanhedrin* 7b, whenever Zutra Chasida was asked to lecture in his old age, he was carried shoulder-high through the assembly so that people would not have to wait too long for him to make his way slowly through the throng by foot.

Zutra of Darishba (fourth/fifth century)

Also known as Mar Zutra of Darishba.

Babylonian amora. *Bava Batra* 126b records a dispute between Zutra of Darishba and his brothers regarding their father's estate. Zutra had divided a basket of peppers with his brothers in equal shares, thus, as the firstborn in the family, renouncing his claim to a double portion of the peppers. The question arose whether by his action Zutra was renouncing his rights to share in the balance of his father's estate. The case came before Ashi, who ruled that since Zutra had renounced his rights to part of the estate, he implicitly was renouncing his rights to the entire estate.

Zutra Rabbah (fourth century)

Also known as Mar Zutra Rabbah.

Babylonian amora. Known in English as Zutra the Great, he is noted in *Beitzah* 8a and *Shabbat* 50a as a teacher of Zutra.

Zutra the Great

See Zutra Rabbah.

Zutrai (third century)

Babylonian amora. He is quoted in *Shabbat* 124b where he differs with Yehudah, who was a disciple of Shemu'el.

Glossary

~

The terms defined below appear in the body of the text.
Please note that a listing of the Talmudic tractates and
their contents can be found on pages 59–78.

Abba (plural, *avot*) Literally, "father." A title of honor given to many Rabbis of the Talmud as a sign of affection and respect. Abba is also used as a personal name.

Acharonim Literally, "later ones." Talmudic commentators who followed the *rishonim. See* Rishonim.

Adar The twelfth month of the Hebrew calendar, starting with Nisan.

Aggadah (Aramaic; plural, *aggadot*; in Hebrew, *haggadah*) Literally, "narrative," referring specifically to those sections of the Talmud that do not deal with legal matters (*halakhah*). *Aggadah* includes homiletic expositions, Bible stories, legends, anecdotes, and moral teachings. *See* Halakhah.

Agunah (plural, *agunot*) Literally, "chained woman." A woman who is forbidden to remarry because she lacks proof that her husband is dead or because her husband refuses to grant her a Jewish divorce (*get*).

Am ha-Aretz (plural, *ammei ha-aretz*) Literally, "person of the land, country folk." An uneducated person, one ignorant of Jewish law and tradition.

Amidah Literally, "standing." This prayer, which is recited in a standing position, is also referred to in rabbinic literature as the *Shemoneh Esrei* (meaning "eighteen," the original number of benedictions in the prayer) or *Tefillah* ("prayer").

Amora (plural, *amora'im*). Literally, "speaker, interpreter." A Palestinian or Babylonian scholar who discussed, analyzed, and interpreted the teachings of the Mishnah.

Apikoros   (Greek) Literally, "heretic." In the Talmud, the term is applied to one who does not believe in God or the divine origin of the Torah, as well as to a Jew who does not accept the rulings of the Rabbis.

Arba'ah Minim   *See* Etrog.

Aris   Literally, "tenant farmer." An individual who leases land rather than owns it.

Asmakhta   (Aramaic) Literally, "support." A biblical text cited to support a law enacted by the Rabbis of the Talmud. The term *asmakhta* is also used to describe an obligation one assumes but does not expect to be called upon to fulfill.

Av   The fifth month in the Hebrew calendar, beginning with Nisan. The fast of Tishah b'Av ("Ninth Day of Av") commemorates the destruction of the First and Second Temples.

Av Beit Din   Literally, "father of the court." In early Talmudic times, the *av beit din* was deputy to the president (*nasi*) of the Sanhedrin and presided over the court when it was in session.

Avot   Literally, "fathers." The patriarchs Abraham, Isaac, and Jacob—fathers of the Jewish people—are collectively referred to as the *avot*. Also, the name of one of the Talmudic tractates.

Babylonian Talmud   Known in Hebrew as *Talmud Bavli*. This commentary on the Mishnah, the creation of scholars who lived in Babylonia, was compiled and edited around the year 500 C.E.

Baraita   (Aramaic; plural, *baraitot*) Literally, "external [to the Mishnah]." The term used to denote a teaching similar to those in the Mishnah that was not included in the Mishnah proper. These *baraitot*, which were gathered into a collection known as the Tosefta, are often quoted in the body of the Talmud. *See also* Tosefta.

Bat Kol   Literally, "daughter of a voice [echo]," referring to a heavenly voice that delivers a divine message to one or more individuals on earth.

Batel be-Shishim   Literally, "void by a sixtieth." This expression refers to the law which states that if a particle of dairy food falls into a pot of meat, and the particle is not more than one-sixtieth the volume of the contents of the pot, the meat is not considered unkosher.

Bavli   *See* Babylonian Talmud.

Beit Din Literally, "house [court] of law." In Temple times, there existed two major courts, the Sanhedrin Gedolah and Sanhedrin Ketannah. *See* Sanhedrin.

Beit ha-Mikdash *See* Temple.

Berabbi *Also spelled* Beribbi. A contraction of the two words *bei* ("house") and *rabbi* ("my master"), this honorific title is generally, but not exclusively, applied to disciples of Yehudah ha-Nasi (Judah the Prince), who was referred to simply as "Rabbi."

Bikkurim Literally, "first fruits [of the new harvest]." In Talmudic times, farmers would bring at least one-sixtieth of their harvest as an offering to the Priests. *Bikkurim* is also the name of a Talmudic tractate.

Birkat ha-Kohanim Literally, "blessing of the Priests," referring specifically to the threefold benediction, recorded in *Numbers* 6:22–27, that was conferred by the Priests upon the Congregation of Israel.

Chalitzah Literally, "removal [of the sandal]." Described in *Deuteronomy* 25:5–10, this ceremony is performed by a childless widow if her brother-in-law refuses to marry her in order that she may bear a son and perpetuate the deceased husband's name.

Chavruta Literally, "study partner." In *Berakhot* 63b, the Rabbis suggest that students learn best when they study in pairs. This system, practiced in the academies of Palestine and Babylonia, is followed in *yeshivot* to this day.

Chazakah Literally, "holding," referring to presumption of ownership. By possessing an article (including land) uncontested for a definite period of time, a person establishes ownership (Mishnah *Berakhot* 3:1).

Chuppah Literally, "canopy," referring specifically to the covering under which the bride and groom stand at a Jewish wedding.

Dinar *See* Zuz.

Elul The sixth month of the Hebrew calendar, beginning with Nisan. During this month, preparations are made for the approaching High Holidays.

Eretz Yisra'el Literally, "Land of Israel." The land that was promised by God to the patriarch Abraham and his descendants.

Eruv (plural, *eruvin*) Literally, "merging, mixture, amalgamation, or blending [of activities or rights]." In its legal sense, the term refers to an instrument that permits the performing of an activity that is normally forbidden on the Sabbath and holidays. *Eruvin* is also the name of a Talmudic tractate.

Essenes Known in Hebrew as Isiyyim ("Pietists"), the Essenes were a small Jewish sect that led a communal existence from the second century B.C.E. until the destruction of the Second Temple in 70 C.E. Qumran, on the western shore of the Dead Sea, near the caves in which the Dead Sea Scrolls were discovered, is believed to have been an Essene settlement. The Essenes were strict in their observance of ritual purity and the laws of Shabbat. They disagreed with the Pharisees and Sadducees on many theological issues.

Etrog (plural, *etrogim*) Literally, "citron." One of the four species (*arba'ah minim*) that comprise the *lulav* bouquet used on the festival of Sukkot.

Exilarch *See* Reish Galuta.

Gehenna The English form of the name Geihinnom, the valley (of Hinnom), where in ancient times children were sacrificed in fire to the god Molech, as described in *2 Kings* 23:10.

Gemara Literally, "learning, teaching." The commentary on the Mishnah. Together, the Mishnah and Gemara comprise the Talmud, although the term "Gemara" is sometimes used to refer to the Talmud as a whole. The word *gemara*, when written with a lowercase initial letter, refers to a commentary on a specific *mishnah*. *See also* Mishnah.

Ge'onim (singular, *ga'on*) Literally, "[people of] grandeur, eminence." Talmudic expositors active between the seventh and eleventh centuries.

Get (plural, *gittin*) Literally, "bill of divorce." A Jewish divorce document may be issued only by the husband and delivered to the wife in the presence of a *beit din*.

Great Assembly *See* Keneset ha-Gedolah.

Great Sanhedrin *See* Sanhedrin.

Haftarah (plural, *haftarot*) Literally, "conclusion." The portion of the Prophets with which the Torah reading is concluded on Shabbat and festival mornings.

Haggadah The book containing the rituals and liturgy of the Passover Seder. Also, a synonym for *aggadah*. *See* Aggadah.

Halakhah Literally, "walking [on the correct path]," referring to Jewish law as first stated in the Bible and then interpreted and expanded upon by the Rabbis of the Talmud and later scholars. *See* Aggadah.

Havdalah Literally, "separation." The ceremony conducted at the conclusion of Shabbat and holidays marking the separation between the holy day and the rest of the week.

Jerusalem Talmud *See* Palestinian Talmud.

Jubilee *See* Sabbatical Year.

Kallah Literally, "bride, assembly." The term refers to the biannual assembly of scholars, held in Babylonia during the *kallah* months of Adar and Elul, at which lectures were delivered by the leading scholars of the Babylonian academies. *Kallah* is also the name of a minor Talmudic tractate dealing with the laws of marriage and sexual relations.

Kashrut Literally, "ritual fitness," referring specifically to the Jewish dietary laws or to the status of religious articles.

Keneset ha-Gedolah Known in English as the "Great Assembly." According to tradition, this body was formed under Ezra's leadership by a distinguished group of 120 Sages. It was during the period of the Keneset ha-Gedolah that the biblical canon was finalized. The members of the Keneset ha-Gedolah were the first to systematically study the biblical text, interpret it, and expound upon it.

Keneset Ketannah *See* Beit Din.

Ketubbah (plural, *ketubbot*) Literally, "marriage contract." The *ketubbah* details the husband's obligations to his wife, including provisions that apply in the event that the marriage is dissolved.

Kiddush Literally, "sanctification." The prayer recited over wine on Shabbat and holidays.

Kilayim Literally, "mixtures." Jewish law forbids the mixture of diverse kinds of seeds, trees, animals, or fabrics. *Kilayim* is also the name of a Talmudic tractate.

Kohen (plural, *Kohanim*) Literally, "Priest." A descendant of Aaron, the brother of Moses, of the tribe of *Levi*. The *Kohanim* were the officiants in the Temple in Jerusalem.

Kohen Gadol Literally, "High Priest." The High Priest was the chief officiant in the Temple. The office was conferred upon

Aaron and his descendants.

Lag B'Omer   *See* Omer.

Levi   (plural, *Leviyyim*) Literally, "Levite." A descendant of the tribe of Levi, the second son of the patriarch Jacob. The *Leviyyim* were assigned the more mundane tasks connected with the operation of the Tabernacle in the wilderness and, later, the First and Second Temples.

Levirate Marriage   Known in Hebrew as *yibbum*, this biblical concept (*Deuteronomy* 25:5–10) states that the brother of a man who dies childless is required to marry his widow in order to provide an heir for him.

Levite   *See* Levi.

Lulav   (plural, *lulavim*) Literally, "palm branch." One of the four species used on the festival of Sukkot.

Mar   Literally, "mister." An honorific title accorded some Talmudic scholars.

Massekhta   (plural, *massekhtot*) Literally, "tractate." The body of knowledge that comprises the Mishnah and Gemara is divided into orders, and each order is divided into tractates. The entire Talmud is divided into sixty-three tractates. See pages 59–78 for a listing of the tractates in each order. *See also* Seder.

Mazzal   Literally, "star, constellation." In popular parlance, *mazzal* means "luck."

Megillah   (plural, *megillot*) Literally, "scroll." The word commonly refers to the Scroll of Esther (*Megillat Esther*), which is read on Purim. *Megillah* is also the name of a Talmudic tractate.

Meturgeman   Literally, "interpreter," referring specifically to a scholar who stood beside a lecturer and "translated" his words into common parlance and also sometimes expanded upon them.

Minor Sanhedrin   *See* Sanhedrin.

Minyan   (plural, *minyanim*) Literally, "quorum." Ten Jewish adult males (over the age of thirteen) are required for a communal prayer service, including the recitation of certain prayers and the reading of the Torah. In recent years, non-Orthodox communities have counted post-Bat Mitzvah age women in a *minyan*.

Mishnah   (plural, *mishnayyot*) Literally, "study, learning." A legal codification, compiled by Yehudah ha-Nasi (Judah the Prince) in the third century C.E., which constitutes the core of the Oral Law. The term *mishnah*, when written with a lowercase initial letter, is also used to describe a unit of study. See *Gemara* and *Oral Law*.

Mitzvah (plural, *mitzvot*) Literally, "commandment." Although often generally defined as "good deed," the term refers to a biblical commandment that a Jew is obligated to obey. The Torah contains 613 commandments, 248 of which are positive (*mitzvot aseh*), that is, those that a person is obligated to perform; and 365 of which are negative (*mitzvot lo ta'aseh*), that is, prohibitions.

Musaf Literally, "additional," referring to the additional public sacrifices that were offered in the Temple on Shabbat and festivals. In post-Temple times, the name came to designate the additional synagogue service recited following the reading of the Torah on Shabbat and holidays.

Nasi (plural, *nesi'im*) Literally, "prince, president." In the Bible, the term refers to the leader of a tribe or clan. In the Talmud, it is used to denote the president of the Sanhedrin.

Niddah Literally, "menstruating woman." According to the Bible, women are considered ritually impure during menstruation, and a wife is prohibited from having sexual contact with her husband until she has waited seven days after menstrual discharge and immersed herself in a ritual bath (*mikveh*). *Niddah* is also the name of a Talmudic tractate.

Nisan The first month in the Hebrew calendar, in which the Exodus from Egypt took place and in which the festival of Pesach is celebrated.

Noahide Laws Seven laws, derived from the early chapters of Genesis (9:4–7), which the Rabbis of the Talmud maintained are binding on all mankind, Jew and non-Jew alike. Six of the laws are negative—specifically, prohibitions against idolatry, blasphemy, murder, adultery, robbery, and eating the flesh of a living animal. The single positive law calls for the establishment of courts of justice.

Omer Literally, "[offering of a] sheaf of newly harvested barley." This offering was made on the sixteenth day of the month of Nisan, the second day of Pesach. The seven-week period between the second day of Pesach and the holiday of Shavu'ot is referred to as the *Omer*. The holiday of Lag b'Omer is celebrated on the thirty-third day of the *Omer* (*lag* has a numerical value of thirty-three).

Oral Law The teachings of the Torah (referred to as the Written Law) as interpreted by the Rabbis of the Talmud and transmitted orally to their students. So that it would not be forgotten, the Oral Law was eventually committed to writing in what is presently known as the Talmud.

Order *See* Seder.

Palestinian Talmud Also known as the Jerusalem Talmud or, in Hebrew, as the *Talmud Yerushalmi*. This commentary on the Mishnah, the creation of scholars who lived in Palestine, was completed and edited around 400 C.E.

Parah Adummah Literally, "red heifer." Chapter 19 of the book of *Numbers* describes the process by which ritual impurity is removed from a person who has come into contact with a human corpse. A red heifer is slaughtered and burned, and its ashes are mixed with water and sprinkled on the defiled person on the third and seventh day following his contact with the dead. Oddly enough, the person who prepares the ashes becomes defiled in the process.

Patriarch *See* Avot.

Perozbol *Also spelled* prosbul. Derived from the Greek for "official notice," the term refers to the legal document through which a lender turns over to the court for collection all loans that are due him during the sabbatical (*shemittah*) year. *See* Sabbatical Year.

Pharisees Known in Hebrew as Perushim ("Separatists"), they were one of the main religious and political parties of the Second Temple period, along with the Sadducees. Strict observers of the laws of purity and tithing, the Pharisees "separated" themselves from others who were less observant. Unlike the Sadducees, the Pharisees regarded the Oral Law with the same sanctity as the Written Law. *See* Oral Law *and* Written Law.

Pittam (Aramaic) The protuberance at the tip of an *etrog*, used as one of the four species on the holiday of Sukkot.

Rabban, Rabbana Literally, "our teacher, our master." An honorific title given to outstanding Talmudic scholars and to the president (*nasi*) of the Sanhedrin in particular.

Rabbi   Literally, "my master." An honorific title given to Talmudic scholars who were ordained in Palestine. Yehudah ha-Nasi is referred to in the Talmud simply as "Rabbi." *See also* Rav.

Rav   Literally, "master, teacher." The Babylonian equivalent of "Rabbi." Since ordination was not permitted outside of Palestine, the greatest Babylonian scholars were referred to as "Rav."

Red Heifer   *See* Parah Adummah.

Reish Galuta   Literally, "exilarch [head of the exile]." This title for the leader of the Jewish community in Babylonia originated with King Jehoiachin in 597 B.C.E. and remained in use until the middle of the eleventh century. The office of the *reish galuta* was hereditary, its occupants descendants of the House of David.

Reish Kallah   Literally, "head of the assembly." The title given to the leading scholar who lectured during the *kallah* months. *See* Kallah.

Rishonim   Literally, "early ones." Scholars from Europe and North Africa who, between the eleventh and sixteenth centuries, analyzed the Talmud, wrote commentaries on it, and prepared responsa to questions from around the world.

Rosh Chodesh   Literally, "head [first day] of the month." The arrival of the New Moon marks the beginning of a month in the Jewish calendar.

Sabba   Literally, "elder, old man, grandfather." A term appended to a personal name to indicate seniority.

Sabbatical Year   Known in Hebrew as *shemittah*, meaning "abandoning." The Torah (*Leviticus* 25:3ff.) ordains that the land in Palestine be allowed to lie fallow every seventh year in order that the land may rejuvenate itself. The year following seven *shemittah* years—that is, the fiftieth year—is called the jubilee year (*yovel*).

Sadducees   Known in Hebrew as Tzedokim or Tzedukim ("Righteous Ones"). The name probably is derived from Zadok, whose descendants had served as High Priest since Solomon built the First Temple. The Sadducees, along with the Pharisees, were one of the main religious and political parties of the Second Temple period. Comprising the wealthy Priestly class that officiated in the Temple, they encouraged strict adherence to the letter of the Written Law, as opposed to the Pharisees, who accepted the Oral Law. *See* Oral Law *and* Written Law.

Sanhedrin   Derived from a Greek word meaning "assembly," the Sanhedrin was the name of the High Court that functioned during the Second Temple period and in Talmudic times. The Sanhedrin Gedolah ("Great Sanhedrin") consisted of seventy-one judges who sat in Jerusalem. Many of the larger towns throughout Palestine convened their own smaller courts consisting of from three to twenty-three judges, varying with the nature of the cases brought before them. Each of these was known as a Sanhedrin Ketannah ("Minor Sanhedrin"). *Sanhedrin* is also the name of a Talmudic tractate.

Savorah   (plural, *savora'im*) Also spelled *saborah.* Literally, "expositor." The first group of post-Talmudic commentators, active primarily in the sixth century.

Seder   (plural, *sedarim*) Literally, "arrangement." Each of the six orders of the Mishnah is referred to as a *seder.* The term is also the name of the family service conducted on Pesach, at which time the Haggadah is read.

Sela   Literally, "rock, stone." In Talmudic times, the *sela,* the largest silver coin in circulation, was of great value, being worth four dinars, a full day's wage for an average worker.

She-hecheyanu   Literally, "[God] Who has kept us in life." A blessing of thanksgiving recited at the beginning of a festival or upon enjoying something new for the first time, such as wearing a new outfit or eating the first fruit of the season.

Shekel   (plural, *shekalim*) A silver or gold coin in use during the biblical and Temple periods.

Shekhinah   Literally, "Divine Presence." The manifestation of God in the human realm. The term, of biblical origin, is commonly used in Talmudic literature.

Shema   Literally, "hear." The first word of one of the most important prayers in the Jewish liturgy: "Hear, O Israel, the Lord is our God, the Lord is One." Its source is *Deuteronomy* 6:4.

Shemittah   *See* Sabbatical Year.

Shemoneh Esrei   *See* Amidah.

Shivah   Literally, "seven [days]." This seven-day period of intense mourning for a deceased, which begins immediately after the burial, is observed for a parent, sibling, child, or spouse.

Shochet Literally, "ritual slaughterer." A person trained to slaughter animals in accordance with the Jewish dietary laws.

Shofar (plural, *shofrot*) Literally, "ram's horn." In ancient times, the ram's horn called men to war and heralded the jubilee year (*yovel*). It is traditional to sound one hundred blasts of the *shofar* on Rosh Hashanah and a single long blast at the conclusion of Yom Kippur.

Simchat Beit ha-Sho'evah Literally, "ceremony of water libation." This joyous ceremony, held on the second day of the Sukkot holiday in Second Temple times, consisted of pouring drawn water on the altar.

Sukkah (plural, *sukkot*) Literally, "booth, hut." Jews are commanded to dwell in a *sukkah* for the duration of the festival of Sukkot (*Leviticus* 23:42–43). The roof of this temporary structure is covered with branches or other vegetation. *Sukkah* is also the name of a Talmudic tractate.

Talmud Literally, "learning, study." The encyclopedic compilation of Jewish law and lore that discusses, interprets, and comments upon the text of the Bible. Comprised of the Mishnah and Gemara, the Talmud was composed between the years 200 B.C.E. and 500 C.E. *See* Babylonian Talmud *and* Palestinian Talmud.

Talmud Bavli *See* Babylonian Talmud.

Talmud Yerushalmi *See* Palestinian Talmud.

Tanna (plural, *tanna'im*) Literally, "teacher." A scholar whose views are expressed in the Mishnah. *See* Mishnah.

Targum The Aramaic translation of the Bible.

Tefillah (plural, *tefillot*) Literally, "prayer." In the Talmud, *Tefillah* refers specifically to the *Amidah* prayer. *See* Amidah.

Tefillin (singular, *tefillah*) Literally, "phylacteries." Black leather cubes containing slips of parchment on which are handwritten four passages from the Torah (*Exodus* 13:1–10, 13:11–16; *Deuteronomy* 6:4–9, 11:13–21). Attached to leather straps, one cube is worn on the worshipper's head (*tefillah shel rosh)* and the other on the arm (*tefillah shel yad).*

Temple The First Temple, built in Jerusalem by King Solomon in the tenth century B.C.E., was destroyed by the Babylonians in 586 B.C.E. Seventy years later, the Temple was rebuilt by those who returned from the Babylonian exile. This Second Temple, as it came to be called, was destroyed in 70 C.E. by the Romans. In Hebrew, the Temple is referred to as the Beit ha-Mikdash. *See also* Av.

Terutz   Literally, "answer." A solution to a difficult question argued by Talmudic scholars.

Tishah b'Av   *See* Av.

Tosafot   Literally, "additions." Commentaries on the Talmud written between the twelfth and fourteenth centuries by Rashi's grandsons and others.

Tosefta   (Aramaic) Literally, "addition." The teachings collected by Yehudah ha-Nasi and his associates are presented in the Mishnah. Teachings of a similar nature gathered by others and not incorporated into the Mishnah comprise the Tosefta, which closely follows the arrangement of the Mishnah. *See* Baraita.

Tractate   *See* Massekhta.

Tzedakah   Literally, "righteousness." In popular parlance, the word refers to doing the right thing by giving charity and performing charitable acts.

Tzedokim (Tzedukim)   *See* Sadducees.

Tzitzit   (plural, *tzitziot*) Literally, "fringes," specifically those worn on the four corners of garments (*Numbers* 15:37–41) as a reminder of God's commandments.

Viddu'i   Literally, "confession." *Numbers* 5:6–7 requires that a person confess his wrongdoings and make restitution. That confession is referred to as *Viddu'i*. Also, the name of a prayer asking for forgiveness.

Written Law   The Torah, which according to tradition was received by Moses on Mount Sinai. *See* Oral Law.

Yerushalmi   *See* Palestinian Talmud.

Yetzer ha-Ra   Literally, "evil inclination," as opposed to the *yetzer ha-tov*, the "good inclination."

Yetzer ha-Tov   *See* Yetzer ha-Ra.

Yibbum   *See* Levirate Marriage.

Yovel   *See* Sabbatical Year.

Zaken   Literally, "elder." A title of reverence conferred upon elderly Talmudic scholars.

Zohar   Literally, "brightness." The central work of literature of the Kabbalah, believed to have been authored by the thirteenth-century Spanish kabbalist Moses de Leon.

Zugot (singular, *zug*) Literally, "pairs," referring specifically to the five pairs of scholars who followed the men of the Keneset ha-Gedolah and who dominated Torah study from about 200 B.C.E. until the destruction of the Second Temple in 70 C.E.

Zuz (plural, *zuzim*) An ancient silver coin, sometimes called a *dinar*.

Bibliography of English-Language Sources

Bergman, Me'ir Zvi. *Gateway to the Talmud.* Brooklyn, New York: Mesorah Publications, 1985.

Blackman, Philip. *The Mishna.* Seven volumes, translated with notes. London: Mishna Press, 1951.

Chajes, Zevi Hirsch. *Student's Guide Through the Talmud.* London: East and West Library, 1952.

Cohen, Abraham. *Everyman's Talmud.* New York: E. P. Dutton, 1949.

Danby, Herbert. *The Mishnah.* Oxford, England: Clarendon Press, 1933.

Encyclopaedia Judaica. Seventeen volumes. Jerusalem: Keter Publishing House, Ltd., 1971.

Epstein, Isidore, editor. *The Babylonian Talmud with Introduction and Commentary.* Volumes 1–36. London: Soncino Press, 1935–1952.

Jacobs, Louis. *Structure and Form in the Babylonian Talmud.* Cambridge, England: Cambridge University Press, 1991.

Kaplan, Julius. *The Redaction of the Babylonian Talmud.* New York: Bloch Publishing Co., 1933.

Mielziner, Moses. *Introduction to the Talmud.* Fourth edition. New York: Bloch Publishing Co., 1968.

Neusner, Jacob, editor. *The Study of Ancient Judaism.* New York: Ktav Publishing House, 1981.

Singer, Isidor, editor. *The Jewish Encyclopedia.* Twelve volumes. New York: Funk and Wagnalls, 1901.

Steinsaltz, Adin. *The Essential Talmud.* New York: Basic Books, 1976.

————, editor. *The Talmud.* Twenty-one volumes. New York: Random House, 1989–2000.

Strack, H. L. *Introduction to the Talmud and Midrash.* Philadelphia: Jewish Publication Society of America, 1931.

Urbach, Ephraim, E. *The Halakhah: Its Sources and Development.* Jerusalem: Masada Ltd., 1986.

Alison Brown

10/07

8.47/3.47 3795